Communication Pathways

Joseph M. Valenzano III • Melissa A. Broeckelman-Post• Erin Sahlstein Parcell

customized for George Mason University by
Melissa A. Broeckelman-Post · Lance E. Schmeidler
2016-2017 edition

FOUNTAINHEAD
PRESS

Our "green" initiatives include:

Electronic Products
We deliver products in nonpaper form whenever possible. This includes PDF downloadables, flash drives, and CDs.

Electronic Samples
We use a new electronic sampling system, called Xample. Instructor samples are sent via a personalized Web page that links to PDF downloads.

FSC Certified Printers
All of our printers are certified by the Forest Service Council which promotes environmentally and socially responsible management of the world's forests. This program allows consumer groups, individual consumers, and businesses to work together to promote responsible use of the world's forests as a renewable and sustainable resource.

Recycled Paper
Most of our products are printed on a minimum of 30% post consumer waste recycled paper.

Support of Green Causes
When we do print, we donate a portion of our revenue to Green causes. Listed below are a few of the organizations that have received donations from Fountainhead Press. We welcome your feedback and suggestions for contributions, as we are always searching for worthy initiatives.
    Rainforest 2 Reef
    Environmental Working Group

For information, please call or write:

        1-800-586-0330

        Fountainhead Press
        Southlake, TX 76092

        Web site: www.fountainheadpress.com
        E-mail: customerservice@fountainheadpress.com

ISBN: 978-1-68036-326-5

Printed in the United States of America

TABLE OF CONTENTS

COMM 101: Interpersonal & Group Communication

Department of Communication

2016-2017

Instructor: _____   E-Mail: _____

Office: _____   Office hours: _____

Communication department phone: 703.993.1090

Names, emails, phone numbers, and Skype contact information for at least two classmates:

Name	Phone	Email	Skype

Required Texts

Valanzano, J. M., III, Broeckelman-Post, M. A., Sahlstein-Parcell, E. & Schmeidler, L. E. (2016). *Communication Pathways Customized for George Mason University*, 2016-2017 Edition. Southlake, TX: Fountainhead.

Note: This book is only available at the GMU campus bookstore. You must purchase a new copy because many of the pages will be used and turned in as part of assignments throughout the semester.

We will also be using Blackboard in this class.

Course Description

This course examines various principles underlying effective communication in the interpersonal, public speaking, and small group contexts. This course presents principles to help develop appropriate and effective communication strategies in one-to-one and small group communication settings. This course places emphasis on analyzing and assessing the communication skills necessary to create and sustain effective communication in personal and professional relationships.

Mason Core Outcomes for Oral Communication

Oral communication competency at George Mason University is defined as the ability to use oral communication as a way of thinking and learning as well as sharing ideas with others. The Mason Core program identifies numerous learning goals in oral communication, which are addressed specifically in two Communication courses, COMM 100: Public Speaking and COMM 101: Interpersonal and Group Interaction. Common to both courses are these four learning outcomes:

1.   Students will demonstrate understanding of and proficiency in constructing and delivering multiple message types.
2.   Students will understand and practice effective elements of ethical verbal and nonverbal communication.
3.   Students will develop analytical skills and critical listening skills.
4.   Students will understand the influence of culture in communication and will know how to cope with cultural differences when presenting information to an audience.

Course Learning Objectives

It is important that you learn to develop your communication skills and that you learn how to present your findings to others. *This is both a theory and a skills course, and our primary goal is for you to gain competence in a variety of interpersonal, public speaking, and small group communication situations.* In order to achieve our goal, we will engage in various activities, assignments, etc. By the end of this course, you will be able to:

1. Monitor your own verbal and nonverbal communication practices, understand the role of culture and perception in interactions, and communicate ethically and effectively in interpersonal, public speaking, and group communication interactions.
2. Identify and explain fundamental communication processes, including models of communication, language, nonverbal communication, and listening.
3. Practice effective listening in order to understand, evaluate, and respond to others' messages.
4. Understand how interpersonal relationships develop and are maintained, and analyze and manage interpersonal conflict situations.
5. Conduct research and evaluate the quality of support materials and their appropriateness for use when explaining complex ideas to non-expert audiences.
6. Prepare full-sentence outlines and deliver speeches that include appropriate organization, well-supported claims, reasoned arguments, effective delivery, presentation aids (including PowerPoint), and adaptation to a specific audience and rhetorical situation.
7. Participate effectively in a small group to accomplish a team-based problem-solving task and be able to analyze and utilize the most appropriate leadership styles, task roles, and maintenance roles for that specific small group situation.

Academic Integrity

The integrity of the University community is affected by the individual choices made by each of us. Mason has an Honor Code with clear guidelines regarding academic integrity. Three fundamental and rather simple principles to follow at all times are that: (1) all work submitted be your own; (2) when using the work or ideas of others, including fellow students, give full credit through accurate citations; and (3) if you are uncertain about the ground rules on a particular assignment, ask for clarification. Under no circumstances is it permissible to cheat, plagiarize, steal, or lie in matters relating to academic work. No grade is important enough to justify academic misconduct, and cases of academic misconduct will be treated seriously, will most likely result in a failing grade on the assignment or in the course, and will be reported to the Mason Honor Committee. Another important aspect of academic integrity includes the free exchange of ideas, and we will often have vigorous discussion in this class. We fully expect that all aspects of this class will be conducted dialogically with civility and respect for differing ideas, perspectives, and traditions. For more information, visit: http://oai.gmu.edu/the-mason-honor-code/. Instructors are mandated reporters of academic integrity violations and may use Blackboard SafeAssign on assignment submissions in this course.

Attendance and Participation Policy

You are expected to be in class on time every day and should come to class prepared and ready to participate in class activities and discussion. Attendance and grades are highly correlated in any class, and most in-class assignments cannot be made up if you are not present in class. You are expected to attend class for the entire duration of the semester, including the last day of class and through the reading days and the designated Final Exam period for all your classes.

However, we understand that emergencies, illnesses, the death of loved ones, participation in university sponsored activities (e.g.: debate tournament or basketball game in which you are competing as a university representative), and important religious observances sometimes make it impossible for you to attend class. For these excused absences and emergencies, you are expected to provide written third-party documentation in advance whenever possible. Examples of third-party documentation include a calendar of religious observances, a letter from your coach that specifies the days on which you will need to miss class because you are away from campus for a competition, an obituary or funeral program, or a note from your doctor. In the case of illnesses or emergencies for which it is impossible to notify your instructor in advance, you should contact your instructor as soon as possible via email and then provide documentation as soon as you are able to return to class.

Campus Emergencies, Closures, and Class Cancellations

George Mason University is dedicated to preparing staff and students in the event of an emergency. All students in this class are encouraged to register for Mason Alert, a system that allows university officials to contact the community during an emergency by sending a text message. In addition, we all need to take a minute to view the emergency procedures poster in our classroom. This poster explains what to do in the event of medical emergency, fire, tornado, violence, power outage or other bad event. Please let your instructor know if you would like to discuss these procedures or any information on emergencies. If you are not currently registered for Mason Alert please text MASON to 411911 or visit the website: https://alert.gmu.edu.

If campus is closed for any reason (power outage, snow, etc.), you should not assume that class activities are cancelled. In the event of a snow day or other campus closure that prevents us from meeting in our normal classroom, we will typically hold class online. You should watch your email for a message from your instructor that will provide instructions about how the class will proceed.

If your instructor is not present at the start of class, please check your emails for updates. If there is not an email from your instructor, please wait until 5 minutes after the start of class and have one member of the class notify the Basic Course Coordinator (bcc@gmu.edu). The BCC may not respond immediately, but the BCC or your instructor will reply to the class within 24hrs. If the instructor is not present within 15 minutes after the start of class you are free to dismiss. Check your emails regularly over the next 24 hours for updates.

Campus Resources

There are numerous campus resources that are available to help you succeed in this class, your academic career, your career after you leave GMU, and to manage the many challenges that all of us face at some point. For more details, please see a list of some of these resources online at http://ctfe.gmu.edu/teaching/student-support-resources-on-campus/. A few of these include

- University Writing Center
- Learning Services
- Academic Advising and Transfer Center
- Student Health Services
- Counseling and Psychological Services

- University Career Services
- Military Services
- WAVES
- ODIME

One of the extra resources that is available exclusively to students who are taking this course is the **Speech Lab.** The Speech Lab is staffed by volunteers from our nationally-ranked Forensics Team, who are some of the best college-level competitive speakers in the nation. The Speech Lab is available to assist you with planning, preparing, and presenting any of your speeches or presentations. See the course Blackboard site for information about the location and hours of the Speech Lab throughout the semester.

Appointments are required and you must provide *at least* 24hrs-advanced notice of your requested appointment. Please see the Speech Lab tab in Blackboard for information about scheduling appointments.

Chain of Responsibility

You are the person most responsible for your learning experience throughout your time here at George Mason. Your instructor is second in that chain. It is your responsibility to communicate with your instructor about anything that you feel may inhibit your learning experience. If the results of those discussions are unsatisfactory, try again. If your instructor still does not seem to understand the concern, your next level of responsibility is to bring the issue to the attention of the Basic Course Coordinator (bcc@gmu.edu) for the Department of Communication. Anything that still can't be resolved will go next to the Basic Course Director. Only after these steps have been taken should you consider going to the Assistant Department Chair, Department Chair, Dean, Provost, or University President.

"Jumping rank" and going directly to the Dean or Provost is a very ineffective communication strategy for a number of reasons and is very likely to hurt your chances of a favorable resolution.

Classroom Conduct and Professionalism

Professionalism includes coming to class with a positive attitude, engaging in dialogic communication (e.g., respecting others' opinions, not interrupting in class, being respectful to those who are speaking, working together in a spirit of cooperation), and arriving to class on time and prepared for the class session. If you are engaging in any type of inappropriate behavior, you may be asked and required to leave for the remainder of that class session. If all goes well in the class, students tend to share information of an "interpersonal" nature"- it goes with the territory. You wouldn't want something said about you to people all around campus, so keep others' revelations confidential and do not talk about your classmates outside of class, and that goes for all of your classes. Each student is expected to be conscious and respectful of classroom diversity. While students may disagree on many topics, every person should respect the perspective of his/her fellow classmates, instructor, and invited guests.

Bring the course textbook, syllabus, your class notes, any needed assignments and drafts, paper, and a writing utensil with you to each class meeting. Laptop computers, tablets, mobile phones, and other electronic devices may be used before and after class, but please do not use them during class unless you have been asked to use them for a specific class activity. Electronic devices tend to be a distraction for you and for other students, and research even shows that using your mobile phone during class reduces note taking by 62% and reduces subsequent grades on exams by 1 ½ letter grades (Kuznekoff & Titsworth, 2013). Silence all cell phones before class begins and put them away. If you are using your cell phone or laptop during class, I reserve the right to confiscate it until the end of the class period or to ask you to leave the class.

Students who interrupt class discussions by frequently arriving late to class, who constantly interrupt others without thoughtfully listening to their comments, or who ask questions (in class and over email) that would more appropriately be answered by a simple glance at the syllabus (e.g., "When is this due?," "What do we have to read for next class?," "Did we do anything important when I missed class?," etc.) not only reflect poorly upon themselves, they also actively devalue the educational experience of others. Keep a copy of the course syllabus and schedule on hand and refer to them often; we expect you to take responsibility for your learning and to keep track of assignments and deadlines throughout the semester.

Disability Accommodations

If you have a learning or physical difference that may affect your academic work, you will need to furnish appropriate documentation to the Office of Disability Services. You can contact ODS at http://ods.gmu.edu, 703.993.2474, or stop by SUB I Room 4205. If you qualify for accommodation, the ODS staff will give you a form detailing appropriate accommodations for your instructor. In addition to providing your professors with the appropriate form at least two weeks prior to the requested accommodation, please take the initiative to discuss accommodation with them at the beginning of the semester and as needed during the term. Because of the range of learning differences, faculty members need to learn from you the most effective ways to assist you. If you have contacted the Office of Disability Services and are waiting to hear from a counselor, please tell your instructor.

Diversity

George Mason University promotes a living and learning environment for outstanding growth and productivity among its students, faculty and staff. Through its curriculum, programs, policies, procedures, services and resources, Mason strives to maintain a quality environment for work, study and personal growth.

An emphasis upon diversity and inclusion throughout the campus community is essential to achieve these goals. Diversity is broadly defined to include such characteristics as, but not limited to, race, ethnicity, gender, religion, age, disability, and sexual orientation. Diversity also entails different viewpoints, philosophies, and perspectives. Attention to these aspects of diversity will help promote a culture of inclusion and belonging, and an environment where diverse opinions, backgrounds and practices have the opportunity to be voiced, heard and respected.

The reflection of Mason's commitment to diversity and inclusion goes beyond policies and procedures to focus on behavior at the individual, group and organizational level. The implementation of this commitment to diversity and inclusion is found in all settings, including individual work units and groups, student organizations and groups, and classroom settings; it is also found with the delivery of services and activities, including, but not limited to, curriculum, teaching, events, advising, research, service, and community outreach.

Acknowledging that the attainment of diversity and inclusion are dynamic and continuous processes, and that the larger societal setting has an evolving socio-cultural understanding of diversity and inclusion, Mason seeks to continuously improve its environment. To this end, the University promotes continuous monitoring and self-assessment regarding diversity. The aim is to incorporate diversity and inclusion within the philosophies and actions of the individual, group and organization, and to make improvements as needed.

Extra Credit

Your instructor will not entertain requests for extra credit opportunities in this class. Extra credit is extra work, and students who are having difficulty completing the required coursework seldom have the time to complete additional assignments. Students who perform poorly on course assignments may not be devoting adequate time and effort to their academic responsibilities. Please see your instructor immediately if you are having difficulty in this course.

Grades

Your final grade will be based on the following points scale:

A+	97-100 (970-1000)	B	83-86 (830-869)	D	60-69 (600-699)
A	93-96 (930-969)	B-	80-82 (800-829)	F	59 or less (599-0)
A-	90-92 (900-929)	C+	77-79 (770-799)		
B+	87-89 (870-899)	C	70-76 (700-769)		

Incomplete grades will not be given in this course except in rare cases in which students have completed the course but are prevented from attending the final exam due to a documented serious medical emergency or other excused absence that truly cannot be avoided. In these cases, you should first attempt to reschedule the exam during the final exam period and an Incomplete will only be considered if this is impossible. In these cases, you should contact your instructor immediately to make arrangements. If your instructor has not heard from you by the end of the exam, it is highly likely that you will receive a zero on the exam. Your instructor may defer to the Basic Course Coordinator to determine if an Incomplete is warranted.

Grade Appeals

The time to challenge the merit of an individual assignment is during the semester and within seven calendar days after the assignment evaluation is returned. Once the semester has ended and your final semester grade is posted, it is not appropriate to then challenge the merit of individual assignment grades earned during the semester. Students often are not aware of what conditions qualify for a grade change after the completion of a semester. The appeal request must fit into one or more of the following categories:

1. A change from a temporary to a final grade either before or after a University deadline (such as an "Incomplete" to an "A")
2. A computational or technical error (such as an issue with an auto calculation)
3. A recording error (such as a professor recording an "18" instead of an "81").

If you believe there is an error in your final semester grade, you should first approach your instructor with clear and concrete justification and evidence to support your appeal in the category or categories above. If you're not able to resolve the issue with your instructor then bring your appeal and justification to the Basic Course Coordinator. Once the semester has ended, the BCC will not hear appeals regarding the merit of individual assignment grades earned during the semester, as those should be resolved with the instructor during the semester.

Late Work Policy

Unless otherwise announced, all assignments are due at the beginning of class on the day that they are due. Late work will not be accepted except in the case of a documented personal emergency or excused absence, and you will not be allowed to make up assignments or exams unless you have third-party documentation of an excused absence or emergency. It is your responsibility to provide **written documentation** from a third party of your emergency or university-excused absence. Except in the very rare case of last minute emergencies (e.g.: you were hit by a car as you were walking to class and were taken to the emergency room), you should let your instructor know about any excused absences, provide documentation, and make arrangements for making up any missed work in advance. When the nature of the emergency makes it impossible to make up work in advance, students will be given a deadline to complete missed work, usually within one week of the original deadline. Technology failures, work-related absences, work in other classes, oversleeping, or meetings with other professors are not considered a personal emergency. Even if students have a documented, excused absence, there are some types of work in this class that might be impossible to make up, such as in-class activities, workshops, group work, and individual or group presentations.

Privacy

Student privacy is governed by the Family Educational Rights and Privacy Act (FERPA) and is an essential aspect of any course. Your instructor cannot discuss your educational record with your parents, your friends, or anyone except for you. Because your GMU email is the only one that we can explicitly identify as belonging to you, your instructor will only communicate with you via email using your GMU address, and your instructor will not discuss grades via email. Students must use their MasonLive email account to receive important University information, including messages related to this class. See http://masonlive.gmu.edu for more information.

Course Requirements and Assignments

Details about all assignments are included in this textbook, and additional resources for completing the assignments and examples of these assignments are available in Blackboard. Grades will be posted on Blackboard and will be earned by completing the following assignments:

Assignment	Points Earned	Points Possible	Assignment	Points Earned	Points Possible
Introductory Speech		**5%**	**Explanatory Speech**		**20%**
Introductory Speech		25	Explanatory Outline Draft		5
Introductory Speech Responses (5)		25	Annotated Bibliography		50
			Explanatory Final Outline & PPt		25
Exploring Culture & Perception		**10%**	Explanatory Speech		100
Interview Questionnaire		25	Explanatory Self-Evaluation		10
Interview Workshop		25	Explanatory Peer Evaluations (2)		10
Paper		50			
			Deliberative Dialogue		**15%**
Interpersonal Communication Journal		**15%**	Individual Position Statement		25
Journal Entries (18)		90	Group Proposal		25
Reflection Paper		60	Presentation & Q&A		50
			Reflection Paper & Group Assessment		50
Content Assessment		**25%**			
Preparing to Participate (PtPs-22)		110	**Participation**		**10%**
Final exam		100	Research Participation (2)		30
Pre-Survey		20	Informative Peer Workshops		10
Post-Survey		20	In-Class Speaking Activities		60
		TOTAL: _____ /1000			

INTRODUCTION TO THE COURSE

Welcome to COMM 101!

This course meets your Oral Communication requirement for the Mason Core and is designed to help you build the foundational interpersonal, public speaking, and small group communication skills that you will need in your future courses, career, and everyday life as a member of your community. This class is unique in that it is both a theory and a skills course. By the time you finish this class, we want you to both <u>understand</u> the theories that are foundational to communicating in a variety of contexts and <u>be able</u> to communicate effectively in those personal and professional contexts. This is why there are some assignments (e.g., exams and Preparing to Participates) that are intended to assess whether you understand the concepts that underlie oral communication, while others (e.g., presentations and papers) are intended to assess your performance and give you opportunities to practice your communication skills. Becoming a highly skilled communicator is a lifelong process that cannot be mastered in fifteen short weeks, but this class will help you build a foundation for becoming an effective communicator and will significantly improve your skills over the course of the semester.

In order to succeed in this class, there are a few things that you should keep in mind:

1. **Your growth and learning in this class is directly related to the amount of work that you put into it.**
   You wouldn't expect a basketball player to become a better three point shooter if they never practiced shooting three pointers, and you wouldn't expect to be able to gain muscle mass and strength if you only lifted weight once every few weeks. Likewise, you should not expect to learn the concepts in this course well and to become an outstanding communicator unless you are taking time to prepare and practice several times a week. At the college level, you are expected to spend 2-3 hours outside of class for every hour that you spend in class, which means that you should plan to spend 6-9 hours per week reading, doing homework, conducting research, developing outlines, doing written assignments, and practicing your presentations.

   You will earn your grade in this class through the work that you do, and you are responsible for your own learning in this class. In high school, your teachers might have been responsible for making sure that you did the work, might have reminded you about missed assignments, and let you make up work that you did not complete on time. That is not going to happen at the university. If you choose not to show up or do the work, nobody is going to start issuing reminders or sit down with you to force you to do the assignments. If you have a lower grade than you wanted at the end of the semester, you are not going to be allowed to make up missed work or convince your instructor to give you a higher grade. Instead, you should plan ahead, keep up with the assignments, and come to class from the very beginning of the semester so that you can learn as much as possible in this class. If you start to struggle with the concepts or assignments, visit your instructor during office hours, and he or she will be happy to work with you. Please take advantage of the other resources that are available, such as the speech lab and writing center.

2. **Use your syllabus and course schedule to plan ahead.**
The deadlines for all of your assignments are included in the course schedule, and you are responsible for keeping track of these deadlines and turning in your assignments on time. The assignments in this class take time and should not be put off until the day before they are due. Make sure you give yourself plenty of time to complete all of your assignments. Plan to complete your research credit options early in the semester, before those opportunities disappear or you find yourself busy completing final projects and preparing for exams in all of your classes.

3. **Come to class prepared.**
Before each class period for which reading is due, you will need to complete the Preparing to Participate (PtP) assignment associated with each chapter that you will be discussing in class that day. To complete each PtP, you should download the Word file, respond to the questions, save the file, and then upload and submit it in Blackboard. These PtPs will sometimes be used in class discussions and activities, so please print and bring a hard copy of your PtPs to class with you and save them to use as a study guide at the end of the semester.

Most days, you will have PtPs, outlines, journal entries, papers, or other assignments due. Almost all assignments in this course are submitted on Blackboard and must be submitted before the beginning of class on the day that they are due. Please give yourself plenty of time to submit your work before the deadline and have a backup plan for completing the assignment on time in case your computer unexpectedly crashes or your wireless network goes down. Even if you must miss class due to an excused absence, you will be expected to complete any work that must be turned in before the deadline.

When you arrive in class, you should not expect your instructor to simply regurgitate the textbook content in another lecture. Instead, you will spend most of your time during class practicing the skills that you read about, clarifying difficult details, analyzing examples, and engaging in other types of active, hands-on activities. On most days, you will also do some type of informal public speaking in class as a part of these learning activities and will earn points for your participation in these speaking exercises.

4. **Come to class on time every day.**
You are responsible for getting yourself to class on time every day. If you come to class late, you will not be allowed to make up any assignments that you might have missed or turn in assignments that were due at the beginning of class. *If you miss your assigned speech day, you will not be allowed to make up your speech unless you have a documented, excused absence.* Please see the syllabus for more details about absences, attendance, and late work.

5. **Use the resources provided on Blackboard.**

   There will be many resources posted on Blackboard that are intended to help you succeed in this class. Visit your course Blackboard site frequently to check for course updates, check your grades and see feedback on assignments that were submitted online, see examples of outlines and speeches, and more. Your instructor will probably use Blackboard as the primary means of communicating with you outside of class, so we highly recommend that you log in at least once a day to check for updates.

6. **Practice, practice, practice.**

   One of the best ways to improve any of your presentations is to practice it out loud several times before you give your speech in class. It is normal to be a little bit nervous before you give a speech, but practicing will help to calm your nerves and make it easier to remember what comes next if you start to have a memory lapse while speaking. Practicing your speech several times will also help you be more confident that you know your material, help you not rely on your note card as much so that you can have better eye contact and delivery, and help you be certain that your speech fits within the time limits. If you can, get a friend or family member to listen while you practice.

As you progress through the semester, please remember that *we want you to succeed* and will do everything that we can to help you learn and do well in this class.

INTRODUCTORY SPEECH

Overview:

The purpose of this speech is for you to introduce yourself to your classmates and to begin to get to know each other as the semester begins. Additionally, we want you to gain practice speaking in a low-stakes speaking environment so that you can become more comfortable speaking in front of others and become familiar with some of the technology that we will be using in this class.

For this speech, your job is to introduce yourself to your classmates. In your speech, you should accomplish three things:

1) Tell us a little bit about your biographical history. What previous experiences, accomplishments, and family/cultural/environmental factors have helped shaped you into the person that you are today?

2) Tell us a little bit about who you are today (personal characteristics, attitudes, and values). Compare yourself to a concrete object and explain how you share an important characteristic with that object. Are you like an Asics Gel Kayano because you have the persistence and determination of a marathon runner? Are you dependable and efficient, but not particularly flashy, like a Honda Civic? Or are you more like a Tesla, which is modern, uses cutting edge research, and is almost always the center of attention?

3) Tell us a little bit about your goals and future plans. What is your major and/or intended career? What are some of your goals for the future? What is your passion in life?

You should begin by preparing some notes or an outline for yourself to help plan what you want to say. Practice your speech several times so that you are familiar with what you want to say and how you want to say it. Record your speech using your smartphone, tablet, webcam, the One Button Studio in the Gateway or Fenwick Library, or another recording device. If you need to borrow a video recorder or need assistance with your own technology, start by contacting the University's STAR Lab. As you record your speech, make sure that you look into the camera so that your audience feels like you are making eye contact with them as they watch the recording. After you have recorded your speech, please upload it to the Introductory Speech Assignment Discussion Board on Blackboard. Please refer to the "Recording Speeches" tab in Blackboard for detailed instructions on how to record and upload your speech.

You will prepare this speech, record it, and upload it to the appropriate discussion forum in the Blackboard Class Discussion Board at the very beginning of the semester, and we encourage you to do this even before the first day of class. **You must upload your speech video via Kaltura,** and instructions for doing so are provided on Blackboard. After you have completed your speech and given others an opportunity to do the same, please watch your classmates' videos and write responses to at least five other classmates' videos.

<u>Sources</u>: You do not need to cite sources in this speech.

<u>Length</u>: 2-3 minutes

Introductory Speech Instructor Evaluation Form

(will be graded in Blackboard)

VIDEO PRESENTATION	Missing 0	C 17.5-19.5	B 20-22	A 22.5-25	
Biographical History: (C) shares something about the speaker's past, (B) explains why the experience had significant impact on the speaker, and (A) describes how that experience shaped the speaker into the person they are today					
Who You Are Today: (C) shares personal characteristics, attitudes, and values that are important to the speaker, and (B) uses a concrete object as a metaphor for who the speaker is, and (A) provides explanations for why the object represents or shares some of the same characteristics as the speaker					
Future Goals & Plans: (C) shares something about goals or future plans, (B) explains why they want to achieve those goals or plans, and (A) conveys how these plans are related to their passion or a deeply held value					
Delivery: (C) can easily hear, understand, and see speaker in video, and (B) speaker conveys enthusiasm in vocal and nonverbal delivery and looks into the camera during parts of speech, and (A) speaker looks into camera and gives audience a sense of connection through most or all of the speech					___/25
RESPONSES	Missing 0	C 17.5-19.5	B 20-22	A 22.5-25	
Response 1: (C) posted a written response to a peer's speech, and (B) response refers to something specific that was discussed during the speech, and (A) response discloses something about the respondent's experiences, attitudes, or beliefs in response to something that was shared during the video					
Response 2: (C) posted a written response to a peer's speech, and (B) response refers to something specific that was discussed during the speech, and (A) response discloses something about the respondent's experiences, attitudes, or beliefs in response to something that was shared during the video					
Response 3: (C) posted a written response to a peer's speech, and (B) response refers to something specific that was discussed during the speech, and (A) response discloses something about the respondent's experiences, attitudes, or beliefs in response to something that was shared during the video					
Response 4: (C) posted a written response to a peer's speech, and (B) response refers to something specific that was discussed during the speech, and (A) response discloses something about the respondent's experiences, attitudes, or beliefs in response to something that was shared during the video					
Response 5: (C) posted a written response to a peer's speech, and (B) response refers to something specific that was discussed during the speech, and (A) response discloses something about the respondent's experiences, attitudes, or beliefs in response to something that was shared during the video					___/25

Total Score: ___/50

The Basics of Communication

As the world around us becomes increasingly accessible, communication skills become more important than ever. Whether we are speaking with family over dinner, going out on a first date, working with a sales team to market a product, delivering a graduation address, or using technology to interact with friends across long distances, the one constant in all our days is communication. It is important to develop good communication skills so that we maximize our ability to be successful in all our endeavors with other people.

People often believe they know how to communicate well and that the same style or mode of communication works in every scenario. With our increasingly complex and digital world, this is simply not the case. Communication skills, like any other skill, require practice and continual development. In this chapter, we introduce you to the basic principles of communicating in any context so that as we progress through the book you begin to see how these principles work to inform how we adapt our communication in a variety of situations. We will begin with briefly describing the various reasons why and how we communicate in today's global world. We will then discuss some common myths about communication and what people erroneously believe it can do. Finally, we will explain models for when communication works and discuss what makes a person a competent communicator.

Why We Communicate

A quick answer to why we communicate could very well be "to get something done"; however, as we will see in this section of the chapter, there are more reasons that drive us to interact with others than simply accomplishing tasks. In fact, there are five fundamental motives that drive our need to communicate with others. These needs all feed into some level of noted psychologist Abraham Maslow's hierarchy of needs (see Figure 1.1).[1] His model shows that people first need to fill physiological needs, such as food and sleep, before then seeking safety for themselves and their family. Once these two needs are met, they move on to filling their needs to love and to belong to a group, which in turn allow them to seek out a way to fill their needs for self-esteem and confidence. Finally, they seek to fill their moral needs through what Maslow calls self-actualization. Maslow's hierarchy demonstrates that for communication to be successful and fulfilling, it needs to be driven by a purpose.

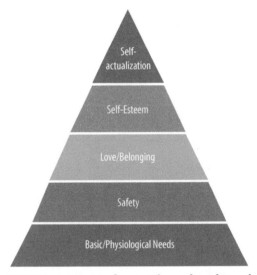

FIGURE 1.1   **Maslow's Hierarchy of Needs**

Physical Needs

Communication enhances our physical and mental health. This fact is what undergirds such programs as cancer support groups, Alcoholics Anonymous, and even suicide help lines. People can feel better when they talk to other people, because in doing so they feel connected to the world around them. For example, according to the American Cancer Society, research indicates that participation in support groups can help reduce stress, tension, and fatigue, while also potentially helping patients achieve greater tolerance for the grueling treatment they are undergoing.[2]

The benefits of communication on a person's health are rooted in the fact that we are social beings. Sometimes it is as if we cannot survive without social contact, something German Emperor Frederick II proved in a grossly unethical experiment in the thirteenth century. In an effort to determine what language children would speak without being exposed to any language, he took 50 newborns and had nurses feed and clean them, but not speak or otherwise hold them. All of the infants eventually died.[3] In more current and less dangerous research, scholars have shown how important human contact, especially touch, is to newborns. In fact, more recent work has demonstrated that talking to babies, even at very early ages, helps them develop language skills.[4] Contact and communication are clearly directly related to health for children and adults, and help people fill their physiological and safety needs.

Instrumental and Task Needs

Despite the health benefits provided by interacting with others, communication also often results in the fulfillment of practical needs. For example, without communication we could not exchange phone numbers, relay sales figures, share a diagnosis with a patient, or even build a bridge.

From ordering dinner, to calling emergency services, we use communication to complete important tasks that allow us to remain safe and even find food. The role communication plays in completing everyday tasks is as important as the benefits it accords our health and well-being. Without communication, we most assuredly would not be able to survive, but since we have survived, we can look to the other needs communication fills in our lives.

Relational Needs

In addition to personal health and safety, we need companionship with others. This companionship helps us receive and give affection to others, as well as find ways to relax and escape from the stresses of life. These are things made possible through connection to other people, which would not be possible without communication. Communication is how we establish and maintain relationships with other people.

In today's global, digital world, there are myriad ways in which we can create relationships with others. There are the traditional avenues, such as face-to-face communication with our neighbors, classmates, and colleagues, and we can also maintain relationships at a distance, thanks to the telephone, video chat programs like Skype and FaceTime, and social media sites like Facebook, Instagram, and Pinterest, just to name a few. Furthermore, we can create relationships with people we have never met in person using these same digital media.

Despite the abundance of communication tools, sometimes the more connected we are, the less connected to other people we feel. This is precisely the worry that has been raised by several scholars and cultural experts. For example, MIT professor, Sherry Turkle, delivered a TEDx talk entitled, "The Innovation of Loneliness," where she argued our increased use and reliance on social media and electronic communication has created an atmosphere where we feel more isolated from each other.[5] The medium of the computer has created a barrier preventing us from truly learning how to relate with other people. Nevertheless, communication helps us fulfill our need to develop and maintain relationships with others, despite the challenges some forms of communication may present in doing so.

Identity Needs

Our conversations with others help shape how we see ourselves. The resulting communication thus provides us with how others understand us, and also provides us the language to define how we present ourselves to other people. Our identities are always in a state of flux, changing based on how new people see us, and how we choose to interact with them. This constant feedback allows us to adapt our self-images based on the different contexts in which we find ourselves.

For example, you define yourself differently and communicate differently with your parents than you do with your friends from school. In turn, you define yourself differently and speak differently with your college friends than you do with your friends from high school.

MEDIATED MOMENTS

The Artist Formerly Known As Prince

One of the more popular and successful musicians in recent years, Prince, changed his name to a symbol in 1993 during a dispute with his record label, Warner Bros. Appearing before the press with the word "slave" written on his face, Prince declared his new "name" and explained its meaning:

> The first step I have taken toward the ultimate goal of emancipation from the chains that bind me to Warner Bros. was to change my name from Prince to the Love Symbol [♀]. Prince is the name that my mother gave me at birth. Warner Bros. took the name, trademarked it, and used it as the main marketing tool to promote all of the music that I wrote. The company owns the name Prince and all related music marketed under Prince. I became merely a pawn used to produce more money for Warner Bros...

> I was born Prince and did not want to adopt another conventional name. The only acceptable replacement for my name, and my identity, was the Love Symbol, a symbol with no pronunciation, that is a representation of me and what my music is about. This symbol is present in my work over the years; it is a concept that has evolved from my frustration; it is who I am. It is my name.

In this statement, Prince publicly announced the symbol he would be referred to as from that point on. He tied it to his sense of self and what he believed he represented. Since people could not verbalize the symbol, they referred to him as "The artist formerly known as Prince." This action by the famous artist shows how close the tie is between communication and our identity, and it depicts how communication can work to fulfill those needs.

Our identities shift based on what we let people see in us, what we choose to hide, and even what we do not know we are sharing or presenting to others. Later, in Chapter 3, we will explore self-esteem in greater detail, but for now it is enough to say we use communication to construct our self-image.

Spiritual Needs

In 2012, 77 percent of Americans still claimed a Christian label,[6] and even those who do not adhere to a faith still grapple with questions like "what is the meaning of life?" and "why are we here?" Spirituality does not mean religion; rather it refers to deep feelings and beliefs about the values, purposes, and meaning of human existence. Spirituality is not synonymous with religion, but rather religion is one form of expression of spirituality. As individuals, regardless of our faiths, we use communication to satisfy our longing for answers regarding these profound questions that cannot be directly answered. Some use prayer, while others employ meditation or read philosophy.

For those who use prayer, there is an even deeper question related to the spiritual needs fulfilled by communication. Communication scholar, Quentin Schultz, refers to this question as the "God Problem,"[7] wherein some people may use prayer to communicate to God, but how do we know he answers us? How does God actually speak, himself? These are profound questions about communication rooted in its ability to help us seek answers to and fulfill our spiritual needs. Intrapersonal communication, or communication with oneself, is also a vital part of other forms of spiritual communication that employ meditation and self-reflective practices.

Understanding How We Communicate

Communication takes many different forms. In this section of the chapter, we will dissect communication to better understand how messages are constructed and how they are delivered. We will first discuss the nature of symbols and their relationship to our thoughts, and then we will discuss three models of communication that explain how messages travel (and sometimes don't) between people in virtually any situation. As we will explain, communication does not function in one way, as there are several paths through which messages can travel.

The Building Blocks of Communication

Many disciplines break down their subject matter into things called **units of analysis,** or the "what" that the researcher is trying to understand or study. Biologists use cells, chemists use molecules, mathematicians use numbers, and communication scholars use symbols. Symbols are not just words; they can take many forms. One of the simplest ways to understand the study of symbols in all their forms is provided by C. K. Ogden and I.A. Richards in their book, *The Making of Meaning*.[8]

Ogden and Richards proposed that meaning is in people, not words. This proposal can also be extended to the use of other symbols. People give words and other

Unit of analysis
the item that the researcher is trying to understand or study

symbols meaning through interpretation, because words and symbols mean nothing until we give them their essence. Ogden and Richards illustrated how the process of interpretation works. There are three parts of a semantic triangle: the referent, the symbol, and the thought. The symbol is a representation, such as a word or image. A referent is an actual object that you are trying to communicate to another person. We use thought to connect the symbol to the referent. It is in our minds, through thought, that we connect the symbol and the referent. Once this relationship has been established, we can use the symbol (such as the word "table") to represent the thing (an actual table) when we are communicating with others who share our same symbol system (our language: English, Latin, Spanish, Arabic, etc.). This allows us to share meaning with other people, even if the things that we are communicating about are not actually present. See Figure 1.2 for an illustration.

FIGURE 1.2   **Semantic Triangle**

As you can see, Ogden and Richards provided a clear way to analyze communication by treating symbols as the units of analysis. We do not, however, communicate using just a symbol, but rather by using symbol systems. Language is a type of symbol system, as are traffic signs, and even the Periodic Table of Elements. These systems allow people to communicate with each other, but the processes by which we send messages using symbols systems is more complex than this.

Models of the Communication Process

There are three primary models used to explain the communication process, and each contains the same basic elements. The process begins with a sender **encoding**, or creating, a message. They then send the message through a **channel,** or pathway through which the symbols travel to a receiver or receivers. Some examples of channels are text messages, television, radio, phone, email, and even your own voice. When travelling through the channel, the message invariably encounters **noise,** or anything that interferes with the receiver's ability to properly receive the message. For some examples of types of noise our messages typically encounter, see Table 1.1. On the other end of the channel is the receiver, who **decodes,** or interprets, the symbols within the message, thus giving them meaning.

Encoding
the process of creating a message using symbols

Channel
pathway through which the symbols travel

Noise
anything that interferes with the receiver's ability to properly receive the message

Decoding
the process of interpreting the symbols within a message

TABLE 1.1   **Types of Noise**

Physical Noise	Psychological Noise
Other sounds (people talking, air conditioner, shuffling papers, etc.)	Preoccupation with other thoughts
Visual barriers	Emotional reaction to the topic
Poor volume and projects	Prejudice or ill will toward the speaker
Distractions in the room	Unwillingness to listen
Hunger, tiredness, and other bodily limitations	Resistance to the message

These basic components serve as the foundation for each of the three models of the communication process we will now explore in further detail.

Action Model of Communication. The action model of communication goes by two other names: the Shannon-Weaver model, and the linear model. The first of these alternate names represents the scholars responsible for the model's development, and the latter name reflects how the model works, as you will see. In the action model, communication is understood as a one-way process, in which the sender sends a message to a receiver, who decodes it. According to this model, the process stops there, as represented in Figure 1.3, but over time communication scholars recognized the process of creating and communicating meaning is not so linear.

FIGURE 1.3   **Action Model of Communication**

Interaction Model of Communication. The interaction model expands the action model, using all the same elements, but adding two more in order to show communication as a two-way process instead of a linear one-way process as shown in Figure 1.3. The first of the added elements to the model is **feedback,** or the various verbal and nonverbal responses to the message by the receiver. In the interaction model, feedback takes place after the receiver decodes the sender's message. The second added component is **context,** or the physical, emotional, and psychological environment in which the communication event takes place. When we communicate, we take the context into consideration when it comes to the words we use, the way we act, dress, and respond, and so the interaction model, Figure 1.4, acknowledges this aspect of the communication process. Despite these additions, the

Feedback
the various verbal and nonverbal responses to the message by the receiver

Context
the physical, emotional, and psychological environment in which the communication event takes place

two-way nature of the interaction model still does not completely capture the nature of the communication process, and so scholars developed a third, more complete model.

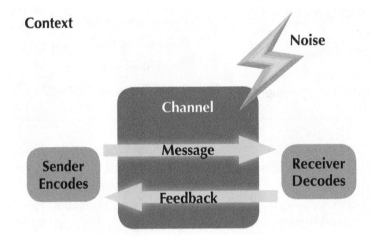

FIGURE 1.4   **Interaction Model of Communication**

Transactional Model of Communication. The transactional model updates both the action and interaction models of communication in one key way. The model does not differentiate between the sender and the receiver, seeing both parties as sender and receiver, as illustrated in Figure 1.5. This feature of the model shows the simultaneous nature of communication, where we are sending messages to the other person even while we are decoding the message they are sending. In this model, communication flows both ways at the same time, which is a much more realistic characterization of the communication process.

Now that we have explored both what communication can do for us, and how it works, we need to dispel some misconceptions about communication that many people hold.

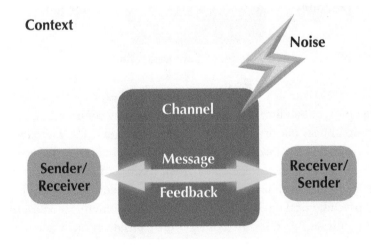

FIGURE 1.5   **Transaction Model of Communication**

Communication Myths

Starting from birth, when we cried to let our caregivers know we needed food or a new diaper and continuing on through our acquisition of language, we have always communicated with others. This may explain why many people believe they understand communication so well, even though they likely do not. In this section, we will explore five common misconceptions many people have about communication.

Myth #1: Everyone is an adept communicator. As noted in the previous section, we all have extensive experience with communicating, but just because we do something often does not make us experts in it. For example, a person may keep track of her personal finances, but this does not make her an expert at finance. Many people also cook, but that does not make them all chefs. What does make someone an expert in something is extensive training in his or her field, and most people do not have extensive training in communication. This is not to say that your experiences are bad or that you are impolite or even a bad communicator, but rather that there is a host of information on communication with which you are unfamiliar. This book will provide you with some of that information in a practical way so you can improve your communication skills.

Myth #2: Communication can solve any problem. Although communication can help to repair relationships and solve problems in many different circumstances, there are times when communication can actually make things worse. As social as people are, they also need their space, and it can be frustrating when we fill that space with constant communication. Additionally, not everything needs to be discussed or even addressed, and so leaving some topics alone is better than confronting them. More communication in these cases is not better; it can make things worse. In certain cases, communication can also let people know it may be time to move on, even when the intent is to bring two people back together. We will return to this myth in more detail when we cover interpersonal conflict in Chapter 12.

Myth #3: There is only one type of communication. Communication is a very broad field, and it covers a lot of activities, but there is no one way to communicate properly. The type of communication we choose to engage in is dependent on the situation in which we find ourselves. Debate and argumentation work in some cases, but dialogue can be more effective in others. Sometimes, listening is the best thing we can do. Our choice depends on the purpose of the interaction and with whom we are speaking. If a person does not adjust the way in which they communicate based on the context in which they find themselves, they increase the probability of misunderstandings and potential problems.

Myth #4: Any communication is good communication. Not all communication is positive, and sometimes we need to exercise restraint and not share certain comments or thoughts with others. Just because you want to say something, or even have the right to say something, does not mean it is good to say it. Just like any tool, communication can be used in a negative way, and, therefore, it is not always good. As an example, think about interruptions. Just because you feel the need to contribute at that moment does not mean it is a good idea to do so. Interrupting others, though communication, is not going to create a positive experience.

Myth #5: More communication will ultimately make people agree with you. Many people believe that the reason others disagree with them is that they have not been clearly understood. As a result, they continue pushing their ideas in an effort to help the other person understand, and thus agree. It can often be the case, however, that the other person does understand what is being said, and yet still does not agree with it. More communication does not produce agreement in these instances, but may instead invite the opposite. It is important to recognize when a point is made and the other person just does not agree, because the more you talk in these cases, the more entrenched the other person is likely to become in the disagreement.

So far we have illustrated the complex nature of communication, how it works, and some common misunderstandings about the process people hold. In the final section of this chapter, we will define what it means to be a competent communicator.

DIALING DIVERSITY

The Culture of Business Cards

When two professionals meet, it is common practice to exchange business cards. The business cards often contain a company name, the individual's name and job title, contact information, and sometimes even a picture. In the United States, it is common to see people take a business card, not look at it, and simply place it in a pocket or even fold it up. They also may take the card and write some notes on it during the meeting. Americans do not find this practice offensive; however, other cultures do. For instance, many Asian professionals expect a person to whom they give their business card to read it and then put it in a place that will keep it from being crinkled. They see this as a sign of respect, because the business card for them is a shorthand for who they are and what they have accomplished, a resume of sorts. To write on it, fold it, or ignore it tells them that not just the card, but who the card represents, is not of any value to the receiver. When interacting with people from different backgrounds, it is important to take their expectations into account. If you do not, you risk damaging or even destroying the relationship. Ignore business cards at your own risk!

The Competent Communicator

Just as there are several misconceptions regarding communication, there are things communication scholars know make up good communication between people. When we think of good communicators we have encountered, we often think of those people as being able to effectively and appropriately interact in any situation. This is also how scholars define **communication competence**. The effectiveness of communication refers to how well it achieves its purpose, and embedded within this definition is the idea that the strategic choices we make about how we communicate with others in a given situation directly influence the degree to which our message can be successful. The appropriateness of communication refers to our ability to pay attention to the rules and expectations of a given situation, something made very difficult when it comes to interacting with people from different cultural backgrounds. In this section of the chapter, we will detail five characteristics exhibited by competent communicators.

Communication competence the ability to effectively and appropriately interact in any given situation

Self-awareness

A competent communicator pays attention to his or her behaviors and comments, and how those influence or affect other people. The process of being attuned to how our actions and messages impact others is called **self-monitoring**. People who are high self-monitors pay close attention to how they look, sound, and react, as well as what they say when in situations with other people. By contrast, low self-monitors pay minimal attention to these things, and are thus not aware that they may be making a negative impression on others. Being a high self-monitor allows people to adjust to different responses and situations.

Self-monitoring the process of being attuned to how your actions and messages impact others

Responsiveness and Adaptability

Good communicators must not only be cognizant of their own actions and reactions, but also must be able to act upon those observations in a way that is appropriate to the situation. Responding to others and adapting your messages and behaviors in different social situations is an important skill exhibited by competent communicators. Remember that communication is not a one-size-fits-all tool, and thus competent communicators know how to adapt their communication to the responses of others and the various situations in which they find themselves.

> *The fundamental problem of communication is that of reproducing at one point either exactly or approximately a message selected at another point. Frequently the messages have meaning; that is they refer to or are correlated according to some system with certain physical or conceptual entities.*[9]
>
> —*C. E. Shannon*

Generalized other
a composite mental image we use to bounce our potential statements or behaviors off of before we actually enact them

Empathy
the ability to understand and feel the same way as another person

Cognitive complexity
the ability to recognize multiple potential ways in which a situation or message could be understood or interpreted

Person-centered Messages

Too often we get lost in ourselves and forget to consider other people. Good communicators consistently take other people's thoughts, ideas, and feelings into account and create what researcher Jesse Delia calls "person-centered messages."[10] Noted scholar, George Herbert Mead, proposed a concept called the **generalized other**, which is a composite mental image upon which we practice our potential statements or behaviors before we actually enact them.[11] This allows us to anticipate how we think other people might react, and thus adapt accordingly. It also helps us experience **empathy**, or the ability to understand and feel the emotions that another person is experiencing. People who are other-oriented have strong generalized others, while those who are more focused on themselves skip the step of anticipating reactions through the generalized other altogether.

Cognitive Complexity

In most cases, there is more than one potential explanation for a behavior or message, and **cognitive complexity** is the ability to recognize multiple ways in which a situation or message could be understood or interpreted. This skill involves being attuned to the dimensions of the context in which people find themselves, and their ability to appreciate the different variables that could influence what, why, and how another person acts and speaks the way he or she does in a given circumstance. Increasing cognitive complexity involves patience and a willingness to have an open mind.

Ethics and Civility

Competent communicators understand and act upon what they believe is the right way to interact in a given situation. They communicate honestly, use good manners, are polite, and also are assertive. All but the last of these qualities may be something you readily understand, but it is important to note that assertiveness does not mean aggressiveness. Competent communicators know how to respectfully state a position in a way that does not offend others or make them defensive, and that is what we mean by being assertive. Competent communicators also know when to exercise self-restraint and to not share something with another party. Communicating in a civil and ethical fashion involves knowing the right and wrong way to communicate, acting on the former, and doing so in a manner that respects both yourself and those around you.

Being a competent communicator is much more involved than many people realize. In this book, we use the best research by experts in the field to provide you with a detailed understanding of how to improve your communication skills.

Summary

In this chapter, we defined communication and provided insight into the benefits good communication produces for people. We also explained the various components of the communication process, and dispelled some widely held myths regarding communication. Finally, we introduced some qualities and characteristics of competent communicators that will be further explored throughout the remainder of this book. Communication is a complex process that works differently in different situations, and as we go further, we will delve into different communication contexts and share the tools that will help you improve your interactional skills in those situations.

Chapter 1 Key Ideas

- We communicate because communication fulfills physical, instrumental, relational, identity, and spiritual needs.
- We communicate using symbol systems that include referents (actual things), thoughts (mental constructs or ideas about those things), and symbols (words or images that represent both the referent and thought).
- There are three models of communication: the action model, the interaction model, and the transaction model.
- There are five common misconceptions or myths about communication: everyone is an adept communicator, communication can solve any problem, there is only one type of communication, any communication is good communication, and more communication will ultimately make people agree with you.
- The five characteristics exhibited by competent communicators include (1) self-awareness, (2) responsiveness and adaptability, (3) person-centered messages, (4) cognitive complexity, and (5) ethics and civility.

Chapter 1 Key Terms

Generalized other	Unit of analysis	Noise
Empathy	Encoding	Feedback
Cognitive complexity	Decoding	Context
	Channel	Self-monitoring

References

1 Maslow, A. H. (1943). A theory of human motivation. *Psychological Review, 50,* 370-96.

2 American Cancer Society. Find support and treatment, http://www.cancer.org/treatment/treatmentsandsideeffects/complementaryandalternativemedicine/mindbodyandspirit/support-groups-cam.

3 Perry, B. D. (2002). Childhood experience and the expression of genetic potential: What childhood neglect tells us about nature and nurture. *Brain and Mind, 3,* 79-100.

4 Medina, J. (2014). *Brain rules for baby (updated and expanded): How to raise a smart and happy child from zero to five* (2nd ed.). Seattle, WA: Pear Press.

5 Connected and disconnected: Technology, empathy and loneliness. *Ashoka's Youth Venture.* https://www.youthventure.org/connected-and-disconnected-technology-empathy-and-loneliness

6 Newport, F. (2012). Seven in ten Americans are very or moderately religious. *Gallup.com,* Dec. 4. Retrieved from   http://www.gallup.com/poll/159050/seven-americans-moderately-religious.aspx

7 Schultze, Quentin J. (2005). The God Problem in Communication Studies. *Journal of Communication and Religion,* 28, 1-22.

8 Ogden, C.K., & Richards, I. A. (1923/1989). *The making of meaning.* Orlando, FL: Harcourt Brace Jovanovich, Inc.

9 Shannon, C. E. (1948). A mathematical theory of communication. *The Bell System Technical Journal,* 27, 379-423.

10 Jesse Delia, Barbara J. O'Keefe, & Daniel O'Keefe. The Constructivist Approach to Communication, in *Human Communication Theory*, F. E. X. Dance (ed.), Harper & Row, New York, 1982, 147–191.

11 Mead, G. H. (1934). *Mind, self, and society from the standpoint of a social behaviorist.* Chicago, IL: University of Chicago Press.

INTERPERSONAL COMMUNICATION
JOURNAL

Each week, you will be asked to observe and think about a specific aspect of your communication behavior in your everyday life. For each exercise, you will be asked to keep a journal documenting your interactions for the week and then reflect on your observations. You should add an entry to your journal **at least three separate days each week**, and each entry should be single spaced and at least half of a page in length. In your entries, you should make a point of using terminology and concepts discussed in the textbook and using **boldface** text to highlight key terms and concepts. After six weeks of journaling, you will re-read your entries, consider what you have observed and learned, and develop some goals for improving your communication interactions with others.

Your journal entries will be submitted via Blackboard in three sets of six entries. All entries should be single spaced using 12 point Times New Roman font and one inch margins. Please download the Interpersonal Communication Journal Templates that are associated with each set of assignments from Blackboard and type directly into those templates to complete your entries.

Week 1: Perception
For each entry this week, consider how perception influences the assumptions that you make about others. For each entry, write about an interaction that you had with another person during the day. During that interaction, what assumptions did you make about the other person's motives? Were these situational or interpersonal attributions? What are some other possible explanations or attributions for the other person's behavior? What are some of the factors that might have been influencing your perception in that interaction?

Week 2: Listening and Nonverbal Communication
For each entry this week, pay attention to how you listen during your conversations and what types of nonverbal communication you use during those conversations. What types of nonverbal communication are you using, and which of the six functions on nonverbal communication are those nonverbal behaviors fulfilling? For which purpose and in which type of listening were you engaging? Which good listening behaviors and nonlistening behaviors are you using in this particular conversation?

Week 3: Culture & Diversity
This week, make a point of having conversations with several people whom you perceive as being from a different culture or co-culture than you. Identify you and your partner's culture or co-culture. What are some of the similarities and differences between your cultures or co-cultures?

What communication challenges might arise from your cultural differences? How might you adapt your communication in order to communicate more effectively and dialogically with others from this culture or co-culture (especially in relation to national cultural dimensions)?

Week 4: Disclosure in Developing Relationships
This week, pay attention to what you talk about in conversations with people that you met recently or with whom you have never had a previous conversation. What topics do you discuss? How does the other person respond to your self-disclosures, and how do you feel you should respond when the other person discloses information to you? How do those disclosures impact your perceived closeness of that relationship? Identify which stage of Social Penetration Theory your relationship with the other person is in by the end of the conversation and provide a rationale for that choice. For at least one of your entries this week, start a conversation with somebody with whom you have never had a previous conversation and report on that interaction.

Week 5: Dialectical Tensions
This week, your entries will focus on communication in three of your intimate relationships: your close friends, family, and romantic partners. For each entry, choose one relational partner. What are some of the specific dialectical tensions that you experience in that relationship? What are some of the ways that you and your partner have tried to manage those tensions? Are there other strategies that you have learned about in this class that you might consider using to manage those dialectical tensions in the future?

Week 6: Conflict
For each entry this week, think about a conflict that occurred this week (or if not this week, sometime fairly recently). What was the conflict about? What are the reasons that you believe the conflict occurred (information, interpretations, or self-interest)? What communication behaviors did you and the other person engage in that were problematic, and which behaviors were helpful? Which conflict styles did you and your partner use? Were you able to resolve the conflict in a way that both parties were satisfied?

Interpersonal Reflection Essay
After all of your journal entries are complete, re-read all of your Interpersonal Communication Journal entries that you have written over the last six weeks. Write a reflection paper with at least one paragraph that responds to each of the following questions:
- What patterns do you notice in your journal entries?
- What are your communication strengths and areas of weakness?
- How has your communication with others changed as a result of observing and reflecting on your communication behaviors over the time?
- How do you plan to continue to improve your communication skills and address the weaknesses that you have identified over the course of the rest of the semester?

Address each of these questions in a 2 ½ - 3 page single-spaced essay using 12 point Times New Roman font with one inch margins. Upload your essay via Blackboard.

Interpersonal Communication Journal Grading Rubric

These assignments will be uploaded to Blackboard and graded online using the rubrics shown below:

FOR EACH JOURNAL ENTRY	Missing 0	C 3.5-3.9	B 4-4.4	A 4.5-5	
Journal entry is (C) at least half of a page in length and shares detailed experiences that are related to the prompt, (B) incorporates terminology (in boldface font) and concepts from the course that are appropriate for the prompt and interaction, and (A) draws clear, appropriate connections between the concepts and experiences					___/5

FOR THE REFLECTION ESSAY	Missing 0	C 42-47	B 48-53	A 54-60	
Patterns: (C) Paper includes a paragraph that discusses several patterns that the writer noticed across his or her journal entries, and (B) provides detailed, specific examples to support the writer's claims about patterns observed, and (A) links those patterns to specific concepts learned in class and uses boldface text to highlight those key terms and concepts					
Strengths & Weaknesses: (C) Paper includes a paragraph that discusses strengths and weaknesses that the writer noticed across his or her journal entries, and (B) provides detailed, specific examples to support the writer's claims about strengths and weaknesses, and (A) links those strengths and weaknesses to specific concepts learned in class and uses boldface text to highlight those key terms and concepts					
Change: (C) Paper includes a paragraph that discusses ways that the writer's communication has changed as a result of these exercises, and (B) provides detailed, specific examples to support the writer's claims about changes, and (A) links those changes to specific concepts learned in class and uses boldface text to highlight those key terms and concepts					
Improvement Plan: (C) Paper includes a paragraph that discusses ways that the writer plans to improve his or her communication skills, and (B) provides detailed, specific examples to support the reasons why improvement is needed and how it will be accomplished, and (A) links those patterns to specific concepts learned in class and uses boldface text to highlight those key terms and concepts					
Proofreading: (C) Reflection essay is written in complete sentences and contains several significant grammar, syntax, or spelling errors. (B) Reflection essay is written in complete sentences and clearly organized paragraphs. Essay contains only a few minor grammar, syntax, or spelling errors. (A) Reflection essay is free from grammar, syntax, and spelling errors. Essay reflects careful attention to word choice and language structures.					
Formatting: (C) Paper is missing two of more of the required formatting elements, (B) Paper is missing one of the formatting elements, (A) essay is 2 ½-3 pages in length, single-spaced, and written in 12 point Times New Roman font with one inch margins					___/60

Chapter 2

Perception and the Self

Even though we all live in the same world, we do not experience, define, or describe it the same way. A group of people can watch a movie or listen to a song and walk away with different ideas about its worth, quality, and value. How is it we can all experience the same thing, yet walk away with different ideas regarding what happened? How can people have two different ways of describing the same emotions, attitudes, events, and actions? The fact is we each pick and choose the things we pay attention to, and then we give them meaning through communication. So, when you watch a movie with a friend, you may focus on the outstanding performance by the lead actress and walk away with a positive impression of the film, while your friend might form a more negative view because he or she focused on the poorly constructed special effects. Neither person is objectively wrong; each emphasizes different aspects of the same thing and reaches different conclusions. This phenomenon is human perception at work.

In this chapter, we explore the concept of perception, specifically how it relates to the way we understand and present ourselves to others. We will first identify the stages of the perception process, and then discuss how we attribute meaning to our surroundings and ourselves. We will then explore the idea of the self-concept, or self-image, and from there explain how we manage our public image. Although it may not seem so at first, perception is a key component to understanding how communication influences our identity and the world around us.

How Perception Works

We don't often think about how we choose what to pay attention to in our surroundings; we just do it. To fully understand the unconscious and conscious choices we make about such things, it is important to define and discuss how perception works. **Perception** is how we establish meaning for our experience of the world around us and the people in it. The process unfolds in three distinct stages, each of which we will examine in this section. We will also discuss the various things that can influence our perceptual abilities, including cultural variables and personal biases.

Three Stages of the Perception Process

There are three stages of the perception process, and they follow a specific order that should make intuitive sense. In many ways, the perception process is a lot like constructing a speech in that you first pick a topic and collect information about that topic, then create a structure so the information makes sense, and finally you offer your assessment of what the information means. As you will see, this is what we do all day as we pay attention to the things that occur around us.

Stage #1: Selection. We learn at a very early age that our five senses enable us to know the world around us. We feel, smell, hear, taste, and see things and then make determinations about those experiences by evaluating our sense experience. Either consciously or subconsciously selecting what to experience is the first stage of perception. When you choose certain stimuli in your environment to experience, you are involved in **selection**. We typically choose things out of the vastness of the world around us for a few different reasons. First, we tend to pay attention to things that are unusual, unexpected, or unique, like a loud sound in a place you normally would not expect to hear it, such as in a library. Second, we pay attention to mundane things that we see repeatedly, like a person who wears the same tie three or four days in a row, or an announcer who uses the same opening line every broadcast. Finally, intense experiences also cause us to heighten our attention, such as when we smell something really intense or see something shocking in a picture or video. We select different things because the uniqueness, commonality, and even intensity of things differ for each of us. What is unique for one person might be common for another.

Step #2: Organization. Once we choose an experience to attend to, we classify it by determining which things we already know that are and are not similar to it. This categorization of stimuli is called **organization**. Just like the selection part of the process, when we organize stimuli we use our unique frames for understanding. When doing this, we employ mental frameworks, called **schemas,** and use them to connect the new stimuli or ideas to others that are already stored in our brain. As a metaphor, you might think about your brain as being like a computer with numerous folders. Each folder is filled with files about related concepts, memories, experiences, individuals, and thoughts. When you encounter a new concept, experience, or thought, you compare it to the files in each folder and store it in a folder with related concepts. For example, if you were to eat a starfruit for the first

Perception
the process of giving meaning to the things we notice in the world around us

Selection
the act of choosing to attend to, consciously or subconsciously, specific stimuli in the environment

Organization
the categorization of stimuli we select to pay attention to

Schema
mental frameworks for organizing information about experiences

time, you would access your mental folder with memories of other types of fruit to compare the taste and texture, and then store a memory of eating the starfruit with the memories of other fruits.

Researcher Peter Andersen suggests that our schemas about other people typically take four forms (Table 2.1): physical constructs that emphasize things like appearance, role constructs that focus on a person's position or job, interactive constructs that hone in on the way people behave, and psychological constructs that stress a person's mood, emotions, and feelings.[1] Schemas apply to certain situations and environments, as well as people, so that we have a general construct for what our rooms look like and how stores, such as grocery stores, are laid out. This allows us to take new information and determine what it is like to better appreciate what the experience or person may share with someone else and thus develop appropriate responses.

TABLE 2.1 **Four Schemas about Other People**

Physical	Is the person a man or woman? Is the person tall, short, or medium height? Is the person old, middle-aged, or young?
Role constructs	Is the person my friend? A coworker? A family member? A neighbor? A police officer? A doctor?
Interactive constructs	Is this person acting appropriately? Is this person acting insensitively? Do I think the person is friendly?
Psychological constructs	Is the person in a good mood? Is this person happy? Sad? Does this person seem to care about what we are discussing? Is he or she bored with our conversation?

Step #3: Interpretation. Noticing something and even categorizing the experience does not complete the perception process; you still must provide it with its meaning. Interpretation, the final step of the perception process, occurs when we assign meaning to an experience or person. It is here, where we interpret stimuli, that we likely see the most differences across people, as they assign different significance and even meaning than another person to the same experience.

Our interpretations are always influenced by many different variables. For instance, our interpretations can be affected by what we know about the other person or the experience. We can read an email from a close friend and know when she is joking, but if the same thing is written by someone we don't know very well, we may not see the joke—and it may not even be intended as a joke at all! Our own personal experiences also color how we interpret different events. Someone who has had to go without food at some point in his or her life may see donating money to a food pantry as the most important act of charity a person could do, while someone else who went homeless for a time may see the most important charity as one providing shelter, such as Habitat for Humanity. Our own experiences affect how we interpret different situations, experiences, or even the actions of others. Finally, our level of agreement or degree to which we identify with a person may influence how we see

Situational attribution
the assumption that another person is doing something because of factors in the environment or the situation they are in

Interpersonal attribution
the assumption that another person is doing something because of her or his character or disposition

Fundamental Attribution Error
the tendency to overestimate the influence of internal characteristics and underestimate the influence of situational factors when evaluating someone else's behavior

that person's positions, statements, or behaviors. Ultimately, each of us brings different sets of internal lenses to the same occurences, and therefore interpret them differently despite seemingly experiencing the same exact thing.

Perception and Attribution

When we observe others engaging in various activities, we often make assumptions about why the other person is engaging in that particular activity. These assumptions about motive, or attributions, generally fall into one of two categories: situational and internal.[2] When we make a **situational**, or external, attribution, we assume that another person is doing something because of factors in his or her environment or the situation. For example, if someone is late to a meeting with us, we could assume he or she had trouble finding parking or got stuck in traffic, or would otherwise be on time for our scheduled conversation. When we make an **interpersonal**, or internal, attribution, however, we assume that the person did something because of his or her character or disposition. For example, we might assume that the person who was late for our meeting is bad at time management, and that if he or she cared about our conversation, he or she would not be late. It's important to note that when we are trying to explain others' behavior, we have a tendency to overestimate the influence of internal characteristics and underestimate the influence of situational factors. This is known as the **Fundamental Attribution Error.**[3] For example, when someone does not call us back, we are more likely to think he or she forgot or doesn't care about the relationship, both internal attributions for the behavior, rather than thinking his or her professor kept the class late or that someone else called him or her before he or she could call us.

MEDIATED MOMENTS

Symbols are all around us, and we each can interpret different things from them. For a case in point, simply look at the critically acclaimed book and television series *Game of Thrones*, created by George R. R. Martin. At the beginning of the second book and second season of the television series, a red comet streaks across the sky. Some characters perceive this as an omen for war and blood and others as a symbol of the family's rise to power. Others still see it simply as a red comet. The same experience was observed by several different characters, who organized it according to their knowledge and beliefs, and then interpreted it to mean something very different. In each case, the interpretations led to choices the characters would make in subsequent chapters and episodes. Our perception becomes our reality, and we all experience different realities in the same world, a fact that George R. R. Martin used to set the stage for a part of his award-winning stories.

Influencing the Perception Process

Just as many different forms of noise can interfere with the communication process we discussed in Chapter 1, there are a multitude of different things that can interrupt, influence, and affect our perceptions of the world around us. It is important to remember that how we perceive things and people is constantly impacted by who we are and what experiences we have had.

Physical Influences. Our own bodies affect what we choose to attend to in our environments, as well as how we interpret them. In any given moment we experience a **physiological state** of being, or temporary condition of the body. All of us know what it feels like to be tired, hungry, or sick, and each condition results in a different response. We might be quick to anger when we are tired, focused only on food when we are hungry, or unable to focus on anything when we are sick. Even for adults, these conditions impede our ability to interact successfully with other people, because they change our perceptions of the actions and statements of others, as well as the environments in which we find ourselves.

We also have more permanent conditions that affect us throughout or lives. These **physiological traits** rely on our senses and manifest in a variety of different ways. For example, different people are more productive at different times of day. Researcher John Medina breaks down this trait into three types, aptly named after different birds. **Larks** are people who are most productive in the morning, and their attention and abilities trail off in the afternoon and evening. Larks constitute 10 percent of the population. **Owls** are 20 percent of the population, and they fittingly operate best at later times in the day and often are found working well past midnight. The remaining 70 percent of us are **hummingbirds,** who are ready for action at any time—though some of us will be a little more larkish or owlish than others.[4] The point here is that this trait is both physical, as it has to do with your body's rhythms, and enduring, meaning it is a characteristic that you exhibit throughout your life. You can easily see how, depending on which category you are in, your perception of events and people can be influenced by time of day.

Cultural Influences. Culture plays a significant role in how we perceive things, more so than what we recognize. In the previous chapter, we discussed different dimensions of culture, and to illustrate how those dimensions influence perception, let's look at a few examples. Recall that collectivist cultures place more of an emphasis on the family or community than individual achievement. Certain Asian cultures tend to be more collectivistic than Western cultures, so it may come as no surprise that it is sometimes much more acceptable to copy someone else's work in those cultures than it is in Western societies.[5] This is because copying is perceived as sharing to help the larger community and not as stealing from another individual.

As an example of gender differences, women in the United States have been socialized to speak more to express emotions and seek emotional support, whereas men have been brought up to talk for more functional problem-solving purposes. So, when a wife comes home from work and starts to share some of the difficulties she had that day with her colleagues, her husband might immediately launch into a list of suggestions for how

Physiological state
temporary condition of the body

Physiological traits
permanent enduring physical conditions that impact us throughout our lives

Larks
10 percent of the population who function best early in the day

Owls
20 percent of the population who function best at later times of the day

Hummingbirds
70 percent of the population who function well throughout the day

she can do something different to fix those problems. The wife gets upset and an argument ensues. Why? Because the wife just wanted to express her feelings without receiving advice in return, and the husband thought he was helping with her workplace relationships. The potential communicative differences between the genders are evident here.

The power distance dimension of culture also influences perception. Recall that high power distance cultures exist where the population is far removed from authority, and low power distance cultures share power among individuals. With that in mind, think about someone who works for a company with very clear lines of authority, where individual creativity is not necessary or encouraged. Now think of this person leaving that job after years of experiencing that culture and going to work for Google, where there is almost the complete opposite corporate structure. At Google, people are encouraged to explore ideas, and the company's headquarters looks like a combination of a playground and a corporate office building. This person may have certain challenges adjusting to the different corporate culture.

Occupational Influences. What we do for a living also influences what we see and how we see it. Professions come with particular sets of training that allow people to be attuned to specific things in certain situations. Physicians see more than most people about how the body functions, and even within that profession, there are subspecialties where doctors are more adept at seeing things in particular areas of the body. Attorneys notice nuances in the law, farmers pay attention to different nutrients in soil, and mechanics are attuned to various cars' sounds and what they might mean. Content knowledge and specific training allow people to pay attention to certain things others may not notice.

Additionally, individuals might have a different view of how things fit together, depending on their level of responsibility within an organization. For example, in higher education, individual instructors know very well what is going on in their classrooms and what resources they need. The chairs of departments know the needs of the entire unit as a whole, and are best able to make decisions about where to allocate resources within the department. The same is the case for deans when it comes to overseeing resource requests and needs for all the different departments in a college. The higher up the administrative ladder, the broader the view and understanding of how the needs of different departments can and need to be addressed. Higher-level administrators are aware of more issues across the university, so they notice more things that individual instructors may not see.

Stereotyping generalizations about groups of people that are applied to individuals we believe are members of that group

Psychological Influences and Biases. There are a variety of other psychological influences that play a role in our perceptions. The first, and perhaps most familiar, of these is **stereotyping**. Stereotyping occurs when we create generalizations about groups of people and apply them to individuals we believe are members of that group. Stereotyping itself is not a bad thing; in fact, it allows us to function when we initially meet someone. The problem occurs when we hold tight to these rigid expectations and act as if they are true, and not just conceptual schemas that need to adapt once we understand individuals and how they might differ from their group. We also need to understand stereotypes as malleable, knowing we must adjust our assumptions when we encounter someone who is a part of the group for which we have a stereotype but who does not conform to all parts of the stereotype. Stereotypes can lead us to perceive what we expect but also to notice things we don't necessarily expect.

Two other factors that influence perception relate to the order in which we experience things. One of the most critical moments is the first, whether it is in a speech, an interview, a date, or a sales meeting. The principle known as the **primacy effect** explains that people are prone to emphasizing the first impression of something over any subsequent impressions when forming their perception of an event or person. Psychologist Solomon Asch, one of the early pioneers in exploring the primacy effect in interpersonal interactions, found that when people are evaluated favorably at first, they are more likely to be seen in a good light going forward, with the impact of later negative information about that person diminishing.[6] The same can be said for things like actors and authors, whose initial work we tend to emphasize more than their later ones, even if the followups are disappointing. On the other hand, if someone sets a negative first impression, positive information that is shared later is likely to be weighed less heavily or discounted altogether.

In addition to what occurs first, the **recency effect** also helps explain our perceptual abilities. It refers to when we allow our most recent impressions to hold more sway than earlier ones. This is important when we consider how we leave interactions. Consider job interviews, where your first impression is no doubt very important, but so is how you end the interview. A firm handshake, leaving a business card or resume, and following up with a quick thank-you note are all ways to leave a lasting recent impression on your prospective employer. Just getting up and leaving when the questions are concluded is not likely to leave a good recent impression with them.

Timing of impressions is one thing, but so is the type of information we choose to focus on when creating impressions of people and events. In some cases, such as during the initial stages of a romantic relationship, people tend to highlight and overemphasize positive information and characteristics when creating an impression. This is called the **positivity bias**. In other cases, we can be overly critical and focus our efforts on picking out negative information or qualities in a person or situation, and this is called the **negativity bias**. People who are unhappy or otherwise disinterested in a situation are more likely to use the negativity bias when evaluating information about experiences than people who are either happy or even ambivalent.

The final influence on perception we will cover is our own capacity to focus on how things affect ourselves. For most of us, we are our favorite topic to talk about, but we are not everyone else's favorite topic. This creates a need for us to manage our own desire to talk about ourselves with the desires of other people to tell stories of their own. People who are not able to do this are considered **egocentric,** or completely focused on themselves and ignorant of the needs of others. This focus on the self is something everyone experiences as a child, but most grow out of by adolescence and young adulthood. When we allow our own egocentrism to impact our perceptions, two things happen. First, we tend to believe the people around us do, see, and experience things in the same manner we do. Second, we tend to see things happening as directly related to ourselves, thus we see people acting in particular ways toward us because we think they either really like us, or perhaps they are out to get us.

Primacy effect
people are prone to emphasizing the first impression of something over any subsequent impressions when forming their perception of an event or person

Recency effect
people are prone to using their most recent experience with someone as their overriding impression of the person

Positivity bias
the tendency to highlight and overemphasize positive information and characteristics when creating an impression

Negativity bias
the tendency to focus our efforts on picking out negative information or qualities in a person or situation

Egocentric
people who are completely focused on themselves and ignorant of the needs of others

Perception and the Self

It should come as no surprise that perception affects how we define ourselves, and also influences how we define our environment and the people in it. Communicating about what we perceive begins with how we see ourselves. In this section of the chapter, we turn our attention to the idea of the self-concept, or the set of perceptions you have about yourself that define who you are, also known as your identity. We will first examine the three characteristics shared by all self-concepts before moving to a discussion of how we manage our self-concepts. In doing so, we will discuss the notion of "faces" and the process of negotiating our understanding of our various faces in different situations.

Defining the Self-Concept

Self-concept
the image we have
of who we believe
we are

Our **self-concept** is the image that we have about who we believe we are. Our identities are quite complex. We may think we are simple people, and that we might be an "open book" to others, but our self-concept involves more than we realize. We cannot keep track of or remember everything that has happened to us, but those experiences all influence the way we see ourselves. So, in short, despite being unable to remember everything, it all leaves its mark on how we understand ourselves. Additionally, even though we all have different self-concepts, our identities all share four characteristics.

Self-concepts are shaped by others. How each of us perceives our self is due in large part to how others respond to us and what others say about us. George Herbert Mead[7] explains that we experience the "self" indirectly from the standpoint of others, so we could think of other people as being the mirror that shows us who we are. Part of this influence is through direct communication; when others repeatedly tell us that we are smart, funny, athletic, kind, or outgoing, we begin to believe those things about ourselves and behave in ways that reflect those beliefs. Part of this influence is through indirect communication or reactions that we see from others; your self-concept will be impacted in different ways if others listen to you with respect when you speak, versus whether others ignore you or look at you with disdain. We are also influenced by what we *think* other people are thinking about us. We imagine how we appear to others and consider how others might be evaluating or judging us based on that appearance, and that imagined perception influences our self-concept. As is shown in Figure 2.1, John Kinch[8] summarized this process by explaining that our self-concept influences our behavior, and others respond to our behavior. How we perceive the responses of others then influences our self-concept, which in turn influences our behavior, making this an ongoing cycle.

Self-concepts are multifaceted. People often think they are the same person no matter what situation they are in, but that is just not true. In fact, we define ourselves differently depending on the situation and the people we are with. Sometimes we focus on our religion, at other times our gender, still other times our age or profession, or even our own estimation of our values and behaviors. We do not have one self, but rather we are the sum of many different smaller selves, each representing a part of our overall self-concept. To assume that

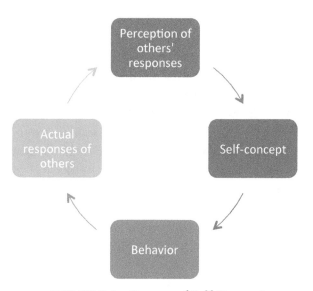

FIGURE 2.1   **Process of Self-Concept**

one part is the sum total of who you are is to essentialize yourself by one demographic or characteristic and to deny the other parts that make you, you.

Perhaps the best way to understand the multifaceted nature of our self-concept is to differentiate between the parts we know with the parts others know about us. Psychologists Joseph Luft and Harrington Ingham proposed a simple image that represents the various dimensions of the self. Creatively called the **Johari Window**, after grafting their two names together, the model—Figure 2.2—breaks down what we and others know about ourselves into four distinct areas.[9] The first of these is the open area, which contains those things that both we and others know about ourselves. The second area, the hidden area, contains things you know about yourself but do not share with others. The blind area includes the reverse of the hidden area; it includes things we do not know about ourselves that others know about us. The final quadrant, the unknown area, involves parts of ourselves that neither we nor others know about, such as how we might respond to certain situations in the future. In the Johari Window, not all quadrants are of equal emphasis or importance for each person, and the importance of each area can increase or decrease in different circumstances, but they all influence how we see ourselves and how others see us, as well.

Johari Window
a four-quadrant model describing the different aspects of our self-concept based on what we and others know about ourselves

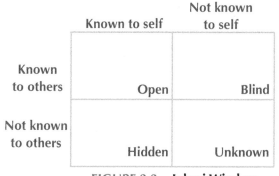

FIGURE 2.2   **Johari Window**

Self-concepts are somewhat subjective. What we know about ourselves can be broken down into two types of information: subjective and objective. Objective facts include things like height, weight, age, hair color, or even shoe size. When we interpret a fact such as a person weighing 115 lbs, we do so by examining the objective fact through the lens of the person's age, sex, or even occupation. For example, we come to different conclusions about a teenage boy who weighs 115 lbs (underweight) than we would about a twenty-something young woman (more appropriate weight). Most of our self-concept is driven by subjective interpretations and opinions. What this means is that people cannot be counted on to evaluate themselves objectively or accurately.

Sometimes, people overestimate their positive attributes. For example, many recent graduates of college rate themselves as better than average or excellent communicators, and yet employers have repeatedly told colleges that graduates need to improve their communication skills. Clearly there is a disconnect between these two groups; perhaps the individuals responding to the survey have a much higher estimation of their communication skills than their employers and colleagues.[10] Sometimes, the opposite is true, and people negatively evaluate their own abilities and attributes. This is particularly prevalent with people who suffer low self-esteem and depression. In either case, there is a subjective assessment of a person's self-concept that is more powerful than any objective element of her or his identity when it comes to defining how the person sees himself or herself.

DIALING DIVERSITY

The idea that a person's self-concept is both enduring and changeable can best be seen through any of the hundreds of success stories in America. For example, perhaps you have heard of John Paul Mitchell Systems? No? What about Paul Mitchell salon products? Well, the salon products are just one of many ventures run by John Paul Mitchell Systems, a company founded by John Paul DeJoria. DeJoria's upbringing was not of the silver spoon variety; his parents divorced when he was 10 years old, and he entered foster care in Los Angeles. DeJoria even was a gang member for a time before entering the military. After leaving the military, he worked at Redken laboratories for a brief period of time before managing to secure a loan to start John Paul Mitchell Systems, a company that began with shampoo products he tried to sell door-to-door while living in his car. Now, JPMS is worth an astounding $900 million annually.[11] Throughout his life story, there are both enduring aspects of his self-concept as well as some things that changed. For example, he always seemed to work hard, despite what life threw at him, but he also adapted his occupational interests as he grew older, thus demonstrating the changing nature of how he defined himself.

Self-concepts endure and change. We develop our self-concepts over a long period of time as we accumulate experiences with our surroundings and the people we encounter. It is a slow process, and one that does not change on a whim, which makes a self-concept relatively enduring. These characteristics are further enhanced by the fact that as we get older, we tend to associate with people who confirm our understanding of ourselves.[12] This simply serves to reinforce our constructed self-concept, but just because it is built and reinforced does not mean it cannot change.

Like a house, the foundation may remain but we can change the structure from time to time. As our brains develop, it can impact our self-concept, and as John Medina notes in his book *Brain Rules,* the two most active developmental times for our brains are when we are around two years old and in our teenage years. Once we reach adulthood, major changes to our self-concepts are much less common.[13] Significant life events such as marriage, a death of a loved one, a serious illness, or moving to a new area can also change our self-concepts. Strong self-concepts adjust and adapt to the changing circumstances brought about by life. Even though there are aspects foundational to our self-concepts, our definitions of who we are can change over time and with new experiences.

Understanding Our Many Faces

Now that the complicated nature of our self-concept is becoming increasingly clear, we might start wondering how different situations interact with aspects of our identity. After all, our friends know us in ways our parents do not, and our instructors know us in ways both of those groups do not. It is a good question, so we will now investigate the mental work we do to manage the perception of ourselves in different contexts.

Facework

Regardless of the situation, we always want people to have a positive impression of us. No one wants to portray himself or herself in a negative light. The behaviors we exhibit to create and maintain the positive perception of ourselves is called **facework**.[14] We conduct facework within three different contexts, and we are also always looking out for and responding to things that might damage our own self-concept.

One of the primary contexts in which we work to create a positive image of ourselves is in social situations. These include efforts to create friendships, romantic relationships, and other social interactions with people. This desire to have others like and respect us is called our **fellowship face**.[15] We want others to perceive us as friendly, so we do our best to come across that way with others when we meet them. This type of behavior plays a very important role when you take the primacy effect into account.

The second face we seek to create concerns respect more than friendliness and likeability. The **competence face** refers to efforts to promote our expertise to others, and it manifests in professional settings or places where you want people to believe you are

Facework
the behaviors we exhibit to create and maintain the positive perception of ourselves

Fellowship face
an effort to fulfill the need to have others like and respect us

Competence face
the effort to promote our expertise on subjects to others so they respect us

knowledgeable on a topic. When we want people—whether they are they friends, family, or colleagues—to respect us for what we do and know, we are concerned with our competence face. When people do not get respect from others, it hurts their competence face and can negatively impact their own self-esteem.

The third, and final, face we seek to maintain with others is related to our desire to be seen as independent. We all want to be seen as capable of doing things on our own, something that comes into play when students transition from high school to college. This, and other times when we want to be seen as responsible and capable in our own right, represents the expression of our **autonomy face**, which refers to when we seek to avoid others making decisions and doing things for us by being seen as capable. In individualistic cultures, the autonomy face is a much larger part of a person's self-concept and thus must be managed more carefully in different situations.

Sometimes we encounter things that threaten to damage the image we work to present to others, and these are referred to as **face threats**. For instance, college students sometimes grapple with the idea that they are autonomous adults living on their own during the school year, but they are still dependent upon their parents for some forms of aid. That dependence is a threat to the autonomy face element of their self-concept. We may also experience threats to our fellowship face when a first date does not go well and someone does not want to see us again romantically. This type of face threat can be very disheartening, but it illustrates that how we manage threats to our face is just as important as the face itself, because we could hole up and never go out again, or reevaluate the situation in a way that does not cause us stress or anxiety.

> *"When our social poise is attacked or teased, we feel the need to restore or save face. When we are being complimented or given credit for a job well done in front of others (i.e. in an individualistic culture), we feel our social self-worth is enhanced and stroked."*[16]
> —S. Ting-Toomey & A. Kurogi

Managing Our Many Faces

Despite the fact that we define ourselves differently in different situations to different people, we also try to maintain consistency with the images each group has of us. **Image management** is the process of coordinating the presentation of our self-concept with various groups in different situations. Managing multiple images across various groups is collaborative and complex, but essential for successful relationships in any context. Image management is collaborative in that our self-concept is constantly influenced by the interaction between ourselves and others. We seek to present ourselves in a specific manner, and when people accept that image, we continue to behave in ways that are consistent with the image they reinforce. If, however, our image does not seem to be accepted by others, we adjust it until it is accepted, or we simply move on from the potential relationship with that individual.

Autonomy face
the perception that we can do things on our own and our desire to avoid others making decisions for us

Face threats
things that threaten to damage the image we work to present to others

Image management
the process of coordinating the presentation of our self-concept with various groups in different situations

Image management is also complex because of the multiple audiences we encounter and the need to monitor all the different parts of ourselves we show to others, both intentionally and inadvertently. One skill we can develop to make this management easier is self-monitoring, which, as we learned in Chapter 1, is the ability to be aware of our own behaviors and statements and how they affect other people. Low self-monitors will speak without thinking about how another person might respond, while high self-monitors tend to consider how their statements might be received. Low self-monitors can often create the image of a selfish person, because they say and do things without attention to their surroundings. Sometimes we say that these people have no "internal filter." It is important to work on monitoring your statements and actions so you can cultivate the best possible perception of you by others.

Additionally, it is important for us to help others manage their image, or face, while also allowing others to help us manage our own face. Each of us occasionally does something embarrassing, makes mistakes, and engages in conflict with others at various times in our lives. In these types of situations, there are many things we can do to help one another prevent losing face before the situation, support the face of others during the interaction, or to repair face afterward.[17] For example, we can pre-apologize, consult with others during the interaction, and even justify our statements and actions after the fact. All of these can help mitigate any damage to face that might occur.

Summary

In this chapter, we defined perception and how it impacts the way we see ourselves as well as how others see us. We first detailed the three stages of the perception process before explaining the various situational influences and personal biases that can impact how we perceive the world around us. We then spent time exploring the notion of the self-concept and how it manifests in various ways through our desire to be seen in specific ways by other people. Finally, we explored how we can manage our self-concepts and images in our dealings with others through the process of self-monitoring.

Chapter 2 Key Ideas

- The three stages of the perception process are selection, organization, and interpretation
- We have a tendency to overestimate situational factors when making attributions about our own behaviors, and overestimate the role of interpersonal factors when making attributions about others' behaviors, which is known as the Fundamental Attribution Error
- Perception is influenced by physiological states and traits, culture, occupation, and psychological biases
- Our self-concept is the image we have about who we believe we are. Our self-concept is shaped through our interactions with others, is multifaceted, is subjective, and will both endure and change over time
- The Johari Window breaks what we and others know about ourselves into four distinct areas: open, blind, hidden, and unknown

- We engage in facework to create and maintain a positive perception of ourselves. There are three primary types of face that we seek to maintain: fellowship face, competence face, and autonomy face

Chapter 2 Key Terms

Perception	Larks	Self-concept
Selection	Owls	Johari Window
Schema	Hummingbirds	Facework
Organization	Stereotyping	Fellowship face
Situational attribution	Primacy effect	Competence face
Interpersonal attribution	Recency effect	Autonomy face
Fundamental Attribution Error	Positivity bias	Face threats
Physiological state	Negativity bias	Image management
Physiological traits	Egocentric	

References

1 Andersen, P. A. (1998). *Nonverbal communication: Forms and functions.* New York, NY: McGraw Hill.

2 Heider, F. (1944). Social perception and phenomenal causality. *Psychological Review, 51,* 358-374.

3 Ross, L. (1977). The intuitive psychologist and his shortcomings: Distortions in the attribution process. In L. Berkowitz (Ed.), *Advances in experimental social psychology* (173-220). New York, NY: Academic Press.

4 Medina, J. (2008). *Brain rules.* Edmonds, WA: Pear Press.

5 Handa, N., & Power, C. (2005). Land and discover! A case study investigating the cultural context of plagiarism. *Journal of University Teaching and Learning Practice, 2* (3b), 64-84; Sutherland-Smith, W. (2005). The tangled web: Internet plagiarism and international students' academic writing. *Journal of Asian Pacific Communication, 15,* 15-29.

6 Asch, S. E. (1951). Effects of group pressure upon the modification and distortion of judgment. In H. Guetzkow (ed.) *Groups, leadership and men.* Pittsburgh, PA: Carnegie Press.

7 Mead, G. H. (1964). *Mind, self, and society from the standpoint of a behavioral scientist.* Chicago, IL: University of Chicago Press. (Original work published in 1934.)

8 Kinch, J. W. (1963). A formalized theory of self-concept. *American Journal of Sociology, 68,* 481-486.

9 Luft, J., & Ingham, H. (1955). The Johari window, a graphic model of interpersonal awareness. *Proceedings of the Western Training Laboratory in Group Development.* Los Angeles, CA: UCLA.

10 Hart Research Associates. (January 20, 2015). Falling short? College Learning and Career Success. Association of American Colleges and Universities. Retrieved from https://aacu.org/leap/public-opinion-research/2015-survey-results

11 Swann, W. B., Rentfro, P. J., & Guinn, J. S. (2003). Self-verification: The search for coherence. In M. R. Leary & J. J. P. Tangney (Eds.), *Handbook of self and identity* (367-383). New York, NY: Guilford.

12 van der Meulen, M. (2001). Developments in self-concept theory and research: Affect, context, and variability. In H. A. Bosma & E. S. Kunnen (Eds.), *Identity and emotions: Development through self-organization* (10-32). Cambridge: Cambridge University Press.

13 Goldschein, E. & D. Eisenberg. (December 28, 2011). 15 inspirational rags-to-riches stories, Business Insider Retrieved from http://www.businessinsider.com/rags-to-riches-stories-2011-11?op=1

14 Goffman, E. (1967). *Interaction ritual.* New York, NY: Anchor Books.

15 Lim, T. S., & Bowers, J. W. (1991). Facework: Solidarity, approbation, and tact. *Human Communication Research 17,* 415-450.

16 Ting-Toomey, S. & Kurogi, A. (1998). Facework competence in intercultural conflict: An updated face-negotiation theory. *International Journal of Intercultural Relations,* 22, 187-225. doi: 10.1016/S0147-1767(98)00004-2.

17 Cupach, W., & Metts, S. (1994). *Facework.* Thousand Oaks, CA: Sage; As cited in Em Griffin, *A First Look at Communication Theory* (8th Edition), New York, NY: McGraw Hill, 70.

Chapter 3

Dialogic Communication

We need only scan the cable news networks and assorted newspaper columns to notice that American society is frequently shaped as aggressive, polarized, and uncivil. Popular news and entertainment shows model communication as combative, not as a means to understand each other or critically examine statements and evidence. The same can be said for expressions on Facebook, Twitter, and other social media tools, where it is not uncommon to find people making disparaging, hateful, and even violent statements about others. Mass media tools can enhance our communication with each other, but sometimes they seem to encourage us to treat others poorly.

As we have already discussed, to be a competent communicator means you are able to understand and respect other people in a variety of contexts. In this chapter, we discuss how to communicate effectively and respectfully in any situation. In subsequent chapters, we will explain how this method of interaction works in specific contexts. The method is called **dialogue**, which, simply put, is communicating in a way that both respects others and encourages them to want to listen, while also listening in a way that encourages others to want to speak.[1] Scholar John Poulakos expounds upon this definition by identifying three components necessary for dialogue to take place: the self, the other, and the in between. For Poulakos, the focus is on the "actual happenings between" people where they "stand

Dialogue
a style of communication that respectfully encourages others to want to listen, while also listening in a way that encourages others to want to speak

before each other prepared to meet the uniqueness of their situation and follow it wherever it may lead."[2] Dialogue thus requires an openness to change and appreciation for the other person's perspective.

In this chapter, we will first explore the concept and discuss the various components of good dialogic communication identified by communication scholars. In the second part of the chapter, we will examine various attitudes of dialogue to illustrate not just what dialogue is, but also what it looks like. Finally, we will offer some suggestions for developing dialogic communication in any context.

Defining Dialogue

Like many things in this book, dialogue may sound simple on the surface, but it is more complicated than meets the eye—and challenging to put into practice! Perhaps you associate the term dialogue with conversations in movies or plays, or maybe you regard any exchange between people as a dialogue. As we will illustrate, dialogue is much more nuanced. In this section, we will investigate the four key elements of dialogue, paying particular attention to the notion of civility. This will then allow us to see how each of these components serves as the foundation for the dialogue characteristics we will discuss later in the chapter.

Civility
the ability to treat others with respect so that we can have a lasting, peaceful, and positive interaction

Civility

The first, and perhaps most essential, component of dialogue is civility. We always want people to treat us with respect, and so it stands to reason we should do the same in our dealings with others. **Civility** is the ability to treat others with respect, so we can have a lasting, peaceful, and positive interaction. Many people associate being civil with being passive, fake, or weak, but as we will see, that is not the case. In fact, behaving in such a way is actually uncivil and unfair to yourself and others.[3] There are three fundamental parts of civil behavior, and as we explore each, keep in mind that just because people may be familiar with some of these concepts does not mean they always know how to consistently put them into practice.

Politeness
the act of showing consideration for others in accordance with societal expectations

Politeness. Parents always remind their children to be polite to others, but how is it that when people become adults they sometimes model aggressive and hostile behavior toward others? **Politeness** is a simple concept, simply meaning to show consideration for others in accordance with societal expectations. The difficulty is not with showing consideration for others, but rather with navigating the societal expectations in given contexts. We have different social norms and rules for different places, people, events, and cultures. More succinctly, politeness is the use of tact when speaking to others.

Politeness often gets confused with "being nice," or as a tactic for manipulating others. Some people view politeness in others as an attempt to hide something, making them skeptical of the motives of others. We propose that people view politeness as a contrast to rudeness rather than as a veil for some ulterior motive that may not be there. Rudeness consists of behaviors that make others uncomfortable, violate social decency, and are inappropriate or demeaning, while politeness consists of none of those things. Civil communicators exercise a degree of self-monitoring, assessing the contexts in which they find themselves to determine the best way to be considerate toward other people and thus avoid being seen as rude. Politeness often manifests itself through the exhibition of good manners. **Good manners** refer to those polite behaviors that encourage positive relationships with others. Good manners are sometimes legislated, like not using cell phones while in flight, but most are social expectations people have of others. Here are a few good manners that apply to most communication settings:

1. Be on time for meetings and appointments.
2. Patiently wait in line.
3. Don't talk with your mouth full.
4. Say "please" and "thank you."
5. Respect other people's property.
6. Don't look at, or answer, your mobile phone while in the middle of a conversation.

As you can probably imagine, engaging in each of these behaviors can help create a positive perception of a person by others. Just think about what we tend to think of people who do the opposite.

Respect for Others. **Respect** is acknowledging the inherent dignity of the other person as a human being, regardless of what we may think about him or her. Respect does not mean subservience or deference, but rather an effort to understand another person and an acknowledgement of his or her ideas and presence. Scholar Richard Johannesen refers to this as a spirit of mutual equality, and describes it this way: "although society may rank participants of dialogue as of unequal status or accomplishment, the participants themselves view each other as persons, not as objects to be manipulated or exploited. The exercise of power and superiority is to be avoided. Participants do not impose their opinion, cause or will."[4] In other words, everyone has an equal stake in the discussion, and no one person is privileged over another. Communication with a spirit of mutual equality entails not forcing one's perspective on someone else but instead remaining open to receiving the perspective of another as equally significant as one's own position or ideas. No one likes to be ignored or to go unnoticed, and so providing that minimum level of recognition is a good baseline for treating people with respect. When we do this to others, we encourage them to reciprocate, and this creates a positive relationship in which we can have honest and frank discussions, even when we disagree.

Respect for Self. Civility is not only about how we treat others, but it is also about how we treat ourselves. We must respect our own opinions, ideas, and humanity in interactions just as much as we need to do that for other people. To do this is an important, if generally

Good manners those polite behaviors that encourage positive relationships with others

Respect the practice of acknowledging the inherent dignity of other people as human beings

Assertiveness
the practice of clearly, calmly, and confidently making positions and ideas known to others

unacknowledged, component of civility whereby we are assertive. To be **assertive** means to clearly, calmly, and confidently make our positions and ideas known to others. It is important that we feel comfortable expressing our opinions and hearing those of other people. It is disrespectful to ourselves and devalues what we have to say if we sit quietly and never share our own ideas, thus eliminating a chance for other people to understand our perspective and perception of the situation.[5]

Assertiveness is not to be confused with aggressiveness. Aggressiveness implies a desire to win, compete, or otherwise move the other side to silence. Aggressiveness is rude and creates a very uncomfortable situation for everyone and can come across in the words we use, the volume and tone of voice we use, and the facial expressions and hand gestures we make. When we are assertive, we are comfortable knowing we have made our contribution, regardless of whether the idea is adopted by others. On the contrary, when we are aggressive, we seek to win and dominate the conversation. Knowing how to be assertive, but not aggressive, is a key component of being civil.

Presentness

Presentness
a commitment to the moment and the other person in the moment with us; giving your undivided attention

Being civil does not in and of itself create dialogue; there are other important components to this form of communication we must note. One of the biggest challenges to engaging in dialogue with another person or group of people is giving them your undivided attention. When we give our full attention to someone and avoid mental distractions, or noise, we are then practicing **presentness**. Presentness involves a commitment to the moment, and more specifically, the other person in the moment with us. As communication scholar Ron

DIALING DIVERSITY

Seeds of Peace: The Maine Experience[9]

In the early 1990s, journalist John Wallach began a program called Seeds of Peace designed to bring young people from areas of conflict together with youths from their respective "enemies." The youths range in age from 13–18, and spend parts of their summer with each other at a camp in Maine where they live and interact together. The goal is that through meeting and talking with each other for an extended period of time that these "seeds" will return home and build a foundation for peace as they grow older and become more active in their communities. To ensure that the impact is not restricted to the summer, the participants in this very selective camp receive continual support after they leave in the form of dialogue sessions, cross cultural visits, and development workshops. As of 2014, there have been participants in the Seeds of Peace program from the Middle East, Afghanistan, South Asia, and India. It is an astounding example of how dialogue can help improve relations between parties who are seemingly in endless conflict.

Arnett puts it, "relationship centered communication that is sensitive to what happens to both self and other approaches dialogic communication."[6] This is harder than it sounds; just think about a time where you received particularly good or bad news and then had to pay attention in class. You were likely not able to give undivided attention to the class because of the distraction the news became.

It is important to note that the human attention span is finite, which means we can only can maintain attention for a certain period of time because doing so requires a great deal of mental effort. Our ability to focus is a skill we can build with practice[7]. Many people erroneously believe they can multitask and pay attention to someone while doing something else. For any cognitive function that requires you to focus, such as driving, reading, or paying attention to a speaker, it is actually physically impossible to multitask. As molecular biologist John Medina notes, "We are biologically incapable of processing attention-rich inputs simultaneously."[8] So, as you can probably see, it is impossible to do something else that requires cognitive effort while participating in a dialogue, because you simply would not be paying attention to what the other person is saying. It also should be noted that doing something else while someone is talking to you is considered rude in almost any social setting.

Unconditional Positive Regard

So far we have explored how dialogue involves civility and presentness, but those are only parts of the equation. The third element of dialogue is what psychologist Carl Rogers referred to as "**unconditional positive regard**," or accepting others with a positive attitude. Although he applied it specifically to therapists, it works in any interactions we might have with people. Keeping an open mind and seeing the potential good in others creates an environment where people feel comfortable expressing ideas and speaking about potentially controversial topics. Unconditional positive regard does not mean you agree with the other person, only that you believe the other person wants the best for you and you want the best for her or him.

Operating with unconditional positive regard is not easy, and it involves taking some risks, but the rewards outweigh potential costs. Of course, if a person repeatedly shows you he or she is deceitful or cannot be trusted, then your positive regard will diminish. Without the presence of deceit, however, you should believe in the best of others. Most interactions are not competitive, and so we should not operate within them as if the other person is "playing us." The idea of unconditional positive regard illustrates the importance of character in any communication situation.

Mutual Equality

In any social, familial, or professional setting there is a power distribution. Parents have power over children, supervisors have power over employees, and so on. This can, and often does, influence the communication patterns and styles people use when interacting with each other, and in many cases, the simple presence of positional authority can diminish the chance of a true dialogue between people. In a dialogue, the expressions and ideas of every

Unconditional positive regard the tendency to accept other people with a positive attitude, having an open mind for the potential good in other people

Principle of mutual equality the premise that each person can make an equal contribution to the interaction

party are valued at the same level; no one person is valued less or seen as unable to provide a positive contribution. The premise that each person can make an equal contribution to the interaction is the **principle of mutual equality**, and it is the fourth and final component of a good dialogue.

A dialogue depends on the free exchange of ideas between parties, even when those ideas might be at odds. As Ron Arnett puts it, dialogue conducted with a spirit of mutual equality seeks the "unity of contraries," or a way to bridge positions that seem at odds. These tensions occur when authority is present, but also when interests seem mutually exclusive, such as a concern for self versus the community or power and responsibility. For mutual equality to happen in a system or environment where one has authority or power over another requires setting aside the power dimensions and communicating in a way that values the contributions made by everyone. Here are some actions that create mutual equality:

- Collaborating on a solution
- Sharing your goals with all involved
- Paraphrasing what others say to ensure understanding

Now look at these behaviors that stress the power dimensions between participants, and see how they might discourage dialogue:

- Responding to every statement others make
- Keeping information from other participants
- Beginning the discussion with your desired decision

Engaging in communication with others in a civil manner and setting aside any existing power dimensions creates a dialogic environment where people are comfortable expressing ideas, even when they conflict. Creating this type of environment, though, is much harder than explaining what it looks like. Now that we have defined what dialogue is, let's briefly take a moment and illustrate what dialogue is not.

> *"Dialogue is public engagement with difference and offers no assurances for correctness or resolution. The absence of dialogue propelled by tenacious hope to meet ideas contrary to one's own assures societal demise."*[10]
>
> —*Ronald Arnett*

What is Not Dialogue

People commonly misconstrue two other forms of communication as dialogue, when, in fact, they are not. True dialogic communication contains a deep respect and recognition for the other parties in the interaction, and it is also not about winning anything but rather about understanding peoples' unique positions and perspectives. This is not to say these other forms of communication do not have their place; they do. In most interactions with others, dialogue works far better.

Just because we are talking with someone else does not mean we are in a dialogue with him or her. In fact, sometimes we are actually conducting a monologue. A **monologue** is a style of communication where only one voice is respected. This does not mean it is the only voice that is heard, but it does mean that only one voice matters in the discussion. In certain contexts, monologues work well, such as in the military where commanding officers need their troops to follow a directive. Without such a structure, the military loses discipline and is far less effective. Monologues are also sometimes helpful in crises when time is of the essence, such as when emergency personnel are coordinating search and rescue efforts after a tornado or other natural disaster. Monologues, though, are not helpful in situations where group participation and commitment are necessary for success.

In addition to monologues, some people also confuse dialogue with a more competitive form of communication, **debate.** In debates, parties critically listen to each other with the goal of defeating the opponent's argument rather than understanding a perspective or finding common ground. This is, unfortunately, the type of communication modeled for most people through television news programs. Two people with opposing views are asked to speak in short periods of time and argue his or her side against the other person's side.

Monologue
a style of communication where only one voice is respected

Debate
a competitive form of communication where parties critically listen to each other with the goal of defeating the opponent's argument, not understanding the other's perspective or finding common ground

MEDIATED MOMENTS

Science vs. Faith: Bill Nye vs. Ken Ham

One of the most popular PBS television programs to run in the 1990s was *Bill Nye the Science Guy*, hosted by scientist and former Boeing mechanical engineer Bill Nye. Since his show finished airing, Nye has made numerous appearances promoting science education to people across the United States. Ken Ham is CEO of Answers in Genesis, and founder of the Creation Museum in Petersburg, Kentucky. Ham established the Creation Museum to make the case to the public that the Christian bible's Book of Genesis explains creation literally. In February 2014, the two men, one a proponent of evolution, and the other an adamant evangelical creationist, met to debate their positions. The central goal for both parties was to prove the other wrong. They did not attempt to understand each other or explore the positions the other articulated, but rather sought to demonstrate how the opponent's evidence was erroneous. This is an example of a debate, not a dialogue. It is also one of the more common approaches to communicating ideas in the public forum, whether in a formal setting like this, or in a two-minute clip on a cable news show. The idea is to push one's position at the expense of the other.

There is no attempt to build common ground but rather to "win points" by undermining the ideas and evidence of the other person. This type of communication does not promote collaboration, and although it is necessary and even appropriate in some situations, it often can get in the way of true understanding.

Attitudes Necessary for Dialogue

Now that we have uncovered the philosophy behind dialogue, we can better understand the different attitudes one needs to effectively participate in dialogue. These attitudes help illustrate what the proper context is for dialogue to take place. Without the right attitude, true dialogue and understanding are difficult to come by. In this section, we will examine four different attitudes that contribute to a strong positive dialogic experience between people.

Open-Mindedness

Central to dialogue is the belief that no one has a monopoly on good ideas, and that the ideas of others might be better than our own. When we enter into a dialogue, we must be ready to critique our own ideas as well as those of other people. Often, someone else may see something in our ideas that could be improved or notice something we missed, and we must be ready to accept this feedback. Dialogue is a matter of identifying the best idea possible through an understanding of multiple perspectives. Being open-minded calls us to withhold judgment while we completely listen to our conversational partners; in doing that, we can gather all the information possible about an issue. This attitude flows from the central premise of dialogue related to respecting other people.

Genuineness

Genuineness
the act of being direct, honest, and straightforward regarding what we believe and think

Recall that in a dialogue we must respect ourselves as well as the other party, and in order to do so, according to Richard Johannesen, we must enter into an interaction with an attitude that is genuine.[11] **Genuineness** means being direct, honest, and straightforward regarding what we believe and think. This allows us to be true to ourselves as well as the other person by not hiding our thoughts or denying ourselves the right to contribute to the dialogue. People who try to communicate strategically or tactically are more likely engaging in debate, and, in trying to manipulate the course of the discussion, prohibit true dialogue from taking place. This is self-centered rather than other-centered communication, which carries great risk for the relationship if uncovered.

Being genuine can carry its own risk, as you might be operating in a genuine manner while the other person is not, thus creating a situation where you might be taken advantage of by the other party. We must be genuine to create trust, but being genuine also makes us vulnerable in interactions with people who are not trustworthy. In these situations, you might want to reveal truths in a gradual manner as you get to know the other person. This will minimize, but not eliminate, the risk; as long as your contribution is true and honest, you are still being genuine.

Agreeableness

One of the key characteristics of a good dialogue is being agreeable. Being agreeable means remaining open to the idea that you might agree with the other person. We often focus on the overall argument or position and not its parts. If we enter into a discussion with an attempt to be agreeable, we allow ourselves to recognize points we might agree with as opposed to a totalizing statement of agreeing or disagreeing with a person. We might disagree with her or his conclusion but find places of agreement in the evidence the person uses to get there. When we stress areas of agreement rather than the things on which we disagree, we create a much more comfortable climate for communication and generate a positive impression of ourselves for other people.

Agreeable communicators not only seek to find the things on which they agree with another person, but they recognize the person is not the argument. They do not equate a person's character or identity simply with a position he or she may take on an issue.

Ethical Integrity

As you might imagine, an attitude derived from a sense of morality and desire for fairness is important for anyone engaging in dialogic communication. **Morality** is our inner sense of right and wrong. Our desire for fairness is shaped by that understanding in specific contexts. Holding true to our sense of right and wrong and consistently applying it in any situation we might encounter is a hallmark of **integrity**, or the maintenance of a consistent application of our values in every situation. There are a whole host of different ethical approaches, some derived from philosophy and others from theology. Regardless, they each inform our sense of what is right and good in a particular situation. Strong ethical character has long been a hallmark of communication, going all the way back to the Roman philosopher and teacher Quintilian, who required his students to demonstrate that they were "a good man speaking well."[12]

No matter the philosophy or theology that informs one's moral center, a good person always seeks what is good for his or her community, not necessarily what is best for his or her self, and is clear about that motive when explaining a position to others. Law professor Steven Carter describes this type of moral integrity as having three main components: "(1) discerning what is right and what is wrong, (2) acting on what you have discerned, even at personal cost, and (3) saying openly that you are acting on your understanding of right from wrong."[13] In dialogue, we must be willing to examine ideas—even our own—for how they reflect our values and then act according to those values.

Each of the attitudes we have discussed—open-mindedness, genuineness, agreeableness, and ethical integrity—all serve as the foundation to actual communicative behaviors that create a dialogue born from the definition of dialogue we explored earlier in the chapter. In the next, and final section of this chapter, we will explore some of those behaviors.

Dialogic Behaviors

Knowing what dialogue is and even approaching it with the right attitude does not guarantee a successful interaction using this style of communication. What we can

Morality
an inner sense of right and wrong

Integrity
the maintenance of a consistent application of our values in every situation

control, however, is our attempt to create what group communication scholar Jack Gibb calls a supportive communication climate. Gibb contrasts a supportive climate, where people are comfortable exchanging ideas and differing opinions with each other, with a defensive communication climate. A defensive climate is one where people feel attacked and threatened by the other party. Gibb identified six contrasting behavior types that could create either supportive or defensive communication climates. In Table 3.1, you can see his communication behavioral typology[14]:

TABLE 3.1   Supportive and Defensive Behavior Types

Supportive Behaviors		Defensive Behaviors	
Description	Nonjudgmental statement or account	Evaluation	Statement that passes judgment in some way
Problem orientation	Seeks to find a good solution to a problem	Control	Seeks to impose a specific solution
Spontaneity	Thought up at the moment	Strategy	Preplanned approach designed to manipulate a person or situation
Empathy	Cares about the other person's feelings	Neutrality	Doesn't care about others' feelings
Equality	Two people are equal as humans	Superiority	One person is greater than the other in some characteristic (e.g., power, wealth, intellect)
Provisionalism	An idea seems promising, pending further consideration	Certainty	An answer is final and requires no further consideration

In this section, we will build upon Gibb's categories and offer six specific behaviors you can employ to conduct a successful dialogue by creating a supportive communication climate. Be forewarned, however, that these behaviors are easier explained than implemented; they take a lot of patience and practice.

Separate Facts from Interpretation

In the previous chapter, we covered the perception process, and the final stage in that process is interpretation. As you recall, interpretations take symbols, events, and experiences and give them meaning, but we all do not give the same meaning to the same things. These interpretations are not facts, and to have a good dialogue we must avoid treating them as such. When people offer interpretations or judgments that are different from ours, they do not necessarily have the facts wrong; they just have a different way of seeing something. Rather than suggesting others are incorrect, interpretive differences illustrate a perceptual gap between ourselves and the other person that we need to bridge through dialogue.

We often deny the opportunity for dialogue by issuing opinions as though they should be accepted as facts. For instance, saying, "The cost for car insurance is $750 a year," is a statement of a fact. If you instead said, "The car insurance here is expensive," you would be offering an interpretation, not a fact. You could adjust this second statement to make it more dialogic by adding the qualifier, "I believe that" to the beginning of the interpretation, making it clear that your statement is an interpretation and not a fact. The more specific and factual we can be in a dialogue, the easier it will be to understand why someone believes the way she or he does.

Ask Clarifying Questions

As you can probably imagine, in many situations it can be difficult to either keep up with a conversational partner or differentiate between fact and interpretation. The most effective dialogic tool for managing these challenges is asking clarifying questions. These questions must be handled in a manner consistent with the principles and attitudes inherent in dialogic communication, meaning they are not judgmental nor do they implicitly state a position in the form of a question. Nondialogic questions might look like the following examples in the left column of Table 3.2.

TABLE 3.2 **Nondialogic and Dialogic Questions**

Nondialogic Questions	Dialogic Questions
"So, you are telling me you did not take out the garbage last night despite what our neighbors said?"	"What time did you take out the garbage last night?"
"Don't you think that spending money on that dress is a waste of your hard earned cash?"	"How much money will you have left after buying that dress?"
"Can't you see how that job is beneath you?"	"What new responsibilities will you have in this position?"

Each of these questions is not designed to achieve understanding but is rather a tool to forward a position disguised as a question. These are examples of leading or loaded questions. These questions do not encourage dialogue, as they do not demonstrate open-minded communication.

Clarifying questions, on the other hand, are focused on furthering understanding through the solicitation of information from another party. These questions do not attack or express judgment, but rather invite further explanation on a topic or issue. Look to the right column of Table 3.2 for some examples of clarifying questions that encourage dialogue.

Each of these seeks information and does not imply judgments. By asking questions this way, communicators invite discussion without putting a person on the defensive.

Allow Other People to Speak Fully

We all can think of a time when we got excited and wanted to either add to the conversation or respond to what someone was saying. In order to create a climate that encourages dialogue, however, we must allow the other person to finish their thoughts before we jump in. This is one of the most common conversational miscues people make: believing they know where someone is going with a statement and so, in their excitement, jumping in and finishing the statement for the other person. Although it may be done with a desire to show support for the other person, this interruption can be construed as rude and may actually end up hurting more than helping to facilitate dialogue. Interruptions often hurt the listener as well as the speaker by denying them the opportunity to hear everything.

To allow other people to speak fully and thus avoid interruptions, it is essential to put your desire to speak to the side so you can focus on your role as a listener. This role is just as important as speaking in a dialogue, and demonstrating the ability and desire to pay attention to the speaker throughout his or her statement helps create an environment in which you listen in a way that encourages others to speak. Additionally, when you listen carefully to the speaker throughout his or her statement, you are modeling that behavior and communicating to others that they should also listen in a way that encourages you to speak.

Take Notes

One thing you can do to keep yourself from interrupting someone and keep pace with what is being said is to take notes. Students do this in most all classes, mainly to create organized study materials for upcoming exams. Little do they realize that note taking would benefit their ability to have constructive and successful interactions with other people. We simply cannot recall everything another person says. The more time that passes between the action and the time we try to remember it, the more we forget. This cognitive loss makes it even more important to keep a written record of important points in conversations so that later, when we need to revisit what was covered, we can return to our notes.

Taking notes also assists us during conversations or presentations in that rather than interrupting a person in the moment he or she says something, we can write down our questions or comments and wait until it is our turn to speak. This keeps us from forgetting the comment or question and allows us to contextualize it with the statement to which our question or comment is responding. Note taking also demonstrates to the other people in the conversation that you are paying attention, which creates a comfortable communication climate where people feel as if you value their contributions. This is a way of physically demonstrating respect for the other person by giving her or him your attention.

Give Complete Attention

Earlier in the chapter we pointed out how multitasking interferes with effective dialogue. Many professors have policies regarding the use of computers and cell phones in their classes, likely because they have witnessed students using computers to do things other than follow along in class. The same thing happens in business meetings, where colleagues often will text or look at their phone during meetings. These activities are disrespectful to the other people in the conversation because they show that person is not paying complete attention. Not only do distractions increase the risk of important information being missed, but relationships and personal credibility could be damaged as well.

Whether it is in class or in a meeting, it is important to give someone your complete attention. You would want the same when you speak, and so giving others your attention is equally important. Keep in mind that attention does not mean simply staring at the other person; it rather involves being fully present and expressing interest in what is being said.

Own Your Own Statements

The final behavior we will discuss that encourages a dialogic climate for communication is owning your own statements. This involves using "I" language instead of "you" language. "You" language puts people on the defensive because it can come across as accusatory. We often do this when we have negative feelings and begin blaming other people or events for the way we feel, thus abdicating our ability to control our own emotions. This diminishes respect for ourselves and comes across as though others can control us. Take a look at Table 3.3.

TABLE 3.3   "You" and "I" Language

"You" Language	"I" Language
"You are a liar."	"I think I need more convincing."
"You never let me finish."	"I have not fully explained myself."
"You are driving me crazy!"	"Please give me a moment."

Each of the "I" statements focuses on the speaker and illustrates his or her ability to both be in touch with emotions and feelings and express them in a way that does not attack the other party. "You" language shows that the communicator is not able to express emotions well and relies on attack or blame to express how he or she feels. It is easy to see how such language choices could destroy opportunities for dialogue.

Summary

Dialogue can be a truly effective tool when interacting with other people. Its goal is mutual understanding, not necessarily agreement. It is a style of communication that encourages people to want to listen and speak. We first examined what dialogue is, breaking it down into four key parts. We then discussed the four attitudes necessary for engaging in dialogue with another person, before ending the chapter with a discussion of six behaviors that encourage dialogue in any situation.

Chapter 3 Key Ideas

- The four key characteristics of dialogue are civility, presentness, unconditional positive regard, and mutual equality
- Civility requires politeness, respect for others, and respect for self; without a willingness to assert one's feelings and thoughts, true dialogue cannot take place. Civility is more than just "being nice"
- Dialogues differ from monologues in that monologues respect only one voice; they differ from debates because in a dialogue the goal is understanding, not necessarily agreement
- The four attitudes one must have to enter into a true dialogue are open-mindedness, genuineness, agreeableness, and ethical integrity
- When engaging in a dialogue, it is important not to confuse interpretations with facts, ask clarifying questions when you do not understand something, do not interrupt others, give full attention, and take notes

Chapter 3 Key Terms

Dialogue	Assertiveness	Debate
Civility	Presentness	Genuineness
Politeness	Unconditional positive regard	Morality
Good manners	Principle of mutual equality	Integrity
Respect	Monologue	

Endnotes

1 Edited and paraphrased from Pearce, W. B. and K. A. Pearce (2000). Extending the theory of the coordinated management of meaning (CMM) through a community dialogic process. *Communication Theory 10* (pp. 405-423); and Pearce, W. B. and K. A. Pearce (2000). Combining passions and abilities: Toward dialogic virtuosity. *Southern Communication Journal 65*, 161–175.

2 Poulakos, J. (1974). The components of dialogue. *Western Journal of Speech Communication. 38*, 199.

3 Forni, P. M. (2002). *Choosing civility: The twenty-five rules for considerate conduct.* New York: St. Martin's Press.

4 Johannesen, R. L. (1971). The emerging concept of communication as dialogue. *Quarterly Journal of Speech. 57*, 376.

5 Forni, P. M. (2002) *Choosing Civility: The Twenty-Five Rules of Considerate Conduct.* New York, NY: St. Martin's Press.

6 Arnett, R. C. (1986). *Communication and community: Implications of Martin Buber's dialogue.* Carbondale, IL: Southern Illinois University Press.

7 Goleman, D. (2013). *Focus.* New York, NY: HarperCollins.

8 Medina, J. (2008). *Brain rules.* Edmonds, WA: Pear Press.

9 Seeds of Peace: Maine Seeds Program. Retrieved from www.seedsofpeace.org

10 Arnett, R. C. (1986). *Communication and community: Implications of Martin Buber's Dialogue.* Carbondale, IL: Southern Illinois University Press, p.7.

11 Johannesen, R. L. (1971). The Emerging Concept of Communication as Dialogue. *Quarterly Journal of Speech, 57*, 376.

12 Quintilian. (1856). *Quintilian's Institutes of Oratory; Or, Education of an Orator.* J. S. Watson. London: G. Bell and Sons, 12.1.1.

13 Carter, S. L. (1996). *Integrity.* New York: Harper Perennial, p. 7.

14 Gibb, J. R. (1961). Defensive communication. *Journal of Communication.* 11 (3), 141–148.

Chapter 4

Language

Communication is only made possible through the use of symbol systems, the most common of which is language. Without language, relationships of any kind would struggle to develop, which would fundamentally alter the nature of what it means to be human. Languages, though, are not simple things; just ask anyone who has ever tried to learn a second language. The very nature of languages is what makes them difficult to learn and use, even for people speaking in their native tongue. The wrong word said in the wrong context can create misunderstandings, misperceptions, and poor impressions. Language is a tool for connecting people with one another, and like any tool, it must be applied correctly to achieve the user's desired ends.

In this chapter, we explore the nature of language in an effort to illustrate its complexities and help you improve your ability to use it effectively in your lives. We will first examine the four basic characteristics all languages share. We will then explore different ways language can be used to create meaning and enhance understanding between people. Next, we will discuss some cross-cultural challenges to understanding when conversational partners speak two different languages. Finally, we will present some suggestions for how to employ language in a way that encourages dialogue.

Language Characteristics

Symbols are the building blocks of language, and a fundamental component of a symbol is that it has meaning. A sound, image, or utterance by itself does not mean anything unless we give it meaning. For example, when someone clears his or her throat, we may not pay it any heed and thus afford it no meaning; we also might take it to indicate the individual wants to say something—thus providing the sound its own meaning. In short, words only have meaning insofar as we give it to them. When we give signs and symbols meaning, like we do with words in a language, they are composed of four characteristics: they are arbitrary, they are ambiguous, they are abstract, and they are negative.

Arbitrary

Arbitrary
term that describes symbols themselves as having no direct connection with the things they represent

Semiotics
the study of the social production of meaning from sign systems like language

Signifier
the physical thing as we perceive it in the world around us

Signified
the meaning associated with the sign, or rather the combination of the sign and the thing it is meant to represent

Sign
an arbitrary symbol; something that can be interpreted as having meaning

The first characteristic of language is that it is **arbitrary**, meaning the symbols themselves have no direct connection with the things they represent. For example, the word "selfie" has no real relationship with a picture of yourself; it only has a connection through the thought the symbol creates in our minds. The term "selfie" could have been something else entirely, but as a community of people using the same language, we essentially agreed that the symbol "selfie" represents a picture you take of yourself using a mobile device. The term is merely a label that has been coordinated by people to mean roughly the same thing to everyone in that group. We say "roughly," because when someone says "selfie," we all get a different image of a selfie in our minds; some of us picture one that we took of ourselves, others perhaps a photo posted to social media, and still others might envision someone actually taking a selfie. The fact that the labels we choose to represent things are arbitrary in nature explains how different languages can have different words for the same thing.

Semiologist and linguist Ferdinand De Saussure helped illustrate how we make sense out of arbitrary signs.[1] He was very interested in how signs functioned and became known as one of the fathers of **semiotics**, or the study of the social production of meaning from sign systems like language. De Saussure breaks down the system into three parts. The first is the **signifier**, which is the physical thing as we perceive it in the world around us. For example, as we see in the diagram below, an example of a signifier might be an actual table. The second is the **signified**, which is the idea or mental construct of that thing. This is the meaning associated with the signifier. Even though there are a lot of different ways particular tables might look for feel, the signified is the general idea we carry around in our minds of what a table is like. The third part of this system is the **sign**, or the arbitrary symbol that represents both the signifier and the signified.

In this case, the word "table" is the sign that represents both a specific, physical table, and the idea of what a table is. There is no necessary relationship between the word "table" and the actual object and idea of what a table is, but over time those who speak the English language have come to an agreement to use the word "table" as the sign that represents the thing and the idea, while those who speak Spanish use the word "mesa" as the sign that represents this same signifier and signified; take a look at Figure 4.1 for a visualization of this relationship. Due to the arbitrariness of language and signs, there are many different signs for the same signifier, which can create confusion. Nevertheless, that there can be many signs for the same signifier illustrates the fundamental characteristic of language, where the words are not the things, but rather representations of those things that we interpret.

FIGURE 4.1   Sign

Ambiguous

A second fundamental attribute of language is that it is **ambiguous**. By that, we mean that words do not have absolute meanings and can be used for a variety of different contexts and purposes. The ambiguity of language allows terms and symbols to mean different things in different contexts. For instance, the "peace sign" of holding up two fingers has also meant "victory," and in some cultures it is actually a profane expression. The word "wicked" can also be interpreted in several different ways; it is the name of a musical, it can mean something that is evil, and it can also mean something that is very enjoyable or interesting.

   The ambiguity of language comes from its connection to a history of usage and understanding. As Roland Barthes explains, symbols (especially words) have two different types of meaning, which creates ambiguity for an audience.[2] The first is **denotative meaning**, which is attached to a sign without understanding its history of usage and application. This type of meaning is, for all intents and purposes, a sign's dictionary definition. But words are not always used according to their literal definitions, as most of the time we use words for their connotative, not denotative meanings. **Connotative meaning** is that which comes from a set of associations a word brings to mind in a person. Individuals and groups can have different connotative meanings for the same word, because of the emotions and experiences tied to that term.

   Both denotative and connotative definitions reflect correct meanings of words, but we usually use words based on their connotative meanings. To illustrate the difference, look at the nature of synonyms, or words that have the same literal meaning. For example, synonyms for the word "car" include "carriage," "wagon," "motor vehicle," and "truck," but when we use each of these terms, we create a different image in someone's mind as to what we are speaking about. We depend on those associations to reduce the ambiguity of the terms we use, and it is evident that the ambiguity of language can easily lead to misunderstandings and misperceptions.

Ambiguous
term that describes words as being without absolute meanings

Denotative meaning
the meaning prescribed to a sign without understanding its history of usage and application; its dictionary, or literal, definition

Connotative meaning
meaning that comes from a set of associations a word brings to mind in a person

Abstract

The third characteristic of language is that it is abstract—not tangible or concrete. It cannot be held, moved, or physically experienced. The mind must understand and interpret language, and words cannot be processed any other way. The abstract nature of language allows human beings to think about and talk about things that could be or might have been. Language does not need to refer to something specific or physical, but rather it can refer to things like ideas, values, and beliefs.

Abstract language can also refer to a set of terms that refer to things that are intangible or not specific. To this end, some terms are more specific than others, and can generate more concrete images in a receiver's mind. The more precise the language, the less abstract the ideas, and the closer two parties can come to sharing meaning. Figure 4.2 is an example of how this works in a visual representation often called the ladder of abstraction:

FIGURE 4.2 Ladder of Abstraction

More Abstract

Book

Novel

Fantasy fiction novel

A Game of Thrones series

A Feast of Crows

More Concrete

Negative
the idea that language separates things from their natural state, thus telling us not only what something is, but what it is not

Negative

Language is also inherently **negative**—not negative in the sense that language is bad, but rather that it creates a void or separation. Scholar Kenneth Burke, who contributed a great deal to our understanding of language, noted that through the process of labeling something we are both saying what the thing is as well as what it is not. He proposed that this gives language a negative quality because the label divides things between what is and what is not. In communication, sometimes the best way to help people understand what you are saying is to explain the negative, or what you don't mean, with a statement.

Terms and Structures of Language

The flexibility of language allows it to take several forms when we use it. The different words and structures allow us to create interesting messages that encourage other people to listen and can also help people understand our meaning in a variety of ways when we try to explain something complicated. The varied word choices and structures of language make speeches, conversations, and ideas memorable to an audience or conversational partner. In this section of the chapter, we will examine several different language structures that can make what we say more appealing to others.

Metaphoric Language

Since all language represents something else, all language is metaphoric. A metaphor is a linguistic device that highlights qualities of two objects in an explicit comparison. There are six different types of metaphors we will discuss in this section, and each does different things.

Simile. One of the more common language structures we use when speaking to others is a simile. **Similes** are language devices that compare two things through the use of "like" or "as." Similes allow the comparison to focus on a specific attribute shared by two different things rather than saying those two things are exactly the same. Similes also contain both of the compared items in the statement, which is to say the comparison is explicit. Let's look at an example: "You are like a kid at Christmas." The qualities shared by the two items (the person and a child at Christmas) relate to their excitement, while it is clear that the person is not being called a child. It is a distinction with a difference, as both the person and the child that person is compared to retain their core qualities, but share in their degree of excitement. It is important to remember that all similes are metaphors, but not all metaphors are similes.

Similes
metaphoric language devices that compare two things through the use of "like" or "as"

Synecdoche. Similes are a type of metaphoric language that is identified through the explicit statement of "like" or "as," but **synecdoche**, the second type of metaphor we will discuss, does not have such an easy marker. Instead, synecdoche is a metaphor that uses one part of something to refer to the whole thing. Look at the following example of synecdoche: "She is learning her ABCs." In this statement, ABCs refers to the entire alphabet, not just the first three letters, but that part of the alphabet is being used to refer to the whole alphabet. In fact, just about any acronym is a synecdoche. There are others as well, like the navy saying, "All hands on deck," where "hands" refers to all personnel.

Synecdoche
a metaphor that uses one part of something to refer to the whole thing

Metonymy. A third form of metaphor is identified by its use of tangible objects to refer to intangible things. **Metonyms** create a much more vivid, colorful, and concrete vision for things that people have a hard time understanding. Such tools can help explain concepts, theories, ideas, and values in ways most people can understand by taking these abstract items and tying them to an experience or thing people have seen, touched, smelled, or otherwise experienced through their senses. One of the most common examples of a metonym is the use of "blood, sweat, and tears" to imply hard work; another is using "heart" to refer to passion or love. Not every task results in someone leaking blood, sweat, and tears upon completion, but the image conveys hard work in any context. Nor do people actually "wear their heart on their sleeves" when they display emotions, but the metonym here helps paint a vivid, interesting picture.

Metonym
a metaphor that is identified by its use of tangible objects to refer to intangible things

Archetypal. Most metaphors are culturally specific and rely on knowledge of a specific community and their experiences to work. For example, saying that a salesperson needs

Archetypal
metaphors that use common human experiences to help describe another object

to "get across the goal line" with a sale is a metaphor that is unique to Americans, because it is drawn from the version of football only played there, so people from another culture likely will not understand its meaning. That being said, there are metaphors drawn from the human experience that use things every person can relate to because the comparison uses something we all experience or know to shed light on something else. Metaphors that use common human experiences to help describe another object are referred to as **archetypal**. Things like "light" and "dark," as well as "sickness" and "health," are common human experiences that can be used to give meaning to other things. For instance, when we say there is a "light at the end of the tunnel" with a class, we mean the class is almost over. Since light and tunnels are part of the human experience nearly everywhere, this archetypal metaphor is not bound to a specific culture.

Mixed metaphors
phrases that make use of two different metaphors that do not logically fit; compare two things that have no inherent connection with each other, creating incongruous comparisons

Mixed. In everyday conversations we often use metaphors to compare two things that have no inherent connection with each other, creating incongruous comparisons. Some of these **mixed metaphors** make use of two different metaphors that do not logically fit but mean the same thing, like saying "We need to hit the bull's eye or we will have to punt this decision to later." Here, an archery metaphor is mixed with a sports football metaphor, but the meaning is fairly easy to discern. The fact that bull's eyes and punting have nothing to do with each other does not detract from the meaning, but when read literally, the metaphors do not really work and create a pretty funny statement.

Dead metaphors
metaphors that have lost the creative element from which they initially drew their power and now are just accepted as true terms, rather than the metaphor they are

Dead. Metaphors are such a common part of our language that often when we use them we forget their origins and the characteristics of the object used for the comparison. These metaphors have lost the creative element from which they initially drew their power and now are just accepted as everyday phrases rather than the metaphors they are. Such commonplace phrases have become **dead metaphors**. Just think about the following and see if you can resurrect the original source of the comparison for the metaphor: "eye of the needle," "body of an essay," "flowerbed," "seeds of doubt," and "branches of government." Each of these words and phrases contains a metaphoric element that implicitly compares it to something else, but we don't actually make the comparison in our minds. Thus, we have killed the original metaphor used for the comparison.

> *Many people who disagree on one or many issues are said by some to have a "communication problem." I, however, would argue that these people don't have "communication problems" but rather problems of substance which in turn cause them to have difficulties in communicating with each other.*
>
> —*Richard Vatz, Towson University*

Language Structures

Metaphoric terms are not the only way we can create interesting and appealing messages. We can also play with the structure of the terms we use and organize our messages into forms that invite people to listen. In this section of the chapter, we will detail five ways to structure language that can increase the appeal of a message for its audience, regardless of whether it is one person, a small group, or a large gathering.

Repetition. One of the old maxims of communication is that if you want people to remember something important, tell it to them, tell it to them again, and tell it to them a third time. This approach can also be applied for effect with words and not just information, and when we repeat words and phrases either immediately following the initial statement or in the same location in a message we are using **repetition**. By "the same location" we mean at the beginning of consecutive sentences or paragraphs. So, when Martin Luther King Jr. used the phrase "I have a dream" in consecutive sentences, he used repetition to make his phrase memorable for his audience.

Alliteration. There are only so many sounds we can make, and speakers can add aural interest when using the same sound in consecutive words. When we use the same vowel or consonant sound at the beginning of consecutive words, we are using **alliteration**. This makes particular content much more noticeable to an audience, and increases the likelihood an audience will retain what was said. Just think of childhood tongue twisters like, "Sally sells sea shells by the sea shore," and you will see the power of alliteration. The key to making alliteration work is that each of the words must relate to each other and the topic at hand, because if you just use words that start with the same sound but do not have anything to do with each other, it will create a message no one understands. Just look at the previous example of Sally, who was selling sea shells on the sea shore—something you might actually believe was happening because the content tells a story that makes sense. Conversely, the alliterative effect would be lost if the sentence was "Sally smites smiles on the septic state."

Parallelism. A third strategy for using terms to create maximum appeal involves placing related words or phrases in a pattern that highlights what they have in common. When we similarly structure words, phrases, or clauses in this way we are using **parallelism**. Let's look at a few examples:

> "She is an actress, writer, director, and producer."
> "Water, food, shelter, and love are all necessary for a happy life."
> "He is a passionate, dedicated, and enthusiastic advocate for his cause."
> "Peace leads to progress and prosperity."

Each of these statements uses similar properties to describe something. In the first statement, all of the jobs described are related to the production of theater or television shows. The second statement contains four things humans need to survive. The next statement uses adjectives rather than nouns to create the parallel structure. The final example is even more interesting because it uses alliteration in the parallel structuring, which illustrates these linguistic devices are not mutually exclusive, but

Repetition
the practice of repeating words and phrases either immediately following the initial statement, or in the same location in a message

Alliteration
the practice of using the same vowel or consonant sound at the beginning of consecutive words

Parallelism
the practice of placing related words or phrases in a pattern that highlights what they have in common

can, when appropriate, be combined to create an even more memorable and effective message.

Parallelism is especially important when you have a single subject accompanied by a series of verbs or a series of nouns accompanied by a single verb. For example, you might say, "My puppy Einstein likes to run, to play, and to sleep," or "My puppy Einstein likes running, playing, and sleeping." However, you would be violating principles of parallelism if you were to say, "My puppy Einstein likes to run, playing, and to sleep."

Antithesis. The fourth way to structure language is a specific application of parallelism, but because of its unique qualities, we treat it separately. Antithesis occurs when two contrasting ideas are placed side by side in a parallel structure. John F. Kennedy gave perhaps the most famous example of antithesis in his inaugural address when he declared, "Ask not what your country can do for you, but what you can do for your country."[3] John Milton also made use of antithesis in his book *Paradise Lost,* when he wrote about the devil, "Better to reign in Hell, than serve in Heaven."[4] One final example comes from the popular adage, "You can please some of the people some of the time, and even some of the people all of the time, but you can never please all of the people all of the time." In each of these statements, contradictory phrases are used to play off of each other to make a point. Antithesis is a creative tool that forces the audience to think about what was said to discern the meaning, but it also generates a very memorable phrase or sentence in the message, increasing the likelihood it will stick with the audience.

Narrative. Metaphoric language and creative turns of phrase like those we have discussed so far are effective tools, but their appeal can be made even stronger when included within larger stories. Not all stories, though, are equal, so it is important to consider what we know about good stories when constructing messages for others. Narrative theory proposes that all humans are story-telling animals, and that everything we say, no matter how short or long, is a story. Most of the time the characters are implied and the action is all that is stated, like when we explain to a partner or friend how our day went. Other times, characters need to be more explicitly stated, such as when we recount something we witnessed or heard about. Regardless, stories are a powerful tool when trying to explain or argue something with an audience, because we always control how the story unfolds through how we tell it.

According to Walter Fisher, the theorist responsible for developing the narrative paradigm, there are two important qualities for judging stories you should use when both crafting your own messages and examining the messages of others.[5] The first is called **narrative coherence**, which refers to whether the story itself hangs together and whether the content of the story makes sense. It asks questions such as: Do the responses of characters to events seem rational? Are the characters consistent? Do events seem plausible and believable in the world of the story? Do things happen in an appropriate order that makes logical sense? In addition to narrative coherence, we

Narrative coherence feature exhibited by a story with content that hangs together and makes sense must also consider **narrative fidelity,** or whether the story rings true to the audience. Narrative fidelity tests how well the story reflects the values and beliefs of the audience. If stories do not reflect the values of an audience, then they are not very appealing or effective devices.

Narrative fidelity term for describing how well a story reflects the values and beliefs of its audience

Guidelines for Dialogic Language

Engaging in a dialogue necessarily involves language, but how we employ that language and what we say makes the difference between a successful encounter and one that is uncomfortable and potentially hostile. When you wish to achieve understanding between two or more people, it is important to take great care with the language choices you make when describing how you feel and what you think. The linguistic choices we make often make the difference between establishing an atmosphere conducive to dialogue, or creating a more combative environment that makes genuineness and understanding difficult to achieve. In this section, we will explore some guidelines for using language that encourages dialogue.

Use Inclusive Language

One of the key components to generating support and creating a dialogic environment is letting the other party know you identify with his or her needs. One way of doing this is by using the pronoun "we" instead of "I," "me," or "you." When speaking with "I" and "me," you set yourself apart from the other party and create division, whereas if you use "we" language you create the perception you are on their side and one of them. Inclusive language goes even further than pronouns, though.

Whenever possible, use gender neutral language. If you use gender specific terminology like "he," "she," or "man," you make assumptions about the makeup of that particular subject that might not be true. For example, you should say "member of Congress" instead of "congressman," "service member" instead of "airman," "flight attendant" instead of "stewardess," and "businessperson" instead of "businessman." The gendered versions of these terms tend to exclude people who you may not want to exclude, and create a negative perception of you and your perspective. It is a matter of courtesy and politeness to use the nongendered terms, and it will go a long way toward creating a comfortable communication environment with others, particularly people who do not know you.

Avoid Profanity

There is hardly a place in American society where **profanity,** or vulgar and irreverent language, is not used. Television programs, both cable and network, depict characters who use it; books and magazines now even place it on their covers; and people use it throughout their daily lives in conversations, memos, and emails. Profanity, however, often does not gain you anything and comes with the risk of insulting, offending, or otherwise irritating people. It also creates the impression that you are not well-spoken and that you are rude. Limiting profanity and knowing the risks to your image that come with its use are important.

Profanity vulgar and irreverent language

MEDIATED MOMENTS

In the 2014 Marvel superhero action hit, *Guardians of the Galaxy*, a team of interstellar misfits comes together to save the universe. Among this group is the brusque and violent Drax the Destroyer, played by Miguel Batista. One of the characteristics of Drax that makes him both frustrating to his teammates and hysterical for the audience is his inability to understand metaphors. Drax takes everything literally, including in a scene where the character Rocket Raccoon complains that some things just go over Drax's head. Drax immediately responds, "It would not

go over my head. I would catch it." Drax also fails to appreciate the synecdoche metaphor offered by Chris Pratt's Star-Lord when he tries to convince Drax not to harm a teammate. Star-Lord mimes the action "cut her throat," meaning to kill, and Drax replies he did not plan to cut her throat, but kill her in a different way. These interactions create comedic confusion, but also illustrate the power of metaphoric language and the necessity to understand that not everyone understands metaphors the same way—especially if they come from another (intergalactic) culture.

Avoid Hate Speech

Profanity is not the only form of language that people find offensive; phrases and terms that attack a person or group of people based upon their gender, ethnicity, religion, sexual orientation, social actions, or any other category that indicates applications of a negative unwarranted stereotype can also destroy the potential for dialogue. Some people use these types of terms in an attempt at humor, but they fail to see how others might receive the message and thus take an unnecessary risk of offending someone else. Remember that being sensitive to the audience's perspective is essential for dialogue.

Use Culturally Appropriate Metaphors

As enticing as metaphors can be when writing a speech or telling a friend a story, it is important to recognize not every metaphor works for every audience. Often, metaphors are tied to experiences within a specific culture and do not translate to those who come from outside of that group. This creates one of two problems in translation that can make understanding more difficult to achieve.

Idioms
metaphoric expressions whose meanings are not predictable from their usual use, but must be inferred from cultural markers

The first problem is called idiomatic equivalence. Some metaphors we use are included in expressions called idioms. **Idioms** are metaphoric expressions whose meanings are not predictable from their usual use, but must be inferred from cultural markers. An example of a culturally specific idiom is the phrase "to stop on a dime." Clearly, to understand this phrase one needs to be familiar with American currency, both in terms of its name and its size. Using this phrase with someone who is not familiar with dimes can cause them to feel embarrassed and even defensive that they do not know what it means, thus hindering the ability to engage in dialogue.

The second problem is related to the fact that different people in different cultures potentially do not share the same experiences or cultural values. Thus, using language that depends on shared experiences or values creates problems with what we call experiential-cultural translation. Basically, if someone has not seen or experienced something, then using that object as a metaphor for something else will only serve to further confuse the situation. Being other-centered and dialogic requires us to pay attention to our language choices and use phrases we believe our audience will understand.

Use Familiar Language

Being dialogic requires a person to be honest with herself or himself as well as others, and nothing damages credibility like trying to use words with which you are not familiar. Mispronouncing words or using them inappropriately only creates a negative impression of you by others. Additionally, if others believe you are trying to portray yourself as more knowledgeable or experienced than you are, then they will see you as insincere, which will damage your ability to engage in a dialogue. It is important that you acknowledge what you do and do not know and that you use words, metaphors, and phrases with which you are comfortable. This is not to say you should not develop a better vocabulary, but you should make sure that you understand the meaning of terms to ensure you are using new words and phrases correctly. At the very least, acknowledge you may not be using them correctly.

Be Specific and Concrete

One of the common errors people make in conversations is "dancing around the issue," or not being clear. In a dialogic environment, it is essential that you try to be as specific and concrete as possible to facilitate understanding between yourself and your audience or conversational partner. The more vague or abstract the description you provide, the less likely the other party will be able to accurately interpret your meaning. Concrete language, which may include the use of vivid examples, helps an audience see things how you intend those things to be seen. Specific details also help remove emotion from controversial situations and allow people to focus on a clear issue and topic without the trappings of the emotions the topic may carry on an abstract level.

Use Descriptive, Not Evaluative, Language

Related to the idea of specificity is the practice of using descriptive rather than evaluative language, which you may recall from Gibb's categorization of supportive and defensive language types from the last chapter. Descriptive language simply lays out objective facts or observations without any form of judgment, whereas evaluative language either expressly or implicitly provides an evaluation of those facts or observations. We often

DIALING DIVERSITY

In 2010, columnist Dan Savage created a YouTube video with his partner Terry Miller to help stem the tide of youth suicides by teenagers bullied for their sexual preference. Their goal was to serve as an illustration of the thousands of gay adults who survived the challenges and difficulties of growing up gay in a heteronormative world. Their video inspired others to do the same and led to the creation of the It Gets Better Project. According to www.itgetsbetter.org, more than 50,000 videos have been created that have been viewed over 50 million times. Submissions have come from politicians, actors and actresses, social activists, and everyday people. Each of these videos, however, serves as a synecdoche for a larger community and goal.

issue judgments and evaluations as though they are facts and not interpretations, but this does not contribute to a dialogic environment. In situations where controversial ideas or topics are being engaged, it helps create a supportive dialogic communication environment when we simply describe things rather than render judgments.

Take the following example: a person is late for work and his boss calls him in and says, "You must not care about your job because you seem to want to show up whenever you feel like it." This takes the behavior, supplies an evaluation, presents it as a fact, and destroys any opportunity for dialogue. Instead, imagine if the manager said, "I noticed you were twenty-five minutes late today. It's the third time this has happened this week. What is going on?" This is a description of the behavior and an opportunity for the employee to explain himself. Perhaps he has a sick child or had to take mass transit to work. By phrasing the observation as a description, the manager does not put the employee on the defensive and instead invites him to a dialogue in which the behavior can be explained. In the first example, where the boss issued an evaluation, the employee is far less likely to engage, and if he does so, it will likely not be in a productive manner.

Summary

In this chapter, we unraveled several of the mysteries of language. We provided the four characteristics that all languages share before exploring the terms and structures that make language interesting and evocative. In that discussion, we covered metaphors, detailing several different types and providing examples of each. We also examined some strategies for structuring language to both enhance its appeal and its ability to be remembered by a receiver. Finally, we provided seven practical guidelines for using language in a way that encourages dialogue and understanding between two parties.

Chapter 4 Key Ideas

- Language is arbitrary, ambiguous, abstract, and negative
- Language systems have three parts: the signifier, the signified, and the sign. The sign (symbol) is comprised of both the signifier (the object), and the signified (the mental picture that we have of the object)
- There are six types of metaphors: simile, synecdoche, metonymy, archetypal, mixed, and dead
- Five of the language structures that can help increase the appeal of a message for its audience include repetition, alliteration, parallelism, antithesis, and narrative

Chapter 4 Key Terms

Arbitrary	Negative	Alliteration
Semiotics	Similes	Parallelism
Signifier	Synedoche	Narrative coherence
Signified	Metonymy	Narrative fidelity
Sign	Archetypal	Profanity
Ambiguous	Mixed metaphors	Idioms
Denotative meaning	Dead metaphors	
Connotative meaning	Repetition	

References

1 De Saussure, F. (1959). *Course in general linguistics.* New York: Philosophical Library. Original work published in 1916.

2 Barthes, R. (1967). *Elements of semiology* (trans. Annette Lavers & Colin Smith). London: Jonathan Cape.

3 Kennedy, J. F. (January 20, 1961). Inaugural Address. *Americanrhetoric.com.* Retrieved from http://www.americanrhetoric.com/speeches/jfkinaugural.htm

4 Milton, John. *Paradise Lost.* (Ed. Scott Elledge). 2nd ed. New York: Norton, 1975.

5 Fisher, W. (1989). *Human communication as narration: Toward a philosophy of reason, value and action.* Columbia, SC: University of South Carolina Press.

Chapter 5

Nonverbal Communication

Words are not the only way people communicate with one another. In fact, we interpret more meaning from nonverbal communication than we do from the content of what is said. **Nonverbal communication** refers to the elements of communication that do not involve words but nevertheless transmit messages. Whereas words have meanings that people can look up, there is no such dictionary for nonverbal communication, making it dependent on the receiver's interpretation. We can change our speaking style and either avoid or use particular words and phrases in different situations, but nonverbal communication is much more difficult—yet incredibly important—to control.

To put the importance of nonverbal communication into context, just imagine different speaking situations. In job interviews, employers examine not just what you say, but how you say it, the manner in which you are dressed, the posture you keep in your chair, and even the strength and quality of your handshake. When out on a date, we pay attention to how other people respond to our stories, how they sit, how their voice sounds, and how much eye contact they make. We also employ appropriate nonverbal behaviors when speaking to teachers or supervisors, such as standing until they ask us to take a seat. The list goes on and on, but the theme is the same: appropriate nonverbal communication is essential in any interaction.

Nonverbal communication the elements of communication that do not involve words but nevertheless transmit messages

In this chapter, we explore the various dimensions of nonverbal communication. First, we will briefly outline the three basic principles of nonverbal communication. Then, we will discuss the numerous functions it plays in communication, before examining the different types of nonverbal communication people exhibit in their interactions with others. We will conclude with some guidelines for using nonverbal communication in a way that encourages dialogue and a supportive communication climate.

Principles of Nonverbal Communication

Like any concept, nonverbal communication has its foundation in certain principles. These principles help guide our understanding of how nonverbal communication works and why it functions the way it does. There are three basic principles we will explain, and each is equally important. The first relates how nonverbal messages convey information regarding emotions and relationships. The second principle refers to how nonverbal communication works in tandem with verbal messages to help maintain relationships. Finally, and perhaps most importantly, is the principle that explains how nonverbal messages are context based, where the same nonverbal display can mean something different to various groups in different situations.

Conveys Emotional and Relationship Information

Verbal messages contain information about both the logical coherence of what is being stated as well as information that could potentially influence the emotional disposition of an audience toward that topic. Since it lacks the ability to be structured and argued, nonverbal communication does not contain any information regarding the logical dimensions of a message. Instead, it helps people understand the emotional aspects of a message and the relationship between the speaker and his or her audience or conversational partner. Although words can carry emotional meaning, nonverbal expression carries the emotional weight.

Think about trying to understand if someone is happy without seeing a smile or hearing a laugh, or consider whether you can determine if someone is upset or distraught without some sort of nonverbal cue from her or his facial expressions or body language. It's very difficult to be certain about the emotional content of messages that are not accompanied by nonverbal cues, particularly in written forms, because our actions convey the emotions that underlie our words. For example, consider all of the possible emotional meanings that could accompany the verbal message, "That's great." Depending on the nonverbal messages accompanying the words, along with the tone of voice, that statement could convey excitement, anger, frustration, disappointment, happiness, or so many other emotions. In fact, according to some communication research, vocal cues like tone of voice, volume, and rate of speech are more accurate tools for decoding emotions than even gestures and facial expressions![1]

In addition to emotional information, nonverbal behaviors also tell us what the relationship is between two parties. Consider watching a person enter an office. How do you know whose office it is, or who the boss is in this situation? You can tell by looking at who sits, who stands, and even who invites the other person to sit. Additionally, the structure of an office can tell you things about the types of relationships people wish to have with those that enter. Head nods, hugs, and handshakes (particularly who extends his or her hands first) also serve as indicators of the relationship between people.

Maintains a Relationship with Verbal Messages

Nonverbal communication helps us interpret verbal messages, and verbal messages also can help us understand nonverbal behaviors. The two forms of communication are related and have a sort of symbiotic relationship. Neither one alone can accurately convey all the information we want to send, but together they have that potential. Communication scholar Judee Burgoon estimates that between 65-70 percent of meaning in a message comes from nonverbal communication, with the rest coming from language.[2] As we will see later in this chapter, nonverbal behaviors can function in accordance with our verbal messages, and sometimes they can present information that is opposite of what we are saying. For effective communication, we must strive to keep a degree of consistency between what we say and what we do while we say it.

Relies on Context for Its Meaning

No dictionary for translating nonverbal communication exists, making it a challenge to accurately interpret nonverbal messages. What we do have available to help us understand the meaning behind nonverbal behaviors is context, but we do not read the situation correctly all the time. In interpreting what we perceive as relevant nonverbal messages, we look at things like the situation, events that may influence the person sending the message, what we know about the person sending the message, and even what is said while delivering the nonverbal communication. What goes on around the nonverbal communication essentially feeds the meaning we assign it.

Additionally, the meaning of nonverbal communication is directly tied to culture. Although emotions are universally human in nature, how we express them varies from group to group. In certain Arab cultures, for instance, grief is expressed openly, while in certain Asian cultures it is seen as inappropriate to express emotions in such a way. In Europe, a sign of friendship between people, even of the same sex, is to embrace and kiss, while in the United States this is not a common practice. Different behaviors are used in various cultures to express the same emotions, and appreciating these differences in context is important for becoming a skilled and effective communicator. Even so, certain basic emotions have been found to be interpreted similarly across cultures. Psychologist Paul Ekman shared photographs of behaviors that indicated happiness, fear, disgust, anger, sadness, and surprise to participants from five non-European countries and found they were all equally accurate in identifying the emotional display in the photographs.[3] Cultures have different norms for expressing certain emotions and messages, but there are certain behaviors that seem to be universally attached to particular emotions.

Even the behaviors themselves can contain multiple possible meanings, and identifying the correct one largely depends on how you read the context in which the nonverbal message is conveyed. This underscores the ambiguity of symbols and gestures, in that a smile in one situation can mean happiness, while in another it could be an indicator of someone hiding something. A head nod could also mean a great many things, such as agreement or a sign of respect and deference to the speaker. Context is key in reducing this ambiguity and interpreting nonverbal communication, and so appreciating the contextual dimension of nonverbal message interpretation is a foundational principle of nonverbal communication.

Functions of Nonverbal Communication

Nonverbal communication can serve any one of six different functions in our delivery of messages to others. Most often it works hand in hand with verbal communication; however, that is not always the case. At one time or another everyone experiences a situation where they misinterpret a nonverbal display, or they create confusion through their own nonverbal messages. Additionally, we have all been in situations where if the nonverbal elements of the interaction are stripped away it loses its charm, uniqueness, and enjoyable nature. In this part of the chapter, we will define the six functions of nonverbal communication, and show how they can help, and in some cases hinder, the effectiveness of your communication.

Repeating

Repeating
the function
of nonverbal
communication
whereby the
physical actions
that follow verbal
messages reinforce
what is said

Although there is no dictionary that helps us to discern the meaning of nonverbal actions and messages, we can often infer what they mean through their immediate context, or how they are used. One aspect of that context can be when a nonverbal message follows a verbal statement. This can occur when we say hello and then extend our hand for a handshake. We may also refer to a person and then point at him or her, or state a location and then motion in the direction that we referenced. When our physical actions that follow verbal messages reinforce what is said, we are using the **repeating** function of nonverbal communication. Nonverbal messages that repeat verbal messages can serve a wide array of purposes for us, and often we do not think about them as repeating when we use them.

Accenting

One of the most powerful aspects of nonverbal communication is that we do not have to always wait until we finish speaking to take advantage of it. Often, we can use nonverbal behaviors while we are speaking to help get a point across, underscore the importance of a statement, or express an emotional dimension of a message. When we use nonverbal behaviors to augment a message while we deliver it, we are using them to **accent** the verbal meaning we sent. Public speakers sometimes pound a podium when making an important point, for example. Accenting verbal messages with nonverbal behaviors helps highlight parts of the message as important for the receiver and is a useful function in a host of situations.

Complementing

A third function of nonverbal communication that shares some qualities with accenting, but is different in that it is more subdued, is **complementing**. When the nonverbal behavior occurs at the same time as the message and displays the same content, then the nonverbal behavior complements the message. This is similar to accenting, in that the behavior and spoken message are consistent with each other; however, in accenting, the behavior is meant to increase the intensity of the message, whereas with complementing, there is no such amplification. We find nonverbal behaviors that complement messages in cases where people smile while saying hello, laugh while telling a funny story or joke, and cry when delivering sad or disappointing news. These behaviors do not increase the intensity of the message or repeat the message after it is spoken, but rather simultaneously display the same message as the verbal statement itself, thus complementing the content.

Substituting

In some circumstances, we may not either want or be able to say anything right away. In those situations, it does not mean we are restricted from communicating, because we can still send messages through our nonverbal behaviors. The function of nonverbal communication whereby our physical actions take the place of our verbal messages is called **substituting**. People substitute nonverbal behaviors for verbal messages quite often. During conversations we issue head nods rather than saying, "I understand;" we smile to indicate we like someone, rather than saying it outright; and we shrug our shoulders when we don't know something. Even the University of Texas Longhorns have a hand gesture that symbolizes an affiliation with the school!

Regulating

Perhaps the most essential function performed by nonverbal communication relates to its ability to help order our interactions with others. We rely on nonverbal behaviors more than verbal ones to know when it is our turn to speak, ask questions, or when a conversation is over or beginning with someone else. The actions that govern the course of an interaction with another person perform the **regulating** function of nonverbal communication. These types of behaviors include things like raising your hand to speak, putting up a hand to stop someone from interrupting while you finish a statement, or pausing in a conversation after asking a question to indicate a response is desired. These nonverbal actions, and others, allow us to conduct conversations and dialogues with other people in a relatively orderly manner.

Accenting
the function of nonverbal communication whereby nonverbal behaviors augment a message while it is delivered

Complementing
the function of nonverbal communication whereby nonverbal behavior occurring at the same time as the message displays the same content

Substituting
the function of nonverbal communication whereby physical actions take the place of verbal messages

Regulating
the actions that govern the course of an interaction with another person

Conflicting

Nonverbal communication is not an exact science, and ensuring our actions correspond to our words the way we intend them to is not an easy task. As a result, we sometimes issue verbal messages that say one thing, while employing nonverbal communication that indicates another. When this happens, our nonverbal communication serves a conflicting function, and it can create, at minimum, confusion between the sender and receiver. In interpersonal relationships, we can smile and laugh with a date, and even say to her or him that we would like to get together again—except our nonverbal behaviors can indicate the opposite is true. In less awkward moments, we might say to turn right but point to the left. These conflicting messages present barriers to effective communication and underscore both the important role our nonverbal communication plays in creating meaning and sending messages, and how difficult they are to control.

Types of Nonverbal Communication

Many people believe that nonverbal communication is simply about hand gestures and facial expressions, but those are only two small aspects of the larger realm of nonverbal communication. Recall the definition from the beginning of the chapter: elements of communication that do not involve words, but nevertheless transmit messages. This encompasses more than just how we use our hands or express emotions through our face. It actually involves things like how we treat time, decorate our personal space, and even the clothes we choose to wear. All in all, there are eight different types of nonverbal communication and in this part of the chapter we will describe each of them in turn.

Kinesics

Gestures
physical movements used to convey a message

Posture
the physical framing and orientation of the body to another person

The first type of nonverbal communication we will discuss is the one with which most people are typically familiar. Kinesics refers to nonverbal behaviors related to the movement of the body. These include everything from **gestures,** which are physical movements used to convey a message, to how we frame and orient our body to another person or audience, or our **posture.** For a brief list of gestures commonly used to express emotions, take a look at Table 5.1.

TABLE 5.1 **Gestures Used to Express Emotions**

Gesture	Emotion Conveyed
Smile	Joy, happiness
Frown	Sadness, disappointment
Grimace	Pain, displeasure
Open arms	Friendliness, fondness
Furrowed brow	Confusion, anger
Tapping fingers	Nervousness, boredom

"Nonverbal behaviors not only provide essential context for making sense of verbal statements, they convey messages in their own right. Communicators ignore the nonverbal signals at their own peril."

—*Judee Burgoon, University of Arizona*

Our posture also sends messages to the other party. If we have an **open posture**, or have the majority of our body facing the audience or other person, we indicate interest and attention. On the other hand, if we have a **closed posture** in which we shield our body from the other person, it can indicate not only lack of interest, but also possibly fear. Additionally, people have a tendency to **mirror**, or replicate, the posture of the other person when they are interested in him or her and believe he or she is interested as well. Whether it is through gestures, posture, or eye contact, kinesics can serve a variety of purposes for the messages we convey, and they come in several different forms.

Emblems. Emblems are the relatively small number of nonverbal behaviors that can usually be correctly translated into words. Examples of emblems include shaking hands, pumping a fist, or holding up one's hand.

Illustrators. These serve to emphasize a spoken message, and include things like pounding a fist on a table, nodding your head while saying something you wish to stress, or furrowing your brow when asking a question.

Affect Displays. These are displays of emotions through the use of our bodies, and manifest in a variety of different ways. We might jump up and down when excited, laugh when happy, cry when sad, or change our position toward the other person when we are upset.

Regulators. Kinesics often serve the regulating function of nonverbal communication. We indicate turn taking in conversations by raising our eyebrows or holding out our hands; we also use it to order classroom participation by raising hands and pointing to who might speak.

Adaptors. These nonverbal behaviors work to satisfy bodily needs, but may create confusion in others when used. Think about shifting your position in a chair when it is uncomfortable, something that another person might interpret as your desire to end the conversation. Using adaptors frequently can lead to the perception that you are nervous or even being dishonest.[4]

Oculesics

Related to kinesics is the use of eye contact to send messages, something researchers also refer to as **oculesics**. We use eye contact to convey interest or lack of interest in another person, respect or disdain for the person or her or his message, and a host of other emotions, attitudes, and thoughts. In Western cultures like the United States, maintaining eye

Open posture
the posture achieved when the majority of one's body faces the audience or other person

Closed posture
the posture achieved when one shields his or her body from the other person

Mirror
the practice of replicating the posture of the other person to indicate mutual interest

Oculesics
the use of eye contact to send messages

contact is seen as a sign of respect and attention, while in other cultures it is interpreted as aggressive and negative. When dating, we show our interest in the other person through how we look at him or her. The eyes are, as the saying goes, truly "the windows to the soul."

Proxemics

Proxemics
how we use
space to convey
information

Whereas kinesics and oculesics involve the use of our bodies to send a message, **proxemics** involves how we use space to convey information. A person's use of space can say a lot about her or his identity, interest in another person, personality, and power. Edward T. Hall, the researcher responsible for coining the term "proxemics," also identified four *distance zones* that are typically used by Western cultures. Each zone invites a particular interpretation of how a person views and is viewed by others.

Intimate Distance. This zone stretches from touching to about a foot and a half apart. This is what most people consider their own space. Encroachment on this space by those who are not invited to do so can create a high degree of defensiveness, discomfort, and even aggression. It is a space typically reserved for those with whom a person is intimate.

Personal Distance. This space extends from a foot and a half to about four feet apart and generally indicates friendship or collegiality. For instance, when you walk with your friends to lunch, you do not walk hand in hand, but you are generally within a few feet of each other.

Social Distance. This zone stretches from about four feet to twelve feet apart and is an area that people with whom we have little to no connection might pass through. We might conduct business transactions in this zone, but it is not the place where we keep our intimate or personal friends.

Public Distance. From twelve feet on, the distance conveys a formal situation. Teachers and presenters speak to audiences at this distance, and it conveys a very professional and formal atmosphere with little personal association. At this distance, some might feel the speaker could be cold and uninterested, which is a risk, particularly for those in the teaching profession.[5]

Haptics

Haptics
the study of how
touch expresses
meaning

One of the behaviors that occurs within intimate space is touching, and the study of how touch expresses meaning to others is called **haptics**. Different types of touch can serve to amplify a verbal message, reinforce it, and even at times contradict it, but the one constant is that touch is key for sending emotional dimensions of a message to another person—perhaps more so than any other form of nonverbal communication. It may come as no surprise that touch is closely related to a baby's attachment to a caregiver, particularly a mother. We also use touch to exert control, convey emotion, and express an affiliation with another person, and the meaning and values placed on expressing messages through touch are culturally driven. Perhaps the most obvious way touch conveys messages occurs when partners or parents hold hands, kiss, or hug to display their love for one another.[6]

Chronemics

Not all nonverbal communication relates to tangible objects like the body and space. One abstract way in which we send nonverbal communication involves time. **Chronemics** is the branch of nonverbal communication that involves how people treat, value, react to, and structure time. In terms of their use of time, people typically fall into one of two chronemic categories: monochronic and polychronic. **Monochronic** people like to do things one at a time, break their time up into small manageable units in a schedule, and value promptness. **Polychronic** people, on the other hand, tend to try and do several tasks at the same time, tend to keep much more fluid schedules, and are not particularly concerned about whether someone is "on time." Whether someone is monochromic or polychromic is influenced heavily by culture. For a list of differences between monochronic and polychronic people, take a look at Table 5.2.

Chronemics
the branch of nonverbal communication that involves how people treat, value, react and structure time

Monochronic
the category of chronemics marked by liking to do things one at a time, breaking time up into small, manageable units

Polychronic
the category of chronemics marked by trying to do several tasks at the same time and having a more fluid approach to scheduling time

TABLE 5.2 Differences Between Monochronic and Polychronic People

Monochronic People	Polychronic People
Do one thing at a time	Do many things at once
Concentrate on the job	Are highly distractible and subject to interruptions
Take time commitments (deadlines, schedules) seriously	Consider an objective to be achieved, if possible
Are low-context and need information	Are high-context and already have information
Committed to the job	Are committed to people and human relationships
Adhere religiously to plans	Change plans often and easily
Are concerned about not disturbing others; follow rules of privacy and consideration	Are more concerned with those who are closely related than with privacy
Show great respect for private property; seldom borrow or lend	Borrow and lend things often and easily
Emphasize promptness	Base promptness on the relationship
Are accustomed to short-term relationships	Have a strong tendency to build lifetime relationships

The use of time conveys emotions and indicates what a person values. For instance, who you choose to spend your time with shows how you feel about people and how you prioritize them in your life. The treatment of time also functions as a regulatory expression of nonverbal communication through the allowance of turntaking in conversations. Respecting another person's desire to respond and not "hogging the air" illustrates an understanding of time in a conversation and the right all people have to a share of that time.

Olfactics
the dimension
of nonverbal
communication
related to smell

Olfactics

Another nonverbal aspect of communication that does not involve the body or space is **olfactics**, the dimension of nonverbal communication related to smell. As with all nonverbal messages, the meanings attached to smells differ by culture. For example, some cultures do not cover up the odors their body produces because it is understood as a natural phenomenon, while other cultures go to great effort to cover up scents. A person's sense of smell is directly tied to his or her memory, and certain aromas can create an inviting and relaxing atmosphere because they remind someone of home or the beach, while other smells create a negative reaction in a person based on bad experiences or memories. These memories, in turn, influence the perception a person has regarding another individual or situation. Smells are most often unintentional messages, but they help people create meaning nonetheless.

Vocalics

Vocalics
those things that
contribute to the
maintenance or
creation of sound in
your voice that help
to convey meaning

The final type of nonverbal communication we will discuss is often confused with verbal communication because it emanates from people's vocal chords and mouths, but it is not verbal because it does not involve words. **Vocalics** are those things that contribute to the maintenance or creation of sound in your voice that help to convey meaning. These are not language, but rather a nonverbal element closely tied to how we send verbal messages to others. Our vocalics can help to express emotions, attitudes, and interest in subjects or people. There are several different types of vocalics: volume, tone, rate, vocalized pauses, and gasps and sighs.

Volume. Volume refers to how loud or soft a person's voice is. When someone is quiet, we might infer he or she is shy or perhaps not interested in the subject. When he or she is loud, we might see it as an expression of excitement or perhaps anger.

Tone. Tone is the emphasis we place on syllables, sounds, words, and phrases that result in the overall sense of "warmth" and interest in our voice. Monotone delivery of a message that has little or no variation might both convey and create disinterest in a subject. In fact, research on tone indicates people find those who speak in a monotone voice unattractive.[7] Tonal variation can enhance our audience's interest, convey our own interest in the subject, and add an emotional quality to what we are saying.

Rate. Rate refers to how fast you deliver a message. When people speak too fast we might infer they are trying to deceive us, but there are also cultural components that impact the rate at which we speak. For instance, people in the Northeast speak much more quickly than those who live in the southern part of the United States. The average rate of speech is around 150 words per minute, but certain circumstances influence whether we speak slower or faster than that.[8,9]

Vocalized Pauses. There are two types of pauses: silent and vocalized. Silent pauses occur when there is a momentary cessation of any sound, while vocalized pauses occur when people use sounds and words like "uh," "um," and "y'know" to fill the void. Excessive use of vocalized pauses might create a perception in the audience that you do not know what you are talking about or are an incompetent speaker, while the strategic use of silent pauses can enhance your credibility and give the audience time to catch up to you.

Gasps and Sighs. One final type of vocalic is the use of breath to convey a message. We do this through gasps and sighs. Gasps usually indicate surprise or fear, while sighs demonstrate frustration or even that a person is tired and uncomfortable.

We employ vocalics whenever we speak, but how and to what end people use different levels of volume, tone, rate, or pausing is, as with all of nonverbal communication, tied to cultural expectations.

Artifacts

The eighth type of nonverbal communication takes place through artifacts. Artifacts are objects used to communicate information about yourself to those around you. They express your attitudes, feelings, mood, beliefs, interests, hobbies and even ideology. For example, how people dress gives clues to the other person or audience about what they value, how they interpret the situation, and what type of personality they have. Consider the meaning people place on tattoos or the concept of the "power tie." How you look conveys a great deal

MEDIATED MOMENTS

Understanding and respecting how others use time and space is a key component to creating and sustaining positive relationships with them. Even when people do not have the same understanding of time or keep their living spaces the same way we do, it does not mean that their approach is necessarily wrong. In an episode of the hit television sitcom *The Big Bang Theory,* Sheldon Cooper makes the mistake of inferring that his neighbor Penny is crying out for someone to help her clean her apartment when he notices it is in tremendous disarray. Unable to allow this to continue, and unable to accept that his neighbor has a dirty apartment, Sheldon ultimately sneaks into her apartment in the middle of the night and cleans it for her. This enrages Penny, who was obviously not seeking the assistance Sheldon believed she needed. Here we see the ambiguity of meaning inherent in Penny's use of space, as well as the imposition of Sheldon's own way of interpreting events on to Penny. If he saw her apartment as dirty, he assumed that she must be dirty as well. The results caused a serious confrontation between Sheldon and Penny.

s_bukley / Shutterstock.com

of information for others to interpret. Artifacts are also prominent in dorm rooms, living spaces, and offices. People who keep a desk between them and the visitor's chair might be seen as rigid and authoritative, while those with a more open setup typically are seen as warmer. What we surround ourselves with, what we wear, and even the colors with which we choose to decorate ourselves and our environment reveals a great deal about us without saying a word.

Guidelines for Dialogic Nonverbal Communication

A dialogic environment is built not simply on verbal messages, but nonverbal ones as well. Recall that genuineness is a component of dialogue, and we are neither genuine nor civil with others when our nonverbal messages contradict what we say. We perceive others as being deceptive when we see inconsistencies in a person's verbal message and nonverbal behaviors. Nonverbal communication can also be a source of confusion for people because its meaning is so ambiguous. To help you navigate the complexities and vagaries of non-verbal communication, we will now provide five guidelines for creating and maintaining a dialogic environment through nonverbal communication.

Ask Clarifying Questions

Nonverbal behaviors can vary in their meaning, and we all might interpret the same action differently. We can remove ambiguity from our interpretations by asking a person what a specific action meant to her or him. If someone furrows her brow while you explain a topic, you might want to ask her if she is following along. She may be confused, and you will not be able to adapt appropriately unless you ask. Asking what people mean by their facial expressions, use of touch, or even how they have their office structured can help to gain clarity about the meaning inherent in those nonverbal expressions. Clarity is essential for creating understanding and a comfortable communication climate between two parties.

Don't Assume Others Understand

Just as we may need to ask clarifying questions of others regarding their nonverbal expressions, we must be ready to answer those same questions from others. Additionally, we must understand the ambiguity of nonverbal behaviors and appreciate that others may infer something other than we intend in what we do. Finally, this guideline should serve as a caution not to use excessive nonverbal communication with people you don't know well, as they lack the experience to accurately infer your meaning in those expressions. Do not expect others to understand what your nonverbal expressions mean.

Control Your Nonverbal Reactions

Practicing self-restraint and self-monitoring are key elements of establishing a dialogue that must be practiced with nonverbal and verbal communication. We may insult someone by grimacing or laughing at the wrong time during an interaction, and we may also express interest when none exists if we do not monitor and restrain our nonverbal reactions. This is not to say you should not have any nonverbal reactions, for that is impossible, but you should monitor your physical reactions so they do not reveal what you might be feeling or thinking at times when it is inappropriate to share that information.

Use Situationally Appropriate Nonverbal Expressions

Not every situation allows you to express your thoughts or feelings as directly as others might, so you must stay tuned into the context of the interaction to know what is appropriate and what is not. For instance, if you interview for a position with a company and know the person who is conducting the interview, should you greet him or her with a hug or handshake? If you arrive at the office of a professor for an unannounced visit, do you walk right in and sit down, or do you knock and wait to be invited in? Do you end a first date with a kiss, hug, or high five? The situation dictates the nonverbal expression that is most appropriate, and so it is important to be aware of what would be expected in a given circumstance and act accordingly.

Learn Cultural Differences in Meaning

As we have noted throughout the chapter, different cultures give different meanings to various nonverbal expressions. Learning those meanings and what might be expected is essential for successful communication in intercultural interactions. Do not behave in an ethnocentric manner and expect the other party to understand your nonverbal expressions and values,

DIALING DIVERSITY

One of the most significant challenges for American professionals travelling abroad is adjusting to the different treatment accorded to time in other cultures. In most parts of the United States, there is a high value placed on punctuality and timeliness. It is generally expected that meetings will begin at the time they are scheduled, and that everyone will be there at the agreed upon time. Additionally, meetings in American culture typically are task oriented, hence the phrase "Let's get down to business." In some Latin American and European cultures, however, the value is placed less on time and more on relationship building. People can typically run late to meetings without any negative connotation to their tardiness, and the initial meetings typically contain less "business" and more socializing. This is because these cultures value interpersonal connections and getting to know those with whom they do business. So, when trying to expand or develop business interests with people from these cultures, it is also just as important to build personal interests.

nor hold others to behaving the same way you do. Understand the cultural expectations and behaviors as best as you can before entering into the situation. In some international businesses, this can mean the difference between closing a deal and closing off an opportunity.

Summary

In this chapter, we explored the complex nature of nonverbal communication and discussed the various forms through which we send messages without words. We provided three foundational principles of nonverbal expression and detailed the six functions nonverbal messages perform in our lives. Then we explained the seven different types of nonverbal communication before concluding with five guidelines for effectively using nonverbal communication to create a dialogic environment.

Chapter 5 Key Ideas

- Nonverbal communication conveys emotional and relationship information, maintains a relationship with verbal messages, and has meaning that is based on the context
- Nonverbal communication can serve six different functions: repeating, accenting, complementing, substituting, regulating, and conflicting
- There are eight different types of nonverbal communication: kinesics, oculesics, proxemics, haptics, chronemics, olfactics, vocalics, and artifacts

Chapter 5 Key Terms

Nonverbal communication	Posture	Chronemics
Repeating	Open posture	Monochronic
Accenting	Closed posture	Polychronic
Complementing	Mirror	Olfactics
Substituting	Oculesics	Vocalics
Regulating	Proxemics	
Gestures	Haptics	

References

1 Kappas, A., Hess, U., & Scherer, K. R. (1991). Voice and emotion. In R. S. Feldman & B. Rime (Eds.), *Fundamentals of nonverbal communication* (200-237). Cambridge, England: Cambridge University Press.

2 Burgoon, J.K. (1985). Nonverbal signals. In M. L. Knapp & G. R. Miller (Eds.), *Handbook of Interpersonal Communication* (344-390). Beverly Hills, CA: Sage.

3 Ekman, P. & Friesen, W. V. (1975). *Unmasking the face: A field guide to recognizing emotions from facial cues.* Englewood Cliffs, NJ: Prentice-Hall.

4 Vrij, A. (2006). Nonverbal communication and deception. In V. Manusov & M. L. Patterson (Eds). *The Sage Handbook of nonverbal communication* (341-359). Thousand Oaks, CA: Sage.

5 Hall, E. T. (1963). System of notation for proxemics behavior. *American Anthropologist, 65,* 1003-1026.

6 Floyd, K. (2006). *Communicating affection: Interpersonal behavior and social context.* Cambridge, England: Cambridge University Press.

7 Zuckerman, M. & Miyake, K. (1996). The attractive voice: What makes it so? *Journal of Nonverbal Behavior 17,* 119-135.

8 Wolvin, A. & Coakley, C. (1996). *Listening.* Dubuque, IA: Benchmark.

9 Pointer, M. R. & Attridge, G. G. (1998). The number of discernible colors. *Color Research and Application* 23, 52-54.

Chapter 6

Listening

Mark Twain once quipped, "If we were supposed to talk more than we listen we would have two tongues and one ear." Twain could not have hit the mark better if he tried, and the numbers bear this out. Just think, there is one of you, while there are numerous other people you interact with throughout your life. With that many different voices, you will naturally listen more than you speak. Still not sure? Studies have consistently found that people listen approximately 45 percent of the time, compared to speaking 30 percent of the time, reading 16 percent of the time, and writing a mere 9 percent of the time.[1] Clearly, listening is an essential part of being an effective communicator.

Listening is more complicated than people realize. Often, we confuse it with **hearing**, which is the physiological process of capturing sound conducted by the ears to the brain. **Listening**, however, as defined by the International Listening Association, is "an information processing task carried out in a social, interactive, or communicative environment."[2] More succinctly, listening is the process of receiving and interpreting spoken or nonverbal messages. Listening, therefore, is communicative, while hearing is physiological. Hearing is something our bodies do, while listening is a skill we can develop and improve. In this chapter, we will first determine what listening is by dispelling some common misconceptions people have about it. We will then explain the different purposes

Hearing
the physiological process of capturing sound conducted by ears to the brain

Listening
the process of receiving and interpreting spoken and/ or nonverbal messages

listening serves for us, and the primary types of listening we use to achieve those ends. Third, we will cover the challenges we face to using effective and accurate listening in a variety of communication situations. Finally, we will provide tips for how to engage in listening that encourages others to speak, which you will recall is one of the core components of dialogue.

Listening Myths

Listening is perhaps the most misunderstood element of the communication process. People often feel that since they have been listening most of their life then they know how to do it. The fact of the matter is that in the traditional education system we do very little to train students how to listen properly, and yet it is one of the most fundamental skills for being a good communicator. Listening is more than just receiving sounds; it is an important and complex cognitive process that is difficult to master. In this chapter, we will examine six common misconceptions people typically have about listening.

Listening Is the Same as Hearing

People often mistakenly treat listening and hearing as synonymous. People who are hearing impaired have some form of physical obstruction or structural difference in their ear that impedes the reception of sound. This can be mitigated in some cases with hearing aids, cochlear implants, or even surgery. On the other hand, when people are not good listeners,

DIALING DIVERSITY

According to the National Institute of Deafness and Other Communication Disorders (NIDCD), roughly 17 percent of Americans report some form of hearing loss. Additionally, roughly 15 percent of Americans between the ages of 20-69 experience hearing loss due to exposure to loud sounds at work or during leisure time.[3] Those who are born deaf enter into a very specific subculture in society, one with several different languages (in the U.S. it is often American Sign Language) and its own university (Gallaudet University in Washington, DC). Among this

group is an even more special subset. The Hearing Health Foundation reports that roughly 60 percent of combat veterans who return from Iraq and Afghanistan return home with hearing loss, making it the number one war wound.[4] Hearing loss can significantly impact a person's ability to acquire language skills and socialize because they can feel as if others are not listening to them. However impaired their hearing, a person with hearing loss can still listen and be listened to because listening is a communicative process, not simply a physiological activity.

it has nothing to do with a physical challenge and more to do with difficulties in concentrating. Listening is, therefore, a skill that can be developed and improved through practice and effort.

I'm a Good Listener

Just because you listen more than you perform any other communicative behavior does not mean you are good at it. In fact, people tend to overestimate how good they are at listening, and underestimate how good others are at listening. This basically means everyone thinks they are better listeners than everyone else—something that cannot be true. When we believe we are good at something, we tend not to work at it, and so when we overestimate our own listening abilities, we don't work to improve our listening skills. This is a cycle that creates poor listeners. The only way to break the cycle is to work at being a better listener.

Effective Listening is Hard to Learn

The skills needed to be a good listener are not that hard to learn or understand, but the challenge is putting them into consistent practice. There are a lot of distractions that keep us from implementing good listening behaviors consistently. To that end, the most important ability to develop for good listening is concentration and attention. When we can train ourselves to focus and not be easily distracted, good listening comes quite easily. Later in this chapter, we will provide you with some guidelines for behaviors that will help you improve your listening ability, and you will see they are not difficult, but making them a habit is the real test.

Intelligent People are Better Listeners

There are several problems with this notion, not the least of which is the poor definition of intelligence. Psychologist Howard Gardner has levied some fairly groundbreaking criticisms of IQ tests and how they privilege only two types of knowledge acquisition over the many other ways people learn,[5] while using things like college or advanced degrees to determine intelligence are obviously problematic as a measurement of intelligence. Additionally, the more people believe they know, the more they typically want to speak—not listen.

There is, however, a correlation between people who are emotionally intelligent and their listening ability. **Emotional intelligence** is defined as the ability a person has to assess, identify, and manage his or her own emotions, while also appreciating and responding to the emotions of others in a civil manner. Those with high emotional intelligence are other-centered and consequently better listeners than those who cannot pay attention and respect the feelings and emotions of their audiences or conversational partners.[6] So, emotional intelligence is related to listening ability, while intellect is not.

Emotional intelligence the ability a person has to assess, identify, and manage his or her own emotions, while also appreciating and responding to the emotions of others in a civil manner

Older People are Better Listeners

Although we increasingly encounter situations where we need to exercise our listening skills as we get older, age does not automatically improve our ability to listen. With age comes habits, and these can be either good or bad. If we practice good listening skills earlier in life and incorporate them into our communicative repertoire, then we will be better listeners as we get older. If, however, we practice poor listening skills, those habits will be difficult to break as we get older. Put simply, age has little to do with our listening skills.

Women Are Better Listeners than Men

Rapport talk
language meant to develop relationships and exchange emotional information

Report talk
the exchange of information, solutions, and problem-solving strategies

Our listening capacities do not depend on gender or sex. Instead, research tells us that women and men communicate differently, and one approach is not necessarily better than the other. According to scholar Deborah Tannen, women tend to communicate through **rapport talk,** or language meant to develop relationships and exchange emotional information. Thus, they tend to listen for this type of talk as well. Men, on the other hand, tend to engage in **report talk,** or the exchange of information, solutions, and problem-solving strategies. Thus, when men listen to messages, they often focus on what can be done, not necessarily the relationship element or purpose of the message.[7]

As you can see, there are many erroneous perceptions regarding listening. Listening is also not a one-size-fits-all concept, as there are different purposes for which we listen and different types of listening in which we engage. In the next part of the chapter, we will explore these purposes for and types of listening.

Why and How We Listen

Listening allows us to tune in to the world around us, and the information we gather through listening helps form our perceptions of people, places, objects, and ideas. There are four primary purposes listening serves in this respect. These range from listening for enjoyment, to listening to glean information. In this part of the chapter, we will discuss each in turn. We will also explain the difference between the two ways we process information when we listen.

Listening Purposes

We do not always engage in listening for the same reasons. There are four primary purposes for which we use listening, and each can manifest in any type of communication situation, whether it is an interpersonal environment, a speech, or in a small group context. It all depends on what you want to focus on and what you hope to retain or achieve in that moment. To that end, it is important to know why you are listening and what you hope to get out of the event, because that will help you identify your listening purpose.

Listening for appreciation
listening for enjoyment; it is not high in cognitive commitment

Listening for Appreciation. The first reason we engage in listening is for appreciation. When we **listen for appreciation,** our goal is to enjoy something on which we focus our attention. The most common examples of this type of listening are listening to music while driving or working out, listening to dialogue in a movie or television show, listening to a comedian on the radio, and listening to a story told by a friend. There is not a high degree of cognitive effort when we listen for appreciation. The goal here is to have fun with what you are listening to, and not necessarily to understand the motives behind what is said or to disagree with what the other party may be proposing.

Listening for Comprehension. The second reason we listen is to comprehend or understand something. When we **listen for comprehension,** we want to understand something we do not know so that we can learn something new. We engage in comprehension listening when we take a class and listen to a lecture, go through orientation with a new employer, and even when we meet someone new and she or he shares information about herself or himself. This type of listening requires more mental effort than appreciative listening, and the goal is not necessarily enjoyment, but rather understanding.

Listening to Show Support. The third reason we listen is to **show support** in a relationship. When we listen to show support, we are listening to someone else because we want the other person to feel like she or he is valued and that we care about what this person has to say. The goal in this type of listening is to develop or maintain a relationship and to demonstrate how much we care about the other person. When we listen as someone tells us about her day, share in a friend's good news, or lend a sympathetic ear to someone who needs to vent about a tough situation, we are listening to show support for that relationship.

Critical Listening. The fourth and final purpose listening serves is criticism, but not in the form of negative attacks on someone else. **Critical listening** is when we evaluate a message and assess whether or not we agree with what is said. When we listen critically, we also are open to disagreeing with a part or even all of a message, yet we take in everything offered by the other side before making our judgment. To do this requires the largest degree of cognitive effort of any listening purpose. We may listen critically to a political speech, a proposal for weekend plans by friends, and sometimes lectures on controversial topics or materials.

Two Ways We Listen

Regardless of what our goal is with listening, we use listening in one of two different ways. The first is **active listening,** which occurs when we pay a high degree of attention to a message. We process, store, and potentially evaluate the content of the message to reach conclusions or an understanding about what was said. We usually show that we are actively listening by using eye contact and facial expressions to respond to the message, and perhaps also by leaning in or nodding. We use active listening at times for each of the four purposes we just explained.

We might be watching a murder mystery or someone may be telling us a very engaging story about a trip he or she just took, and we pay those messages a great deal of attention because we want to understand or evaluate what is being relayed to us. That would constitute active listening for appreciation. Active listening for comprehension or criticism would involve paying attention so you completely understand what is said and can either integrate it into your own body of knowledge (comprehension) or determine

Listening for comprehension listening to understand and learn something new; requires a significant degree of mental effort

Listening to show support listening to a speaker to make him or her feel valued, and to show the person we care about what he or she has to say

Critical listening listening to evaluate a message and assess whether or not we agree with what is said; requires the most cognitive effort of any listening purpose

Active listening listening with a high degree of attention to a message; we process, store, and potentially evaluate the content of the message to come to conclusions or an understanding about what was said

Passive listening
listening without
engaging the topic
in any noticeable
way, trying only to
absorb what is said

whether you agree with what was proposed or not (criticism). For example, you might be transitioning into a new position and thus you need to listen to the details of your new job so you understand what you need to do. On the other hand, when we listen to political speeches, we might try and focus on the proposal and how it might impact our own life so we can make a judgement regarding whether or not we support the candidate's ideas.

The second way we might listen is passively. **Passive listening** occurs when we do not engage the topic in any noticeable way and just try to absorb what is said. When we listen passively, we do not engage in much evaluation, nor do we question our own understanding of what is said. Most listening for appreciation is passive listening, but you can also see examples of passively listening for comprehension or criticism when you look around a classroom and see people who do not participate or ask questions about the content. Passive listening can be risky, because you elevate the chances of daydreaming and losing your ability to follow the speaker.

Regardless of which listening purpose we try to achieve and whether we do so actively or passively, we do not always listen the way we want to, and sometimes we fail to listen at all. In the next part of this chapter, we will unpack several different behaviors people may mistakenly think are listening.

Much of the exciting research in listening studies how the senses affect how well we listen and how we can make use of the powers of our brains to listen, use and remember things. You can save yourselves a great deal of time, effort, and even money, if you work harder to listen throughout your life. The failure to listen results in lost friendships and lost resources.
—*Melissa Beall, University of Northern Iowa*

Nonlistening
providing the
appearance of
listening without
actually paying
attention to the
message

Nonlistening

Due to the high degree of cognitive effort involved in effective listening, we cannot maintain it for long periods of time. Just like exercise, we tire out after a while. We often try to hide the fact we lost focus on the message by maintaining an appearance of attention without the actual attention. We sometimes spot others engaging in these behaviors, but it is very hard to prevent ourselves from falling into the trap—especially if a conversation is lengthy. When we do this, we are engaging in **nonlistening**. Nonlistening typically takes six different forms, which we will now examine.

Pseudolistening
the practice
of hiding our
inattention by
appearing to
actually listen
through nonverbal
and verbal
responses that
make it appear
as though we
understand what is
being said

Pseudolistening

One of the most common forms of nonlistening occurs when we hide our inattention by appearing to actually listen, a process called **pseudolistening**. We all have either done this or noticed someone doing this in a conversation when he or she nods or offers some other simple response like "yeah" to appear as though he or she is processing what is said, but then are unable to repeat what was said. This form of deceptive interaction looks like listening, and even sounds like listening, but it is not listening. This also negatively impacts the ability to have a dialogue because without someone's full attention, true understanding cannot be achieved—although the speaker may believe it has occurred because of the "yeah" statements by the pseudolistener.

Glazing Over

Often called daydreaming, **glazing over** is when a person loses complete attention with what is going on around him or her and thinks about something else entirely. We notice people who glaze over when they stare blankly at us when we are speaking, or when they focus on something outside or in a different direction than where the message comes from. Glazing over might not initially appear as a negative behavior, but it can create feelings of frustration and even depression in the speaker because the speaker feels he or she is boring her or his conversational partner or audience. This can often come about when the message or story may not be very interesting to the person listening, or perhaps the listener has other more pressing concerns on his or her mind at the moment. Nevertheless, glazing over is not listening, and barely pretends to be.

A significant contributing factor to both glazing over and psuedolistening is the fact that we all have **spare brain time**. This is the gap between the roughly 150 words a minute we can speak, and the 650 words per minute we can mentally process. The gap creates openings for our brains to do something else, thus leading to opportunities for glazing over or turning our internal attention to something else.

Ambushing

Often times when we listen critically to a message, we focus only on the weaknesses of what the other person is saying and ignore the strengths of her or his position, thus we only hear what confirms our opinion. When we listen with a goal to attack the weak points of the other person, then we are not truly listening; we are **ambushing** the person. We are not processing and evaluating the other person's message in its totality and are simply seeking to argue. Sometimes we confuse ambushing with constructive criticism, but they are not the same because constructive criticism is offered in a way that takes the positive and negative dimensions of a position into account and does not focus solely on the weak points. Ambushing does not promote collaboration or dialogue and often exacerbates interpersonal tension.

Prejudging

With today's technology, we can easily find out the background of a speaker with who we may not be familiar; we also know our friends and family members well, and so we tend to have an idea of what they will say when we get into discussions with them. This information can be useful, but when we use it to evaluate speakers and their message before they even have a chance to deliver it, then we prevent ourselves from listening. Even if we sit through the entire presentation or statement and do not

Glazing over losing complete attention with what is going on and thinking about something else entirely, often staring in a different direction than the speaker

Spare brain time the gap between the roughly 150 words a minute we can speak, and the 650 words per minute we can mentally process

Ambushing the practice of focusing only on the weaknesses of what the other person is saying and ignoring the strengths of his or her position interrupt or challenge what was said, we are not truly listening to our conversational partner if we simply hold to what we thought our partner was going to argue or say before he or she even spoke. When we enter an interaction with a judgment about what we believe will be said before the person has a chance to present it, we engage in **prejudging**, not listening. This eliminates any potential for dialogue, understanding, or relationship building.

Selective Listening

We do not always enter interactions with a closed mind and prejudgments rendered about the speaker and his or her message. Sometimes we stop listening in the middle of a statement because we believe we have heard the main points. When we do this, we stop listening to the entire message and filter out things we deem unimportant, regardless of whether or not the speaker believes those details are essential or interesting. This process of **selective listening**, where we choose what the main points are in a message regardless of what the speaker says, creates the potential for miscommunication, disagreement, and confusion. Listening is hard work, and using this shorthand that privileges your own listening abilities in a way that likely overestimates them tries to get around this cognitive effort. Remember that one of the fundamental misconceptions of listening is that we all believe we are better listeners than other people.

MEDIATED MOMENTS

In the Oscar-winning film *Good Will Hunting,* a judge sentences the title character to counseling after getting into a fight. Dr. Gerald Lambeau, Will's reluctant benefactor, sets Will up with a series of different counselors, and at each meeting Will interacts in a rude manner in order to not undergo therapy anymore. Finally, he meets Dr. Sean Maguire, played by Robin Williams, and again he enters with a preconceived notion of how the therapist will act, behave, and what he will care about. He proceeds to engage in a series

of behaviors designed to have the same effect, but Maguire continues to see Will. In one scene, Maguire tells Will a story about his late wife and how he met her by giving up tickets to the 1975 World Series. Initially, Will is focused more on the fact Maguire did not go to the game than the relationship that Maguire developed with his wife as a result of the decision. Will heard what he wanted to hear, and not what Maguire meant with his story. This scene thus serves as an example of selective listening exhibited by Will.

Advising

There are times when we want to support and help other people when they talk about problems or challenges they face, and this is only natural. But we must only offer advice in these situations when the person actually seeks it, and to make that determination we must listen attentively and fully. When we interrupt the person or offer suggestions and opinions when they were not sought, then we make the mistake of **advising**. We may believe this is being supportive, but it actually represents a form of nonlistening through which we did not pay attention to what other people were saying or what they were looking for from us. Offering advice in this situation ignores their message and illustrates ineffective listening in the guise of offering support.

It might seem like there are more ways not to listen effectively than there are to listen well, which might be true. Nevertheless, there are some good practices that will improve your listening skills and create a communication environment in which you can interact with others.

Advising
the practice of interrupting a person to offer suggestions and opinions in an effort to be helpful even when they were not sought

Guidelines for Dialogic Listening

Creating a dialogic environment necessarily involves treating listening as an important behavior. Not only must we focus on being good listeners, but we must also encourage and help others to do the same. As we have mentioned in this chapter, there are numerous challenges to effective listening, thus making it sound easier than it actually is. Knowing how to work on your listening skills and how to spot nonlistening in others will help you engage in dialogic communication and increase the chances that you and the person you converse with truly understand what is being discussed. In this last part of the chapter, we will provide you with six guidelines for improving your listening. These are in addition to the suggestions offered in the dialogue chapter, which as you recall, also focuses on listening behaviors.

Stop Talking

This sounds trite and crude, but it is true. You cannot listen to the other person if you are talking. This includes when we talk over people, interrupt them, and even finish sentences for them. These all involve you talking, and therefore not listening, to the other party. When we speak, we are not listening to the other person, and when we speak a lot, we are both not giving the impression we care about the perspective of the other and also not providing them with the opportunity to share their thoughts. Being aware of the amount of time you spend talking and making a conscious effort to allow others to speak and finish their thoughts is a cornerstone of dialogue. So, the first, most basic guideline for listening effectively is to stop talking.

Make Listening a Goal

There are many different ways in which people can appear to be listening but actually aren't, so simply being quiet and not talking does not mean you are listening. Listening to the other person's message must be a conscious goal, and so we need to enter into interactions with a goal of listening to the other party. If we choose to spend time with another person, we should want to hear what the other person has to say, so we must work to be attentive and set a goal to listen well. This can be accomplished by making sure there are minimal distractions around when you are spending time with the person. Think about things like putting your phone away, stepping away from your computer, and even closing the door.

Remove Distractions

Given that so many things can interfere with our ability to listen, from noise, to other types of distractions, we must try to minimize these obstacles as best we can to create an opportunity for a dialogue. Environmental obstacles can usually be resolved by moving to a quieter space or a room that keeps such distractions to a minimum. If you are not feeling well, this can also impede your ability to listen. If possible, changing the time of the meeting to one where you will be feeling better is a good course of action. Your own beliefs and attitudes can also prove to be significant impediments to listening effectively and accurately, so make sure you are in a positive frame of mind and willing to set aside personal biases to openly hear another person's message. None of these options are easy, nor are they always viable, but knowing what might distract you from listening and trying to mitigate its impact is a great step toward creating a comfortable, dialogic communication environment.

Listen for Ideas

There is no way you will be able to remember everything a person says. In fact, two concepts we covered earlier in the book tell us what we are most likely to remember from a message or interaction. Recall from Chapter 3 that the recency effect suggests we will remember the most recent thing we hear, and the primacy effect suggests we will remember the first thing someone says. Rather than focusing on the first and last things a person says, we should try and listen for the ideas being presented and not the minute details surrounding those ideas. If you understand the ideas being presented, then you can understand the message even if you would use different words to express the same ideas.

Listen to the Nonverbals as Well as the Content

Content often gets the bulk of our attention, but content alone does not encompass the message someone sends—a point made clear in high context cultures. How someone says something can be just as important as what he or she says or does not say, so listening for tone, rate, and pitch and staying attuned to eye contact and other physical mannerisms can help you listen more closely to what the person is actually saying. If you get caught up trying to follow just the content of a speaker's message, you may miss out on nonverbal indicators he or she uses to tell you what is truly important, whether he or she believes the message to be true or not.[8]

Focus on Agreement and Not Disagreement

When we listen to people make a case for something, we often listen for the things with which we disagree. This is a defensive position and a behavior that is hard to change.

Instead of looking for what is different or that which you oppose in someone's statement, look for places of agreement. You might not agree with every point, but if you can find some common ground, it is possible to build from there and perhaps eventually find a compromise. Listening for agreement also lets the other person know you are listening with an open mind and not simply seeking to shut down the person or make the person appear as though he or she is wrong. This creates a relaxed environment where people become more open to expressing their ideas and thoughts with each other. When we just look for disagreement, that is all we will find, and we will not be able to change minds or move to common ground. This tactic requires you to be patient, open, genuine, and critical all at the same time.

Summary

In this chapter, we delved into the concept of listening, a fundamental aspect of communication. We first dispelled six different misconceptions about listening and how it works. We then defined the three main purposes for listening and the two ways in which we listen. Next, we outlined the six different ways in which people appear to listen, but are not actually processing messages in their entirety, if at all. Finally, we provided six guidelines for developing good listening skills that encourage dialogue and effective communication.

Chapter 6 Key Ideas

- There are four purposes of listening: listening for appreciation, listening for comprehension, listening to show support, and critical listening
- We engage in active listening when we pay a high degree of attention to the message, but we engage is passive listening when we just try to absorb what is being said without significant mental or conversational involvement
- There are six types of nonlistening behaviors: pseudolistening, glazing over, ambushing, prejudging, selective listening, and advising

Chapter 6 Key Terms

Hearing	Listening to show support	Spare brain time
Listening	Critical listening	Ambushing
Emotional intelligence	Active listening	Prejudging
Rapport talk	Passive listening	Selective listening
Report talk	Nonlistening	Advising
Listening for appreciation	Psuedolistening	
Listening for comprehension	Glazing over	

References

1 Wilt, M.E. (1950). A study of teacher awareness of listening as a factor in elementary education. *Journal of Educational Research,* 43 (8), pp. 626-636; Tricia Hedge, *Teaching and learning in the language classroom,* Oxford University Press.

2 International Listening Association, Priorities of Listening Research: Four interrelated initiatives. Retrieved from http://www.listen.org/Resources/Documents/White_Paper_PrioritiesResearch.pdf, p. 9.

3 Quick Statistics. (n.d.). Retrieved from http://www.nidcd.nih.gov/health/statistics/pages/quick.aspx.

4 Hearing Loss & Tinnitus Statistics. (n.d.). Retrieved from http://hearinghealthfoundation.org/statistics.

5 Gardner, H. (1983). *Frames of mind.* New York: Basic Books.

6 Goleman, D. (1995). *Emotional intelligence.* New York: Bantam Dell.

7 Tannen, D. (1990). *You just don't understand: Women and men in conversation.* New York: William Morrow and Company, Inc.

8 Buller D. B. & and Burgoon, J. K. (1996). Interpersonal Deception Theory. *Communication Theory 6,* 203-242.

Chapter 7

Communication, Culture, and Diversity

Our ability to instantaneously communicate with people over great distances has had numerous effects on our lives, not the least of which is exposure to myriad different people, cultures, languages, and beliefs. We encounter these diverse audiences in classrooms, on social media, as business clients, medical patients, and even as family members. Such richness and diversity is both exciting and challenging. It makes appreciating the backgrounds and the experiences of others an essential part of becoming an effective communicator. More than ever, we must ensure that we are sensitive and respectful toward others when we speak, which makes it more likely they will listen to what we have to say.

In this chapter, we explain how culture and diversity impact our communication with others. First, we will define culture and investigate its different dimensions. We will then provide some detail on specific categories that constitute and influence the diverse audiences we encounter when we communicate in any context. Finally, we will offer some concrete suggestions for enhancing your ability to interact successfully with diverse groups of people in a variety of situations.

Understanding Culture

Culture
the distinctive ideas, customs, social behavior, products, or way of life of a particular nation, society, people, or period

According to the Oxford English Dictionary, **culture** is defined as "the distinctive ideas, customs, social behavior, products, or way of life of a particular nation, society, people, or period."[1] Geert Hofstede, one of the first social psychologists to study culture, offers another take, defining culture as "the collective programming of the mind distinguishing the members of one group or category of people from another. The 'category' can refer to nations, regions within or across nations, ethnicities, religions, occupations, organizations, or the genders."[2] No matter which definition you prefer, culture is a complicated, powerful component of human development and life. It influences self-images, priorities, personalities, and how we communicate with one another.

We are not part of only one overarching culture. Instead, we belong to and are impacted by a variety of smaller, more specific cultures. These smaller groups, called **co-cultures,** exist within and alongside larger cultural groups, allowing individuals to simultaneously belong to several cultures and co-cultures. Sometimes we even feel conflicted between the different cultures in which we belong.

Co-cultures
smaller specific cultures that intersect in our lives

Let's look at an example to illustrate how cultures work and collide in our lives. Darius grew up in a Russian-American family and is a practicing Roman Catholic. Darius happens to be quite proud of his ethnic heritage, and also makes sure he attends mass every Sunday. He does not speak Russian, however, nor does he agree with all the church's teachings. Nevertheless, many of the customs and beliefs of both groups inform Darius's perspective on the world around him. Many of his friends in his neighborhood are Russian, and he belongs to the Knights of Columbus, a Catholic charity dedicated to helping the sick, disabled and needy in their communities, but none of his Russian neighborhood friends are affiliated with that organization. Darius belongs to both cultures, which constitute co-cultures within the larger American or Western culture.

One type of culture that is particularly influential is national culture. The specific traditions of a national culture vary greatly between countries, but according to Hofstede, national cultures can all be understood through six consistent dimensions.

High vs. Low Power Distance Culture

Cultures with high power distance have high levels of inequality in power distribution in organizations, families, and other institutions, whereas cultures with low power distance have less inequality. Democratic countries typically have low power distance, for instance, because everyone has an equal share in decisions, while high power distance is more likely in monarchies and dictatorships where only a few have access to power and others are removed from decision making. In terms of families, those with high power distance tend to adhere to parents' decisions and seek the permission of elders for certain actions. Those families with low power distance embrace a more inclusive approach, where major decisions, like moving or choice of school for children, is arrived at through a group discussion and decision, not the edict of a parent or elder. Power distance, or more aptly put, distance from power, plays a large role in how individuals and groups behave and helps identify things they value. For instance, low power distance cultures seem to value freedom of expression and dissent more, while high power distance cultures value stability, tradition, and experience.

High vs. Low Uncertainty Avoidance Culture

Cultures with high uncertainty avoidance have a low tolerance for ambiguity and minimize the possibility of uncomfortable, unstructured situations by enforcing strict rules, safety measures, and a belief in absolute truth. Cultures with low uncertainty avoidance have fewer rules, take risks, and are tolerant of change. This cultural characteristic can also be seen in interpersonal relationships, as we will discuss later. For example, individuals who hail from cultures with high uncertainty avoidance will ask questions to reduce their uncertainty over the status of a relationship, while those who are more comfortable with uncertainty will allow things to move along naturally and not inquire about the status of a relationship to reduce their own stress. Again, this characteristic of cultures provides a view as to what a particular group may value. High uncertainty avoidance cultures may value things like planning and stability, while low uncertainty avoidance cultures tend to be more flexible and open to spontaneity and change.

Individualist vs. Collectivist Culture

Individualistic societies have loose ties between individuals and expect each person to look out for himself or herself and his or her immediate family. Collectivist cultures have strong ties between individuals, strong communal bonds, and often live in extended families that are deeply loyal to the group. Individualistic cultures value things like personal achievement and personal opinions, while collectivistic cultures tend to value things like group harmony over any one person in the group. This cultural characteristic manifests in some unique ways. For example, in individualistic cultures, such as the United States, people tend to pride themselves on speaking their minds and saying what they mean, regardless of the impact it might have on another person. Conversely, in collectivistic cultures, people will tend to "talk around" an issue until the other side realizes what is being said. This maintains group harmony while still getting a point across, but it takes much more time and effort than the direct nature embraced by individualistic cultures.

Masculine vs. Feminine Culture

Masculinity and femininity refer to the distribution of emotional roles between the genders and the difference in the values of men and women. In masculine cultures, men are typically highly assertive and competitive, and women are somewhat assertive and competitive. In feminine cultures, men and women are both much more modest and caring. Masculine cultures tend to emphasize competition, whereas feminine cultures emphasize cooperation and consensus. These masculine and feminine cultural behaviors have been identified through extensive research on gender and communication. Linguistics scholar Deborah Tannen coined the term "genderlect" to more clearly illustrate that gender is a cultural difference and that men and women simply communicate differently, thus creating their own cultures through their different styles of interaction. One fundamental difference she found was in the purpose of communication, as a masculine style of communication is one seeking to establish or defend status and express competition, while a feminine style of communication is one where the purpose is establishing connections and creating cooperation.[3]

Long-term vs. Short-term Orientation Culture

Cultures with long-term orientation are pragmatic and focus on future rewards, with an emphasis on saving, persistence, and adaptation. Cultures with short-term orientation focus on the present and past and emphasize national pride, tradition, social obligations, and saving "face" in the here and now. What is interesting about this cultural characteristic is that "long" and "short" mean different things in different places and to different people. To some, a long-term orientation means thinking about next week, next month, or perhaps next year. It might even pertain to thinking about long-term career goals and where one wants to be in five years. To others, that type of thinking is still short-term. Keep in mind some cultures have existed for thousands of years, and as such they have a very different conception of longterm. They may plan in terms of decades or even generations—a very different way of thinking about time than looking at the next few days, months, or even years. Like other cultural characteristics, long-term versus short-term orientation should be viewed on a linear scale, and not as a "one or the other" form of existence. Some cultures are more long-term in their thinking than others.

> *"For effectively cooperating with people who are from other nations, there are two basic conditions that have to be fulfilled. The first is speaking or having learned a shared language, and the second is acting according to shared rules and standards."*
>
> —*Geerte Hofstede*

Indulgent vs. Restrained Culture

Indulgent cultures freely allow gratification of desires that allow individuals to enjoy life and have fun. Additionally, indulgent cultures value things like individual happiness, vacation, and leisure time, and the expression of emotions and thoughts. Restrained cultures have strict social norms and discourage acting simply out of want. In fact, in restrained cultures, many of the indulgent behaviors are curbed and governed through strict social and familial norms and rules, because they are seen as potentially rude. Leisure and vacation are not seen as that important in more restrained cultures. Although this is the newest of the cultural dimensions to be identified and studied, there have been some thoughts on its impact in a globalized workplace. For instance, those who come from more restrained cultures may not freely express dissent or unhappiness, and this could be detrimental to a working environment; conversely, those from more indulgent cultures may be more likely to speak out of turn or to say something inappropriate that can also have a detrimental impact on work productivity and group cohesion.[4]

It is easy to see how different nations and countries can differ along these spectrums. It is important to note, though, that Hofstede believed these dimensions fall along a continuum, and do not exist as simply "either-or." For example, a culture is not either collectivistic or individualistic, but falls somewhere in between each on a line.

In addition to the six dimensions of culture identified by Hofstede, Edward T. Hall[5] explains that most national cultures can also be identified by how much importance is placed on nonverbal cues. In **low-context cultures**, such as the United States and Germany, meaning is derived mostly from the language used in an interaction, and less emphasis is placed on the nonverbal communication, environment, and situation. In **high-context cultures**, such as Korea and Saudi Arabia, a great deal of meaning is derived from the nonverbal expressions, environment, and situation in which the communication is taking place, and less emphasis is placed on the words.

Hofstede's original six dimensions of culture, along with the one proposed by Hall, allow us to begin to understand the complexity of different cultures. This understanding can enhance our ability to interact with people by helping us see how they might differ from us in terms of values along these continuums. Next, we will explore some different cultural categories in addition to nationality, beginning with race and ethnicity.

Race and Ethnicity in Culture

Race is a common cultural marker as well as a demographic category we find on college and job applications, census data, and other types of reports. **Race** refers to a set of physical characteristics shared by a group of people, such as skin color, body type, facial structure, and hair color. These physical characteristics are genetically inherited and reflect adaptations to the geographic region in which someone's ancestors previously lived. However, there is no biological difference between races in other characteristics, such as intelligence, athleticism, or other abilities. Due in part to the fact these characteristics developed in particular groups in specific regions, those groups created a culture themselves because of the fact they lived in close proximity to each other. However, definitions of race have been formed and reformed numerous times throughout history, and race has often been used as a marker to treat groups of people differently throughout history, so race is also a reflection of the different social, political, and economic experiences of groups of individuals and is often an important part of an individual's cultural identity.[6] For example, a history of slavery, Jim Crow laws, segregation, and other types of unequal treatment have shaped the experiences of many black Americans over time. Many Japanese-Americans were placed in internment camps during World War II, and many people of Middle Eastern descent have faced intense discrimination since the World Trade Centers were attacked. Whether or not

Low-context cultures
meaning is derived mostly from the language used in an interaction, and very little emphasis is placed on the nonverbal communication, environment, and situation

High-context cultures
a great deal of meaning is derived from the nonverbal expressions, environment, and situation in which the communication is taking place, and less emphasis is placed on the words

Race
a set of physical characteristics shared by a group of people, such as skin color, body type, facial structure, and hair color

Ethnicity
a group of people who identify with each other based on a common experience, which might include geographic or national origin, ancestry, history, cultural and social norms, religion, race, language, ideology, food, dress, or other factors

each of these labels reflects race, nationality, or ethnicity is often a matter of intense debate, and the ways that we define racial categories will continue to change over time. Even so, the experiences associated with being identified as a member of a particular race is often associated with either a certain set of privileges or challenges that shape one's experience and can be a way of establishing communities with others who share similar experiences.

Another cultural marker that developed due to the close proximity of people is ethnicity, but ethnicity should not be confused with race. **Ethnicity** refers to a group of people who identify with each other based on a common experience, which might include geographic or national origin, ancestry, history, cultural and social norms, religion, race, language, ideology, food, dress, or other factors. Ethnicity is sometimes (but not always) related to national heritage. At times, violent conflicts and disputes evolve out of differences in ethnic heritage and values between two or more groups. At other times, several ethnic groups might coexist peacefully in the same nation. In fact, Tufts Professor Colin Woodard argues that the United States is really made up of eleven nations, each of which has a different history, ancestry, and set of deep-seated attitudes.[7]

A recent example of ethnic tension can be seen in the Crimea region of the Ukraine. In 2014, Russian-speaking citizens of Ukraine sought support from the Russian Federation when the political situation in the country became unstable, and ultimately voted to secede from Ukraine and join the Russian Federation. Ukrainian nationals in Crimea disagreed with this approach, and an international crisis ensued that still dominates much of the eastern border of the Ukraine shared with Russia.

Ethnic heritage can also be a source of reinforcement for individual identity through cultural celebrations. In major American cities, Italian Americans celebrate the Feast of San Gennaro, a food festival central to their culture. Many other cities hold a celebration for *Dia de Los Muertos*, a holiday that originated in Mexico and is now celebrated in many countries to honor and remember friends and family members who are deceased. A number of cities also have areas designated Little Italy, Little China, and so on, where people who share that ethnic heritage settled. These areas offer a great opportunity to explore some of the ethnic differences between people in fun, interesting, and, if you like food, tasty ways.

Sex, Gender, and Sexual Orientation

Another set of significant cultural categories refers to one's physical, psychological, and romantic definitions of his or her identity. To properly appreciate how these aspects of a person's self-concept relate to culture, we must first differentiate between the various ways we define our sexuality. According to the American Psychological Society[8], **sex** refers to one's biological classification as male, female, or intersex (having both male and female physical characteristics) based on one's reproductive organs and chromosomes. Sex is an objective way of identifying the group to which a person belongs based on biology. Often, job applications and college applications ask for this information but are prohibited from using it to make decisions. Males and females are also often depicted with images as shown in Figure 7.1.

Sex
one's biological classification based on reproductive function

FIGURE 7.1   **Male and Female Images**

Sex is also often incorrectly used as a synonym for gender, which is quite different. **Gender** is a social construction that includes all of the beliefs, attitudes, actions, and roles associated with being masculine or feminine. One's biological sex informs one's gender identity, but gender is more than simply a reflection of physical characteristics. Gender includes one's sense of self as being male or female regardless of physical biology. Gender also includes the societal expectations for behaviors, attitudes, and roles filled by feminine- or masculine-minded individuals. It is important to note that these expectations vary across cultures. Whereas biology defines one's sex, communication creates one's gender.

If a person's gender identity matches the sex characteristics with which they were born, they are considered **cisgender**, and would likely categorize themselves as male or female. If a person's gender identity is different than the sex characteristics with which they were born, they are considered **transgender**, and would likely categorize themselves as trans male or trans female. Someone who does not consider themselves to be male or female in gender might identify themselves as **gender queer** or **gender nonconforming**.

Gender
a social construction that includes the all of the beliefs, attitudes, actions and roles associated with being masculine or feminine

DIALING DIVERSITY

In many cases, laws are written using categories of sex, and not the more fluid concept of gender. In June 2014, this conflict of terminology and practice resulted in a controversy in the state of South Carolina. Chase Culpepper, a 16-year-old male self-identified gender nonconformist, went to the Department of Motor Vehicles to have his driver's license photo taken dressed as a girl. In fact, Chase reportedly prefers to wear girl's clothing but identifies with male pronouns. When he arrived at the DMV, they required him to take off his makeup, stating he did not look like a boy and that the makeup constituted a disguise (their reasoning being that it is illegal to wear a disguise for a driver's license photo). Although he ultimately wiped off the makeup for the photo and received his license, he, along with his family and the Transgender Legal Defense and Education Fund, complained that this requirement violated his right to gender expression protected by the First Amendment. Chase's story serves as a clear example of the difference between sex and gender, and how communication assists people in expressing their identity. Furthermore, the episode shows how certain labels carry certain expectations for society and cultural groups.

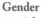

Sexual orientation
the sex and gender
to whom a person
is romantically and
sexually attracted

In addition to the physical and psychological aspects of one's sexuality, there is an emotional and romantic dimension as well. A person's **sexual orientation** refers to the sex and gender to which a person is romantically and sexually attracted. Sexual orientation includes many categories along a continuum, but the three most common categories include whether one is attracted to members of the opposite sex (heterosexual), of the same sex (gay or lesbian), or members of both sexes (bisexual). The declaration and enactment of sexual orientation is both an intensely personal decision and, for some people, a public declaration of belonging to a group.

Chase Culpepper's public declaration of belonging to a group presents us with an example of how sexual orientation can be construed as a culture. Many cities across the globe hold Gay Pride Parades that are public celebrations of lesbian, gay, bisexual, and transgender (LGBT) culture. These parades reinforce ties between individuals who identify with this culture and help serve to promote their beliefs, attitudes, and values.

Age

We do not often think of age as a cultural marker, but it definitely operates as one in any society. While none of us will be the same age for the rest of our lives, a person's age tells others something about his or her life experiences as well as some possible attitudes, and beliefs he or she may hold. Let's look at a few examples of different generational cultures in the United States[9]:

The GI Generation: sometimes referred to as the Greatest Generation, this is the generation that fought during World War II

The Silent Generation: too young to fight in World War II, but came into adulthood during the rise of the middle class and relatively prosperous time that followed

The Baby Boomers: the children of the GI generation, grew up with Woodstock and the Vietnam war, tended to focus on careers and set high expectations for their children

Generation X: graduated from high school in the '80s and '90s; tend to be independent, resilient, and adaptable

The Millennials (also sometimes referred to as Generation Y): graduated high school after 2000, and they tended to be very protected by their parents and had high expectations set for them

The generation that each person lives in shapes his or her experiences, expectations, and attitudes toward others. Not everyone from a specific generation acts and believes the same way, but people always identify with the times in which they grew up. As these different generational groupings illustrate, age as a cultural group is not as simple as "old" and "young" or "elderly" and "middle-aged." Those labels are defined purely by a number and fail to recognize the importance of each person's experiences and how those inform a person's generational culture. In fact, we will all be labeled "old" or "middle-aged" at some point, but the generation to which we belong will not change.

Physical and Cognitive Diversity

Age, ethnicity, race, and sexuality are not the only ways in which we are different. In fact, unless you have an identical twin, you are probably the only person who looks exactly like you, acts like you, and thinks like you. Considering there are now more than seven billion people on Earth, there is a great deal of physical diversity among humans. However, our differences go beyond appearances and also include abilities. Some people have especially high levels of specific physical abilities (for instance, Usain Bolt holds world records in both the 100- and 200-meter dashes due to his ability as a sprinter), while others have lower levels of specific physical abilities (for example, Helen Keller could not see or hear). These differences make us no better or worse than someone else, but rather add to the richness of human experience.

At some point, most, if not all, of us will experience some type of physical or cognitive impairment. Some of these are permanent, while others are temporary; some are due to genetics, others the result of an illness or accident. Some people are born blind, for example, while others may develop blindness due to macular degeneration later in life. Some others may lose their sight temporarily, such as after surgery. This variety of causes is important to note because not all people with the same impairment are the same; instead, they may share a similar limitation or level of ability. These differences also do not define the person, but rather are a part of us, just as age, ethnicity, and race are a part of us.

Likewise, there is great diversity in our cognitive abilities and preferences. There is a broad range in IQ, learning styles and preferences, interests, memory, and experience among people. Many cognitive challenges are not immediately apparent when we meet someone, such as dyslexia, Attention Deficit Hyperactivity Disorder (ADHD), Alzheimer's disease, or memory loss. Like physical impairments, some people live with these challenges for their entire lives, while others might experience them for a shorter period of time. Medication, for example, can impact a person's short-term memory, as can a concussion.

Additionally, there is a wide degree of variability in how people cognitively process information and learn about the world around them. Some people understand concepts by reading about them, while others prefer to see a picture, and others still may prefer to examine a model. The idea of different modalities for human learning has been explored extensively by psychologist Howard Gardner, and formalized under his theory of multiple intelligences. **Multiple intelligence theory** proposes that although all individuals can access and learn about the world through each of the seven intelligences he identified, people differ in the strength of their aptitude or preference for those various intelligences.

Multiple intelligence theory although all individuals can access and learn about the world through each of the seven intelligences, people differ in the strength of their aptitude or preference for those various intelligences

Although controversial, Gardner's theory illustrates how all people develop differently and experience the world in different ways.[10]

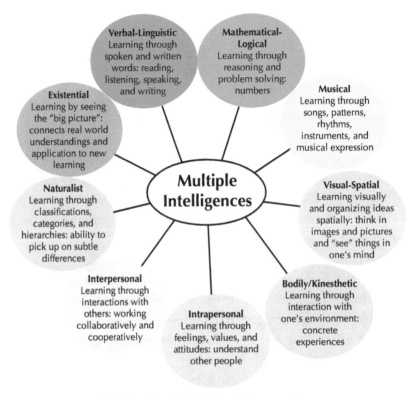

FIGURE 7.2   **Multiple Intelligence Theory**

Ideological Diversity

Ideology
set of ideas, beliefs, and ideals that form our worldview and provide a basis for action; forms the basis for political beliefs and is heavily influenced by both the family and society in which we grow up

We have thus far focused on largely physical differences between people, but diversity of thought is just as important. This type of diversity often emerges in politics, where people hold different ideas on policy and effective governance. These views are the result of a commitment to an **ideology,** or set of ideas, beliefs, and ideals that form one's worldview and provide a basis for action. Ideology is the basis for political beliefs and is heavily influenced by the family and society in which we grow up. As Colin Woodard showed when defining the Eleven Nations in the U.S.[11], there is a great deal of ideological diversity even within the United States, and that ideological diversity expands even more when we consider the entire globe. Not every country has, or even wants, a democracy. Let's focus a bit on ideological diversity in the United States specifically.

We often think of the United States as practicing a two-party system, and for all practical purposes this is true, but to believe the two parties contain individuals that completely agree or share worldviews would be foolish. The Democratic Party, for example, consists of people who place different priorities on various issues, and this sometimes manifests in intraparty squabbles. Some Democrats care about limiting government spending (they are called Blue Dog Democrats), while others are more concerned with civil rights and social issues. They do not agree on every issue. The same can be said for Republicans, who contain some Libertarians who believe in very small government, others who care about advancing social issues from a religious perspective, and others still who want to lower taxes and promote business. The fact of the matter is the two parties merely cloud the vast political and ideological diversity that exists in the United States. To use "liberal vs. conservative" dichotomies to describe people and groups does not come close to acknowledging the variety of thought on public issues that exists in the United States.

Religious Diversity

One final area of difference that both creates its own cultural norms and enhances diversity in America and around the world is religion. There are numerous different faiths practiced in the United States, and despite the prevalence of the Abrahamic faiths (Judaism, Christianity, and Islam) each contributes to the fabric of our culture in its own way. In 2009, the US Census Bureau issued a statistical breakdown of the religious affiliations of people in the United States. In it they found a tremendous amount of diversity, including within Christian faiths, where they identified 30 different denominations. Each of these faiths has different religious perspectives, practices, and beliefs. The report also included a note regarding the growing number of Muslim, Wiccan, Buddhist, and non-religious people in the US.[12]

The growth of non-religious and "unaffiliated but spiritual" individuals requires some discussion. It is a mistake to assume knowledge of someone's beliefs based on his or her specific affiliation, just as it is unwise to assume someone has no faith or belief in morality/spirituality because he or she is unaffiliated with a religious group. Many people still hold beliefs privately, and should not be discounted or counted simply based on the religious groups with whom they identify. Understanding and appreciating these differences, while not necessarily agreeing with them, is essential for developing a respectful community.

Religious groups also play important roles in local, state, and national communities. They often do good work on behalf of the community in which their members live and help to promote charitable endeavors across the world. Churches, synagogues, mosques, and temples all also practice their own culture by providing members opportunities to connect with each other and share stories and experiences. These efforts build their religious culture, but also contribute to the larger community's culture. However, some religious groups also have a history of violence, discrimination, and hatred toward other groups of individuals and have often wielded that influence in powerful political ways.

Socioeconomic Status

Another way in which individuals' experience differ is socioeconomic status, or the experiences that accompany someone's access to economic resources. **Socioeconomic status** is usually measured as a combination of someone's education, income, and occupation. What

Socioeconomic status measured as a combination of someone's education, income, and occupation each person considers to be a "normal" part of life, the careers we choose, our expectations the types of support we might or might not receive from family members, what we believe is attainable, what we eat, where we shop, the type of entertainment we tend to seek out, the types of exercise we select (if any), how we expect to be treated by others, what we think of as expensive or inexpensive, and more are influenced by our own socioeconomic status and the socioeconomic status of the family in which we were raised.

Communicating in a Culturally Diverse World

To be a competent communicator in any situation you need to understand, acknowledge, and appreciate the diversity that cultural differences provide our society. The differences in language, experiences, values, beliefs, and perspectives can enrich our lives in many ways, but require communication grounded in the purpose of understanding others rather than trying to convince them of anything. It requires us to be perceptive of the context in which we find ourselves, as well as the ways that context might be different for someone else.

So far, this chapter has focused primarily on describing some of the differences experienced by groups of individuals to help us build a greater understanding of others and to help to provide a shared language for identifying and describing those differences. However, we must go beyond simply understanding that differences exist and work toward understanding one another, respecting each person's dignity and individual experience,

MEDIATED MOMENTS

In today's world, where people tweet comments and use cameras to record events, it is almost impossible to hide something. Such is the lesson several celebrities have learned in recent years. Famously, 2012 Republican presidential candidate Mitt Romney was recorded calling out 47 percent of the population for what he claimed was wanting handouts from the government, and the video arguably cost him the election. In 2013, a video surfaced of Philadelphia Eagles wide receiver Riley Cooper using a racial slur after being denied access backstage at a concert, and he was subsequently suspended by his team. Donald Sterling, owner of the Los Angeles Clippers, was also recorded telling his girlfriend not to bring "black people" to his games. Celebrity chef and restaurateur Paula Deen also lost her employment with the Food Network after she was accused of, and admitted to, using a racial slur. The Twitter-verse and webpage comment areas are littered with people using culturally insensitive terminology and labels for others. This may be due to the belief people have that their comments and actions are anonymous, but it does not hide the fact that our communication as a society needs to improve to better respect and understand the differences of the people with whom we live.

and communicating effectively in ways that help us see beyond our differences. In this final section, we provide several tips to help enhance your ability to use communication to understand and respect differences between people.

Don't try to define others based on a single demographic characteristic.

While it is helpful to understand the ways that various demographic and personal characteristics might influence a person's experience and ways of communicating, we should recognize that a single characteristic does not make up someone's entire experience. Each person's perspective is shaped by a complex combination of experiences, including but certainly not limited to each of the dimensions discussed in this chapter, and those unique combinations help each of us see the world a little bit differently.

Use appropriate terminology that is respectful of differences.

Much of this chapter was descriptive and helped to provide terminology that is generally considered appropriate and respectful when describing specific differences, but is certainly not comprehensive in doing so. When you are speaking with or describing others, use the most respectful possible language. If someone shares terminology that they prefer to have used to describe specific characteristics of themselves, use their preferred terminology. Language is constantly evolving to reflect our changing world and experiences, and this includes the language that we use to describe aspects of our identity.

Make the Message Accessible

As a speaker, it is important to consider the range of abilities in your audience and to adapt your presentation where possible to help the entire audience understand what you are saying. For instance, you might need to add captions to film clips, avoid combining red and green on slides so that those with colorblindness can read your text, and include signposts and transitions that make it easy for your audience to follow along if their attention wavers for a few moments. Using microphones, handouts, and other assistive methods may help people better follow your message, regardless of any limitations or challenges they may have. Another way to make information more accessible is to create stories that use references with which the audience might be familiar so they can understand how the concepts relate to their lives.

Focus on Similarities, not Differences

Though you might think that acknowledging the different abilities or backgrounds of others may make you seem like you understand them or are trying to help them, they may take issue with this. It calls them out in front of others and specifically heightens the differences they may not want others to know. So, act no differently and whenever possible if you need to make an accommodation of sorts, do so in a way that everyone shares in it so as not to segregate your audience. If at all possible, it is far better to focus on the ties that bind an audience together than the things that make people feel different.

Avoid "ist" Language

This is the type of language that demeans, ignores, inappropriately calls attention to, or disrespects members of a separate culture or group. This includes ageist, racist, and sexist language that does not respect the humanity of other people. This type of language depicts the other group as a passive object and not an active subject, thus making them seem less than the group of the person making the statement. Remember, the more ways you can emphasize commonalities between people, the more positively received your appeal will be.

Following these three simple tips will enable you to become more effective when developing, sending, and receiving messages in a variety of contexts. They ask that you be a respectful, observant, and thoughtful communicator.

Summary

In this chapter, we discussed the relationship between culture, communication, and diversity. We first explained the theoretical underpinnings of culture and explored the various dimensions all national cultures share to some extent. We then discussed several different categories of difference that both are their own cultural groups and contribute to a diverse society. We also offered some suggestions for how to effectively appreciate differences through communication.

Chapter 7 Key Ideas

- Each of us belongs to and is influenced by several cultures and co-cultures
- Hofstede identified six dimensions of national cultures: (1) high vs. low power distance, (2) high vs. low uncertainty avoidance, (3) individualism vs. collectivism, (4) masculinity vs. femininity, (5) long-term vs. short-term orientation, and (6) indulgence vs. restraint
- Low-context cultures derive meaning primarily from language, while high-context cultures derive a great deal of meaning from nonverbal expressions, the environment, and the situation in which the interaction is taking place
- Race refers to a set of physical characteristics shared by a group of people, whereas ethnicity refers to a group of people who identify with each other based on a common experience
- Sex is one's biological classification as male, female, or intersex, whereas gender is the social construction associated with being masculine or feminine. Sexual orientation refers to the sex and gender to whom a person is romantically attracted
- Humans have diverse experiences related to their generational differences, physical and cognitive ability, ideology, and religion

Chapter 7 Key Terms

Culture	Race	Sexual orientation
Cocultures	Ethnicity	Multiple intelligence theory

Low-context cultures   Sex   Ideology

High-context cultures   Gender   Socioeconomic status

References

1 Culture. (n.d.). In *Oxford English Dictionary online*. Retrieved from http://www.oxforddictionaries.com/us/definition/american_english/culture

2 Hofstede, G., & Hofstede, G. J. (2013). Culture. Retrieved from http://www.geerthofstede.nl/culture.

3 Tannen, D. (2001). *You just don't understand: Men and women in conversation*. New York: Harper Collins.

4 Maclachlan, M. (January 11, 2013). Blog: View on Global Working, *Communicaid*. Retrieved from http://www.communicaid.com/cross-cultural-training/blog/indulgence-vs-restraint-6th-dimension/#.VXmPfM9VhBc

5 Hall, E. T. (1976). *Beyond culture*. New York, NY: Doubleday.

6 Omi, M., & Winant, H. (2014). *Racial formation in the United States* (3rd ed.). New York: Routledge

7 Woodard, C. (2013, Fall). Up in arms. *Tufts Magazine*. Medford, MA: Tufts University. Retrieved from http://www.tufts.edu/alumni/magazine/fall2013/features/up-in-arms.html

8 American Psychological Association (2014). Practice guidelines for LGB clients. Retrieved from http://www.apa.org/pi/lgbt/resources/guidelines.aspx?item=2.

9 Howe, N., & Strauss, W. (2000). *Millennials rising: The next great generation*. New York: Vintage.

10 Gardner, H. (1999). *Intelligence Reframed: Multiple Intelligences for the 21st Century*, New York, NY: Basic Books, 1999.

11 Woodard, C. (2013, Fall). Up in arms. *Tufts Magazine*. Retrieved from http://www.tufts.edu/alumni/magazine/fall2013/features/up-in-arms.html

12 U.S. Census Bureau. (2009). Self-described religious identification of adult population: 1990 to 2008. 2010 statistical abstract. Retrieved from http://www.census.gov/compendia/statab/2010/tables/10s0075.pdf

Chapter 8

Interviewing

Of all the communication situations you will experience during your life, none combines more of the elements of public speaking, interpersonal communication, small group dynamics, and listening than interviewing. There are many different forms and several different types of interviews. Journalists interview witnesses and experts to gather information for a story, and potential clients may interview several different service providers before selecting someone to work with, but the most common interviews occur in the workplace. These can be for prospective employees, or even current employees who are going through a performance review. Interviews are important events in all of our lives.

Interviews are also an opportunity to demonstrate good communication skills. In 2014, a survey by the National Association of Colleges and Employers found that applicants' abilities to make decisions, solve problems, and effectively verbally communicate with people inside and outside of the organization are the most important abilities to potential employers.[1] All of these can be demonstrated through a strong and successful interview, which will increase the likelihood you will be selected for the position. This is because **interviews** are goal-oriented communication events where both sides use question-and-answer techniques to achieve their ends. They are, for all intents and purposes, the epitome

Interviews
goal-oriented communication events where both sides use question-and-answer techniques to achieve their ends

of interactional communication where both parties are senders and receivers simultaneously throughout the engagement.

In this chapter, we examine interviewing and, although we will begin by defining the types of interviews you might encounter throughout your career, we pay particular attention to employment interviews. After defining the interview types, we will explain how an employment interview could take place through a variety of media. We will then explore the structure of an interview and the types of questions you will likely encounter when seeking a position. Finally, we will offer some guidelines for effectively employing dialogue in an employment interview to maximize your ability to succeed in getting a job offer.

Interview Types and Formats

Interviews come in all shapes and forms, and you will find yourself in any one of them at some point in your life. All interviews are goal oriented, but they have different goals for each party. For example, journalists conduct interviews to gather information for stories, while job seekers go on interviews in the hope of getting a position with a company. Additionally, interviews occur in several formats, even through different media. It used to be that all interviews were face-to-face; however, now thanks to programs like Skype, interviews can happen digitally over long distances. Interviews also do not always imply one person interviewing another— today the number of people in the room has even changed! In this section of the chapter, we will describe six types of interviews and five formats for conducting them.

Types of Interviews

Interviews are labeled and defined by the goals the particular interaction seeks to achieve. Regardless of what type of interview takes place, both parties are aware that they are in an interview situation. In this part of the chapter, we will briefly define six different types of interviews, even though the remainder of the chapter will focus on employment interviews specifically.

Information-Gathering Interviews. This interview is commonly practiced by journalists, but managers and researchers also conduct these from time to time. **Information gathering interviews** seek to discover facts, information, and other knowledge about a particular topic from peers, experts, witnesses, or others who may be knowledgeable about it.

Helping Interviews. These interviews occur most often with counselors, psychologists, psychiatrists, and other healthcare providers. When you consult an expert in other areas, such as construction, they also are participating in a helping interview. **Helping interviews** take

Information-gathering interviews
a type of interview that seeks to discover facts, information, and other knowledge about a particular topic from peers, experts, witnesses, or others who may be knowledgeable about it

Helping interviews
a type of interview that takes stock of a problem or challenge faced by an individual and offers informed and expert advice on how to handle it

stock of a problem or challenge faced by an individual and offer informed and expert advice on how to handle it.

Problem-Solving Interviews. There are times when conflict or issues arise within a company or organization that requires investigation. These investigations conduct interviews designed to gather information but do so specifically to identify a problem's source and a solution to it. **Problem-solving interviews** thus operate as a form of very specific information gathering coupled with an emphasis on solving a particular problem.

Performance Interviews. In most organizations, employees undergo an annual or semi-annual review of their achievements, contributions, and behavior. Often, these reviews, also called **performance interviews**, provide employers and managers with information used to determine raises, as well as target areas of improvement for staff. These interviews are official and are added to the personnel file of an employee. As it is an interview, the employee always has a chance to add or comment on points raised by her or his supervisor, thus negotiating the meaning of the performance period.

Exit Interviews. A typical practice of employers is to conduct interviews with employees who either resign or are dismissed. These interviews are conducted by human resources professionals and are designed to gather information about the processes and climate of the organization in an attempt to use that information to improve in the future. The effectiveness of **exit interviews** depends on the candid nature of the outgoing employee and the practical information he or she provides in the discussion.

Employment Interviews. When people speak of having an interview, they typically are referring to an **employment interview**, where employers conduct conversations with applicants for open positions in an effort to determine to whom they would like to offer a position. Additionally, the interviewees seek information about the company that will influence their decision to accept an offer, should one come. Employment interviews come in several different forms, but all typically follow the same pattern and require that applicants do their homework on the company before sitting down for the interview.

Interview Formats

Thanks to today's mediated environment, interviews now take place in several different ways. In fact, you might interview for the same position several different times, each through a different medium, before receiving a job offer. Usually, but not always, interviews occur between one job candidate and anywhere from one to several members of the company. In this section of the chapter, we will discuss five different interview formats you may encounter when searching for a job.

Email Interview. In the initial stages of the job process, prospective employers may send you questions via email. Normally, these questions would only go out to people who meet the

---

Problem-solving interviews
a form of very specific information gathering coupled with an emphasis on solving a specific problem

Performance interviews
a type of interview that provides employers and managers with information used to determine raises, as well as target areas of improvement for staff; also called performance reviews

Exit interviews
a type of interview conducted by human resources professionals with outgoing employees designed to gather information about the processes and climate of the organization in an attempt to use that information in the future to improve

Employment interviews
a type of interview in which employers conduct conversations with applicants for open positions in an effort to determine to whom they would like to offer a position; the interviewees seek information about the company that will influence their decision to accept an offer, should one come

minimum qualifications for the position. The questions during this stage typically ask you to expound upon aspects of your resume or fill in other pertinent information the employer may need to further refine the applicant pool.

Phone Interviews. More common to the interview process is the phone interview, where the employer arranges a time to call the job candidates with whom they wish to speak. These calls range in length, but you typically will have a day or so to prepare. It is important to make sure you know who is on the other end of the phone when interviewing through this medium, and so beginning the conversations with introductions is a good idea. Usually, the candidates chosen for a phone interview represent a "semi-finalist" approach, and some companies use these conversations to finalize their list of candidates for in-person interviews. During these interactions, employers seek to determine something about the candidate's personality, goals, and knowledge about the company.

Skype Interviews. Another advancement in technology allows company representatives to interview job candidates face to face without having to bring candidates to the company's location. Digital programs such as Skype allow these conversations to happen, and they are both inexpensive and useful because you can see nonverbal reactions to questions by both parties. In some cases, Skype interviews are used instead of flying someone in because they can save substantial amounts of money; but, at other times, Skype interviews are used to see how a candidate communicates and works in a mediated environment because increasing numbers of workers are telecommuting from home offices instead of living near and working in a centrally located corporate office. Sometimes, Skype interviews are conducted in addition to phone interviews, but other times they can take the place of either the phone interview or the in-person interview.

Island interviews a type of interview in which prospective candidates are placed in a room together and asked to discuss why they believe they are the better fit for the position

Island Interviews. A somewhat rare form of interview is the **island interview**, where prospective candidates are placed in a room together and asked to discuss why they believe they are the better fit for the position than the other candidates present. This type of interview format is more likely to occur when applying for graduate school, but it does happen in other professional areas from time to time. The prospective school or company watches the interaction to determine whom to select.

In-Person Interviews. The most common interview is the in-person interview, where finalists meet with members of the hiring committee or human resources staff. In-person interviews are often the final step in the process, but it is possible that you would have more than one in-person interview before a job offer is made. These interviews range in length from industry to industry, and could be as short as thirty minutes, or as long as a full day (or even two in some cases!). Even though these interviews are conversations, the employer usually scores answers afterward to help determine to whom to offer the position. In-person interviews also occur in many different places, although most commonly they will take place where the candidate would work. Sometimes, though, they are conducted in restaurants, coffee shops, airports, and even homes.

Interview Process

One of the advantages to employment interviews is that everyone typically knows what to expect. Most interviews follow a similar structure, though there might be slight variations. What is important to understand, however, is that in every case, the interview process begins well before you talk with the employer. First impressions are made through resumes and cover letters, although they can be enhanced or reduced based on the first face-to-face or phone interview. In this section of the chapter, we will go through the various stages of the interview process, thus explaining the structure you should expect during most job interviews.

Getting an Interview

The interview process begins with identifying the positions for which you wish to apply. This might sound easy, but examining job postings and determining your fit for these posts takes work. We will detail a few of the steps for positioning yourself well in the hopes of increasing the chances of receiving a formal interview.

Make sure you fit the minimum qualifications. Many applicants are removed from the pool because they do not meet the minimum requirements for the position. If the job asks for certain certifications or a number of years of experience, make sure you can reasonably make the case that you have those things. If you don't, you are wasting your time and theirs.

Determine any preferred qualifications you fit. In addition to minimum qualifications, many job descriptions contain preferred qualifications. You may still be a viable candidate without having these desired qualities, but having them will elevate your application. Make sure you find a way to highlight these for the employer.

Line up your references. Most employers today do not call references until they are ready to extend an offer; nevertheless, make sure you have spoken with the people you plan to use as references. This is both civil and professional. On a practical level, it also ensures those people will be available to field the call should it come.

Prepare your resume. All positions require a resume with a job application. Make sure yours is prepared, in a legible font and format, and contains an accurate representation of what you have done. Additionally, it is not a bad idea to bold words in the resume that match those in the job advertisement because this helps the reviewer see how you fit the position. Remember, though, that you should edit and adapt certain elements of your resume, like the lists of responsibilities and accomplishments, to the specific job for which you are applying. Don't just send the same resume everywhere—adapt it your audience.

Resume Dos and Don'ts

Do:

Proofread and Edit Your Resume Several Times Before Submitting It. Potential employers will see you as lacking attention to detail if the main document representing you is not produced with care.

Use a Variety of Action Words When Describing Past Experiences. Words like directed, expedited, accelerated, and delivered help describe what you've accomplished and get the reader excited to know more about your potential contributions to their organization.

Quantify Your Impacts in Previous Positions, If Possible. Potential employers like to know in concrete ways how you might make your mark on their company. If you can offer precise figures of how you, for example, increased sales or decreased waste, you will make a stronger case.

Don't:

Use the Same Resume for Every Position. Tailor your resume for each job you apply for.

Lie on Your Resume. If a lie is discovered, it could be grounds for termination. Honesty is the best policy!

Offer Personal Information on the Resume. Potential employers cannot use information such as your marital status or non-work related affiliations to decide your employment, so leave such information off your resume.

Write a strong cover letter. Many, but not all, positions ask for a cover letter to accompany the resume. When writing the cover letter, try to find out to whom you should address it. In the letter, do not simply detail your resume, but instead take the opportunity to elaborate on your accomplishments and explain how they fit the specific job qualifications. This is your first and most important opportunity to make an argument for why you should be considered for the position.

The Opening

The interview process continues to unfold when you are invited in to speak with representatives from the company. Not only should you arrive early for the meeting, but you should also dress appropriately. When your time arrives, the opening is your first real opportunity to make a lasting impression on the employer. Your resume gets you in the door, but your opening captures their attention and interest.

Shake hands with everyone. Although this may seem simple and possibly unnecessary, it is important to shake hands with everyone in the room before sitting down to begin the conversation. This is a sign of respect and acknowledgment, and it goes a long way toward establishing a friendly and comfortable environment. When shaking hands, remember to look the person in the eyes and use a firm handshake.

Establish a rapport with the interviewer(s). Rapport is something that should build throughout the interview, but the process of doing so begins at that start of the meeting. Good rapport is friendly and conversational. Some things that might help would be comments on the office or meeting area, compliments about the staff you have met, references to some current events related to the company, and even asking questions about the person's day. Additionally, it can be helpful to also thank the interviewer(s) for their time and recognize that their jobs are quite busy.

Introduce yourself. A common mistake during the opening is to not remember to state your name and what you prefer to be called. Some people in the room may not be familiar with you and might be meeting you for the first time, so it is always good practice to provide your name for everyone, and this can be done when shaking hands. In some cases, the people meeting with you may not have conducted the phone interview or even reviewed your resume in depth, so making sure they know your name, and how to pronounce it, is important.

The Body of the Interview

After introductions are made and rapport established, the core of the interview begins. This is when the most important work of your interview takes place. The body of the interview is the majority of the time you will spend with the prospective employer, and it functions largely as a question and answer session. In this part of the chapter, we will detail some of the types of questions you may encounter when being interviewed.

Closed-Ended Questions. During the initial stages of the interview process, you may be asked to answer some questions that do not require explanation. These types of questions often also have defined answers from which you will choose the best fit. These **closed-ended questions** are typically used to collect anonymous data about the characteristics of the pool of applicants.

Closed-ended questions questions that have defined answers from which you will choose the best fit

Open-Ended Questions. The most common form of question in an interview is one that requires you to explain and describe your answer in detail. **Open-ended questions** do not provide possible answers, but rather ask you to craft your best answer to the inquiry. The remaining types of questions we will cover all fall under the category of open-ended questions.

Open-ended questions questions that ask you to craft your best answer to the inquiry

The "Tell Me About Yourself" Question. This is often the first question asked during an in-person interview and represents the transition from the opening to the body of the interview. The question is far more complicated than it might seem because many interviewees make the mistake of providing information about their family or re-hashing their resume. In fact, employers simply want to know about your interest areas and work experiences, and how they relate to the job. Additionally, they want you to use this answer to demonstrate how familiar you are with the company and its mission. The unsaid part of this question is "…and how you fit this position with this company."

Resume Questions. During the interview, the employer will explore your resume and will likely ask you to expand on one or two experiences you listed. Be prepared to discuss your responsibilities and accomplishments with a degree of detail that adds to the resume and doesn't simply reiterate what is on the page. If there are gaps in your resume or if you are entering a brand new field, be prepared to explain those aspects of your history.

Situational Questions. Employers will ask questions designed to get you to explain how you would behave in certain situations to determine your fit for the position. Situational questions focus on what you would do if confronted with a specific set of circumstances, and the interviewer gives you the opportunity to lay out a clear approach to handling it that demonstrates your skill sets. The key is to provide as clear and detailed a response as you can to this type of question. Here are a few examples of potential situational questions:

> "How would you handle a dispute with a colleague?"
> "How would you repair a relationship with a disgruntled client?"

Behavioral Questions. Whereas situational questions focus on the future, behavioral questions ask you to delve into your past experiences. There are a few principles behind this form of questioning, which is becoming more and more prevalent in the interview process. First, the idea is that to effectively answer the question, the respondent must have actually had the experience they describe because making up an answer to a behavioral question on the spot would be easy to detect. Secondly, and perhaps even more importantly to the employer, the idea is that if you behaved this way in the past, it is likely you would repeat the same behavior in similar circumstances in the future. Like situational questions, behavioral questions require details in the answer tantamount to telling a story. Additionally, oftentimes these questions ask you to talk about times when you encountered difficulty or failed at doing something. Employers want answers that focus on honesty and the ability to learn a lesson from an experience, so if you failed then say so, but follow it up with a description of what you took away from the experience so that your answer is ultimately a positive one. Here are a few examples of behavioral questions, and as you can see, they focus on the past, not the future:

> "Tell me about a time you disagreed with your boss."
> "Tell me about a time when you failed to complete a project on time."

DIALING DIVERSITY

The interview process must be an even playing field for all potential applicants. To that end there are certain questions employers cannot ask applicants at any stage of the hiring process. They cannot even find creative ways to try to obtain the information, either. There are laws interviewers must follow in an attempt to ensure the integrity of the selection process and to prevent discrimination. Unfortunately, not all interviewers adhere to these regulations and so it is important to know what can and cannot be asked in an interview. For instance, you cannot be asked about your religion, race, sexual preference, age, familial status, or citizenship status. Some examples of illegal interview questions are:

"How do you plan to handle child care while working?"

"Will you require days off for religious reasons?"

"Are you an American citizen?"

"Do you have any problems working for a female boss?"

For a complete understanding of the rules regulating the questions in an interview, see the website of the United States Equal Employment Opportunity Commission (EEOC).[2]

Follow-up Questions. During the course of the interview, you may provide an answer that interests the employer, and so interviewers may continue to ask you about that answer in the hopes of obtaining more detail. These follow-up questions are extremely common, especially during your answers to a behavioral question. Employers know if you get interrupted and are then asked for more detail, you will not be able to provide it if you are not telling the truth, but if you are telling the truth, these details would be easily recounted. Follow-up questions are often a sign of interest by the employer, but they are also an opportunity to correct or expound upon things you have said.

The Closing

Once the employer finishes her or his questions, the closing of the interview begins. There are a few things to keep in mind during this stage of the process because you want to make sure you leave the employer with a positive impression. This may very well be your last chance to make a strong impression in person, so be sure to make every effort to be prepared to close well.

Have questions of your own prepared. At this point, the interviewers will ask you if you have any questions, and there are a few things to remember when this opportunity arises. First, always have a few questions ready, even if you think you know the answer, because this shows interest in the company. Not asking questions makes it seem like you are not very interested in working for the company and are only looking to secure a paycheck. Second, do not tell them "you have already answered my questions," because this comes across as not having prepared any questions and thus demonstrating a lack of interest. This is also not the time to ask about salary. If the company brings up the issue of salary, then that is fine, but do not ask them first about compensation. Finally, don't ask questions that could easily be answered by looking at the company website, as this will show that you did not prepare well for the interview. It is a good idea, however, to mention something you saw on the website and ask for greater detail or clarification. Here are some good general questions that can help you in the event you don't have any specific queries about the company:

> "How would you describe the culture here?"
> "Why did you join this company?"
> "What are some of the greatest challenges and opportunities working here?"
> "What is your timeline for making a decision?"

Re-establish rapport. Just as you need to establish rapport in the opening, you need to re-establish rapport in the closing to remind them of the fact you had a good experience with them and they with you. Say one or two complimentary statements about the interviewers and the company, and refer to something that occurred during the interview. You also could consider reiterating your interest in the position and company, and tying it to things you heard in the interview itself.

Shake hands with everyone. Shaking hands is not just reserved for the opening. It is just as important to conclude the interview by shaking everyone's hands and thanking them for spending their time with you during a busy time. Additionally, express to them that you enjoyed the conversation and look forward to hearing from them soon. Much like the opening handshake, make sure you say their names and maintain eye contact when shaking hands.

"Choose your self-presentations carefully, for what starts out as your mask may become your face."

> —*Erving Goffman,* The Presentation of Self in Everyday Life

---

Following Up after the Interview

The interview process does not end when you leave the in-person interview. An important part of the process is to follow up after the interview. There are several ways you can do this, but the most effective is a "thank you" note. The thank you note is a brief statement you can send through e-mail or postal mail that restates your gratitude for the time spent at the in-person interview, reinforces your interest in the position, recounts something you learned from the interview that makes the position attractive, and provides your contact information one more time. Thank you notes are an effective means of following up on an interview, but they should not be ornate or elaborate.

In some circumstances, it may be possible, and even worthwhile, to follow up with a phone call. When doing so, know exactly who you are calling and why. Additionally, if the person does not answer, simply leave a message about why you called and your contact information. The important thing to understand about follow-up phone calls is that you should only do them once; do not keep calling until someone answers. This can be rude and even come across as desperate—not an impression you want to leave with the prospective employer.

Using Dialogue Effectively in an Interview

An employment interview is nothing more than a dialogue between two parties regarding a job position. Both sides seek to understand each other's expectations and needs, and they do so through the civil exchange of questions and answers. Although it is a positive outcome when each side agrees they are a good fit at the end of the interview, it is equally as positive when they understand why they were not a good fit. That said, interviews can be stressful for job candidates, and so engaging in dialogue can become difficult. In this final section of the chapter, we will provide seven tips for engaging in an effective dialogue during an interview.

Do Your Homework

Much of dialogue depends upon showing respect for the other party and demonstrating genuine interest in his or her position. One way to make this happen during an interview is to research the company and the position before arriving at the interview. This will allow you to adapt your answers to your audience, as well as determine the areas about which you want further information. Coming in prepared with knowledge about the company and job shows an interest in the company and demonstrates a respect for them that goes a long way toward creating a relaxed and supportive communication climate during your interview.

Be Your Professional Self

During the interview do not try to pretend to be someone you are not. This attempt will be noticed, and you will either not get the position or, if you do, you will likely not be happy at the company because you pretended to have different qualities, interests, and values just to get the position. Instead, be yourself and don't try to tell the interviewer what you think she or he wants to hear. Interviewers want to hear honesty, so be honest. Just because you are yourself, however, does not mean you are among friends or can relax your professional attitude, demeanor, or language. Remain respectful and courteous throughout the interview, but do not be insincere or try to anticipate answers you think the company expects.

Use Names When Speaking to Others

Many people hear a name at the introduction stage of the interview and promptly forget it or disregard it. Don't make this mistake. When answering questions from someone, make sure you say his or her name every once in a while. It is not necessary to do so during every answer, but referencing someone's name is a sign of respect and also lets her or him know you truly listened at the introduction.

Understand the Question Being Asked

Sometimes, especially when there is more than one person conducting the interview, the questions can get confusing. There is nothing wrong with rephrasing the question back to the interviewer to make sure you know what she or he is asking. You can also ask interviewers to repeat the question if you feel you missed something. It is impossible to do well in an interview if you do not answer the question being asked, so it is essential that you ask for clarification if you are unclear about something.

Ensure Answers Connect to Question and Claims

Once you understand the question, be prepared to deliver an answer that you can substantiate with data or stories from your own experiences. People appreciate direct claim-data-warrant answers that provide a supported claim that you then connect to the qualities necessary for the job or why you feel that particular story reflects values consistent with your worldview and work ethic. In short, don't just tell a story, but have a point to it that employers would want to hear.

Take Notes

You will not be able to remember everything people say during the interview, so it is important to jot down a few notes you believe are important. It is also a good idea to write down

MEDIATED MOMENTS

In the seventh season finale of the American hit sitcom *The Office*, the CEO of Dunder Mifflin-Sabre Paper forms a search committee to identify a replacement for the branch manager position vacated by Steve Carell's character, Michael Scott. The episode features a parade of guest stars taking turns at making major interviewing mistakes. For example, Darryl (Craig Robinson) believes he is a sure choice for the position and is surprised when told he needs a resume and has to interview.

He quickly prepares an elaborate but unsuccessful four-page resume. Nellie Bertram (Catherine Tate) also proposes eliminating office titles and creating a Zen garden for the Scranton location of Dunder Mifflin-Sabre, much to the confusion of the search committee. Robert California (James Spader), derides the company and the position to office staff before entering his interview. There are more examples, and each highlights a major interview mistake.

the names of those who interview you in case they forget to give you business cards. As the interview progresses, the employer may reveal some things that spark questions, and by taking notes you can ensure you ask those questions when your opportunity to do so arrives. Taking notes also helps prevent you from cutting people off and illustrates to employers you are paying attention to what is going on.

Don't Interrupt Anyone

When we converse with friends and family, we sometimes like to finish sentences for other people or even cut them off to make a point or ask a question. This tendency only magnifies during an interview when we get excited about things we are being told. However, interrupting interviewers and finishing sentences for them is not a good idea and can ultimately create a negative impression of you. Let the interview follow its format and wait to ask questions until the interviewers are done speaking.

Summary

An interview is one of the most common, challenging, and rewarding communication contexts. In this chapter, we differentiated between different types of interviews and the various formats in which they occur. We also explored the interview process, paying particular attention to the types of questions you are likely to encounter when on an employment interview. Finally, we discussed how specific dialogic behaviors can help you create an atmosphere more conducive to success when interviewing.

Chapter 8 Key Ideas

- There are six different types of interviews: (1) information gathering interviews, (2) helping interviews, (3) problem-solving interviews, (4) performance interviews, (5) exit interviews, and (6) employment interviews.
- Interviews might take place via e-mail, phone, Skype, in a group "island" format, or in person.
- Interviews have an opening, a body, and a closing.

Chapter 8 Key Terms

Interviews	Performance interviews	Closed-ended questions
Information-gathering interviews	Exit interviews	Open-ended questions
Helping interviews	Employment interviews	
Problem-solving interviews	Island interviews	

References

1 Adams, S. (2014). The college degrees and skills employers most want. *Forbes.com*. Retrieved from http://www.forbes.com/sites/susanadams/2014/04/16/the-college-degrees-and-skills-employers-most-want/

2 Discrimination by type. U.S. Equal Employment Opportunity Commission. Retrieved from http://www.eeoc.gov/laws/types/index.cfm

EXPLORING CULTURE & PERCEPTION

Overview:

The purpose of this assignment is for you to gain experience preparing for and conducting an interview as well as to help you think more carefully about the ways that culture and prior experiences impact our perception. For this assignment, you will develop an interview questionnaire that is intended to gain a better understanding of the ways that one of your classmate's perceptions and everyday experiences differ from your own as a result of your respective cultures, co-cultures, diverse characteristics, and prior history. These might be large or small differences that impact your day to day experiences or expectations for the future. For example, perhaps one of you expects to be able to choose your life partner by yourself, while the other expects to have family members select your life partner for you. Perhaps one of you only feels safe at social gatherings if you have a friend with you and can keep your beverages covered, while the other may have never been concerned about safety in social situations. Perhaps the two of you have different religious traditions, family birthday and holiday traditions, political ideologies, ways of thinking about and organizing your work, challenges in navigating physical spaces, expectations for encounters with people you meet for the first time, expectations for how you speak with family members, and work and family responsibilities. Perhaps each of you perceives yourself to have a different set of skills and abilities that will contribute to your success in different future careers. All of these differences contribute to the diversity of human experience and impact the way that we perceive and experience the world around us.

Your interview questionnaire should be developed to help you conduct an information-gathering interview with one of your classmates. Your goal is to use open-ended questions to help you understand the other person's experience and the factors that shape their perception as much as possible. You will be given 25-35 minutes in class during the Exploring Culture and Perception Interview Workshop to conduct your interview with your partner, and your partner will be given the same amount of time to interview you. Your interview questionnaire should include a clear introduction, body, and closing. You should include 9-12 open-ended questions that have been carefully constructed to help you learn as much as possible about your partner.

When conducting the interview, you might decide to ask follow up questions or modify questions based on what the interviewee has already told you. You are encouraged to take notes and, if your partner grants permission to do so, may record the interview so that you have an audio or video copy of the interview that you can refer to after class as you write your paper. However, you should respect your partner's privacy by not sharing the interview recording with anyone else and by deleting it after you have completed the assignment.

After you have completed your interview, you will write a reflection essay in which you identify at least four ways that you and your partner's everyday experiences differ as a result of your cultures, co-cultures, diverse personal characteristics, or prior history. Your essay should begin with an introductory paragraph that summarizes the goal of the paper and previews the differences that you will discuss in your paper. Next, you should have a long paragraph for **each** of the differences that you identify that does the following:

- Identify and define the difference in perception or experience.
- Describe how the difference that you identified is related to one of the concepts that you have learned in this class. Bold face any key words or concepts to highlight where you are using concepts and terms used in this class.
- Explain how you and your partner's cultures, co-cultures, or other prior history have led to or contributed to this difference in perception and/or experience.
- Evaluate how this difference might lead to different types of future experiences or perceptions of future events.

At the end of your essay, write a concluding paragraph that reviews your findings and sums up what you have learned from this interview experience.

Your essay should be 2 ½-3 pages in length, single-spaced, and written in 12 point Times New Roman font with one inch margins. (You will probably need to adjust your computer's default settings.) Upload your essay via Blackboard.

Exploring Culture & Perception Interview Questionnaire Rubric

This assignment will be uploaded to Blackboard and graded online using the rubric shown below:

	Missing 0	C 17.5-19.5	B 20-22	A 22.5-25	
Interview Structure: (C) Interview questions appear to be placed in an intentional order, and (B) reflect a clear opening, body, and conclusion, and (A) show careful attention to the flow of the interview and the expected elements of the opening, body, and conclusion.					
Questions: (C) Questionnaire includes 9-12 open-ended questions (B) that are not leading or loaded with an expected "acceptable" answer and (A) that together facilitate an opportunity for an in-depth interview that will help to increase understanding of the interviewee's perceptions and experiences.					
Proofreading: (C) Interview questionnaire is written in complete sentences and contains several significant grammar, syntax, or spelling errors. (B) Questionnaire is written in complete sentences and clearly organized paragraphs. Contains only a few minor grammar, syntax, or spelling errors. (A) Questionnaire is free from grammar, syntax, and spelling errors.					___/25

Exploring Culture & Perception Paper Rubric

This assignment will be uploaded to Blackboard and graded online using the rubric shown below:

	Missing 0	C 35-39	B 40-44	A 45-50	
Introduction: (C) Paper includes an introduction that give some indication of what the paper will be about, and (B) summarizes the goal of the paper, and (A) clearly previews each difference that will be highlighted in the paper					
Difference 1: (C) Paper clearly identifies and describes a difference between the interviewer and interviewee, and (B) connects that experience to key terms and concepts discussed in this course and discusses how those elements of culture, diversity, or prior experience contributed to these differences, and (A) evaluates how these differences might impact future experiences or perceptions					
Difference 2: (C) Paper clearly identifies and describes a difference between the interviewer and interviewee, and (B) connects that experience to key terms and concepts discussed in this course and discusses how those elements of culture, diversity, or prior experience contributed to these differences, and (A) evaluates how these differences might impact future experiences or perceptions					
Difference 3: (C) Paper clearly identifies and describes a difference between the interviewer and interviewee, and (B) connects that experience to key terms and concepts discussed in this course and discusses how those elements of culture, diversity, or prior experience contributed to these differences, and (A) evaluates how these differences might impact future experiences or perceptions					
Difference 4: (C) Paper clearly identifies and describes a difference between the interviewer and interviewee, and (B) connects that experience to key terms and concepts discussed in this course and discusses how those elements of culture, diversity, or prior experience contributed to these differences, and (A) evaluates how these differences might impact future experiences or perceptions					
Conclusion: (C) a conclusion paragraph is included that (B) clearly reviews the differences discussed in the paper and (A) sums up what the writer learned from this experience					
Proofreading: (C) Paper is written in complete sentences and contains several significant grammar, syntax, or spelling errors. (B) Paper is written in complete sentences and clearly organized paragraphs. Paper contains only a few minor grammar, syntax, or spelling errors. (A) Paper is free from grammar, syntax, and spelling errors. Paper reflects careful attention to word choice and language structures.					
Formatting: (C) Paper is missing two of more of the required formatting elements. (B) Paper is missing one of the formatting elements. (A) Paper is 2 ½-3 pages in length, single-spaced, and written in 12 point Times New Roman font with one inch margins					___/50

Chapter 9

Relationship Development

Thus far, we have focused on the different dimensions of the communication process, a process that takes place in a variety of different contexts. Over the next few chapters, we will turn our attention to one of those contexts: interpersonal relationships. **Interpersonal relationships** are close associations or acquaintances between two or more people. These relationships might be based on love, community or business interactions, friendship, family, or some other social commitment. In this chapter, we will first discuss what interpersonal relationships are and why they are an important part of our lives. Next, we will explain four theories about how relationships develop. Finally, we will suggest some guidelines for using dialogue to build and maintain strong interpersonal relationships.

Characteristics of Interpersonal Relationships

Interpersonal relationships include relationships with friends, family, coworkers, neighbors, and others with whom we interact and feel a personal connection. Interpersonal relationships can include **social relationships**, which are informal, voluntary relationships such as acquaintances, coworkers, and casual friendships. We also have **intimate relationships**, which include relationships with romantic partners, family, and our closest friends. Interpersonal relationships are the foundation of communities and help fulfill some of our deepest needs. In addition, because of their voluntary and sometimes fleeting nature, we

Interpersonal relationships close associations or acquaintances between two or more people. These relationships might be based on love, community or business interactions, friendship, family, or some other social commitment

Social relationships informal, voluntary relationships such as acquaintances, coworkers, and casual friendships

Intimate relationships deeply personal bonds that we have with other individuals that are accompanied by affective communication and a sense of belongingness are more likely to treat social relationships like commodities that have costs and benefits. In this section of the chapter, we will highlight six characteristics of interpersonal relationships and illustrate how they serve fundamental and important purposes in our lives.

Create and Maintain Identity

Identity
how we understand our own qualities, beliefs, values, and characteristics as unique as well as different from others

As we discussed earlier in the book, communication through language allows us to label ideas, concepts, objects, and just about anything else, thus giving it meaning. Language functions similarly when we decide to describe ourselves in a particular way and therefore give ourselves particular meaning. That meaning becomes a part of one's **identity**, or how we understand our own qualities, beliefs, values, and characteristics as unique or different from others. Our identities come from both how we see ourselves and how others see us, and both come from the communication within the social relationships we form with others. Put simply, we define ourselves through our associations with others.

Fulfill the Need to Belong

Psychologist Abraham Maslow proposed a hierarchy of human needs, and just above the base needs of shelter, safety, and food was what he identified as the need to belong.[1] We all have a deep need to be accepted by others, and this is accomplished by connecting with people through communication. We seek people who accept us for who we are, and we do the same for them. These social relationships become a source of self-esteem and stability in our lives. The need to be accepted and belong to a larger group is a core part of the human psyche, and communication allows us to create those bonds with other people in our daily lives. Sometimes we seek to belong to groups with similar interests, and sometimes we look for people who share certain experiences. The former of these is part of identifying with whom we wish to become friends, while the latter can have health benefits as seen through organizations like Alcoholics Anonymous.

Allow for the Creation of Communities

Community
refers to both a specific place where people share certain characteristics, or a feeling of fellowship with others who share attitudes, interests, and beliefs

It is no surprise that community and communication share the same Latin root word, *communis,*[2] because without the connections provided by communication we would not be able to create and live in communities. **Community** can refer to both a specific place where people share certain characteristics and communicate with one another, as well as a feeling of fellowship with others who share language, attitudes, interests, and beliefs. The formation of communities occurs when groups of people fulfill their needs to belong by finding in each other common characteristics and talking about them. Before the advent of media, communities were based mostly on the locations where people lived in close proximity to each other. Now we refer to communities in a variety of ways, some using demographic categories (e.g., The African-American community, the LGBTQ community), while others use interests to bind groups, such as when people play video games together. One such online game that links people across continents and time zones is Grepolis, where individuals create alliances within the community to conquer other islands.[3] Although players do not share a location, they share an interest that creates their sense of community.

Communities are also bound by rules that govern the interactions of their members. These rules often refer to communication behaviors that are either expected or required by members. When people violate these rules, they are reprimanded by the community, and if the offense is great enough, the person may be expelled from the group. The process of being expelled from a community is called **excommunication,** because the person is no longer allowed to live among or even speak to those in the group to which they once belonged. This shunning is, in some cases, meant to teach the person a lesson before allowing him or her re-entry into the group, but the exile can be permanent in other instances.

Involve Rewards and Costs

Interpersonal relationships reward us with more than helping us create identities for ourselves or establish a community; they also bring physical and material benefits as well. Friends help us move, listen when we need to vent regarding some emotionally distressing situation, and even might loan us money when we need it on occasion. Friends also provide us with a sense of belonging and connection that, as you may recall from Maslow's hierarchy of needs, is one of the key things all people require for a well-balanced life.

Interpersonal relationships also involve certain costs, and these costs are the mirror image of the rewards we receive. After all, we invest time, emotional energy, and even money into people that we care about deeply, while we probably do not do that with others. Every time you are there when a friend needs you for emotional support, to lend a few dollars, or even to give her or him a ride home, it is a cost of the friendship. As we will learn shortly, there is only so much we are willing to invest in friendships, as these costs can add up to a point where you will no longer work to sustain the relationship.

Now that we have discussed the characteristics of interpersonal relationships, we will investigate four theories about how relationships are formed: Attraction Theory, Uncertainty Reduction Theory, Social Penetration Theory, and the Stage Model of Relationship Development.

Attraction Theory

The process of choosing and selecting our friends and romantic partners is rooted in perception. We observe a characteristic about a person, organize it into a category with which we are familiar, and ultimately interpret it in either a good or bad light. When it comes to determining whether we wish to initiate a relationship, we refer to **interpersonal attraction,** or observing a force that draws us to someone else. There are three types of interpersonal attraction: social attraction, physical attraction, and task attraction.[4] When we have **social attraction** with someone, we see the person as someone with whom we would like to be friends or get to know. When we are **physically attracted** to someone, we are drawn

Excommunication
An exile from a community one belonged to whereby one is shunned into reconciliation, or completely exiled; it requires no communication between the individual and the community

Interpersonal attraction
a force that draws us to someone else

Social attraction
we see the other person as someone with whom we would like to engage in social interaction and be friends

Physical attraction
we are drawn to someone's physical appearance because we like the way the person looks

Task attraction
we like to work
with them and can
count on them to
get a job done

to someone's physical appearance because we like the way the person looks. When we have **task attraction** with someone, we like to work with the person and can count on her or him to get a job done.

Considering these three types of attraction, it should be no surprise that attraction is not restricted to physical attraction for romantic purposes, or that there are different characteristics that attract us to different individuals for a variety of reasons. Sometimes physical qualities intrigue and attract us, while other times we are interested in someone's knowledge, expertise, personality, or dependability. Regardless of the reason we are drawn to someone to form a relationship, there are certain things that serve to enhance someone's attractiveness to us.

Appearance

The first thing we notice about most people we meet is their appearance, and so attraction often begins when someone looks physically appealing to us. What is physically appealing to one person, however, may not be to another, and the standards of beauty have changed over time and differ by culture. For instance, if you look closely at some famous portraits from the Middle Ages, you will see men and women who would not be what society considers attractive today—but in their time they were the height of beauty. Appearance is a fundamental force in interpersonal attraction, but we differ in how we judge it.

Proximity

Typically, people seek out friends and romantic relationships with those people who are around them. Now, however, thanks to the Internet, cell phones, and the increased availability and affordability of travel, the definition of proximity has changed and its importance in terms of attraction has lessened. That reduction in influence comes with risk. Some people have friends they have never met in person with whom they have had extensive relationships online. Sometimes the people they believe they are talking to are not who they claim to be. Regardless, proximity still retains influence over attraction within small communities and neighborhoods where people gather together, because they share a common area of residence.

Similarity

This may not be very surprising, but research shows that we are more likely to establish relationships with people with whom we share interests, values, beliefs, and other characteristics. People who share our experiences and worldviews reinforce our own identities and thus are a more welcome presences in our lives. On a practical level, they also make it easier to find things to do together and to talk about. For example, if you are signed up for a dance class, you might strike up conversations with people there because you know they share that interest with you. We are thus more likely to be attracted to those who are like us. Keep in mind, however, that similarity does not mean that all people interested in the same things as you are will become friends—there are always areas of difference we have with one another.

Complementary Difference

The world would be a boring place indeed if we all were the same and only sought out relationships with those who were like us. This is not to say we seek out people who are completely opposite to ourselves, but rather that we do form relationships with people who are different in ways that we see as adding something to ourselves or our communities. The differences in these relationships are understood as positive elements, not negative ones that create friction. Forming friendships based on complementary differences is challenging, because it necessarily involves being open to changing our views on the world based on the other person's different perspective—and this is very hard to do if we are convinced our way of seeing things is the one true way.

Uncertainty Reduction Theory

Deciding to strike up a conversation with someone in the hopes of gaining a new friend can be a somewhat scary proposition, because you do not know how the other person will react or what he or she might feel. Sharing deep information about yourself with someone is even more of a daunting task because it involves taking a leap of faith and investing trust in the other person. Communication professors Charles Berger and Richard Calabrese understood this reluctance and trepidation we all feel about interacting with other people because of our inability to always accurately predict the outcome of the meeting. Berger and Calabrese developed the **Uncertainty Reduction Theory,** which focuses on "the assumption that when strangers meet, their primary concern is one of uncertainty reduction or increasing predictability about the behavior of both themselves and others in the interaction."[5]

Types and Stages of Uncertainty

There are two kinds of uncertainty that we face when we meet someone for the first time. **Cognitive uncertainty** occurs when we do not know what the beliefs and attitudes of the other person are, and **behavioral uncertainty** occurs when we do not know how the other person will behave in a particular situation. Most people are uncomfortable with uncertainty, so we interact with others to reduce the uncertainty we feel about the possible reactions of others, and the more we communicate with the other person, the less uncertain—or more confident in our ability to predict the response of the other person—we become.

When we meet another person for the first time, we usually go through three stages as we work to reduce uncertainty. The first stage is the **entry stage,** during which we follow culturally accepted rules for interactions and politeness, including greeting one another, making small talk, and laughing at jokes. The second stage is the **personal stage.** In the personal stage, we begin to explore the other person's attitudes and beliefs while also disclosing some of that same information about ourselves. The third and final

Uncertainty Reduction Theory
the idea that increased knowledge of another person improves our ability to predict future behaviors and thus reduces our own uncertainty

Cognitive uncertainty
occurs when we do not know what the beliefs and attitudes of the other person are

Behavioral uncertainty
occurs when we do not know how the other person will behave in a particular situation

Entry stage
first stage of Uncertainty Reduction Theory during which we follow culturally accepted rules for interactions and politeness, including greeting one another, making small talk, and laughing at jokes

Personal stage
second stage of Uncertainty Reduction Theory during which we begin to explore the other person's attitudes and beliefs, while also disclosing some of that same information about ourselves

Exit stage
final stage of Uncertainty Reduction Theory during which both individuals decide whether to continue the relationship or not to pursue the relationship

stage is the **exit stage,** when both individuals decide whether or not to continue the relationship.

We do not always have the desire to reduce uncertainty about another person, and there are three variables that can influence whether we wish to do so.[6] The first of these is whether we anticipate future interactions with the other person. If we believe we will see the person again, we will want to reduce our uncertainty as much as possible so we can better gauge the possible behaviors and reactions he or she might exhibit. If, on the other hand, we do not think we will see the person again, we are not as concerned with reducing uncertainty about him or her. The second variable is whether or not the person has something we want or need. If the other person does, we want to be able to better predict future behaviors so we can maximize our chances of receiving what we want from her or him; however, if the person does have anything important to offer us, we don't feel the urge to reduce uncertainty, because predicting her or his future behaviors will not gain us anything. Finally, we like to reduce uncertainty when the other person acts in some odd way that seems abnormal or inconsistent with our expectations. These weird behaviors can throw us off, and thus call for us to reduce uncertainty so that we can adjust and know what to expect in the future.

Strategies to Reduce Uncertainty

Passive strategy
unobtrusively observing the other person

There are three different strategies we can use when trying to reduce uncertainty when meeting someone for the first time.[7] The first way to reduce uncertainty is by using a **passive strategy**, which involves unobtrusively observing the other person. For example, you might watch as the other person interacts with others, listen in on conversations that are easy to overhear, or observe her or him completing other tasks. The second way to reduce uncertainty is by using **active strategies**, which involve engaging in activities to learn more about the other person while avoiding direct contact with him or her. For example, you might ask a mutual friend about the person or search for the person using Google or Facebook. The final way to reduce uncertainty about another person is by using **interactive strategies**, which involve engaging in direct contact or face-to-face conversation with him or her. For example, you might ask the other person questions or start a conversation.

Active strategy
engaging in activities to learn more about the other person while avoiding direct contact with him or her

Interactive strategy
engaging in direct contact or face-to-face conversation with the other person

All in all, Berger and Calabrese's Uncertainty Reduction Theory helps us understand relationships by explaining that we are motivated to reduce that uncertainty by engaging in and reciprocating information sharing because we are uncomfortable with uncertainty about others when we first meet them. As we reduce our uncertainty, we are also likely to increase the intimacy level of our disclosures and like the other person more. We like to be around those whom we can generally accurately predict their responses and behaviors. We typically don't like feeling uncertain about friends, loved ones, or acquaintances.

Social Penetration Theory

Developing and maintaining strong relationships does not solely depend on attraction or reducing uncertainty in those initial interactions with others; it also involves getting to know more about the other person after the initial attraction draws you together. In an effort to understand this development, social psychologists Irwin Altman and Dalmas Taylor devised a theory to explain how we form these close connections with others. Their theory, **Social Penetration Theory,** proposes that the process of creating and maintaining deeper intimacy with another person takes place through gradual and mutual self-disclosure.[8] **Self-disclosure** occurs when one person voluntarily shares personal history and information regarding attitudes, feelings, values, and experiences with another individual. Altman and Taylor explained that the self-disclosures we make to others have two qualities, and both are important in developing friendships.

Qualities of Self-Disclosure

The first of these qualities is the depth of the penetration, or how much we share on a specific topic or subject with another person. The other is breadth of self-disclosure, which refers to how many topics we share with other people. We can develop friends with whom we share a lot of information about only one or two subjects because that is where our interests collide, and we can have friendships where we share deeply about a broad number of subjects. There are also relationships where we share only superficial information about a lot of subjects, because we are either guarded or not quite sure about the strength of the bond between ourselves and the other person.

Social Penetration Theory
the process of creating and maintaining deeper intimacy with another person takes place through gradual and mutual self-disclosure

Self-disclosure
when one person voluntarily shares personal history and information regarding attitudes, feelings, values, and experiences with another individual

MEDIATED MOMENTS

The longest running television show of all time is the British program *Doctor Who.* The show originally aired from 1963-1989, before taking a 16-year hiatus and returning in 2005 for a run that is still ongoing. The show focuses on a humanoid alien known as "The Doctor," who travels through time and space combating evil. One of the Doctor's abilities is to regenerate into a new body when he is close to death, and this has allowed thirteen actors to play the role throughout the show's history. Each "new" Doctor has all the memories of the previous one but a very different personality. The Doctor also takes on a human travelling companion who becomes one of his closest

confidants. Each time the Doctor enlists a new companion, that person works to get to know the Doctor, initially focusing simply on his quirks and ability to travel through time and eventually understanding the depths of the man himself— someone who is conflicted about his role in history and whether or not he is a good man. The process by which these companions get to know the Doctor is a perfect illustration of social penetration theory, as they begin by knowing only surface level characteristics of the Doctor before he shares deeper core elements of himself with them, thus creating a strong bond of fellowship between them.

Stages of Mutual Self-Disclosure

It is important to know that when we develop relationships, the deep sharing of information on a subject takes place over time and is thus a gradual process. To best understand Social Penetration Theory, think about peeling away the layers of an onion. When we first meet someone, we only know the person's superficial layers, but as we peel away more and more we eventually know her or him in a much deeper and more meaningful way. This process of getting to know someone through mutual self-disclosure involves five potential stages: orientation, exploratory affective exchange, affective exchange, stable exchange, and depenetration.

Orientation Stage. In this stage, individuals engage in small talk and follow social norms for appropriateness and social desirability. You might use simple clichés, but you are mostly engaging in surface-level conversation and are not revealing much information about yourselves. Think about this as the casual, polite conversation that you might have when you meet someone on the first day of class, while walking your dog, or waiting in the checkout line at the grocery store.

Exploratory Affective Exchange Stage. In this stage, individuals begin to reveal themselves by sharing personal attitudes and opinions about some moderately personal topics like government, education, and current events. You are not yet talking about private or personal matters or sharing vulnerable information with others, but individuals in this stage are casual friends or acquaintances and are still feeling out the relationship.

Affective Exchange Stage. In this stage, individuals begin talking about private and personal matters, and they might begin using personal idioms that are unique to that relationship or even begin engaging in criticisms and arguments from time to time. At this stage, you are becoming close friends, and in romantic relationships, this stage might involve more intimate touching or kissing.

Stable Exchange Stage. In this stage, individuals have a deep level of trust and are sharing their deepest personal thoughts, beliefs, and values with one another. Both partners can predict the emotional reactions of the other person, and they are closely connected to the other person in an intimate (though not necessarily romantic) relationship.

Depenetration. In this stage, individuals begin to withdraw from the relationship and stop disclosing information to one another. Often, individuals feel that the costs of the relationship exceed the benefits, and the relationship is terminated.

It is important to note that relationships do not have to go through all of these stages. Most of our everyday interactions and acquaintances never go beyond the Orientation or Exploratory Affective stages. Some of our most intimate friendships, family relationships, and romantic relationships are enduring relationships that might remain at a stable stage through decades of our lives, while others go through depenetration and lead to the end of the relationship.

Stage Model of Relational Development

So far, we have learned about three theories that help us understand the beginning of a relationship, and one theory that explains how relationships grow closer over time and perhaps eventually end the relationship. However, none of the theories we have discussed so far tells us much about how a relationship deescalates over time. Communication scholar Mark Knapp more thoroughly addresses how relationships develop as well as how relationships devolve in his Stage Model of Relational Development (Figure 9.1), which identifies five stages through which individuals come together in a relationship and five stages through which individuals come apart.

FIGURE 9.1 **Stage Model of Relational Development**

"Coming Together"

Stage #1: Initiating. There needs to always be a beginning to any relationship, and so the **initiating stage** occurs when you take the first step to interact with and try to make an impression on someone you are interested in. This includes both verbal initiation, like a greeting or casual conversation, or nonverbal initiation, such as making eye contact and smiling. Thanks to the advent of the Internet and the proliferation of dating sites such as eHarmony, Match.com, and Itsjustlunch.com, the initiating stage is no longer restricted to in-person communication. People can initiate relationships digitally by examining a person's profile and determining if they want to strike up a conversation.

Stage #2: Experimenting. Contrary to what the name may make you envision, this stage does not involve a lab. The **experimenting stage** is where you engage in conversation about surface-level interests and topics with the other person to see if your interest is expanded or not. This helps us determine how much we have in common with the other person, and whether or not we wish to continue relationship development with that person.

Stage #3: Intensifying. In the intensifying stage, you move from surface-level conversation and activity, to deeper, more meaningful interactions. During the **intensifying stage**, you invest

Initiating stage
when you take the first step to interact with someone you are interested in

Experimenting stage
where you engage in conversation about surface level interests and topics with the other person to see if your interest is expanded or not

Intensifying stage
you invest more time in each other, learn more about a person's history, interests, and goals

Integrating stage
partners begin to
develop a sense of
an identity for their
relationship with
each other

more time in each other, begin to share private information, and learn more about a person's history, interests, and goals. During this stage, partners commonly develop nicknames for each other and express their desire for deeper commitment.

Stage #4: Integrating. During the **integrating stage,** the two individuals begin to develop a sense of an identity for their relationship with each other. In the case of a romantic partnership, the individuals think of themselves as a couple and do more things together. There is a high level of investment of time and resources into the relationship and activities the two do together. During this stage of the courtship, friends expect to see the two together, and their connection is largely public knowledge. They socialize with other couples, sign cards together, and perhaps even move in together to more completely integrate the social, financial, and emotional aspects of their lives.

Bonding stage
partners make their
deep commitment
formal and
public through
an engagement,
marriage, or civil
union

Stage #5: Bonding. Relational partners in the **bonding stage** make their deep commitment formal and public through an engagement, marriage, or civil union. These commitment ceremonies are pronouncements of the long-term deep commitment the couple has for each other. For some couples, the bonding stage lasts forever, though for others the relationship will eventually begin to dissolve despite the couple's best intentions when they made a bonding commitment.

"Coming Apart"

Stage #6: Differentiating. As work, family, friends, and other interests begin to exert pressure on the couple, the two people in the bonded relationship might begin to think of each other more as separate individuals than as a partner in a couple. At this point, each person might begin developing her or his own hobbies or begin doing more things separately from the partner—in other words, they are **differentiating** themselves from each other or (re) constructing their identities as more separated than together.

Differentiating stage
occurs when the
partners begin to
separate themselves
from each other

Circumscribing stage
happens when
the partners are
primarily living
different lives and
their conversations
are increasingly
limited in scope
and depth

Stage #7: Circumscribing. When a couple reaches the **circumscribing stage,** the individuals begin to live mostly separate lives. Each person has his or her own friends, activities, possessions, and space, and there are now boundaries for what the couple will and will not talk about together. Some topics are avoided entirely in order to avoid arguments, but the disagreements about those issues persist.

> *Changes in relationships take place for many reasons: partners'*
> *feelings and experiences with one another, health, economics, the*
> *presence or absence of children, relationships with other family*
> *members, work, and professions. In short, change is an intrinsic*
> *and inseparable aspect of close relationships.*[9]
> —*Altman & Ginat, 1996, pp. 14-15*

DIALING DIVERSITY

The Defense of Marriage Act (DOMA) was signed into federal law by President Bill Clinton on September 21, 1996. At the time, DOMA had two important provisions: 1) marriage was defined as a union between one man and one woman, and 2) that states did not have to recognize marriages performed in other states. The first provision was repealed in 2013, which meant at the federal level a marriage could occur between two men, two women, or one man and one woman. This was a significant moment in the history of marriage within the United States, as it created a space for same-sex couples to be formally recognized as couples, for example, on their tax returns. Many states now allow for same-sex marriage, civil unions, or domestic partnerships. These recognitions make it possible for same-sex couples to achieve the bonding stage of relational development just like opposite-sex couples. The piece of paper, and all that comes along with it, is a symbol of the couple's commitment to one another and their relationship.

Stage #8: Stagnation. At this stage, the relationship has become **stagnant**. The couple is still together, but the individuals are living separate lives and rarely talk with one another because they see little point in communicating. The couple might be staying together for their children or out of apathy because a formal separation or divorce might be inconvenient or impossible for other reasons.

Stage #9: Avoidance. By the time a couple reaches the **avoidance stage**, both individuals deliberately avoid contact with the other person. Both people avoid eye contact, do not speak to the other person, are physically detached, and might even try to leave and return at different times so that they won't see each other, even if they are still living in the same home. In some cases, this manifests as married partners sleeping in separate bedrooms to avoid the other person.

Stage #10: Terminating. At this stage, the relationship completely ends. In the case of a married couple, the **terminating stage** might include moving out, filing for divorce, dividing belongings, and making decisions about the custody of pets and children.

Most relationships will not go through all 10 of these stages, but as current divorce rates show, this does happen for some relationships. It is also important to note that relationships can go forward and backward through these stages, so a couple that begins to differentiate can go backward toward being a bonded couple again and are not necessarily doomed to a failing relationship.

Stagnation stage
when couples move into the stagnation stage, they are still a couple, but primarily in name. They are neither moving forward or backward in the relationship but have hit a point when they are not relating on an intimate level

Avoidance stage
the couple actively avoids interacting with each other so they will not have to face each other

Terminating stage
the final phase of relationship deterioration. Couples end their current relationships and move into a post-relationship phase where they may or may not continue to have contact as separated individuals

Dialogic Communication in Developing Relationships

While many of the people we meet will pass through our lives without another encounter, others will become friends, colleagues, neighbors, casual acquaintances, romantic partners, or family members. As the saying goes, first impressions count, and establishing a first impression that demonstrates you care about hearing from the other person will go a long way toward building relationships. Not to mention, approaching new relationships with dialogue allows you to understand and learn about different people, their experiences and their beliefs—even if you won't see them again. Below are a few suggestions for maintaining dialogic communication as relationships begin.

Balance How You Express Your Feelings

You don't want to reveal everything you are thinking and feeling all the time, especially when you are meeting someone for the first time, nor should you keep everything to yourself. Neither approach in the long term will help you if you continue to develop the relationship. In your earliest interactions, observe the rules for politeness in your particular cultural context. As the conversation progresses and you begin to disclose more, communicate honestly about yourself, but also pay attention to what and how much the other person is disclosing so you can reciprocate those disclosures without overwhelming the person with private information that should typically only be shared in a more developed relationship.

Give the Benefit of the Doubt

If the other person you are interacting with says or does something that could be interpreted negatively, consider that you might be making a Fundamental Attribution Error. There might be situational factors impacting the other person's behavior. The person might appear upset or tense because he or she hasn't been sleeping well. He or she might appear distant because of a recent tragedy; he or she might even be sick. The point is, we never know what might be influencing the mood or disposition of another person, and so we owe it to others to give them the benefit of the doubt that some things that may come across as rude or negative were not intended that way. This means we should seek to learn more rather than rushing to judgment.

Exercise Empathy

Be attuned to the emotional state of your partner and try to recognize when he or she needs support and when he or she might need space. Listen to your partner and try to put yourself in his or her emotional shoes. Sometimes all a person needs is someone to listen, so be careful not to interrupt or offer unsolicited advice. Empathy is different from sympathy, and involves listening more than anything. Often, our first reaction is to share a common experience we have had with the person who is having a tough time, but remember he or she needs to express himself or herself more than they need to hear about your experiences.

That is not to say those experiences aren't helpful, but that relaying them at the proper time and place is a must for practicing effective empathy.

Invest Time in Your Relationships

Perhaps the biggest sign that a relationship may be in decline is the reduction in time spent with each other. When you are in a social or intimate relationship with someone, spend time on the relationship through e-mail, phone calls, text messaging, or even letters. Nothing lets others know they are valued and important like spending time with them, or letting them know you spent time thinking about them. But remember: this is not about quantity of time, but rather spending quality time with people. In some of the strongest friendships, people can go long periods of time without speaking, but when friends finally reconnect, it is like there was never a gap. That's because the quality of the time investment is so strong that people know they count and matter to the other party.

Summary

In this chapter, we began by discussing the characteristics of interpersonal relationships—specifically how they develop. We first explored the four characteristics of both intimate and social interpersonal relationships. We then discussed three theories that help to explain why we begin relationships with other people. We then explored Knapp's 10 stages of relational development, before providing some practical ways to encourage dialogue in interpersonal relationships.

Chapter 9 Key Ideas

- Interpersonal relationships help us create and maintain our identity, fulfill the need to belong, allow for the creation of communities, and come with rewards and costs
- There are three types of interpersonal attraction: social attraction, physical attraction, and task attraction. Some of the factors that enhance attractiveness include appearance, proximity, similarity, and complementary difference
- Uncertainty Reduction Theory states we are uncomfortable with uncertainty in interpersonal relationships, so we use passive, active, and interactive strategies to reduce uncertainty. There are three stages that we go through as we reduce uncertainty: (1) the Entry Stage, (2) the Personal Stage, and (3) the Exit Stage
- Social Penetration Theory proposes that we create and maintain deeper intimacy with another person through mutual self-disclosure. The five stages of Social Penetration Theory are (1) Orientation, (2) Exploratory Affective Exchange, (3) Affective Exchange, (4) Stable Exchange, and (5) Depenetration
- Knapp's Stage Model of Relational Development identifies five stages through which individuals come together, and five stages through which individuals come apart

Chapter 9 Key Terms

Interpersonal relationships

Social relationships

Intimate relationships

Identity

Community

Excommunication

Interpersonal attraction

Social attraction

Physical attraction

Task attraction

Uncertainty Reduction
    Theory

Cognitive uncertainty

Behavioral uncertainty

Entry stage

Personal stage

Exit stage

Passive strategy

Active strategy

Interactive strategy

Social penetration

Self-disclosure

Initiating stage

Experimenting stage

Intensifying stage

Integrating stage

Bonding stage

Differentiating stage

Circumscribing stage

Stagnation stage

Avoidance stage

Terminating stage

References

1 Maslow, A.H. (1970). *Motivation and personality* (2nd edition). New York: Harper & Row.

2 Community. Online Etymology Dictionary. Retrieved from http://www.etymonline.com/index.php?term=community

3 Grepolis. *Innogames.com.* Retrieved from www.grepolis.com.

4 McCroskey, J. C., & McCain, T. A. (1974). The measurement of interpersonal attraction. *Speech Monographs, 41,* 261-266.

5 Berger, C. R., Calabrese, R. J. (1975). Some exploration in initial interaction and beyond: Toward a developmental theory of communication. *Human Communication Research, 1,* 100.

6 Sunnafrank, M. (1990). Predicted outcome value and uncertainty reduction theories: A test of competing perspectives. *Human Communication Research, 17,* 76-103.

7 Berger, C. R. (1995). Inscrutable goals, uncertain plans, and the production of communicative action. In C. R. Berger & M. Burgoon (Eds.), *Communication and social processes* (1-28). East Lansing, MI: Michigan State University Press.

8 Altman, I., & Taylor, D. (1973). *Social penetration: The development of interpersonal relationships.* New York: Holt, Rinehart, and Winston.

9 Altman, I., & Ginat, J. (1996). *Polygamous families in contemporary society.* New York, NY: Cambridge.

Chapter 10

Relationship Maintenance

In the last chapter, we talked about how relationships develop, particularly during their early stages. Once we have developed a relationship, we need to find ways to sustain and maintain the interpersonal bonds that are important to us. **Relationship maintenance** refers to the work we do to keep a relationship going in a condition with which both partners are happy. Just as a car will begin to have problems and eventually break down entirely if we do not perform regular maintenance such as adding fuel, changing the oil, and adding air to the tires, our relationships will also deteriorate and eventually die if we do not give them the attention and work that are required to keep them strong.

In this chapter, we explore the complex task of maintaining an interpersonal relationship. First, we will briefly outline the various behaviors that communication scholars identify as being key elements to sustaining strong relationships. We will then discuss several theories of relationship maintenance: Social Exchange Theory, Communication Privacy Management, Everyday Talk, and Relational Dialectics. We will conclude by discussing some guidelines for using dialogic communication in our relationship maintenance practices.

Relationship maintenance the work we do to keep a relationship going and in a condition with which both partners are happy

Relationship Maintenance Behaviors

Communication researchers have come up with a list of relational maintenance behaviors that partners use in their relationship: positivity, assurances, sharing tasks, acceptance, self-disclosure, social networks, and relationship talks.[1] Positivity includes communication that is optimistic and upbeat, such as complimenting one's partner or being cheerful during conversations. Assurances are used when partners communicate their commitment to each other and the relationship, like when a husband tells his wife that he would marry her all over again, or when friends talk about what their relationship will be like in their old age.

When partners share tasks by doing things, such as sharing the chores around the house or helping one another get ready for work in the morning, they communicate that they respect one another. Acceptance occurs when we make our partners feel like we will care for them no matter what, which makes us feel safe and validated in our relationships. You will recall self-disclosure from the last chapter and how it involves revealing things about ourselves such as our feelings, experiences, and goals to our partners. When we self-disclose to another person, we are entrusting the person with a piece of ourselves, which in turn helps to maintain our bond with him or her.

Relationship talks happen when we discuss our relationship with our partners, a process that is **meta-communicative**, or, simply, communication about communication. Taking time to talk frankly about the relationship, how we feel about it, and where we want it to go, shows the other person we care about the relationship and we want to maintain it. Finally, we can do a lot to maintain our relationships through our social networks. We do this by spending time with and getting to know one another's "circles" and families, who

Meta-communitative communication about communication

DIALING DIVERSITY

Maintaining a relationship takes work, but it seems to especially take work in stigmatized relationships such as a same-sex relationship, where friends and family may not be as supportive of the lifestyle or bond between the partners. In Chapter 8, we discussed the Defense of Marriage Act (DOMA) and how its partial repeal has brought public recognition to thousands, if not millions, of couples in the United States. With this official recognition sometimes comes the more interpersonal recognition, and hence support, for these relationships. If a couple is seen as valid in the eyes of the part-

ners' families and friendship networks, then they are likely to spend time with the couple, getting to know them individually and as a unit. They also might offer various forms of support when the partners or the relationship needs it (e.g., grandparents offering to babysit the grandchildren for the parents when they need time alone). When couples do not have the support of their networks, it can be very challenging to stay together when things get rough. While we have a relationship with one other person, we need the support of friends and family to maintain it over the long haul.

will likely serve as sources of support for the relationship in times of need. We also maintain our relationships through our social networks by supporting our partners in spending time with their friends and family.

Theories of Relationship Maintenance

As the advertisement goes, there is no one way to eat a Reese's, just as there is no one way to maintain a relationship. Every relationship is unique, and so it is impossible to craft a one-size-fits-all explanation of how to effectively maintain strong positive interpersonal connections with others. One thing that is certain, however, is that doing so requires work by both parties. Relationships change over time, and so we must always work to maintain them in the event they undergo some wear and tear. In this section of the chapter, we introduce four communication theories that begin to explain the complicated nature of relationship maintenance.

Social Exchange Theory

A common perspective on relationships of all types is to view them through an economic prism, where we evaluate their costs and benefits in order to decide if they are worth maintaining. Psychologists John Thibault and Harry Kelley formalized this economic evaluation into **Social Exchange Theory**, which proposes that relationship behavior is regulated by the evaluation of the perceived rewards and costs of the interaction by both sides.[2] This evaluation is a simple mathematical equation that looks at the benefits gained from a relationship, subtracts the costs, and determines the outcome. If the outcome is positive, then we continue the relationship; if it is not, we let it dissipate, so we try to maximize the benefits and minimize the costs. This is known as the **minimax principle**.

Relationship Worth = Rewards - Costs

Of course, some of the benefits and costs of our relationships are not easily calculated, and the perceived level of benefits and costs of particular interactions will vary from person to person. For example, some of the perceived benefits of relationships might include companionship, emotional support, social support, instrumental support, and feelings of love and belonging. Some of the perceived costs of a relationship might include time doing things you do not enjoy with the other person, emotional distress, or being asked to do things for the other person. If we are happy with the overall perceived balance of costs and rewards, then we are generally satisfied with the relationship.

Our satisfaction with and decision to continue a particular relationship is also impacted by our expectations and prior experiences. According to Social Exchange Theory, there are two different ways in which we make the determinations regarding which relationships we keep and which we replace. The first is the **comparison level**, which refers to our general expectations for a certain type of relationship, such as a friendship or romantic relationship. We have ideas about what each type of relationship should be like based on our previous interactions with others, our family interactions, cultural expectations, and the

Social Exchange Theory a theory suggesting that relationship behavior is regulated by the evaluation of perceived rewards and costs of the interaction by both sides

Minimax principle principle describing the tendency to maximize the benefits and minimize the costs in relationships

Comparison level our general expectations for a certain type of relationship, such as a friendship or romantic relationship ways that each type of relationship is portrayed in the media. If our current relationship meets or exceeds our comparison level, then we are satisfied with the relationship; if it falls short of our comparison level, then we are dissatisfied.

Second, we often compare our current relationship to the other relationship options we believe are possible. Sometimes we try to determine if the outcomes would be better with another person, or what the threshold would be for changing relationships. As we perceive other people as more attractive alternatives, our existing relationships become less stable. When we compare existing relationships to other possible relationships, we use the **comparison level of alternatives**. Ultimately, the best situation is when we believe our relationship is better than our comparison level and our comparison level of alternatives, which means we are satisfied and want to maintain the relationship.

The comparison level of alternatives also explains why some people stay in unsatisfactory relationships. It is common for people to stay in abusive relationships because their abusive partner has convinced them they are worthless, that nobody else would want to be with them, or because they have never been in a healthy relationship and do not believe such a relationship is possible. If a person does not think there is a better alternative, sometimes a bad relationship is perceived as better than not having one at all.

Communication Privacy Management

As the theories in the previous chapter demonstrate, relationships necessarily involve the sharing of personal information with another person. Sometimes we share information with others we do not wish to be shared any further. Communication scholar Sandra Petronio found the management of this process of sharing secrets and private information with other people fascinating, and so she developed a theory to explain how it works. **Communication privacy management** offers a map of sorts to navigate the way people manage private matters that are shared with others.[3]

All of us have **private information**, which is information we believe we have the right to own. When we consider information to be private, we do not believe that information should be shared widely with other people unless we have made an intentional decision to share that information with them. Private information can be information that we see as positive or negative, and as permanently or temporarily secret from other people. Examples of information that someone might consider to be private include medical conditions, new relationships, GPA, immigration status, income, or sexual orientation.

Any time we share information with others, we create co-owners of that information. These co-owners are often deliberately chosen, or **deliberate confidants**, meaning we make a conscious decision to disclose the information to them, but they are also sometimes accidental, such as when others overhear our private conversations. Petronio was primarily concerned with deliberate confidants, because people often establish rules regarding how the information they purposely share with someone should be handled. When you share private information with someone else, you create a **boundary linkage** with that person. The rights and responsibilities we ascribe to the person with whom we share the information are elements of **boundary ownership**, because they establish the boundaries, or rules, for the spread of the information. When we establish with whom the other person can

---

Comparison level of alternatives expectations arising from comparing existing relationships to other possible relationships

Communication privacy management a theory that offers a map of the way people manage private matters that are shared with others

Private information information we believe we have the right to own

Deliberate confidant a person with whom we intentionally share information meant to be kept in confidence

Boundary linkage the practice of sharing private information with another individual

Boundary ownership the rights and responsibilities we ascribe to the person with whom we share private information share the information, we establish the degree to which the information has **boundary permeability**. Sometimes we do not want the information to be shared with anybody else, which establishes a thick boundary. Sometimes there are a few particular individuals with whom we give the person permission to share our private information. Yet other times, we are comfortable having the private information shared fairly widely, which is a thin boundary. When we share private information, we must tell the other person whether the private information should be kept in confidence.

Problems in relationships occur, however, when information we believe is private and shared in confidence is shared with others. This form of **boundary turbulence** can occur for a variety of reasons, but the two most common are a direct violation of established boundaries or the failure of both parties to explicitly state the boundaries for the information. Sometimes our friends or partners deliberately share our private information with others, even though they know we do not want them to, while at other times they accidentally share the information, such as when they are talking with us about the information in a public place. At other times, our partners share the information because they do not realize that you considered that information to be private.

Social relationships with any degree of depth necessarily involve sharing confidential information, but when that trust is broken, we must make a determination of how to proceed with the relationship. In some cases it constitutes an end to the relationship altogether, but in other situations we still retain the relationship because of the rewards it provides us. Ultimately, what communication privacy management shows us is that relationships are complicated phenomena that involve a degree of trust and a leap of faith.

Boundary permeability
the degree to which a confidant can share private information with others

Boundary turbulence
occurs when information we believe is private and shared in confidence is broadcast to other parties

MEDIATED MOMENTS

In the television show *Nashville*, guitar player Deacon Clayborne is diagnosed with liver cancer after years of alcoholism. His niece Scarlett is with him when he receives his diagnosis, and, at first, Deacon is adamant that he does not want anybody else to know he has cancer. Scarlett finds that keeping Deacon's medical condition a secret is a huge burden, because she cannot talk with anybody else about the distress she feels about his diagnosis and the fact that she might lose the family member she has been closest to through her entire life. Keeping this secret for him affects her work and her relationships. Eventually, Deacon shares his diagnosis with a small group of people, including his ongoing romantic interest, Rayna, and their daughter Maddie, both of whom are initially hurt that he kept this information secret from them for so long. While Scarlett was able to maintain a thick boundary around the information about Deacon's medical condition and avoid boundary turbulence, her distress also showed that sometimes it is challenging to be a co-owner of private information about another person.

Everyday Talk

You might assume that it is easy to determine whether a relationship does or does not exist and exactly what type or stage your relationship is in based on the amount of intimate or private information being shared. In reality, though, relationships are much more complex. Once you have engaged in interpersonal interactions with another person, you have begun to develop a relationship history with that other individual. While the nature of your relationship will likely change over time, you can never go back to having never had a relationship. Even if you fall in love, marry, and then divorce someone, the relationship is not actually over; instead, you now have a relationship history together that will influence future interactions (or perhaps the avoidance of future interactions) with that partner. Our feelings about a particular relationship also fluctuate from day to day, and some days we have doubts or anxieties about a relationship that we do not feel on other days.

Everyday talk
interaction that includes mundane, ordinary conversations across our daily experience, making up our relationships in addition to the more noticeable, "bigger" moments, such as our first big fight or a marriage ceremony

Steve Duck explains that our relationships are "unfinished business," and that relationships are always in the process of becoming, rather than in a static state.[4] Relationships are a process that happens over time, and a great deal of a relationship takes place in the context of our joint activities and mundane, ordinary conversations. In fact, Daena Goldsmith and Leslie Baxter found that, even in our most intimate relationships, most of our conversations are comprised of **everyday talk** as we experience and enact our relationships.[5] Goldsmith and Baxter developed a list of 29 different kinds of "everyday talk" that fit into six separate categories. Even in our most intimate relationships, many studies have shown that most of our conversations involve superficial and informal talk (small talk, catching up, gossiping, joking around, etc.), not deep or relational talk (love talk, making up, talking about problems, conflict, etc.).

These findings show us that our everyday interactions and conversations are just as, if not more, important than the big, memorable events in our relationships. While we might keep pictures of birthday celebrations, graduations, weddings, vacations, or other events that mark important milestones in our lives and relationships with friends, romantic partners, or family members, it is the boring, everyday conversations and interactions that do the most to help us to develop and maintain our relationships. Even simple things like watching television shows and movies or playing video games together can help to strengthen our relationships because we are investing time in the other person.

> *"The potential for production, not just reproduction, is present in every new encounter between relationship partners; parties continue to construct the meaning of their relationship and through their adaptations in meaning, they construct new relationship identities."*[6]
>
> —*Baxter, 2011, p. 93*

Relational Dialectics

The final theory about how relationships function that we will discuss is Relational Dialectics Theory. Relational Dialectics is not so much about how relationships form, but rather, how we negotiate our relationships over time. While Social Exchange Theory and Communication Privacy Management Theory help us to understand how we decide whether to stay in a relationship and manage information in that relationship, and Everyday Talk helps us understand the importance of our mundane conversations and interactions, these theories do not give us a complete picture of how we understand and manage competing desires and the ebb and flow of relationships over time.

Leslie Baxter and Barbara Montgomery argue that our relationships are the products and the producers of **dialectical tensions**. These tensions occur because we simultaneously have several essential, yet oppositional, needs or desires within our relationships.[7] For example, as we saw in Uncertainty Reduction Theory, most people want certainty about the other person in their relationships and attempt to gain it through mutual self-disclosure. However, too much certainty might leave us feeling bored when we feel like we know our partner too well, and we might soon be craving a bit of spontaneity and mystery. We want both of these needs to be fulfilled simultaneously, though at times we might fluctuate back and forth about which need is more important. These dialectical tensions are internal struggles both parties experience throughout the relationship and must constantly manage while working to maintain it. Baxter and Montgomery identified three primary dialectical tensions that are experienced in all relationships and found that each manifests itself in different ways within a relationship between the partners themselves, as well as between the relational couple and the outside world.

Integration and Separation. The first is the dynamic between being a couple and being individuals separate from one another. Within a romantic relationship, this is labeled as the **connection and autonomy** dialectical tension, and it manifests, for example, when it comes to how much time you want to spend with a partner and how much time you wish to spend on your own. While you want to feel close to your partner and do things together (i.e., feel connected), you also want to maintain a sense of yourself as an individual with your own separate interests and activities (i.e., have your autonomy). What makes this even more of a challenge is that we need to participate in relationships in order to learn who we are and who we want to be; we also need to do things as individuals and bring those experiences back into our relationships in order for them to grow. The external form of the integration and separation dialectical category is labeled **inclusion and seclusion**, and it involves having a desire to spend time as a couple with friends and family, while also wanting to spend time alone together as a couple.

Stability and Change. The second dialectical tension involves having a desire for the comforts of a stable, consistent relationship, while also having a desire for spontaneity. Relationships without spontaneity can be dull and deteriorate over time, while those that are wildly unpredictable might be too exhausting to maintain. The internal form of this tension is **certainty and uncertainty** and includes the desire to count on some things to occur regularly in a relationship, while also having some novelty in the relationship. For example, a couple might have a tradition of going out for dinner for every birthday (certainty), but one time a partner surprises the other with a homemade meal or a surprise birthday party with friends (uncertainty). The external form of this tension is **conventionality and uniqueness**. Couples may, for example, always go out with the same group of friends, or they may do

Dialectical tensions
tensions that occur because we simultaneously have several essential yet oppositional needs or desires within our relationships

Connection and autonomy
the internal dialectical tension of integration and separation; spending time with a partner and spending time alone

Inclusion and seclusion
the external dialectical tension of integration and separation; spending time alone as a couple and spending time as a couple with others

Certainty and uncertainty
the internal form of the stability and change dialectic; the desire to count on things to occur and the desire to have novelty in the relationship

Conventionality and uniqueness
the external form of the stability and change dialectic; doing the same things with the same people versus doing new things together

Openness and closedness
the internal form of the expression and nonexpression dialectic; refers to the degree of disclosure partners have with one another

Revelation and concealment
the external form of the expression and nonexpression dialectic; refers to what couples share with the community and what they do not

Spiraling Inversion
method of managing tensions that takes place when we alternate back and forth between attending to our needs

Segmentation
method of managing tensions that takes place when we choose to privilege the parts of the dialectical pair based on different contexts

Balance
method of managing tensions that takes place when we try to find a compromise that allows us to partly fill each need while also sacrificing some of each need

something with a different group they have never met. Healthy relationships require that couples balance the ordinary with the unexpected.

Expression and Nonexpression. More so than the other dialectics, this one explicitly refers to communication. The internal form, **openness and closedness,** refers to the degree of disclosure partners have with each other. Some topics are freely shared, while others are not and are kept close to the vest. The external manifestation of this tension is **revelation and concealment,** and it covers what the couple shares with others in the community. This includes the decision whether to publicly announce that two people are in a relationship, or to keep their relationship secret for a while.

Effectively Managing Dialectical Tensions. Although the presence of these tensions is inevitable and may seem challenging, you can and do manage them in your relationships every day. Also, while you might often choose to value one part of the dialectic over another (e.g., you and your partner decide it's time to take some time apart, so you privilege autonomy for a while), you can manage these tensions in a variety of ways. There are six productive ways that couples can manage these tensions:[8]

Spiraling Inversion takes place when we alternate back and forth between attending to our needs. For example, a couple might decide to spend time together on the weekends, but not spend time together during the week so they also have time for their individual work, interests, and friends. They cycle back and forth between autonomy and connection over time.

Segmentation takes place when we choose to privilege the parts of the dialectical pair based on different contexts. For example, you and your partner might decide that you are willing to talk openly about your families and friendships, but you do not want to talk at all about past romantic partners. So, for certain topics you are open with each other while other topics are kept private.

Balance takes place when we try to find a compromise that allows us to partly fill each need while also sacrificing some of each need. For example, you and your partner might decide to give up some of your alone time to be with friends, but also sacrifice some important times with friends to be together.

Integration takes place when we are able to completely fulfill both opposing forces at the same time without sacrificing part of either one. For example, a family dinner might allow you to enjoy time together while also talking about individual experiences and accomplishments that happened during your days.

Recalibration involves reframing contradictions so we do not see the two opposing forces as being in contradiction with one another. For example, you might decide that spending time alone exercising or relaxing to take care of yourself is also helping take care of your relationship, because you will be more relaxed and able to enjoy the time you do spend together.

Reaffirmation involves accepting that contradictions cannot be reconciled, instead celebrating what the dialectical tension means for a couple's unity. For example, you might discuss how the tension between wanting to spend time together and alone shows that you have a healthy, strong, normal relationship.

All four of these theories of relationship maintenance offer us something unique for understanding our relationships and how they are maintained; each gives us specific concepts that help us make sense of our relational worlds. Theories are sense-making devices, and each one makes arguments about the world we can choose to accept and use or not. Hopefully these theories provide new insight into relationships and ways to maintain them better in the future.

Dialogic Communication in Ongoing Relationships

While our relationships should be enjoyable and fun, they require time, attention, and work to maintain. We must consciously work to maintain them in positive ways, or they will eventually fade. Below is a list of suggestions for keeping social relationships alive while privileging dialogue.

Embrace New Experiences

Relationships gain greater depth and strength when the two people share more interest and experiences with one another. When a partner asks you to try something new that he or she enjoys, be open to the experience and try it. Such a leap of faith and spirit of exploration will only deepen your bond, whereas shooting it down will blunt the development of a relationship. But, do remember that maintaining some sense of stability, predictability, and routine in your relationships is also important.

Privilege Quality and "Quantity" Time

Quantity of time matters just as much as quality of time with our relationship partners, whether they're friends, romantic partners, family members, or other social acquaintances. Even simple conversations recounting what happened during our day, talking about current events, and joking around show that we value the other person and enjoy his or her company. Those everyday activities and conversations are what make up our relationship, and when we make plans to do even mundane things together, we are demonstrating an ongoing commitment to our relationship.

Demonstrate Fidelity to the Relationship

Make sure your partner knows you value the relationship through verbal and nonverbal communication. Spend time with him or her, help when he or she asks for it, and inquire about his or her interests, activities, and feelings. These actions reinforce for the other person that you are committed to and value the friendship. We enter into relationships because we value the other person and feel valued by her or him; if you do not consistently express

Integration
method of managing tensions that takes place when you are able to completely fulfill both opposing forces at the same time without sacrificing part of either one

Recalibration
method of managing tensions that involves reframing the contradiction so you do not see the two opposing forces as being in contradiction with one another

Reaffirmation
method of managing tensions that involves accepting that you cannot reconcile the contradiction and celebrate what the dialectical tension means for the couple's unity

that value to the person, you risk damaging and even ending the relationship. Time is the most precious commodity we have, and so how we spend it and whom we spend it with speaks a lot about what relationships we value.

Avoid Judging or Controlling Your Partner

Social relationships are built on mutuality, and when one person begins to judge the actions, beliefs, or attitudes of another or attempts to control his or her choices and behaviors, then the relationship will greatly suffer. Remember, people choose to be in relationships; when they feel they can no longer be themselves because another person is domineering or judgmental, they might seek better alternatives to those relationships.

Celebrate Commonalities and Appreciate Differences

Relational partners share a range of different attitudes, interests, and beliefs. These overlapping activities and perceptions should be celebrated, and that's the easy part of relationships. The hard part is accepting that your partners will not always share your values, beliefs, and ideas. When these differences occur, you should work to understand why the other person sees things the way he or she does, but do not try and change him or her. The differences between partners can, as we mentioned earlier in the chapter, be complementary and thus enhance relationships—so long as we understand and accept those differences.

Give Your Partner Space

Even in the closest of relationships, we still need to have a sense of individuality. Plan activities with your partner, but also continue to explore some interests and activities on your own. Having some separate activities and friendships will help each of you continue to develop as individuals, give you something to talk about to help enrich your conversations together, and help you keep a sense of your own identity as an individual as well as part of a partnership.

Summary

In this chapter, we continued our exploration of interpersonal communication by examining how we maintain relationships with others. We briefly covered key relationship maintenance behaviors identified by communications scholars as key elements of successful interpersonal associations. We then delved into four prominent theories that begin to explain how the maintenance of relationships takes place. Finally, we provided some key tips for using dialogue to maintain healthy relationships with other people.

Chapter 10 Key Ideas

- Relationship maintenance refers to the work we do to keep a relationship going and in a condition with which both partners are happy

- Social Exchange Theory suggests that we evaluate our relationships based on the perceived rewards and costs in order to decide whether to stay in a relationship. Relationship satisfaction is based on comparison level, which is our set of general expectations for a certain type of relationship, and comparison level of alternatives, which is our comparison of our current relationship to other possible alternatives
- Communication Privacy Management Theory helps us understand how people manage private information that is shared with others and how we establish rules for the spread of that information
- Even in our most intimate relationships, most of our conversations consist of mundane, everyday talk. Those ordinary, everyday interactions help us to maintain our relationships and can be just as or even more important than deep relational conversations
- In our relationships, we experience a set of dialectical tensions, which are oppositional needs or desires within our relationship. The three primary types of dialectical tension include integration and separation, stability and change, and expression and nonexpression

Chapter 10 Key Terms

Relationship maintenance	Boundary linkage	Openness and closedness
Meta-communitative	Boundary ownership	Revelation and concealment
Social Exchange Theory	Boundary permeability	Spiraling Inversion
Minimax principle	Boundary turbulence	Segmentation
Comparison level	Everyday talk	Balance
Comparison level of alternatives	Dialectical tensions	Integration
	Connection and autonomy	Recalibration
Communication privacy management	Inclusion and seclusion	Reaffirmation
Private information	Uncertainty and certainty	
Deliberate confidant	Conventionality and uniqueness	

References

1 Stafford, L. (2011). Measuring relationship maintenance behaviors: Critique and development of the revised relationship maintenance behavior scale. *Journal of Social and Personal Relationships, 28,* 278-303.

2 Thibaut, J. W., & Kelley, H. H. (1959). *The social psychology of groups.* New York, NY: Wiley.

3 Petronio, S. (1991). Communication boundary management: A theoretical model of managing disclosure of private information between married couples. *Communication Theory, 1,* 311–335.

4 Duck, S. (1990). Relationships as unfinished business: Out of the frying pan and into the 1990s. *Journal of Social and Personal Relationships, 7,* 5-28.

5 Goldsmith, D. J., & Baxter, L. A. (1996). Constituting relationships in talk: A taxonomy of speech events in social and personal relationships. *Human Communication Research, 23,* 87-114.

6 Baxter, L. A. (2011). *Voicing relationships: A dialogic perspective.* Thousand Oaks, CA: Sage.

7 Baxter, L. A., & Montgomery, B. M. (1996). *Relating: Dialogues and dialectics.* New York, NY: Guilford.

8 Ibid.

Chapter 11

Communication in Intimate Relationships

In the last two chapters, we talked about how relationships are developed and maintained. In this chapter, we turn our attention to some of the most important relationships in our lives: intimate relationships. **Intimate relationships** are deeply personal bonds we have with other individuals that are accompanied by affective communication and a sense of belongingness. Perhaps more than any other type of relationship, the intimate associations we form with others significantly impact both the development and quality of our lives.

The first relationship we ever form is the intimate bond with our parents or caregivers when we are born, and this bond later grows to include the relationship with our entire family. Beginning in childhood we develop close friendships, and, for some, these friendships are among the most important connections. Later in life we also create intimate bonds with partners, wives, husbands, and perhaps children of our own. These relationships are complicated in nature and impacted by culture, but they are all held together through communication.

In this chapter, we explore the basic tenets of intimate relationships by first explaining the fundamental characteristics these types of associations contain. We will begin by turning our attention to the characteristics of romantic relationships and discuss

Intimate relationships deeply personal bonds that we have with other individuals that are accompanied by affective communication and a sense of belongingness how these bonds are formed, developed, and potentially dissolved through communication. We will then examine families and how communication turns these connections into cherished relationships in our lives. Next, we will turn our attention to the unique nature of friendships. Finally, we will discuss how you can use dialogue to create and maintain constructive and rewarding intimate relationships with other people.

Components of Intimate Relationships

Not every relationship we form is intimate and, in fact, most are not. Think about how many different people you come into contact with every day. Now try to remember how many of them whose name you recall. It's probably not that many, and you can probably not remember details about even more. That's because those people, the people we know and recall a great deal about, are those with whom we formed intimate relationships. The reasons why we choose to form an intimate relationship with one person and not another are myriad, but the characteristics of the communication we use in those close associations is consistent. In this section we will explain five basic qualities shared by communication in intimate relationships.

Involve Deep Commitment

When we buy a cup of coffee or have a conversation with the cashier while buying groceries, we typically do so without thinking about the future of the relationship and accept we may not talk to the person again. There are other individuals that we interact with often at school, work, the gym, or in our communities we might talk to on a regular basis, and even socialize with from time to time, but with whom we have a casual social relationship rather than a deep personal connection. Everyday interactions with acquaintances and even casual friends are important in that they often help us to accomplish tasks and provide companionship and a sense of community as we live our lives, but those social relationships are fleeting and usually end if one of the parties moves to a new geographic location or if the activities that brought you together end.

Commitment
the desire to make efforts to stay in the relationship regardless of what happens

When we have an intimate relationship with someone, however, we want to positively connect with the person over and over again in the future, hope to have that desire reciprocated, and work toward facilitating future conversations and activities with that person, even if geographic distance or schedule changes become obstacles to doing so. This is the quality of **commitment,** or the desire to do whatever we can to stay in the relationship regardless of what happens. The commitment is a promise we make to ourselves and the other person that the relationship will not only continue, but will continue to be strong.

Commitments in intimate relationships take many forms, and can even be codified legally through marriage contracts, birth certificates, or adoption certificates. We might make financial commitments to a partner or family. Ultimately, though, the deep commitment of intimate relationships is an emotional and chronemic commitment whereby we value the feelings of the other person and seek to spend a great deal of time with him or her.

This emotional connection is deep and comes with a sense of responsibility for the other person's well-being and the well-being of the relationship. Regardless of the difficulties, arguments, challenges, or problems in a relationship, there is an ongoing promise to work through it and preserve the connection.

Promote Interdependence

One quality that makes intimate relationships so unique and powerful is that the depth of the commitment and connection to the other person creates a high level of interdependence between the relational partners. This means that what affects one person in the relationship affects the others. This can sometimes be said of casual acquaintances as well, but the level at which the interdependence exists in intimate relationships is what distinguishes it from casual acquaintances. Think of it as prioritizing, since we would likely put the needs and desires of our partners or family above those of coworkers.

In one sense, the intimate relationships we form with others make the other person an extension of oneself. Intimate others become part of how we identify ourselves; for instance, in some situations, you might begin to introduce yourself as the partner, spouse, daughter, brother, parent, or close friend of someone with whom you have an intimate relationship. Our intimate relationship partners are the first people with whom we share important parts of our lives, just as they share important parts of their lives with us first. Both parties become part of the other, joined in one category of family, siblings, partners, couples, spouses, or even close friends.

Require Constant Maintenance

Recall the concept of Social Exchange Theory from the prior chapter and how it used a financial metaphor of investment for judging interpersonal relationships. That metaphor carries over here as well. Just like managing investments in the stock market, we choose to invest different quantities of time, effort, emotion, and attention to different relationships. What we expect to get in return is based on what we believe we put into the relationship. In intimate relationships, we invest a significant portion of our resources and hope that it is returned by the other party. The degree of investment is also ongoing. Investment is not a matter of spending one day a week or month with the other person, but instead choosing every day to tend to the relationship. Intimate relationships have a consistent quality to the investment we put in them, and we expect the other party be similarly invested.

Tend to be Fluid Rather Than Static

All relationships have beginnings, middles, and ends, and they fluctuate in intensity during different periods. For this reason, it is important to understand that relationships are not simply static things, but rather processes you undergo or travel through. As we discussed a moment ago, what happens to one person affects the other, and we all experience different things that affect our moods, attentions, emotional states, and perceptions of our surroundings all the time. Sometimes the effect is barely noticeable; at other times it is dramatic and results in a fundamental change in the way we see the world around us. Since we are constantly influenced by our surroundings, so too is the relationship between ourselves and our partners or families influenced and adjusted based on those events. As a result, intimate relationships are fluid and ever changing.

Require Management of Tensions

The external experiences that influence relationships and leave them in a constant state of flux also can create tensions that the parties must manage in order to maintain their relationship over time. As we learned in the previous chapter, relationships are filled with dialectical tensions, or challenges that come from having several sets of essential, but at times oppositional, needs or desires.[1] For example, there are times when we want and need our family's communication to change. Children get older and their relationships with their parents must be revised. The move into adolescence can be the most challenging to negotiate for children and parents. The children are becoming more independent and want to be spoken with in increasingly more mature ways. Parents sometimes struggle with these changes, because they don't want to see their children grow up. The changes are necessary, however, to reach a "new normal," though that new normal will change again in later years.

Romantic Relationships as Intimate Relationships

When we think of intimate relationships, many of us think first about romantic relationships. Romantic partnerships come in many different forms, just like families, but one common characteristic they share is that there are no genetic ties between participants. Romantic relationships evolve, and sometimes even dissolve, over time, and romantic relationships come with their own communication challenges and issues. In this part of the chapter, we will first briefly define the characteristics and types of romantic partnerships that exist in society before explaining the development process these relationships go through.

Characteristics of Romantic Relationships

Not all romantic relationships are the same, as each couple creates, negotiates, and sometimes violates the rules that govern the association. For this reason, it is quite difficult to pin down the characteristics all romantic couples share; rather, we can identify some typical attributes that many, but not all, romantic partnerships contain.

Open vs. Closed Romantic Relationships. The traditional way of defining a romantic partnership is through the exclusive nature of the relationship, meaning that both parties do not have romantic bonds with anyone other than each other. This is a closed relationship. There are, however, some romantic relationships that are open, and both parties are free to see other people while still holding a deep commitment to each other. In fact, polygamy is the practice of marrying more than one partner, and there are cultures that continue this practice of open relationships even today.

DIALING DIVERSITY

In the United States, voluntary marriages are the norm; however that is not the case across the globe. In fact, in India there are a variety of different approaches to marriage. In a tradition rooted in the historic Vedic religion of India, parents of a girl would announce the intention of their daughter to marry and invite interested suitors to come forth at a specific time and place in a wedding hall. The daughter would then choose her husband from

the men gathered there. The Gandharva marriage tradition relies simply on mutual consent between a man and woman with no rituals or even witnesses. Other marriage practices in India include traditional arranged weddings by parents and, recently, voluntary nuptials based on mutual love and affection. The idea of love as the primary reason for a wedding is actually a cultural development rooted in the West.[2]

Voluntary vs. Arranged Marriages. In Western cultures, marriages and romantic pairings are typically voluntary. Each person enters into the relationship freely and has the right to end the relationship. In some cultures, however, marriages are arranged for children by parents to maximize family social standings, financial status, or for other reasons. The parties who are contracted to marry sometimes have no say in the matter, and in some cases they do not even meet until their marriage. In other cases, family members introduce potential partners that the family has approved and give the couple some time to get to know each other before letting the couple decide whether they are compatible and willing to marry. What is interesting about this is that the two individuals could marry someone they do not love, something that typically does not happen with truly voluntary romantic relationships.

Opposite-Sex vs. Same-Sex Couples. Traditionally, marriages and romantic relationships have been defined as existing between opposite sex partners, but recent history has changed that. In the United States alone, states are beginning to rescind bans on same-sex marriage, and the federal government recognizes same-sex couples for tax and benefits purposes. This was not the case at the turn of the century. American culture is becoming more accepting of same-sex couples and supportive of equal rights, as can be evidenced through the changes in legislation and their growing presence in television shows like the popular *Modern Family* and *Glee* sitcoms and reality shows like *Extreme Guide to Parenting*.

Married for Life vs. Divorced. When couples marry, they typically believe it is a lifetime commitment. Unfortunately, divorce statistics illustrate that many marriages are not lifetime commitments. Marriage commitments wane and dissipate for a variety of reasons; however, there are a host of other reasons, such as social, familial, and community support

Interdependence
the quality of intimate relationships whereby one person's actions influence the other and vice versa; refers to the degree of connectedness between the two individuals, including how the couple shares time and space within their home

Ideology
refers to the beliefs and values that the individuals have about what marriage and family life should be like, and can include placing a value on stability and predictability or on spontaneity and relational uncertainty

Conflict
refers to whether the couple tries to resolve differences through open conflict or whether they avoid conflict

that help preserve marriages even through difficult and trying times. One of the most influential factors in the success or failure of a marriage is communication, both before and during married life. For instance, marriage expert and scholar John Gottman found that communication is key to predicting the success or failure of relationships based on how people interact with each other.[3]

Types of Romantic Relationships

Just as there are many different types of romantic relationships, there are also several different types of relationship patterns that can be seen in romantic relationships and marriages. Mary Anne Fitzpatrick and her colleagues[4] have found that there are three dimensions important for classifying marital relationships: interdependence, ideology, and conflict. **Interdependence** refers to the degree of connectedness between the two individuals, including how the couple shares time and space within their home. **Ideology** refers to the beliefs and values the individuals have about what marriage and family life should be like, and can include placing a value on stability and predictability or on spontaneity and relational uncertainty. **Conflict** refers to whether the partners try to resolve differences through open conflict or whether they avoid conflict.

Traditional. Couples who have traditional relationships have a high level of interdependence, share conventional ideologies about marriage, and avoid marital conflict. In these marriages, both individuals take on conventional sex roles; the wife usually takes her husband's last name, the couple spends a lot of time together, and the individuals disclose a lot of information to one another. Traditional couples are also likely to keep regular schedules and share the same spaces in their home. While traditional couples do not avoid talking about problematic issues, they try to do so in a neutral way and avoid engaging in open conflict.

Separates. Separate couples tend to have low levels of interdependence, share conventional ideologies, and avoid conflict. Similar to traditional couples, separates have conventional views about marriage, family, and sex roles and are likely to avoid conflict. However, separates spend far less time together, talk less, disclose less information to one another, maintain a psychological distance, and spend time in separate spaces.

Independent. Independent couples tend to have a high level of interdependence, share unconventional ideologies, and openly engage in conflict. Like traditional couples, independent couples disclose a lot to their partner, spend a lot of time together, and often have long conversations. However, independent couples do not think that relationships should constrain individual freedom and are likely to have less conventional sex roles, are likely to maintain separate spaces (e.g., separate home offices), and do not always keep regular schedules. Independent couples are also more likely to engage in open conflict when a problematic issue arises.

Mixed. Mixed couples include spouses who have different definitions for their relationship. For example, one partner might define the marriage as traditional while the other partner might define the marriage as separate based on the dimensions of interdependence, ideology, and conflict. Mixed couples could see themselves as having any two of the three marriage types described above, and approximately 40 percent of all couples fall into this category.

Families as Intimate Relationships

Now that we have talked about romantic relationships and the marriages that result in some of those romantic relationships, it only seems natural to move on to talking about families. Families are unique and complex forms of intimate relationships. In some ways we have no control over our family, but in others we do. For example, we have no control over the family into which we are born, but we do choose our mates and can build our own families. In this part of the chapter, we will describe the common ways families are defined or created, explain how families function as systems, describe the types of families, and finally explore some of the significant communication issues families confront.

Creating a Family

There are three ways in which families form in society, and many families form in more than one way. The first of these is the most obvious: through genetics. The second way families can be created in a society is through the law, whereby the government recognizes a family unit. The third, and final, way is through role enactment.[5]

Most, but definitely not all, families share genetic information and are biologically related. Keep in mind, though, this relates to parents and children, not the parents themselves, as marriage partners come from different families. The children share half their genetic information with each biological parent, thus connecting the family through genetics. This shared DNA often results in close connections between individuals, especially as they grow up in that particular family structure. It is important to note, though, that there are several different methods through which families form intimate bonds with children who do not share any biological information—for instance, through adoption, foster care, and surrogacy.

Families are such an important element of a stable society that governments and communities care about how they are constituted and managed. It is for this reason there is a legal dimension to and option for establishing a family. When a couple marries, they must get a civil license for the marriage through their local or state government office to certify the union. Legal protections for couples often includes things like tax filing status, custody of children, the right to make medical decisions for a family member when they are unable to do so for themselves, and the ability to share employer-provided healthcare benefits.

Families also always contain roles and typical behaviors for members. It is these roles and behaviors that create the perception of a family unit. These include things like living together, caring for each other, identifying as a family to the community, and showing a genuine interest in the development of each other's lives and interests. These roles can manifest in genetic families as well as adoptive or surrogate ones. The existence of familial roles contributes to the use of "family" as a metaphor for teams, companies, and other typically social groups that do not have the legal designation as a family or genetic ties to one another.

System
interdependent
parts that interact
with and affect one
another

Open system
a system in which
parts both affect
and are affected by
events within and
outside the system

The Family System

The tight bonds that give families their intimate quality also create a **system** of operation within them, meaning they are composed of interdependent parts that interact with and affect one another. Researcher Paul Watzlawick defined families as complex self-regulating arrangements of feedback loops between the people involved that are governed by rules established by its members.[6] In other words, families each have their own unique rules and ways of operating. Families also adapt as things happen and as members interact with one another. These family systems are referred to as **open systems,** or those systems where parts both affect and are affected by events within and outside the system, and they exhibit certain qualities.

Families are influenced by context. As an open system, families and their members are constantly adapting to the things that happen at home and outside. People change, and family systems change with them.

Families foster interdependence. All systems experience the pull and push of individual parts, and families are no different. Resources are shared by all in the system, and conflicts can arise when these are in short supply. Additionally, happiness is shared; when one member has something positive happen, the entire family reacts and responds to that event.

A family is greater than the sum of its members. A family is more than just an individual, creating its own identity that manifests when all or a few members are together. The shared identity influences individual identities, just as the individuals in the system contribute to the overall family dynamic.

Families contain multiple systems. Each family contains certain groups within it that have their own dynamics. Parents and children interact in specific ways, as do siblings with each other. Those siblings also have different relationships with individual parents than they do when the parents are together. These different permutations of members have their own unique system within the larger family system.

Families establish change-resistant systems. It is incredibly difficult to change the ways families communicate once patterns are established within the unit. It is not impossible, but it is challenging. Just think how difficult it is for parents to adjust to the changing dynamic of their relationship with children when they go off to college.

Family Types

Just as marriages can be described as fitting into different categories based on several communication dimensions, families can also be described as fitting into different categories or types depending on how family members interact with one another. Mary Anne Fitzpatrick and her colleagues argue that families can be divided into four different types based on their conversation orientation and their conflict orientation as represented in Table 11.1.[7][8]

Conversational orientation is the degree to which family members are encouraged to participate in unrestrained conversation about a range of topics, and **conformity orientation** is the degree to which the family emphasizes homogeneity of attitudes, values, and beliefs. As can be seen in the table on the next page, families typically fall into one of the following four types: consensual, pluralistic, protective, and laissez-faire.

Consensual Families. These families are high in conversation orientation and high in conformity orientation. These families encourage open conversation and the exploration of ideas, but there is also a high amount of pressure to agree in order to preserve the existing hierarchy. While children are encouraged to speak, the parents ultimately make the decisions for the family and take time to explain those decisions to the family. Decision-making is often distributed among the adults, so that one makes some types of decisions while the other makes other types of decisions.

Pluralistic Families. These families are high in conversation orientation but low in conformity orientation. These families encourage open, unrestrained communication and evaluate all family members' contributions on their own merit. Parents and children participate equally in family decision-making, and children usually become independent and autonomous. Pluralistic families spend time together and share a great deal, but they also value autonomy and spend time apart engaging in individual activities.

Protective Families. These families are low in conversation orientation and high in conformity orientation. These families emphasize obedience to authority, and parents make decisions for their children and rarely explain the reasoning for their decisions.

Laissez-faire Families. These families are low in conversation orientation and low in conformity orientation. Family members are uninvolved, have very limited conversations, believe that all family members should be allowed to make their own decisions, and have little interest in those decisions.

Conversational orientation
the degree to which family members are encouraged to participate in unrestrained conversation about a range of topics

Conformity orientation
the degree to which the family emphasizes homogeneity of attitudes, values, and beliefs

TABLE 11.1   Types of Families

	High Conversation Orientation	Low Conversation Orientation
High Conformity Orientation	Consensual	Protective
Low Conformity Orientation	Pluralistic	Laissez-faire

Communication Issues in the Family System

Communication issues within families can take two primary forms. The first are the communicative actions that help to strengthen the family identity, while the second are those communicative patterns that negatively influence the family and its members. To be clear, communication issues refer to the *ways* in which families communicate rather than the *topics* about which they communicate.

Rituals
repetitive behaviors that contain a unique meaning for members, and each family develops their own traditions

Positive communicative actions within a family include those things that create a sense of history and identity for members. These might include certain family rituals and traditions, like eating certain foods on holidays, modes of celebrating birthdays, and even how and when everyone gets together for meals. **Rituals** are repetitive behaviors that contain a unique meaning for members, and each family develops their own traditions. In many cases, these traditions trace back many generations, while other families begin rituals in the hopes of making it a "new" family tradition to uniquely shape family identity. Research has also shown that importing traditions from one's family past into a new family is especially important in building a sense of cohesion in blended and adopted families.[9]

A second positive communication action that enhances the family identity is that of telling stories. Every family has its own stories about generations past, current members, and important events in the history of the family. Telling and retelling these stories to each successive generation connects a new member not just with those present but also with family members from the past. Families also take comfort in the fact that their stories may be added to this long narrative of the family in future generations.

Complementary interchange
interaction between members of a system that is based on acknowledged differences in power

Symmetrical interchange
communication between members that seeks to neutralize the power difference and treat each person equally

On the opposite end of the spectrum, there are communicative patterns that can negatively impact those in the family system. These patterns are driven by the power, status, and control dimensions inherent to human organizations, including families. In a **complementary interchange**, the interaction between members of the system is based on acknowledged differences in power, such as what exists between parents and children. In a **symmetrical interchange**, communication between members seeks to neutralize the power difference and treat each other equally. When family members seek to exert dominance over one another or exhibit control over another member, they engage in complementary interchanges, and when they do so, they risk creating stress in the entire system despite the

MEDIATED MOMENTS

One of the most successful franchises on the Bravo television network is *Real Housewives*. There have been casts in New York, New Jersey, Atlanta, Orange County, Miami, Beverly Hills, and most recently, Melbourne, Australia. These shows follow the friendships of a group of wealthy women and their families. In the *Real Housewives of New Jersey* series, a brother and sister encounter serious problems in their relationship—so much so a counselor is brought in to help address the deteriorating relationship between the two. The negative communication patterns the two have, along with those exhibited by their respective spouses, are difficult to change as the show illustrates. Their interactions also contain a sibling subsystem within their larger family. These shows are excellent examples of how complex and challenging communication within families can become.

the Real Housewives

fact such behaviors may be necessary at times. Symmetrical interchanges are much healthier approaches to communication where no one seeks to exert dominance over another and everyone is able to communicate and do things based on their own merits. However, these patterns also come with the risk of **enabling communication** that is not assertive, and thus may allow members to continue abusive, addictive, and otherwise negative behaviors.[10] Enabling communication helps create an environment where negative behaviors are not stopped, and thus end up being encouraged to continue.

Enabling communication interaction that is not assertive and thus allows members to continue abusive, addictive, and otherwise negative behaviors

Friendships as Intimate Relationships

Now that we understand the ways in which romantic and family relationships are important intimate relationships, we will turn our attention to one of the most unique relationships in our lives: friendships. While some friendships are acquaintances that would best be categorized as casual social relationships, some of our friendships can be the closest, most intimate, and sometimes even the longest relationships in our lives. First we will cover the five qualities that constitute friendships, before discussing some of the dialectic tensions inherent in these forms of relationships. Anytime we are close to someone, and the person feels close to us, tensions can and do arise.

> *"Because of the conscientious choices and beneficial consequences of friendship, communicating as friends has important ethical and political potentials."*
>
> —*William Rawlins, Ohio University*

The Qualities of Friendships

Friendships are characterized by five different common elements. We don't necessarily think about these things when we form friendships, but they exist nonetheless. In this section of the chapter, we will discuss these five different characteristics that constitute the friendships in our lives.[11]

Friendships are voluntary. Part of what makes friendships so powerful is that they are one of the few relationships we freely choose to make or unmake. While you can't choose your neighbors, classmates, coworkers, or family members, you do get to choose your friends. If you want to end a friendship, all you have to do is make that decision, whereas ending a marriage or family relationship requires a long legal process, and deciding not to be neighbors or coworkers with someone requires that you find a new place to live or acquire a new job. Knowing that you have chosen, and continue to choose, each other as friends can create a very powerful bond between two people.

Friendships are personal relationships. While we sometimes see other individuals with whom we have interpersonal relationships as part of a certain group or class (sister, parent, child, teacher, etc.), we see each of our friends as unique individuals. We privately negotiate our friendship with our friends, and each of our friendships is a distinctive relationship.

Friendships are pervaded by a spirit of equality. Even though we might have different levels of education, socioeconomic status, ability, age, or other characteristics than our friends in other contexts, we view our friends as equals within the context of our friendship and deliberately choose ways of interacting that emphasize that sense of equality.

Friendships are characterized by mutual involvement. As communication scholar William K. Rawlins explains, "The bonds of friendship result from the collaboration of two individuals in constructing a shared social reality. This interpersonal reality evolves out of and furthers mutual acceptance and support, trust and confidence, dependability and assistance, and discussion of thoughts and feelings."[12] Both parties must be actively engaged in a friendship for the friendship to continue to exist.

Friendship implies affective ties. We care about, are concerned for, have positive feelings toward, and often have a deep love for our friends.

Dialectical Tensions in Friendships

Our friendships sometimes serve different purposes depending on the stage of our lives, ranging from childhood playmates, to college friends, to later-life companions. Just as we feel strains from dialectical tensions in our romantic relationships, Rawlins argues that we face a slightly different set of dialectical tensions in our friendships. The first two dialectical pairs are tensions that arise from our cultural conceptions of friendship. The final four dialectical pairs are tensions that emanate from the relationship itself and are referred to as interactional dialectics.

Private and Public. We often feel pressure to interact publicly with our friends in ways that are deemed socially acceptable and expected, while at the same time having our own personal expectations and ways of interacting in that particular friendship. For instance, cross-sex friends might feel like they have to partially disguise their friendship in public out of concern that others might think there is a romantic or sexual relationship, while they might be able to talk and express their friendship much more openly when in private.

Ideal and Real. We have cultural expectations for what friendships should look like and how we should interact with our friends, and this is often sometimes very different from how individuals interact with specific friends in everyday life.

Freedom to be Independent and Freedom to be Dependent. Just as we have a desire for both autonomy and connection in our romantic relationships, we want to be able to pursue our individual interests without interference from our friends, but we also want to be able to depend on our friends when we need help.

Affection and Instrumentality. We want to be friends with others because we care about them as people and have affection for them, but we also want to be friends because friendships are utilitarian or instrumental in that they help us achieve other things.

Judgment and Acceptance. We want our friends to accept and support us in our actions, but at times we also want our friends to give us honest evaluations or criticisms, and vice versa.

Expressiveness and Protectiveness. We want to be able to be open and share vulnerable information with our close friends, which shows a great deal of trust, but at the same time, there is often information we do not want to share with our friends because we consider it private.

Just as we must work to manage dialectical tensions in our other relationships, we must constantly negotiate the dialectics within our friendships.

Dialogic Communication in Intimate Relationships

One of the primary reasons intimate relationships reach the end is a lack of good communication between partners, either at the beginning stages of the relationship regarding expectations and values, or during the period of bonding. Using dialogue with a partner helps to mitigate these problems before they happen, in many cases because it is based on achieving understanding. Understanding your partner, family member, or friend and what his or her beliefs, values, goals, and desires are is a key element to any successful intimate relationship. In this final part of the chapter, we will provide you with some guidelines for successfully enacting dialogue in your intimate relationships.

Be Honest About Your Feelings

This may seem obvious, but it is also quite hard to do in the moment. Many people do not want to hurt or offend their partner, and they feel disagreement can hurt them so they resist the urge to express this disconnect. Asserting your own opinions and helping your partner or family understand your perspective on an issue, however controversial, leads to positive outcomes, not negative ones, for the relationship. Being honest and open about how something makes you feel, how you perceive something, or what you would like to do is part of the foundation of any intimate relationship. Additionally, you must be prepared to accept openness and honesty from your partner and family as well.

Own Your Own Statements

In being open and honest, we also must own our own feelings. This means acknowledging your feeling, instead of placing blame or attributing the feeling to someone or something else.

For example, when we say, "You make me so mad," we are issuing an accusatory statement that also relinquishes our ability to control our own emotions by saying someone else can dictate how we feel through how she or he acts. Instead, point to the specific behavior and say, "I get upset when you don't clean the dishes after you eat." Here you own your own feeling, and are specific about what incites that emotion, so the other party knows what to address.

Focus on the Other Person

Perhaps what makes relationships intimate is not the depth of yourself you share, but the focus, care, and attention you place on the other person. Maintaining that interest and appreciation for his or her beliefs, attitudes, emotions, interests, goals, and activities is what keeps partnerships together. A genuine affection is borne not only out of a sense of sharing oneself, but also in caring enough to let the other person share himself or herself with you.

Approach Conflict Constructively

Later in this book we will address interpersonal conflict in greater detail, but handling it in a constructive and not destructive way is essential for intimate relationships. When you care about the other person and have a deep commitment to her or his well-being, then conflict can be a constructive platform from which relationships can evolve and grow. Do not attack people or assume motives, but rather engage to understand the roots of the disagreement and work to bridge any gaps that may exist.

Welcome Different Experiences

The richness and diversity of experiences people have and are interested in having are what make being in a relationship such a rewarding experience. In initiating a relationship or maintaining a family connection, you must be open to the different opinions and interests of the other person and not approach them as opportunities to dominate and control. Respect a person's background, goals, and experiences, and he or she will likely reciprocate. Also, be open to trying things that might make you uncomfortable, but be sure to share your perception of the experience with your family member or friend.

Discuss the Status of the Relationship

It is important to be on the same page with others with whom you have intimate relationships, and to do this you should periodically check in about the state in which you see the relationship. You might discover the other person disagrees, but you also might get an opportunity to have your perception reinforced. Knowing the relational status allows you to determine the best labels to use or behaviors to exhibit. These types of moments can come about after long periods of noncommunication with family members, but also more commonly happen in romantic relationships at that awkward moment when one person in the couple sees the relationship in one way, but the other person might not. Talking about this issue adds to the intimate nature of the relationship, but does come with risk—and reward.

Summary

In this chapter, we explored different types of intimate relationships. We discussed three primary forms of intimate relationships: those that exist in romantic partnerships, those that occur in families, and those that are our closest friendships. We detailed the characteristics of all three relationship forms, how they develop and change, and what issues are typically confronted in these relationships. Finally, we provided some guidelines for creating dialogue within intimate relationships with family members and romantic partners.

Chapter 11 Key Ideas

- Intimate relationships share five basic qualities: (1) they are marked by individuals deeply committed to one another, (2) they entail interdependence, (3) they require constant investment to maintain, (4) they are fluid, not static, and (5) they require the management of tension
- Three of the most important types of intimate relationships in most people's lives are romantic relationships, family relationships, and friendships
- Marriages can be classified based on the level of interdependence, ideology, and approach to conflict within the couple. The four types of marriages are traditional, separate, independent, and mixed
- Families can be created through genetics, law, or role enactment. Families are systems with their own self-regulating arrangements of feedback loops. Families can be categorized based on their conversation orientation and conformity orientation into four distinct types: consensual, pluralistic, protective, and laissez-faire
- Friendships are voluntary personal relationships that are pervaded by a spirit of equality, characterized by mutual involvement, and imply affective ties. We experience a slightly different set of dialectical tensions in our friendships than in our romantic relationships

Chapter 11 Key Terms

Intimate relationships	System	Complementary interchange
Commitment	Open system	Symmetrical interchange
Interdependence	Conversation orientation	Enabling communication
Ideology	Conformity orientation	
Conflict	Rituals	

References

1 Baxter, L. A., & Montgomery, B. M. (1996). *Relating: Dialogues and dialectics.* New York, NY: The Guilford Press.
2 Meyer, J. J. (1989). Sexual life in ancient India: a study in the comparative history of Indian culture. Motilal Banarsidass Publishers.

3 Gottman, J. M., & Levenson, R. W. (1992). Marital processes predictive of later dissolution: Behavior, physiology and health. *Journal of Personality and Social Psychology, 63,* 221- 233.

4 Fitzpatrick, M. A. (2004). Family communication patterns theory: Observations on its development and application. *The Journal of Family Communication, 4,* 167-179. doi: 10.1207/s15327698jfc0403&4_4; Williamson, R. N., & Fitzpatrick, M. A. (1985). Two approaches to marital interaction: Relational control patterns in marital types. *Communication Monographs, 52,* 236-252.

5 Floyd, K., Mikkelson, A., & Judd, J. (2006). Defining the family through relationships. In L. Turner, & R. West (Eds.), *The family communication sourcebook.* (21-41). Thousand Oaks, CA: Sage. doi: http://dx.doi.org/10.4135/9781452233024.n2

6 Watzlawick, P., Beavin, J. H., & Jackson, D. D. (1967). *Pragmatics of human communication.* New York: W. W. Norton.

7 Ritchie, L. D., & Fitzpatrick, M. A. (1990). Family communication patterns: Measuring intrapersonal perceptions of interpersonal relationships. *Communication Research, 17,* 523-544. doi: 10.1177/009365090017004007

8 Koerner, A. F., & Fitzpatrick, M. A. (2002). Understanding family communication patterns and family functioning: The roles of conversation orientation and conformity orientation. *Communication Yearbook, 26,* 36-68.

9 Braithwaite, D. O., & Baxter, L. A. (1998). The role of rituals in the management of the dialectical tension of "old" and "new" in blended families. *Communication Studies, 49,* 101-120. doi: 10.1080/10510979809368523

10 Rogers, L.E. & Farace, R. (1975). The Analysis of relational communication in dyads: New measurement procedures. *Human Communication Research, 1,* 222-239; Watzlawick, P. & Hoyt, M. (1997). Constructing therapeutic realities: A conversation with Paul Watzlawick. (183-196), in *Handbook of Constructive Therapies,* M. Hoyt (Ed.), San Francisco, CA: Jossey-Bass.

11 Rawlins, W. K. (1992). *Friendship matters: Communication, dialectics, and the life course.* New Brunswick, NJ: Transaction Publishers.

12 Ibid.

Chapter 12

Mediated Relationships

As technology has advanced, the media we use to interact with others has changed a great deal. Prior to the invention of the telegraph in 1832, individuals had to rely on either face-to-face communication or written letters. Letters had to be physically carried across geographic space from the writer to the recipient, which could take a great deal of time if the recipient was far away. The invention of the telegraph allowed messages to be sent long distances almost instantly, though messages still had to be transmitted back and forth one at a time, which allowed for a greater control of message construction.[1] Later, the invention of the telephone finally allowed synchronous communication and interactive conversations across long distances. If we fast forward to today, our options for mediated communication have expanded tremendously, leaving us with more options for communicating and maintaining relationships with others across time and space than any generation before. In this chapter, we will first discuss the types of social media that are now available, and then explain how the use of mediated communication impacts the relationships between—and perceptions of—self and others. Finally, we will provide a few tips for engaging in social media with a dialogic spirit.

Mediated Communication

Earlier in the book, we discussed various models of the communication process. You may recall the linear and transactional models of communication, with the former providing no explanation for feedback, and the latter allowing for constant and continuous messaging by both parties. Communication through media, especially electronic media, which we will focus on in this chapter, can work in either the linear or transactional format. Sometimes, however, there may be a slight or significant time lag between communication by both parties through their electronic platforms. In this section of the chapter, we explain how this time lag helps us further categorize communication before explaining some specific types of mediated communication.

Modes of Mediated Communication

Synchronous communication communication that occurs simultaneously

All mediated communication, including social media, can be categorized in several different ways. The first way considers whether communication occurs simultaneously, or in a back and forth exchange over time. **Synchronous communication** is communication that occurs simultaneously. In synchronous communication, both parties of the conversation are able to respond to one another in the moment. Examples of synchronous communication include a face-to-face conversation, a phone conversation, a Skype or Facetime video call, and even an instant messaging or text message conversation in which both parties are online and engaging in the conversation at the same time.

Asynchronous communication communication that occurs when the communicators are sending and receiving messages at different times

Asynchronous communication, on the other hand, is communication that occurs when the communicators are sending and receiving messages at different times. Examples of asynchronous communication might include mailed letters, emails, online message boards or review sites, Facebook messages, or even text message conversations in which there is a gap in time between responses. Each of these modes of interaction allow people to take their time to respond to the initial message.

Types of Mediated Communication

In the early years of the Internet, most users consumed information from a relatively small number of content producers and information that was posted online was fairly static, meaning that once something was posted on a website, it was likely to stay there and remain unchanged for a while. Around the beginning of the twenty-first century, though, we began to see a transition to Web 2.0, in which almost all Internet users generated online content and frequently updated or added to the information posted online, largely as a result of the development of social media sites. **Social Media** include forms of electronic communication through which users create online communities to share information, ideas, personal messages, and other content. A few examples of social media platforms include Facebook, Twitter, Pinterest, Spotify, Yelp, Instagram, Snapchat, Blogger, YouTube, Groupon, Farmville, and numerous other sites that have likely been developed and become popular since this chapter was written. Now, almost anyone with Internet access and a little bit of experience using Web applications can easily add and edit online content.

Social Media forms of electronic communication through which users create online communities to share information, ideas, personal messages, and other content

The second way to categorize types of mediated communication is on a continuum from impersonal to hyperpersonal communication. **Impersonal communication** is communication that occurs in order to facilitate some type of transaction and is based primarily on social roles in the particular situation. Examples of impersonal communication might include a phone conversation with a receptionist to schedule a dental appointment, a brief interaction at a fast food restaurant to order and pay for a meal, an email reminding you of a deadline, or a review of a product posted on Amazon that shares information about the product with other potential buyers. Researchers used to believe that computer-mediated communication was more impersonal than face-to-face interpersonal conversations, but now some types of computer-mediated communication can actually exceed face-to-face conversation in users' ability to create an impression, present information about oneself to another person, and achieve relational goals.[2]

Hyperpersonal communication occurs when computer-mediated communication has a higher level of affection, emotion, liking, solidarity, and intimacy than face-to-face conversations. Online communication allows communicators to focus more on their message because they do not have to monitor behavioral cues. Online technologies also give communicators the ability to craft the image they convey by emphasizing some characteristics and downplaying others. Such hyperpersonal online communication can allow individuals to find support from others with similar experiences online, but it also makes it possible for individuals to create fake identities and deceive others in what sometimes become painful situations.

Yet another way that we can categorize types of social media is by the type of information shared or the function served by the social media. Some social media sites allow members to connect with others that they know offline or who share similar interests, such as Facebook, GooglePlus, and LinkedIn. Some sites, such as YouTube, Flickr, and Vimeo, allow users to post and watch online photo or video content, while others such as Spotify or Netflix allow you to stream commercially produced media, while also sharing recommendations with

Impersonal communication
communication that occurs in order to facilitate some type of transaction and that is based primarily on social roles

Hyperpersonal communication
computer-mediated communication that has a higher level of affection, emotion, liking, solidarity, and intimacy than face-to-face conversations

Catfishing
the practice of pretending to have a different identity via social media in order to initiate and maintain a relationship with another person

MEDIATED MOMENTS

In 2012, Notre Dame college football player Manti Te'o thought his girlfriend had died. He and the woman had only communicated online, but later he found out that her existence had been entirely faked. An acquaintance, Ronaiah Tuiasosopo, had apparently orchestrated the entire relationship by making up the woman via social media and pretending to be her in phone calls to Te'o. Tuiasosopo has admitted to using another woman's photos to create the made-up girlfriend, Lennay Kekua, who he said was a Stanford University undergraduate student. This is an example of what has been termed **catfishing**, which is when a person pretends to have a different identity via social media in order to initiate and maintain a relationship with another person.

friends in social networks. Blogging sites, such as Blogger and Wordpress, allow users to post entries with text, photos, video, and even music for followers, while a microblogging site, such as Twitter, allows users to post messages that are no more than 140 characters in length.

Mediated Self and Mediated Others

Think about your own Facebook friends list, the people that follow you on Twitter, and the people with whom you have exchanged emails or text messages in the past week. How many of them are people that you have met in person? Chances are, you have met most of the people you communicate with online in face-to-face interactions and probably even see some of them on a fairly regular basis. While mediated communication opens up the possibility of connecting with other people online that you have never met and would be unlikely to encounter in day-to-day life, the reality is that most people connect with people they already know in their "offline" lives when communicating online.[3] Mediated communication often serves as a way to grow, enhance, and maintain relationships with people we already know, such as keeping in touch with old friends when moving to a new place or beginning college, and maintaining and intensifying relationships with people we interact with often.

Interpersonal Relationships and Media Impact

There are three primary ways that media impact messages in interpersonal relationships.[4] First, the medium can modify the message, which means that the medium we choose to communicate certain messages can change how others receive those messages. For example, choosing to use a text message instead of face-to-face communication to break up with a romantic partner might result in a bitter response from your partner and others who perceive your actions as cold; however, using that same technique in another relationship might give your partner a sense of relief that he or she didn't have to have an awkward break-up conversation with you. Choosing to tell someone that a loved one passed away via a Facebook post instead of a phone call might leave some friends or relatives feeling hurt that you communicated such sensitive information in such an uncaring way, while others might view it as your way of getting the information out quickly and simultaneously while saving your emotional energy from having to call so many different people with the same news. In some cases, it is difficult to predict how your choice of medium will affect your interactions with others, but typically you can refer to the richness of the message and match it to the richness of the mode of the communication.[5]

Media Richness Theory states that "lean" messages, such as clarification questions (e.g., "Are we meeting for dinner at 6 or 7 o'clock?"), are best suited for "lean" media, such as email or text messaging, because these types of messages are considered straightforward. "Rich" messages (e.g., telling your spouse that there are problems in your marriage) that include complex and potentially emotional content are expressed best using "rich" media (e.g., face to face or over the telephone); however, these are merely guidelines, and sometimes very "rich" interpersonal interactions (e.g., seeking and receiving social support from others) can occur online.[6] Online interactions can be a lot like face-to-face interactions now, given the advances in technology, which allows us to feel a high level of social presence while relating with others when using these communication media.

Online interaction might also provide certain benefits over face-to-face communication. For example, online support groups can offer you the opportunity to talk to and/or learn from many other people who have faced a similar situation (e.g., your child has a serious illness) but who might have different perspectives.[7] You can also share and discuss these sensitive topics at your convenience and without the challenge of talking in front of others in a face-to-face setting where you might feel apprehensive to talk about such things with strangers.[8] These are some of the benefits of online communication over offline interactions; choosing which is appropriate and functional in a given situation is important and should not be taken lightly.

The second way media impact messages in interpersonal relationships is understood by viewing the medium as part of a causal chain, meaning that the use of one media type might lead to the use of another media type. For example, someone might send a friend a cryptic text message to spark curiosity and get that friend to initiate a phone call. A particularly difficult face-to-face conversation might lead to an apology text or email, or vice versa. A set of Facebook posts about how you are feeling might cause a coworker to stop by your desk and ask you how you are doing and if you need any help at work. If you think about it, probably many of your everyday interactions span across several different communication media. This is not necessarily a bad thing, but you should be mindful when shifting from one form to another to make sure you are not unintentionally violating any norms of communication and/or of the relationship(s) with the other person or people who are a part of the interaction.

Third, the types of media used in a relationship communicate something about that relationship, regardless of the messages that are sent using those media. For example, most people communicate with those they are closest to via several media. For instance, you might communicate with your closest friends or romantic partner face to face, via phone calls, with text messages, through written notes and emails, and through social media such as Facebook, Instagram, or Snapchat on a regular basis. However, you might choose to only communicate with more distant others, such as coworkers with whom you are not particularly close, via face-to-face and email communication. As we become closer to or more distant from particular individuals, the number of channels or types of media through which we communicate might also increase or decrease. Additionally, we might choose to talk with others via specific media to conform to social expectations for that particular type of relationship. For instance, one study found that people tend to engage in everyday talk less often with cross-sex friends than same-sex friends when face to face and on the phone, but these differences are not seen when communicating with same-sex and cross-sex friends online.[9] A female student might be less likely to engage in a lot of everyday talk face to face with a male friend because other friends might begin asking whether they are a romantic couple; instead, those two friends will probably engage in more everyday talk online or through text messages, which allows for less public communication.

As stated earlier, it is important to mindfully choose when to use mediated communication, and the particular form, in order to match it to the message you wish to convey; it is equally important to consider the relationship you have with the person (or want to have with the person). For example, it is likely better to talk to your boss about a salary increase in person instead of sending her an email asking for a raise. This particular message is typically considered a "rich" one, so you should choose a "richer" medium. Also, you want to convey to her that you are assertive, and so talking to her in a face-to-face meeting is the better context for communicating that quality. Emailing her is certainly the less face-threatening choice, but if you want to earn the raise, then showing you are assertive and professional will likely help your case.

Tips for Effective Email Communication

1. Determine whether email is the best medium for your message or interaction. For sensitive topics, you might want to consider having a face-to-face conversation or making a phone call instead.

2. If emailing in a professional relationship, format the email (e.g., use a salutation; include an opening, body, and concluding paragraph; and sign your name) and construct the message accordingly (e.g., use titles when appropriate, such Dr. or Mrs., and use formal language, such as Good Morning or Hello instead of Hey). Always use the person's name versus a generic "Hi" when you are emailing someone in particular. This shows respect as well as attention to detail.

3. Use a meaningful subject line that summarizes your message so the recipient knows what your message is about before she or he begins to read it. If you are emailing a professor about a class, it is also a good idea to include the course number or name in the subject line.

4. Always review your message for typos and other technical errors. This is your message, and it will say something about you and the relationship you have with the person. Don't let the person potentially think you are lazy or don't care about him or her by sending a sloppy message.

5. Consider at what time you send the message. Emails always have a time and date stamp, and these potentially could add meaning to your message in ways you might not immediately recognize. So, think about it before hitting send!

6. Allow adequate time for a reply, if a reply is needed. Once you have received a reply, acknowledge that you received the reply, even if no further information needs to be shared.

7. Remember that email is a written record. Even if you delete an email, the other person may not and it is possible that deleted emails will remain on a server for years after you thought you deleted the message. In some states, all emails on state-owned servers (such as at public universities) are considered public record and can be requested by anyone as part of open records regulations, which are sometimes referred to as "sunshine laws." If you are unsure of whether you want your words kept "on file" or made public, then consider using the telephone or talking to the person face to face instead.

8. Note that ALL CAPS can be interpreted as screaming, so use it and other formatting possibilities with care.

Benefits and Challenges to Mediated Communication

Most of us will initiate, develop, maintain, and/or negotiate our relationships using mediated communication at some point, whether it is in a work relationship, family relationship, friendship, or romantic relationship. There are many benefits as well as challenges to communicating using mediated forms, and it is important to take these into consideration as you choose how to communicate in your various relationships.

One way mediated communication benefits the workplace is when workers use it while telecommuting. Workplaces are increasingly allowing workers to telecommute, which allows employees to spend less time commuting and perhaps have more flexible work arrangements, while simultaneously decreasing the cost of office space for companies. Many large national and international companies frequently need to have teams work together from multiple distant locations. While email and phone communication have been possible in such work situations for years, newer computer-mediated communication has increased productivity and made it easier to navigate time zone differences.[10] The downside to this is that there might also be reduced interpersonal affect and group solidarity, which then can decrease overall team effectiveness over time.[11] However, new technologies that allow for richer communication and increased visual cues during conversations, such as video conferencing, offer the promise of even more effective interpersonal communication in long-distance workplace relationships. At the same time, being online can also have negative effects in the workplace if you become a "cyberslacker" and are too distracted by your technological outlets. A recent Forbes article[12] reported that 64 percent of workers visit non-work related websites daily and waste anywhere between an hour to 10 or more hours of their workday spending time on the Web. There is some evidence, however, that a little bit of "cyberslacking" might increase your productivity if the break in work rejuvenates you for taking on your next task.

> *"Although humans have maintained mediated relationships for millennia, computer technologies create new opportunities for us to maintain relationships. In the coming decades, mediated communication will probably become even more central in our personal and professional lives."*
>
> —*Andrew Ledbetter, Texas Christian University*

You have probably already experienced long-distance family relationships, friendships, and perhaps even romantic relationships, especially if you or some of your friends attended college away from home. It is probably no surprise that the benefits and challenges people face in these types of long-distance interpersonal relationships are different than the challenges they face in workplace relationships.

Military families often experience long-distance relationships (e.g., deployments), and career and educational opportunities often result in people living in separate, physically distant places from their partners or spouses and other family members.[13] Partners and families often use communication technologies because such technologies are cost effective, save time, and allow a sense of connectedness across space. Family members are just a click away, and families may now communicate using Skype or FaceTime, which helps to increase their sense of connection and satisfaction in these relationships. The use of communication technologies can also pose challenges to long-distance family members. The availability of communication via Facebook, for example, can cause some family members to feel too connected and increase their need for clearer boundaries around their relationships.

You likely have friends with whom you communicate using online technologies, and many of them are probably friends who live in different cities, states, and even countries. The advances in communication technologies, such as email and social media sites, have certainly helped people form more friendships and maintain them for longer periods of time. And these relationships are not just with our closest friends; we often create and keep "weak ties" with others, since it is so easy to do so with social media sites such as Facebook. Unfortunately, one potential negative outcome of spending time "catching up" with all of our Facebook "friends" is that it can make us depressed. Recent research has shown that time spent on Facebook is negatively related to one's mood.[14] So, why do we continue to spend time on Facebook? The same research speculated that we make an "affective forecasting error," where we expect the time we spend on Facebook will actually make us feel better, when in reality it can make us feel worse. It's important to remember to spend time talking to your friends on the phone or in person in addition to using these technologies. A careful balance of face-to-face and mediated communication should help maintain these relationships for years to come.

Long-distance romantic relationships also can benefit as well as be challenged by reliance on communication technologies such as texting, email, and social media sites. Of course, the available technologies allow romantic partners to communicate while they are apart, and their regular use has been shown to positively affect these relationships.[15] However, long-distance romantic partners typically limit their conversations to topics that won't provoke conflict. Most couples want to keep the conversations they do have positive.[16] The distance can place pressure on couples to make the limited time they have together extra special. But these patterns of interaction translate into partners **idealizing** their relationship, which means they hold a false sense of the relationship that highlights the positive.[17] The planning and pressure for intensive togetherness time can take a toll on the couple and limit the amount of time they have available to spend with friends and family, which adds even more stress to the relationship.[18]

Fortunately, the availability of numerous forms of mediated communication, including many channels that allow partners to hear changes in vocal tone and see facial expressions, have made it easier for relational partners to initiate, develop, and maintain frequent and meaningful communication across distances. But, as discussed above, we must also be aware of the potential challenges these communication technologies pose for our relationships. In the last section of this chapter, we provide some advice for using these media so you maximize their potential benefits.

Idealization
the practice of perceiving only the positives of a person and/or a relationship

Dialogic Communication in Mediated Relationships

While the opportunities for communication via different technologies are numerous, the possibilities for deceiving, offending, and even hurting someone while using them are

DIALING DIVERSITY

Everyone seems to be online these days. This is increasingly true for people in the United States age 50 and older. Recent estimates report upwards of 77 percent of 50-64 year olds and 53 percent of people 65 and older are online, and one in three are using social media.[19] This picture is quite different from even 10 years ago, when, for example, the number of people 65 or older online was less than half what it is today. Social media, such as Facebook and Instagram, are great places for keeping up to date on immediate and extended family members, and more than 70 percent of senior citizens typically use the Internet daily. It seems that when given the training necessary to navigate the online world, seniors will transform into enthusiastic users. Moreover, the majority of seniors (seven out of 10) own mobile phones. So, if you want to speak with your grandparents and they are not answering their landline, try texting them or messaging them on Facebook—they are likely online!

equally as great. Newspapers are filled with stories every day of someone using Twitter to insult someone else, people losing their jobs for Facebook posts, or even individuals pretending to be someone they are not for nefarious reasons. Despite these potential pitfalls, mediated communication provides many opportunities for dialogue and positive interactions that enhance our quality of life. Below we offer some suggestions for fostering and maintaining dialogue when communicating using technology.

Be Honest

As we've discussed in previous chapters, it is important to be honest in order to facilitate dialogue in your communication with others. This couldn't be more important than when talking via technology. Whether you are talking to a client or coworker, or communicating with a family member, friend, or romantic partner, being sincere will pay off in the long run.

Consider if the Medium Fits the Message

Always choose the technology to fit the message. For example, don't manage conflict with your partner through wall posts on your Facebook page. This not only allows all of your friends to see your conflict, it also creates distrust in the relationship. In other words, think before you post.

Take Care with What You Share

Always remember that what you post on the Internet has the potential to come back and haunt you later on. This is particularly important today, since employers often check the social media sites of job candidates. You also never know who might be seeing your texts; even if you delete a text message from your phone, it is possible for the person to whom you sent the message to share the message with others, and it is sometimes possible for phone companies to retrieve past messages. So, make sure you can live with the consequences if your messages get into the wrong hands!

Avoid Using Media to Maintain Relationships

While technology has added so many opportunities to manage our relationships, we must be cautious that we don't rely too heavily on them. If you want to have healthy, long-lasting ties, you are best served by using a mixture of face-to-face and online communication with your partners. In order for your relational partners to want to continue their ties with you, they must see that you not only want them on your list of friends but also that you care enough to visit them in person or call them on the phone on a regular basis.

Interact Online as if Face to Face

There are numerous examples of people who take to online blogs, comment forums, websites, and even text messages to use the advantage of distance from the recipient to send hostile, rude, or aggressive statements. In 2013, San Francisco 49ers placekicker David Akers was on the receiving end of death threats by fans for his performance, prompting him to quit Twitter. Doubtless, those fans would not have said these things if they were right in front of David Akers. Treat your mediated messages as if the person is standing in front of you, and convey the respect and dignity every person deserves.

Summary

In this chapter, we explored the influence media and technology have had on developing and maintaining relationships. We defined the various types of media and social media available for use today, and then examined the impact these tools have on how we define ourselves and others. We also discussed some of the benefits and challenges that media and social media bring to relationship maintenance. Finally, we provided some tips for engaging in social media and mediated communication in a way that facilitates dialogue and minimizes the potential pitfalls that can occur without your conversational partner in front of you.

Chapter 12 Key Ideas

- Some forms of mediated communication are synchronous, which means that the partners communicate simultaneously, while others are asynchronous, which means that messages are sent and received at different times

- Mediated communication can be impersonal, or based primarily on facilitating a transaction, or hyperpersonal, which is when mediated communication has higher levels of affection, emotion, liking, solidarity, and intimacy than face-to-face conversation
- The medium through which we choose to communicate can impact our interpersonal relationships, lead to the use of other media, and communicate something about the relationships
- Mediated communication can have both rewards and challenges when it is used to maintain local or long-distance relationships

Chapter 12 Key Terms

Synchronous communication	Impersonal communication	Idealization
Asynchronous communication	Hyperpersonal communication	
Social Media	Catfishing	

References

1 Carey, J. (1995). Time, space, and the telegraph. In D. Crowley and P. Heyer, *Communication in history: Technology, culture and society* (154-158). White Plains, NY: Longman.

2 Walther, J. B. (1996). Computer-mediated communication: Impersonal, interpersonal, and hyperpersonal interaction. *Communication Research, 23*, 3-43. doi: 10.1177/009365096023001001

3 Ellison, N. B., Steinfield, C., & Lampe, C. (2007). The benefits of facebook "friends:" Social capital and college students' use of online social networking sites. *Journal of Computer-Mediated Communication, 12*, 1143-1168. doi: 10.1111/j.1083-6101.2007.00367.x

4 Ledbetter, A. M. (2014). The past and future of technology in interpersonal communication theory and research. *Communication Studies, 65*, 456-459. doi: 10.1080/10510974.2014.927298

5 Daft, R. L., & Lengel, R. H. (1984). Information richness: A new approach to managerial behavior and organizational design. *Research in Organizational Behavior, 6*, 191-233.

6 Wright, K. B., & Muhtaseb, A. (2011). In K. B. Wright & L. M. Webb (Eds.), *Computer-mediated communication in personal relationships* (pp. 137-155). New York, NY: Peter Lang.

7 Ibid.

8 Ibid.

9 Ledbetter, A. M., Broeckelman-Post, M. A., & Krawsczyn, A. M. (2010). Modeling everyday talk: Differences across communication media and sex composition of friendship dyads. *Journal of Social and Personal Relationships, 28*, 223-241. doi: 10.1177/0265407510377904

10 Nie, N. H., Hillygus, D. S., & Erbring, L. (2002). Internet use, interpersonal relations, and sociability. In B. Wellman & C. Haythornthwaite (Eds.), *The Internet in everyday life* (pp. 215-243). Malden, MA: Blackwell.

11 Walther, J. B. (1996). Computer-mediated communication: Impersonal, interpersonal, and hyperpersonal interaction. *Communication Research, 23*, 3-43. doi: 10.1177/009365096023001001

12 Conner, C. (September 7, 2013). Who wastes the most time at work? *Forbes.com*. Retrieved from http://www.forbes.com/sites/cherylsnappconner/2013/09/07/who-wastes-the-most-time-at-work/

13 Sahlstein, E. (2010). Communication and distance: The present and future interpreted through the past. *Journal of Applied Communication Research, 38*, 106-114. doi: 10.1080/00909880903483615

14 Sagioglou, C., & Greitemeyer, T. (2014). Facebook's emotional consequences: Why Facebook causes a decrease in mood and why people still use it. *Computers in Human Behavior, 35*, 359-363.

15 Dainton, M. & Aylor, A. (2002). Patterns of communication channel use in the maintenance of long-distance relationships. *Communication Research Reports, 19*, 118-129.

16 Sahlstein, E. M. (2004). Relating at a distance: Negotiating being together and being apart in long-distance relationships. *Journal of Social and Personal Relationships, 21*, 689-702

17 Stafford, L. (2005). *Maintaining long-distance and cross-residential relationships*. Mahwah, NJ: Erlbaum.

18 Sahlstein, E. (2006). Making plans: Praxis strategies for negotiating uncertainty-certainty in long-distance relationships. *Western Journal of Communication, 70*, 147-165. doi: 10.1080/10570310600710042

19 Zickuhr, K. & Madden, M. (June 6, 2012). Older adults and Internet use. Pew Research Center. Retrieved from http://www.pewinternet.org/2012/06/06/main-report-15/

Chapter 13

Interpersonal Conflict

One of the most misunderstood elements of human life is the friction that can develop among people over values, ideas, material objects, respect, and attitudes. These conflicts can be small in scale, like those that occur between romantic partners or colleagues, or larger in scale, such as those that lead to aggressive and sometimes even violent altercations between communities. Regardless of the scope or scale, **conflict** often encourages an uncomfortable feeling in people and the closer proximity of the individuals, the more uncomfortable the conflict feels.

Perhaps if we understood conflict a bit more we might manage it so these situations would become beneficial rather than potentially destructive. Conflict, after all, is natural, and not always a bad thing. If managed appropriately, conflict can result in relationship growth between people. On the other hand, if managed poorly, it can lead to the dissolution of the bond between individuals. Make no mistake, however, we are not proposing communication can always resolve conflicts. It can, however, help avoid some conflicts and work through others. Communication is, after all, both a source of conflict and the way in which we resolve the tensions created by conflict.

Conflict
an expressed struggle between at least two interdependent parties who perceive incompatible goals, scarce resources, and interference from the other party in achieving those goals

In this chapter, we explore the concept of interpersonal conflict by first defining it and examining some reasons why we perceive conflict as negatively as we typically do. We will then identify and explain the primary reasons conflict exists in interpersonal relationships before discussing good and bad ways we manage conflicts. Finally, we will offer some concrete advice for how we can use the principles of dialogue to ensure we maximize our ability to turn conflict into a positive and not a negative.

Defining Conflict

The most widely accepted scholarly definition of interpersonal **conflict** was offered by William Wilmot and Joyce Hocker: "an expressed struggle between at least two interdependent parties who perceive incompatible goals, scarce resources, and interference from the other party in achieving those goals."[1] In this part of the chapter, we will break down this definition, clarifying what actually constitutes conflict and what does not. We will also explore some of the metaphors we use to describe conflict and how they, as powerful language devices, influence our approaches toward conflict.

Expressed Struggle

The key word in this part of the definition of conflict is not struggle, but rather "expressed," because you cannot actually be in an interpersonal conflict with someone unless both of you are aware there is a difference between you. The expression of the conflict is fundamental for conflict, but it does not need to be expressed through verbal statements alone. In fact, romantic partners often realize they are in a disagreement simply by the looks on each other's faces. Nonverbal expression can express a dispute with someone sometimes even more effectively than the content of what is or might be spoken! Think about saying you agree with someone or that you are "OK," when your nonverbal reaction communicates the opposite. Such a behavior may contribute to the expression of a struggle between two people.

The second half of the phrase, "struggle," can mean a variety of things. It can simply mean a disagreement with someone or something stronger than merely disagreeing. Struggle may sound physical in nature, but often it is more a "tug-of-war" over ideas, values, or decisions. Whenever two or more sides present arguments in favor of differing positions on the same topic, then there is a struggle.

Two Interdependent Parties

Not all expressed disagreement constitutes a conflict, as the parties must also depend upon each other for something. For instance, you may disagree with a political leader over his or her position on something. Even if you make that dissent loud and clear, this is not actually a conflict because you do not depend on the leader for anything. Romantic partners and families, on the other hand, often engage in interpersonal conflicts because they depend upon each other. Romantic partners depend upon each other for a host of things, and thus conflict becomes a natural part of their lives. Children in families require the food, housing, and love that parents provide, while parents also want the joy and company of their children.

It is important to note, however, that interdependency does not require a familial or romantic connection. When we dine at a restaurant and interact with a server or cook, there is a small degree of interdependency. The restaurant employee depends on us having a good experience so we pay our bill and tip well, while we depend on him or her for providing a pleasurable experience and delivering delicious food. There is, then, an interdependent relationship that can create conflict. If you have a problem with the food or the service, or on the other hand, if you are rude to the staff of the restaurant, then a conflict can ensue, as it will quickly become an expressed struggle between two interdependent parties.

Perceived Incompatible Goals and Scarce Resources

Here again we find two dimensions of the phrase that require attention. The first is the idea that perception is key to conflict. Recall our conversation regarding perception from earlier in the book, and remember it is different for everyone. That is, we can experience the same event as someone else but perceive it differently. The potential for perceptual differences to create conflict then becomes readily apparent. Often, conflicts emerge when two people seek to achieve different goals, and this results in some rather significant disputes.

People who are interdependent by definition work together, but doing so with different ideas about the aim of their joint efforts invites conflict. In some instances, we do not see that we are working together to achieve different goals until we get to the end, but

DIALING DIVERSITY

In Chapter 2, we discussed cultural influences on communication, and nowhere is this made more apparent than in the strategies people from different cultural backgrounds typically rely on for conflict management. For example, individualistic cultures such as the United States tend to emphasize the competing or avoiding approaches to conflict. This is driven by the individual nature of the culture; people feel like if something is important to them, they must win it. Also, if something is

uncomfortable, people in individualistic cultures often believe they should not put themselves in such a situation if they can avoid it. On the flip side, collectivist cultures like China emphasize compromise and accommodation, because they seek to reduce discord and discomfort for everyone. Just as there are myriad diverse groups in the world, so too are there myriad reasons behind why we choose one conflict management style over another.

Hidden agenda
a goal we keep
secret from other
parties while
working with them

there are also times when people have **hidden agendas**. A hidden agenda is a goal we keep secret from other parties while working with them. It is both disheartening and upsetting when we discover that someone working with us had a hidden agenda, and expressing those feelings to the other person creates conflict.

Different perceived goals are not the only thing that may result in a dispute, as perceived scarce resources also create opportunities for disagreements. We often deal with finite resources, such as time, money, and material objects, and sometimes we cannot equitably share these resources with others. For instance, you and a friend may interview for the same job, but there is only one position to be had. This can create an uncomfortable situation between you. Within romantic relationships, spending time with each other is very important, but if one partner does not feel she or he is being attended to adequately, the person may express this concern and create a conflict regarding time management for the relationship. Money can also come between people, as there is only a finite amount that someone can spend or use. It can prove distressing when choices need to be made about spending funds.

Interference from the Other Party

In addition to perceiving incompatible goals and scarce resources, the parties might believe the other is, or will be, interfering with achieving the goal or acquiring the resources necessary to achieve the goal. Interference can come in many forms, such as physical obstruction, political maneuvering, or even an unwillingness to express or provide support for the effort. Although it may just seem like you are remaining neutral when you fail to provide support or encouragement, the other person actually can understand it as interference. Perceived interference creates a defensive climate between two parties, and a defensive climate suggests there is some assault to defend against.

How We Talk About Conflict

In Chapter 5, we discussed language and explained how some of the ornamental linguistic devices like metaphors are powerful tools in describing how we see the world. Conflict is a prime example of how the metaphors we use to describe this abstract concept reveal our perceptions and feelings about engaging in disputes with other people.

One of the most common sets of metaphoric expressions for conflict used by people reveals an interpretation of it as aggressive, nasty, and something to avoid. Look at the following ways we describe conflict: "conflict as war," "conflict as a fight," "conflict as trial and tribulation," and "conflict as explosive." Each of these invites aggressive tactics aimed at completely dominating the other party. There is no good will, emphasis on collaboration or compromise, and certainly no respect for the other person. When we describe conflict this way, we encourage "surrender" by the other person, and it is no surprise that when we encounter people who see conflict in this manner, we often just want to avoid it.

Another set of metaphors people use to describe conflict illustrates a more strategic and less aggressive construction of it. Think about these metaphoric descriptions of conflict:

CHAPTER 13 • Interpersonal Conflict

"conflict is a game," "conflict is a bargaining exercise," "conflict is a dance." Games, bargains, and dances all require some type of strategy or movement to counter the other side. Those who use these metaphors often enjoy conflict as a mental exercise to achieve their own ends while out maneuvering the other person. These metaphors still see conflict as something to win and not work through, but to these people, winning the conflict involves subtler and less aggressive approaches to making that happen.

The way we describe conflict can influence how we approach disputes when they arise. If we think of conflict as "an opportunity" and "a journey," we might then see the positive prospects it can provide. These types of metaphors encourage a more optimistic and less dreary approach to these challenging situations that allow us to grow as partners, friends, and colleagues.

Reasons that Conflict Exists

When we unraveled the definition of conflict, we identified that its primary sources are perceived incompatible goals and scarce resources. As you might recall from Chapter 3, perception can be impacted by many different factors and plays an important role in our self-concept, how we perceive others, and the reasons to which we attribute others' behaviors. These differences in perception mean that we all see the world a little bit differently, which is why most conflicts arise in the first place. Douglas Stone, Bruce Patton, and Sheila Heen, who are part of the Harvard Negotiation Project, explain that there are three primary reasons why we have different stories about our experiences, which are ultimately the root of most conflicts.[2]

We Have Different Information

Even though we might have been involved in the exact same encounter at the exact same time as another person, we both walked away from the situation with different information and experiences. This is partly due to us noticing different things. For example, consider a person who took her niece and nephew to a parade last year. During the parade, the aunt, who once played in a marching band, noticed which marching bands were in sync with each other, whether certain parts of songs were played correctly, and whether various groups marching in the parade were spaced appropriately to not interfere with each other's performances. After the parade, though, the niece just talked about the dancers and baton twirlers, and the nephew talked about all of the different types of fire trucks and horses. Even though all three watched the same parade, they each had very different information and memories about the parade afterward and were somewhat oblivious to the information the others noticed.

Similarly, we often come away from important conversations and experiences having noticed very different things and are sometimes completely unaware of elements that were especially important to another person. For instance, one person might leave a meeting furious that she was constantly interrupted by one of her colleagues and did not have the opportunity to speak, while another person might leave the same meeting happy that there was so much spirited debate about an important issue.

Additionally, we have access to information about ourselves that others do not, and others have access to information about themselves that we do not. You know more about your own previous experiences as well as the situational factors impacting your behavior in a particular moment, than anyone else does. When you are frustrated that one of your coworkers shows up to work late and is unable to focus, you might not know that she did not get any sleep the night before because she was studying for an important exam, just found out that her grandfather was diagnosed with a serious medical condition, and had a flat tire on her way to work. Your coworker might not know that you arrived early and were hoping to finish work a little bit early in order to get to an important event, and that you are wary of working with others after you have been working on a project with a partner who is not doing his part.

We Have Different Interpretations

Even if we have the same information about a situation, we might interpret that experience very differently based on our past experiences and the implicit rules we live by. We have assumptions about what the world is like and how things should be based on the families, communities, and cultures we were raised in, when in fact others might have vastly different experiences. We might have beliefs about how birthdays should be celebrated, how we should greet friends and family members, whether it's normal to go on vacation every year, how to celebrate important holidays, whether or not to arrive a little bit late for a dinner party, whether it is OK to squeeze the toothpaste tube from the middle of the tube, who in the household does the cooking or mows the lawn, or whether spanking is a normal part of child discipline.

These and many other experiences can seem like ordinary, everyday practices that we take for granted, but when we encounter others who have different sets of assumptions about what the "rules" are for everyday life, conflict can ensue. If you grew up in a community where being invited to dinner at 7:00 meant you should arrive sometime between 7:10 p.m. and 7:15 p.m. to give the host a few extra minutes to prepare, you might think your guests are being rude when they arrive at 8:00 p.m. or 6:45 p.m., instead. If you grew up in a community where it was normal to shake hands when you greet a close friend, you might feel like a friend who greets you with a kiss on the cheek is being inappropriately intimate, while that same friend might think you are being rude and standoffish to offer a handshake. Many of these implicit rules that guide our interpretations are influenced heavily by dimensions of culture, as we learned earlier in the book, while others might stem from everyday local experiences. However, our different interpretations leave us with very different emotional responses, and those differing emotional responses can result in conflict and difficult conversations.

Our Conclusions Reflect Self-Interest

Confirmation bias the tendency to look for and remember information that is consistent with what we believe or what we want to happen

We have a tendency to look for and remember information that is consistent with what we believe or want to see, and to ignore or forget information that contradicts our beliefs and hopes. This tendency is called **confirmation bias**, and it leads to overconfidence in our own beliefs, even in the presence of contradictory evidence. This tendency often occurs when

we are making financial decisions, such as evaluating
deciding which type of car to buy. It is even strong
ally charged issues or deeply held beliefs, such as
allowed. We are usually unaware that our perceptio
ing information that supports our beliefs rather th
fairly. When we disagree with another person abou
individuals are basing their argument on biased i
which might make our differences seem larger t
on issues sometimes become an important part
cult situation if we feel like a disagreement abou
kind of person we are (lovable or unlovable, ki

Because we have differences in wha
shared information, and confirmation biases that make our p
might otherwise be, we often find ourselves in conflict with others, someti...
might seem fairly insignificant on the surface. If we work first, however, to understand w...
the other person is coming from and how he or she sees the situation, rather than jumping to
conclusions about who is right or wrong, what was intended, or who is to blame, we can often
find ways to resolve seemingly difficult situations in a way that satisfies both parties.

Whether or
almost en
is focus
beh

Contempt
the expression
insults and d
for a perso
his beh
idea

Conflict Management

Knowing what conflict is and where it comes from is only part of the process in handling
disputes in a positive and beneficial way. The other ingredient is knowing what behaviors
contribute to a negative conflict communication spiral and what different strategies are
available for resolving conflict. Many conflicts can either be resolved quickly or avoided
altogether if people recognized the behaviors being exhibited and that contributed to the
situation, and worked to change them in a collaborative way. In this part of the chapter, we
will first outline four behaviors that do not help resolve conflict and even make it worse,
and then we will detail the five primary strategies available for managing different conflicts.

Problem Behaviors

There are four primary problematic behaviors that create and sustain negative conflicts between individuals. In fact, these behaviors are so damaging to relationships that
Psychologist John Gottman was able to watch newlywed couples interact and identify
which ones would remain married and which would divorce with more than 90 percent
accuracy just by watching for these behaviors.[3] We will explore each of these four behaviors,
which he refers to as the Four Horsemen of the Apocalypse, before moving on to discuss
various strategies for managing conflict.

Criticism. One of the primary sources of interpersonal conflict are statements that are critical
of the behavior, attitude, or other characteristics of someone else. **Criticism** is the expression
of disapproval of someone or something based upon perceived faults in a person or behavior.

Criticism
the expression
of disapproval
of someone or
something based
upon perceived
faults in a person
or behavior

not criticism makes a negative or positive contribution to a relationship depends entirely on the language used and the manner in which it is delivered. When criticism is based on behaviors, then it can be constructive and helpful because people can adjust behaviors; however, when the criticism is focused on personality or character, then it can be destructive. Providing constructive criticism is a helpful skill not just for romantic partners, but also for managers who often need help changing employee behaviors without seeming to attack the individuals themselves.

Contempt. A second major contributor to negative conflict within a relationship is the expression of contempt. Contempt is different from criticism, because it is almost exclusively negative. **Contempt** involves the expression of insults and disdain for people, their behaviors, and their ideas. Statements exhibiting contempt often are accompanied with nonverbal behaviors that indicate a disparaging opinion of the person, such as a furrowed brow, a snarl, or even a dismissive exhale of breath. Expressions of contempt have a universally negative impact on the receiver and often function to diminish his or her self-esteem within the relationship. Insults and demeaning expressions can have catastrophic effects on interpersonal relationships in any setting.

Defensiveness. In Chapter 4, we introduced communication scholar Jack Gibbs, who identified specific behaviors that create a defensive communication climate. Such a climate reduces listening, increases aggressiveness, and inhibits understanding and dialogue in a relationship. Recall that the behaviors that create a defensive climate include making evaluative statements about the other person, trying to control the behaviors of another or the outcome of the interaction, withholding information to get what one wants, remaining neutral and not expressing empathy or sympathy for the other person, acting superior to the other person, and not engaging in a conversation with an open mind. Defensiveness prevents a person from seeing his or her own role and responsibilities in the situation, and prevents parties from finding common ground when working through conflicts. In some people, this behavior becomes a part of who they are, and they ultimately view themselves as forever a victim of others and of circumstances.

Stonewalling
a complete withdrawal from the conflict, both physically and verbally

Stonewalling. The final problematic behavior people exhibit that contributes to negative conflict experiences is stonewalling. **Stonewalling** involves withdrawing from the conflict interaction. When people stonewall, they might look and/or move away from the other person, and they do not make any comments themselves. Sometimes this occurs because they feel their contributions are not valued or heard, and at other times it is an expression of frustration. Most often it's because they feel overwhelmed by the conflict and use stonewalling to cope with their feelings. Stonewalling can make the situation worse if the other person perceives it as passive-aggressive, whether or not that's the intent. The presence of stonewalling should be a sign that the parties need to take a break, because without both parties present and involved in the conflict, the dispute cannot be overcome and may become worse. If one person continues trying to engage in the conflict and the other person continues to withdraw, then the conflict will likely spiral even further into negativity.

Conflict Management Styles

There are five methods for managing conflict in interpersonal settings, and each approach can be appropriate in some situations and inappropriate in other situations. Most people have a dominant conflict style they tend to use in most conflict situations, but each of us can choose to use any of the five conflict styles based on what will help both parties best resolve the conflict and maintain the relationship. Kenneth Thomas and Ralph Kilmann have developed one of the most-used instruments for identifying conflict styles (see Figure 13.1) and argue that these five conflict styles can be mapped onto two dimensions: assertiveness and cooperativeness.[4] Assertiveness is the degree to which you try to make sure your own concerns are satisfied, and cooperativeness is the degree to which you attempt to satisfy the other person's concerns. In this part of the chapter, we will examine the five strategies for resolving interpersonal conflict and address when each may or may not be the best option available.

FIGURE 13.1   Thomas-Kilmann Conflict Styles

Competing. The **competing** conflict style involves trying to win the argument or to make sure you get the resolution you want, even if the other person is not happy with the outcome. Competing treats an argument like something to win, even at the expense of the other person or any valid points he or she may have. In that respect, this is a win-lose approach to conflict management. There are instances when this approach can be acceptable, such as in a bid for a contract between yourself and another group, or in a job interview. When there can be only one clear winner, this may be a strategy worth employing. However, in interpersonal relationships, a competing approach often yields further discord and unhappiness between partners, because someone always feels like he or she lost out or was not heard, thus leading to feelings of resentment. The competing approach is best used in situations in which you care deeply about the outcome, time is limited, and a decision must be made quickly.

Competing
conflict management strategy that treats an argument like something to win, even if the other person is not happy with the outcome

MEDIATED MOMENTS

In the 2009 film *Couples Retreat*, four couples attend an exotic spa and resort in an attempt to solve issues facing their intimate relationships. Three of the couples go to support their friends, but learn while they are there that they too have issues they need to work through. As part of the retreat package, the couples do numerous activities together while also attending couples therapy sessions. It is in these therapy sessions where each couple exhibits different conflict management styles, all resulting in poor relationship satisfaction for both partners. For instance, the characters of Dave and Ronnie, played by Vince Vaughn and Malin Ackerman, engage in conflict avoidance because they never actually bring up the issues that cause stress between them. Joey (Jon Favreau) and Lucy (Kristin Davis) engage in competing conflict management, which results in quite a few screaming matches between them. Shane (Faizon Love) and Trudy (Kali Hawk), a couple with an age difference of more than twenty years, illustrate accommodating because Shane always gives in to what Trudy wants to do, even when he is exhausted or not interested. Finally, Jason Bateman and Kristen Bell play Jason and Cynthia, who initiated the trip because they had a cold and distant relationship brought about by a consistent clinical approach to conflict management that ignored the emotional elements of the relationship.[5]

Accommodating
A management style defined by a person giving in to the desires and position of the other person. With this approach, the manager loses by sacrificing his or her position and desires to those of the other person

Avoiding
conflict management strategy that involves avoiding the other person, choosing not to express or make a conflict known

Compromising
conflict management strategy by which both sides sacrifice part of what they want while getting something they desire

Accommodating. This second approach represents almost the polar opposite of competing in that you give in to the desires and position of the other person. With **accommodating** you lose by sacrificing your position and desires to those of the other person, thus creating a lose-win scenario. This strategy may work when the issue is not something to which you are attached or on which you hold a particularly strong position. If you can let go and be satisfied with the other person winning the argument or making a decision, then this strategy may help preserve the peace. For example, if your partner cares deeply about seeing his or her family during a particular holiday every year, and you do not feel strongly about seeing your family during that holiday, then that might be a situation in which the best solution is to accommodate your partner's desire to spend that holiday with his or her family every year. However, if you care about the outcome of the conflict and are not comfortable making such a sacrifice, then accommodating is definitely not the best strategy for managing the dispute.

Avoiding. A third strategy available for conflict management is **avoidance**. Avoidance is when there is a brewing conflict, but you choose not to express it and make it known, even going to great lengths to avoid the person with whom you would have the dispute. Avoidance differs from stonewalling in that stonewalling occurs during a conflict, while avoiding tries to ensure the conflict never occurs. Avoiding is a lose-lose approach to conflict management because neither side is able to address the issue and solve the problem, because they are never aware it needs to be addressed. This can lead to festering resentment and distance between two people. Avoidance is not a bad solution when neither you nor your partner feel invested in the issue, but it is not a civil way to approach disputes you or your partner care about, because it denies each of you the ability to assert your own feelings.

Compromising. Many people believe compromise is always the best solution, and this is true in some cases, but not all. **Compromising** represents yet another lose-lose conflict management strategy, because neither partner gets what he or she wants completely, and walks away losing some desired elements. Both sides sacrifice part of what they want, while getting something they want. This strategy takes time, patience, honesty, openness, and understanding to facilitate successfully. In many negotiations, this can be an effective way to proceed, but in more complex conflicts, compromise may not be possible and may not lead to satisfaction for both parties. For example, imagine you and your significant other are trying to decide where to spend Thanksgiving, and each of you wants to spend every Thanksgiving with his or her own family. If you agree to spend Thanksgiving alternate years so that you spend one year with your family and the next year with your partner's family, then you will have reached a compromise that allows each of you to get what you want part of the time, but that also forces each of you to sacrifice your desires part of the time.

Collaborating. The final strategy for conflict management is the most beneficial when used to resolve important issues that both parties care deeply about, as well as the most difficult to accomplish. Like compromise, **collaboration** also requires time, patience, honesty, openness, and effort, but the goal is not to identify aspects both parties can lose. Instead, when collaborating, the goal is to find a solution that allows both parties to win. Win-win scenarios are difficult to manage, and they are not always possible, but when you can employ this approach, you reap relational rewards such as increasing trust, strengthened personal bonds between partners, and satisfaction that everyone won. Collaboration requires that individuals act in good faith and with good will. The key to collaboration is to identify what each party really wants and then try to develop a solution that allows both of those desires to be met. For example, imagine that you and your partner are trying to decide how to spend your evening, and you want to go out to dinner, while your partner wants to go to a party with some friends who are visiting from out of town. If what you really want is a good meal, and what your partner really wants is to have a chance to reconnect with your friends, then through collaboration you might identify a third option that lets you both get what you want, such has hosting a dinner party with your friends or going out to a restaurant to have dinner together. The downside of collaboration is that it can take a great deal of time and can be exhausting, so it is not appropriate to use this conflict style when managing every conflict.

> **Collaborating**
> the most beneficial of the conflict management strategies, one that has as its goal finding a solution that allows both parties to win

Too often we fall into a routine of using one particular conflict management strategy, leading to more and more irresolvable situations and damaged relationships. Instead, treat these as tools in your relational repair toolkit. Not every disagreement can be resolved or managed effectively with the same approach.

Dialogue and Conflict Resolution

As you can probably tell, dialogue is most closely aligned with collaboration as a conflict management style, but its principles allow for effective and rewarding conflict management, regardless of the strategy you employ. Additionally, you may have noticed that there is an emphasis in the chapter on avoiding the creation of a defensive communication climate in conflict situations. To effectively employ dialogue in conflict, it is important to establish a supportive communication climate, and in this section of the chapter, we will provide six guidelines, first identified by communication scholar Jack Gibb,[6] for using good dialogic behaviors when trying to resolve a conflict with another person by doing just that.

Use Description Instead of Evaluation

Descriptive statements focus on behavior and cast no judgments regarding whether the action is right or wrong. They also do not focus on the character of the person. An evaluative statement might look like this: "You are very immature," and this message will almost universally insult the other person and put her or him on the defensive. Instead, a descriptive statement would focus on the behavior, "Talking to the person next to you during a presentation is distracting to the speaker." This statement focuses on the behavior without making the person feel like her or his entire identity is being judged as negative, and is thus more likely to be received better.

> *"Unhappy couples get into what is called a "Markov absorbing state" of negative affect, meaning that it is easy to enter, and hard to exit. The reason for this "Roach Hotel Model" (they check into negative affect but they don't check out) is that Repair processes fail in unhappy relationships; as good as it gets is that we all mess up communication, but only master couples can repair effectively. Effective repair requires having a 'positive story of us.'"*
>
> —*John Gottman,* Author of The Seven Principles for Making Marriage Work

Focus on Solving the Problem, Not Controlling the Outcome

Conflicts always occur due to some problem, and often the two parties either understand the problem differently or have different ways of solving the problem. Rather than trying to control which solution gets enacted, focus on determining which solution is most effective at solving the problem. Don't be concerned with taking credit for identifying the solution, but focus on solving the problem together. A control statement might look like, "Let's just do this the way I suggested; we have talked it through enough." This closes down opportunities for participation by making the decision for everyone else. It results in less buy-in from the partner or group and negative feelings toward you. Instead, use statements that focus on the problem, like: "We have three potential ways forward, so let's see which one gets us to where we want to be with minimal hassle."

Be Spontaneous, Not Strategic

Strategic statements always attempt to either pressure people to do something by using leverage, or they attempt to conceal an agenda from the other party. Spontaneous statements, on the other hand, are open and allow the other person to make a pressure-free decision or contribution to the discussion. A strategic statement like "You owe me for helping you write that report when you had a family emergency, remember?" could easily be turned into something less forceful. The spontaneous version would look something like, "I have a project I could really use some help with. Are you able to spend some time with me on it?" This latter example does not leverage anything and allows the other party to make a meaningful contribution. The strategic version, on the other hand, just served to create a guilt trip for the recipient.

Express Empathy, Not Neutrality

Empathy is the ability to put yourself in the shoes of the other person and try to see things from his or her perspective. This is the opposite of not taking sides and trying to remain removed from the situation. Conflicts always have an emotional dimension to them, and so treating them with a clinical, purely objective approach often leaves people feeling less than satisfied with the solution. A neutral statement of "I do not want to get involved with the disagreement between you and your roommate," could easily be turned into an empathic statement of "I understand that when your roommate lets the dishes pile up it bothers you. Perhaps you should try and talk to her about it." This allows you to acknowledge the emotional dimension of the dispute without coming across as distant, and still keeps you from getting involved.

Empathy
the ability to put yourself in the shoes of the other person and try and see things from his or her perspective

Acknowledge Equality, Don't Be Superior

In some situations, we fall back on our expertise or experience as though it makes us better or more qualified than someone else. When we point to something about us that makes us better than other people it makes them feel disrespected and defensive. Even if you do know something others do not, don't assume this makes you better than or capable of judging them. Statements like, "That was a stupid thing to do," or "Why would you go and do a thing like that?" contain an air of superiority because implicit in them is the idea that you know better than the other person. This creates a defensive climate and creates tension in conflict situations. Instead, express equality for people by developing mutual trust and an openness to their way of thinking or perception of the situation.

Be Provisional and Not Certain

Certain statements close off flexibility and options, making it appear as though there is only one way to proceed. More often than not, flexibility is possible, and when you express an ability to be flexible and open to different ideas, then it can de-escalate tensions between you and your partner. This is called **provisionalism.** Instead of saying something needs to be completed right now, consider softening the claim to "when you have a moment, please take care of this." This allows the other person to negotiate his or her time and effort and feel like there is flexibility in fulfilling the request. Provisionalism expresses good will, while certainty does not.

Provisionalism
the expression of an ability to be flexible and open to different ideas

As you can see, creating a supportive climate takes work, but when you use supportive communication behaviors in any interaction, it becomes more likely those actions will be reciprocated by the other party, making it easier to negotiate the conflict and come to a collaborative resolution where everyone wins.

Summary

Conflict is an inevitable part of human interaction, and the negative stigma that often accompanies it makes managing disputes in a positive fashion a challenge. In this chapter, we defined conflict and explored the different metaphors we use to characterize it. We also examined the various sources of conflict in relationships and identified both problematic behaviors we might use in a conflict and more effective and potentially constructive methods for managing the disputes. Finally, using the work of communication scholar Jack Gibbs, we provided six guidelines for employing dialogue to create a supportive, rather than defensive, communication climate when engaging in efforts to resolve conflict.

Chapter 13 Key Ideas

- Conflict is "an expressed struggle between at least two interdependent parties who perceive incompatible goals, scarce resources, and interference from the other party in achieving those goals"
- Conflict often exists because we have different information, different interpretations, and different conclusions that reflect self-interest, even about shared experiences
- The Four Horsemen of the Apocalypse or behaviors that damage relationships, include criticism, contempt, defensiveness, and stonewalling
- There are five conflict styles based on the level of assertiveness and cooperativeness of each individual. These five conflict styles are competing, collaborating, avoiding, accommodating, and compromising

Chapter 13 Key Terms

Conflict	Stonewalling	Collaborating
Hidden agenda	Competing	Empathy
Confirmation bias	Accommodating	Provisionalism
Criticism	Avoiding	
Contempt	Compromising	

References

1 Wilmot, W. W. & Hocker, J. L. (2001). *Interpersonal conflict.* New York: McGraw-Hill.

2 Stone, D., Patton, B., & Heen, S. (1999). *Difficult conversations.* New York, NY: Penguin.

3 Gottman, J. (2003). *The mathematics of marriage.* Cambridge, MA: MIT Press.

4 Thomas, K. W. (1992). Conflict and conflict management: Reflections and update. *Journal of Organizational Behavior, 13,* 265-274.

5 Stuber, S. (producer), Vaughn, V. (producer), and Billingsley, P. (director). (2009). *Couples retreat* [Motion picture]. United States: Universal Pictures.

6 Gibb, J. R. (1961). Defensive communication. *Journal of Communication 11* (3): 141-148.

ANNOTATED BIBLIOGRAPHY
ASSIGNMENT

For this part of the assignment, you will look for and evaluate sources that you can use for your explanatory speech. After you have selected your topic, you should find **five sources** as follows:
1. One book
2. One scholarly journal article
3. One newspaper or magazine article
4. One credible website or media clip
5. One interview with an expert. For this interview, you will need to identify an expert on your topic (perhaps a professor, a professional, or someone else who has significant experience and expertise in this area), develop a list of interview questions, schedule an appointment, and conduct the interview. You should take extensive notes during the interview that you can then use to complete this assignment. You will need to plan ahead to complete this portion of the assignment!

For each of these sources, do the following:
1. Label the type of source.
2. Write the APA format citation that you would include in your references list.
3. Write a one paragraph summary of the source using your own words.
4. Write another paragraph evaluating the source. Will it be a helpful source to include in your speech? Why or why not?

Please type and single space your responses using 12 point Times New Roman font.

Upload your Annotated Bibliography on Blackboard before class on the day that the assignment is due.

Writing Guide for APA Style

Setting up your APA style document

Before typing, change the document settings as follows:
1. 1" margins all the way around; headers and footers should be set to .5."
2. Double spacing for essays, single spacing for outlines, no spaces before and after.
3. Times New Roman font, Size 12, Black text.

A few tips for writing academic papers:

1. Do not use contractions (don't, didn't, weren't, I'd, etc.).
2. Do not use clichés ("the cat's out of the bag," "at the end of the day," "stop and smell the roses," etc.).
3. Do not use colloquialisms (slang, ain't, nothin', or other local language not shared by most speakers).
4. When citing other sources, talking about others' work, or talking about events that have already occurred, you should use the past tense (was, did, were, etc.). Only use present tense when you are talking about ongoing events.
5. Proofread your document for APA and grammatical errors such as misplaced words, word choice, and spelling. It is a good idea to find three other people who can proofread your paper and mark errors for you as well.

Citing sources in your outline:

In most academic papers written in APA format, you should include the author's last name and the year of publication in parentheses at the end of the sentence. If you use a direct quotation, then you should also add the page number. However, in your speech outlines for this class, you should cite your sources in your outline exactly the same way you plan to cite them out loud in your speech and add a references page to the end of your outline.

Citing sources verbally in your speech:

In the verbal/oral citation, you should include four things: (1) the author or source's last name, (2) the author or source's credentials, (3) the name of the publication, and (4) the date. *Example:* "According to Paul Krugman, a Nobel-Prize winning economist and professor at Princeton University, in the September 2, 2009 *New York Times*, most economists' blindness to the possibility of catastrophe contributed to last year's recession.

The following page includes examples of an APA-formatted reference page, organized by type of source. For further details, please also see the Purdue Owl website at https://owl.english.purdue.edu/owl/resource/560/01/

References

Academic Journal Article (paginated by volume):

Author last name, A. A., Author, B. B., & Author, C. C. (year). Title of article. *Title of Journal, Volume*

    number, pages. doi: XXXXX

> Notice that the words in the article title are not capitalized, but the words in the journal title are capitalized.

Mazer, J. P., & Thompson, B. (2011). Student academic support: A validity test. *Communication*

    Research Reports, 28, 214-224.

    doi: 10.1080/08824096.2011.586074

> Notice that all sources that are more than one line are indented after the first line. To do this in Word, highlight your references list, click on paragraph, and choose "Hanging" in the dropdown menu under "Special." All of your references should also be in alphabetical order.

Book:

Author last name, A. A. (year). *Title of work: Capital letter also for subtitle.* Location: Publisher.

Lipson, C. (2004). *Doing honest work in college.* Chicago, IL: University of Chicago Press.

Interview:

A. Last Name, personal communication, date.

> Typically an interview is cited in text, but not in the references list. For this class, though, please include your interviews in your references list.

L. E. Schmeidler, personal communication, March 20, 2014

Magazine:

Author last name, A. A., Author, B. B., & Author, C. C. (year). Title of article. *Title of magazine,*

    Volume number (Issue number), pages.

Bernasek, A. (2014, March 21). Life in the slow lane. *Newsweek, 1* (162), 1.

Newspaper:

Author last name, A. A., Author, B. B., & Author, C. C. (year). Title of article. *Title of Newspaper,*

    Volume number (Issue number), pages.

> Notice that the newspaper is the only type of source with p. or pp. in front of the page numbers.

Santos, F. (2014, March 20). Two states win court approval on voter rules. *The New York Times,* p. 1.

Website:

Author last name, A. A. (date last updated). *Title of document.* Retrieved from http://address.

National Institutes of Health. (2014, March). *Headache pain: What to do when your head hurts.*

    Retrieved from http://newsinhealth.nih.gov/issue/mar2014/feature2

Annotated Bibliography Assignment Grading Rubric

This assignment will be uploaded to Blackboard and graded online using the rubric shown below. **Each** of your five sources will be evaluated using the following criteria:

	Missing	C	B	A
Source quality	Source is inappropriate for this speech and/or does not meet the source type requirements	Source is not a high-quality source that would be appropriate for use in an informative speech on this topic	Source would be acceptable to use for the informative speech, but is not the best possible source of information	Source would be an excellent source of information for an informative speech on this topic
APA citation	No APA citation is included for this source	Citation is included, but is not formatted properly	Citation is included and is written in APA format, but has one or two minor mistakes	Citation is written in perfect APA format
Summary	No original summary paragraph is included for this source	Includes a few sentences that do not adequately summarize the source	Includes a short paragraph in student's own words and adequately summarizes the source	Includes a well-written complete paragraph in the student's own words that clearly summarizes this source and demonstrates understanding of its meaning
Evaluation	No evaluation paragraph is included for this source	Includes a few sentences that evaluate the source as a separate paragraph, but the evaluation does not assess both the overall source quality and usefulness of the source for the informative speech assignment	Evaluates the quality of the source and its usefulness in a separate paragraph, but does not explicitly draw on concepts from the textbook in the evaluation	Evaluates the quality of the source using concepts from the textbook (is the source clear, competent, objective, etc.) and explains why this will or will not be a useful source for the speaker's informative speech in a well-written, complete paragraph

EXPLANATORY SPEECH

Overview:

The purpose of your explanatory speech is teach your audience something about a topic that is <u>related to your major or intended career</u>. In this speech, you are not trying to change your audience's attitudes, actions, or beliefs— you will do that in your persuasive speech a little bit later this semester. For this speech, you should teach your audience something that is a specialized concept, a key historic figure, or important historic development in your area of interest. For example, an agronomist might talk about how Norman Borlaugh developed hybrids of wheat and rice that would later keep entire nations from dying of starvation, a biologist might explain how unchecked cell growth leads to cancer, a communication student might teach about how the Theory of Reasoned Action explains how we make decisions, a musician might explain the difference between analog and digital music recordings, and a computer scientist might explain how computer security algorithms work and teach the audience how to create more secure passwords.

When brainstorming ideas and selecting a topic for your explanatory speech, you should begin by asking yourself a series of questions about each topic that you consider:
1. Is this topic about something related to your major or career?
2. Is this an appropriate topic for an explanatory speech in a scholarly setting?
3. Is this a topic in which I am interested? Is this topic important to me?
4. Do I have expertise in this area or want to learn more about this subject?
5. Will my audience be interested in this topic?
6. How much does my audience already know about this topic? Will this teach them something new?
7. Will learning more about this topic help or improve my audience in some way?

After selecting a topic, you should develop a specific purpose and thesis statement for your explanatory speech. Decide which pattern of organization (chronological, spatial, topical, etc.) is best for presenting your main points, and incorporate support materials as you develop your speech outline. Use the Explanatory Speech Outline template in the following section to help plan and organize your speech. Make sure that you also incorporate at least one of the strategies to help audiences understand (repetition, show and tell, build on the known, humor, checking for understanding) and at least one of the three strategies for explaining difficult concepts (elucidating explanation, transformative explanation, quasi-scientific explanation).

Research: For this speech, you will need to conduct additional research. You should consult a variety of sources, such as newspaper articles, magazines, peer-reviewed academic journals, books, and websites, as you did in your Annotated Bibliography Assignment. Additionally, you are required to interview someone who is an expert on your topic; the expert might be a professor in your major, a professional who is in the same field as your intended career, or someone else who has specialized experience or expertise. You should include an APA formatted references page with your outline (note that this is a separate list of references from the Annotated Bibliography). During your speech, you should **orally cite at least three different types of sources** and **use at least three different types of support materials**. You may cite a source multiple times, but that will count as only one source. Please label each of your types of sources and support materials in your final full sentence preparation outline using the "Add Comment" function in Word.

<u>**PowerPoint:**</u> For this speech, you are required to use PowerPoint during your presentation. Please refer to your textbook and class discussions for guidelines when developing your presentation.

<u>**Notes:**</u> While planning your speech, you will develop a full sentence preparation outline that you will turn in before giving your speech. When you give your speech in class, you should use only **one note card** with a key word speaking outline.

<u>**Length**</u>: 5-7 minutes

<u>**What you need to upload to Blackboard before you give your speech:**</u>
- Final draft of your full sentence preparation speech outline, including a list of references in APA format. Please label each type of source and support material using the *New Comment* feature.
- PowerPoint file that you will use when you deliver your speech in class.

<u>**What you need to bring to class:**</u>

Day of the Outline Peer Workshop:
- 2 typed hard copies of your draft full sentence preparation outline (also upload a copy on Blackboard)
- Explanatory Speech Outline Peer Workshop Evaluation Form

Day of the Performance Peer Workshop:
- 1 copy of your typed full sentence preparation outline
- Notecard with keyword speaking outline
- Stopwatch or timer
- Explanatory Speech Performance Peer Workshop Form

Speech Days:
- Explanatory Speech Instructor Evaluation Form
- Explanatory Speech Peer Evaluation Form
- Final draft of your full sentence preparation speech outline, including a list of references in APA format. Please label each type of source and support material.
- Notecard with key word outline
- A digital video recording device (such as a smartphone or tablet)

Explanatory Speech Template Outline

I. Introduction (Approximately 1min.)

    A. Attention Getter

    B. Background and Audience Relevance

    C. Speaker Credibility

    D. Thesis

    E. Preview of Main Points

Transition to first main point

II. Body (Approximately 3 ½-5 ½ mins.)

    A. Main Point 1:

        1. Sub point 1

        2. Sub point 2

Transition (summary, signpost, preview)

    B. Main Point 2

        1. Sub point 1

        2. Sub point 2

Transition (summary, signpost, preview)

    C. Main Point 3

        1. Sub point 1

        2. Sub point 2

Transition and signal closing

III. Conclusion (Approximately 30 seconds-1 minute)

    A. Restate Thesis

    B. Review Main Points

    C. Memorable Closer

References
(on new page)

Co-Cultural Theory
By Ashley Thomas

I.   Introduction

    A. **Attention Getter:** Robert Alan Silverstein, an American writer, artist, and social activist, once stated, "Intercultural dialogue is the best guarantee of a more peaceful, just, and sustainable world." Interestingly, the development of formal intercultural communication theories that help us to understand such dialogue only occurred less than fifty years ago.

    B. **Background and Audience Relevance:** As we learned in our culture and diversity unit, and according to the *Oxford English Dictionary*, culture is "the distinctive ideas, customs, social behavior, products, or way of life of a particular nation, society, people, or period" (p. 137). In the 2005 book *Theorizing about Intercultural Communication*, communication professors Tadasu Imahori and William Cupach describe intercultural communication as an interaction among those from different cultural groups. George Mason University's website reported in 2015 that *The Princeton Review* named GMU "#1 in the nation for the 'frequency and ease of interaction among different racial/class groups.'"

> **Comment:** Build on the known
> **Comment:** Supporting Material: Definition
> **Comment:** Book
> **Comment:** Website
> **Comment:** Supporting Material: Statistic

    C. **Speaker Credibility:** Since I am a communication major who will one day enroll in our COMM 305: Foundations of Intercultural Communication course, I thought it was important to share with you all what I have learned about an intercultural communication theory known as co-cultural theory.

    D. **Thesis:** Learning about co-cultural theory will help us to better understand the communication strategies that marginalized groups use in intercultural interactions.

    E. **Preview of Main Points:** First, I will discuss how intercultural communication research and theory have evolved over the years. Second, I will explain co-cultural theory. Lastly, I will provide a specific example of co-cultural theory.

Transition to first main point: Now, let us discuss how intercultural communication research and theory have evolved.

II.   Body

    A. **Main Point 1**: Over the years, intercultural communication research has begun to focus on popular culture, identity, globalization, and theory building.

        1. **Sub point 1**: In 2002, communication professor Dreama Moon wrote a chapter in the book *Readings in Intercultural Communication: Experiences and Contexts* discussing how intercultural communication research in the 1990s focused on popular culture, considering that the media impacts how we view the world and its human interactions. Also, in an interview with Dr. Adam Smith, a public relations consultant, held on September 5, 2016, Smith stated that research from the early 2000s to present has emphasized identity

> **Comment:** Book
> **Comment:** Interview

and globalization, which involves the impact of technology and international trade on the interaction and integration of people and organizations from all over the world. According to Wendy Leeds-Hurwitz, current Director of the Center for Intercultural Dialogue at the University of Wisconsin-Parkside, in the October 2009 issue of the National Communication Association magazine *Spectra*, recent research focuses on vocabulary needed for intercultural dialogue and how to teach concepts helpful for such dialogue.

2. **Sub point 2**: In 1990, Leeds-Hurwitz also writes in the scholarly journal *Quarterly Journal of Speech* that it was not until the 1980s that intercultural communication moved beyond simply providing concepts and examples to using theory to study cultural phenomenon. In our respective majors, it is important to understand what theories are, as they guide much of the work we will do in our fields. An example of a lay theory, or theory we use in our everyday lives, would be that people who work hard succeed. Smith defined theory as a generalization used to describe and predict phenomenon. However, a simple statement of observation, such as "a majority of students in our class speak more than one language," would not be an example of a theory, since it does not predict or explain a phenomenon.

Transition: Since I have shared how intercultural communication research and theory evolved to include popular culture, theory building, and more, I will now explain co-cultural theory.

B. **Main Point 2:** In 1996, communication professor Mark Orbe published his co-cultural theory in the scholarly journal *Communication Studies* to describe the ways in which members of co-cultures, or traditionally marginalized groups, such as racial/ethnic minorities, women, and homosexuals, communicate in their everyday lives with fellow group members and members of dominant groups.

1. **Sub point 1**: Co-cultural theory has several philosophical assumptions. According to Orbe, there is a hierarchy of privilege in which the dominant group has members in places of power who control communication structures. In addition, Orbe notes that when public communication forums do not reflect the lived experiences of co-cultural groups, the dominant structure can hinder advancement of marginalized cultures. Orbe also states that experiences with dominant structures impact communication strategies of co-cultural members.

2. **Sub point 2:** According to Orbe, these strategies include preferred outcomes and communication approaches. Orbe describes preferred outcomes, which include accommodation, separation, and assimilation, as well as communication approaches, which include

Comment: Magazine

Comment: Scholarly Journal

Comment: Support Material: Examples

Comment: Elucidating Explanation
Support Material: Explanation

Comment: Support Material: Examples

nonassertive, assertive, and aggressive communication. Orbe observes that accommodation seeks to maintain some cultural variance while changing existing dominant structures, separation involves the preference of forming bonds with other marginalized communities instead of the dominant group, and assimilation involves removing cultural distances in order to conform to the dominant society. According to Orbe, nonassertive communication is non-confrontational and puts others before oneself, assertive communication improves the self while focusing on the concerns of both self and others, and aggressive communication is more hostile and self-focused.

Transition: Now that we see how co-cultural theory explains the ways marginalized groups communicate in dominant structures, I will provide you with an example of co-cultural theory.

    C. **Main Point 3**: During my interview with Smith, I was able to see how aspects of co-cultural theory appear in his response to unfair treatment in the workplace based on his physical disability.

        1. **Sub point 1:** Smith shared with me that he has a hearing impairment. Based on a hierarchy of privilege, nondisabled people typically experience greater privilege than someone with a disability and can control communication structures. As a result, Smith's employer did not provide the technology or interpreters necessary for him to successfully carry out his work duties. Since his work environment did not reflect the lived experiences of his co-cultural group, Smith faced challenges in moving up from an entry-level position to his goal of being an assistant manager.

        2. **Sub point 2:** Therefore, he decided to use assertive accommodation and work with his nondisabled colleagues to make all employees feel welcome. According to Smith, when some employees would make derogatory comments about those with mental or physical disabilities, he would educate them on appropriate ways to describe and address members of his co-cultural group. Smith wanted people to see him and his colleagues with disabilities as people first and not "the disabled man" or "the handicapped woman." Eventually, Smith left the company to work at a public relations consultant firm in support of businesses that strive to be more inclusive of those with disabilities.

> **Comment:** Support Material: Narrative

Transition and signal closing: Since we have addressed an example of co-cultural theory in the context of the workplace, I would like to review what we have learned throughout this speech.

III.   **Conclusion**
   A. **Restate Thesis:** In conclusion, learning about co-cultural theory will help us to better understand the communication strategies that marginalized groups use in intercultural interactions.
   B. **Review Main Points:** First, I discussed how intercultural communication research and theory have evolved over the years. Second, I explained co-cultural theory. Lastly, I provided a specific example of co-cultural theory.
   C. **Memorable Closer:** All of us have the potential to be a part of at least one marginalized group. While Robert Alan Silverstein may be right that intercultural dialogue brings about hope for a better world, intercultural communication theory sheds light on how we can explain and predict the ways to effectively communicate with others in so many aspects of our lives.

References

A. Smith, personal communication, September 5, 2016.

Culture. (n.d.). In *Oxford English Dictionary online*. Retrieved from

    http://www.oxforddictionaries.com/us/definition/american_english/culture

George Mason University. (2015). Quick facts 2014-2015. Retrieved from

    http://irr.gmu.edu/QuickFacts/QuickFact201415_Final.pdf

Imahori, T. T., & Cupach, W. R. (2005). Identity management theory. In W. Gudykunst

    (Ed.), *Theorizing about intercultural communication* (pp. 195-210). Thousand Oaks,

    CA: Sage.

Leeds-Hurwitz, W. (1990). Notes in the history of intercultural communication: The foreign

    service institute and the mandate for intercultural training. *Quarterly Journal of*

    Speech, 76, 262-281. doi: 10.1080/00335639009383919

Leeds-Hurwitz, W. (2009). NCA's First International Conference a Great Success!. *Spectra,*

    45(9), 10.

Moon, D. G. (2002). Thinking about "culture" in intercultural communication. In Martin,

    J. N., Nakayama, T. K., & Flores, L. A. (Eds.), *Readings in intercultural*

    communication: Experiences and contexts (2nd ed.) (pp. 13-21). McGraw-Hill

    Humanities/Social Sciences/Languages.

Orbe, M. P. (1996). Laying the foundation for co-cultural communication theory: An

    inductive approach to studying "non-dominant" communication strategies and the

    factors that influence them. *Communication Studies, 47,* 157-176. doi:

    10.1080/10510979609368473

216

Explanatory Speech Outline Peer Workshop

Speaker: _____   Evaluator 1: _____

Topic: _____   Evaluator 2: _____

Speaker: List 2 or 3 questions here that you would like your peer reviewer to address while responding to your outline. These questions can focus on aspects you are uncertain about, parts that you would particularly like help or advice, a section you really wrestled with, or a feature that you are particularly proud of.

1.

2.

3.

Evaluators: 1) Read through the outline, writing comments on any areas that you think need changed or that you think are especially good. Check to see whether the outline contains everything it is supposed to and whether it is structured properly. 2) Read the author's questions on the top of this sheet and write responses to them. 3) Write responses to each of the questions below. Be sure to explain your answers—the more you write, the more your comments will help the speaker. If you need more space, write on the back. When you are finished, discuss your suggestions and return this sheet and the outline to the speaker.

Is the topic specific enough to be adequately covered in 5-7 minutes? Should it be more narrow or broad?

Evaluator 1:

Evaluator 2:

Is this speech explaining something new that is related to the speaker's major or intended career? What else would you like to know about this topic?

Evaluator 1:

Evaluator 2:

Does the opener catch your attention? How can it be made better? Are there ways to help maintain audience interest more throughout the speech?

Evaluator 1:

Evaluator 2:

Has the speaker established the significance of the topic, both for the world and for the specific audience? How could the speaker make you care more?

Evaluator 1:

Evaluator 2:

Does each main point clearly support the thesis? Are all main points clear and separate? How can they be better?

Evaluator 1: | Evaluator 2:

What sources have been cited? Are they good quality sources? Are there three different types of sources, including an interview with an expert? Do you think they are credible and relevant to the point being made? Why or why not? How can this be better?

Evaluator 1: | Evaluator 2:

Have a wide variety of support materials (examples, statistics, testimony, analogies, metaphors, narrative, illustrations, descriptions, explanations, definitions) been used? How can the speaker strengthen his/her points even more?

Evaluator 1: | Evaluator 2:

What are your two favorite parts of this speech? Why? Can you think of a way to make them even better?

Evaluator 1: | Evaluator 2:

What are two ways you think this speech could be improved? How? Why?

Evaluator 1: | Evaluator 2:

Speaker: What was the most helpful advice you received today? Write down at least 3 things you plan to do to revise your speech before you present it in class. Be sure to bring this sheet and all comments and outlines on the day that you speak.

1.

2.

3.

Explanatory Speech Performance Peer Workshop

Speaker: _____   Evaluator: _____

Speech Title: _____

Does the opener catch your attention? How can it be made better? Are there ways to help maintain audience interest more throughout the speech?

Does each main point clearly support the thesis? Are all main points clear and separate? How can they be better?

What sources have been cited? Are they good quality sources? Are there three different types of sources, including an interview with an expert? Do you think they are credible and relevant to the point being made? Why or why not? How can this be better?

Have a wide variety of support materials (examples, statistics, testimony, analogies, metaphors, narrative, illustrations, descriptions, explanations, definitions) been used? How can the speaker strengthen his/her points even more and even better teach the audience about this topic?

What are your two favorite parts of this speech? Why? Can you think of a way to make them even better?
1.

2.

What are two ways you think this speech content could be improved? How? Why?
1.

2.

What are two elements of delivery that the speaker is doing well? How can he or she build on these strengths?
1.

2.

What are two elements of delivery that the speaker needs to work to improve? How would you recommend improving these areas?
1.

2.

Speaker: What was the most helpful advice you received today? Write down at least 3 things you plan to do to revise your speech before you present it in class. Be sure to bring this sheet and all comments and outlines on the day that you speak.
1.

2.

3.

How many times do you plan to practice your speech again before you give your speech in class?

Explanatory Speech Performance Peer Workshop

Speaker: _____   Evaluator: _____

Speech Title: _____

Instructions: 1) Read through the questions below so that you know what to listen for while listening to the speaker give his or her speech. 2) Listen carefully as the speaker delivers his or her speech. Take notes and provide written feedback in the space below. 3) Discuss the speech performance and provide constructive feedback to the speaker. 4) When you are finished, give this completed form back to the speaker.

Does the opener catch your attention? How can it be made better? Are there ways to help maintain audience interest more throughout the speech?

Does each main point clearly support the thesis? Are all main points clear and separate? How can they be better?

What sources have been cited? Are they good quality sources? Are there three different types of sources, including an interview with an expert? Do you think they are credible and relevant to the point being made? Why or why not? How can this be better?

Have a wide variety of support materials (examples, statistics, testimony, analogies, metaphors, narrative, illustrations, descriptions, explanations, definitions) been used? How can the speaker strengthen his/her points even more and even better teach the audience about this topic?

What are your two favorite parts of this speech? Why? Can you think of a way to make them even better?

1.

2.

What are two ways you think this speech content could be improved? How? Why?

1.

2.

What are two elements of delivery that the speaker is doing well? How can he or she build on these strengths?

1.

2.

What are two elements of delivery that the speaker needs to work to improve? How would you recommend improving these areas?

1.

2.

Speaker: What was the most helpful advice you received today? Write down at least 3 things you plan to do to revise your speech before you present it in class. Be sure to bring this sheet and all comments and outlines on the day that you speak.

1.

2.

3.

How many times do you plan to practice your speech again before you give your speech in class?

Explanatory Speech Instructor Evaluation Form

Give this form to your instructor before you give your speech

Name:_____ Topic:_____ Time:_____

INTRODUCTION	Missing 0	C 7-7.5	B 8-8.5	A 9-10	
Attention getter is (C) present, (B) uses a meaningful narrative, quotation, statistic, or question that is related to the topic, and (A) involves the audience or creates information hunger					
Background and audience relevance (C) some background information about the topic is provided, (B) the significance of the topic is firmly established, and (A) topic is clearly connected to this specific audience					
Speaker credibility (C) speaker provides a reason for choosing the topic, (B) explains why they care about the topic, and (A) explains why they have compelling experience or expertise in this area					
Thesis (C) The thesis is clearly stated (B) in a clear, complete, single declarative sentence, and (A) uses carefully chosen language that sets the tone and direction for the speech					
Preview of main points (C) tells the audience what main points will be discussed, (B) uses signposts, and (A) uses concise, carefully worded phrasing					___/10

BODY	Missing 0	C 17.5-19.5	B 20-22	A 22.5-25	
Main Point 1 (C) is clearly stated and supports the thesis, (B) is well developed using a variety of support materials and (A) is supported by distinct, clearly worded and supported subpoints					
Main Point 2 (C) is clearly stated and supports the thesis, (B) is well developed using a variety of support materials and (A) is supported by distinct, clearly worded and supported subpoints					
Main Point 3 (C) is clearly stated and supports the thesis, (B) is well developed using a variety of support materials and (A) is supported by distinct, clearly worded and supported subpoints					
Transitions (C) speaker clearly indicates when they are moving to each new main point (B) and has an effective summary, signpost, and preview in **each** transition, and (A) include pauses, gestures, or movement to reinforce the transition					
Explanations: (C) attempts to explain complex idea to non-expert audience (B) using at least one of the strategies to help audience understand (repetition, show & tell, build on the known, humor, check understanding) and (A) at least one of the three strategies for explaining difficult concepts (elucidating, transformative, or quasi-scientific explanation)					___/25

SUPPORT MATERIALS	Missing 0	C 14-15.5	B 16-17.5	A 18-20	
Support Materials (C) uses at least **three** different types of support materials (B) that effectively support the speech and enhance understanding and (A) help to establish significance and make the speech memorable **Types:** examples, statistics, testimony, analogies, metaphors, narrative, illustrations, descriptions, explanations, definitions					
Source Quality: (C) cited **three** different types of sources (B) including an interview with an expert, and (A) all sources were high quality and had strong credibility **Types:** interview, book, academic journal, newspaper or magazine, website or media source					
Source Citations: (C) all sources had some type of oral citation and (B) each citation had the name of the person/organization/publication and date and (A) provided the credentials of the expert who provided the information when possible					___/20

CONCLUSION	Missing 0	C 3.5	B 4	A 4.5-5	
Signals conclusion: (C) transition to the conclusion is indicated (B) using a clear signpost (A) that is reinforced through vocal tone, gestures, movement, and /or a brief pause					
Restates thesis: (C) topic of speech is clearly mentioned (B) in a clear, complete declarative thesis statement (A) using carefully chosen language that reinforces the tone of the speech					
Reviews main points: (C) tells audience which main points were discussed (B) using clear signposts (A) using concise, carefully worded phrasing					
Memorable closer: (C) brings a sense of closure to the end of the speech (B) in a memorable way that has audience impact and (A) ties back to the attention getter					___/5

AUDIENCE ADAPTATION	Missing 0	C 10.5-11.5	B 12-13	A 13.5-15	
Topic (C) is appropriate for this assignment and context, (B) is clearly related to the student's major or intended career, and (A) has clear significance for the speaker and the audience					
Audience Analysis: (C) speech is appropriate for and considerate toward all members of the audience, (B) is clearly adapted for this specific audience and context, and (A) incorporates specific characteristics of the audience into the speech					
Language (C) is appropriate for the audience and occasion, (B) uses several memorable phrases, and (A) incorporates several language structures and devices					___/15

PRESENTATION AIDS	Missing 0	C 7-7.5	B 8-8.5	A 9-10	
PowerPoint (C) supports the speech, (B) utilizes images, graphs, diagrams, and other visual resources that complement the presentation rather than primarily using text that repeats the presentation, and (A) is visually appealing and utilizes blank slides when appropriate					
Visual Citations (C) some type of verbal or visual reference is made to the source of images, graphs, diagrams, etc. used on slides under the images, (B) name of source or URL appears under some of the images in the presentation, or (A) **all** images have the name of a source or URL under them					___/10

DELIVERY	Missing 0	C 10.5-11.5	B 12-13	A 13.5-15	
Extemporaneous: (C) reads heavily from notecards or manuscript throughout the speech, (B) occasionally reads portions of the speech from notecards, (A) student refers to notecards occasionally, but notecard use does not interfere with delivery					
Vocal Delivery: (C) speaker can be heard and understood throughout speech, and (B) vocal delivery conveys enthusiasm for the topic and keeps audience attention, and (A) vocal delivery engages audience and commands the attention of the room throughout speech *Pronunciation, Articulation, Volume, Pitch, Rhythm, Rate, Tone, Vocalized Pauses*					
Nonverbal Delivery: (C) attempts to use gestures, movement, and facial expressions a few times during the speech but may include a few distracting movements (swaying, rocking, repetitive motions, etc.) (B) speech uses gestures, movement, and facial expressions during the speech that at times complement the message, (A) speech uses intentional and effective gestures, movement, and facial expressions to enhance the speech, enhance credibility, and maintain audience attention *Apparel, Posture, Facial Expressions, Gestures, Movement*					
Eye Contact: (C) speaker looks at audience a few times during the speech, (B) makes eye contact with some audience members during significant portions of the speech, (A) makes eye contact with all members of the audience throughout the speech					___/15

POINT DEDUCTIONS	
Over time or under time: deduct 1 point for every 10 seconds	
Missing instructor evaluation: deduct 10 points	

Total Score: ___/100

Explanatory Speech Instructor Evaluation Short Form

Give this form to your instructor before you give your speech

Name:_____ Topic:_____ Time:_____

INTRODUCTION	Missing 0	C 7-7.5	B 8-8.5	A 9-10	
Attention getter					
Background and audience relevance					
Speaker credibility					
Thesis					
Preview of main points					___/10

BODY	Missing 0	C 17.5-19.5	B 20-22	A 22.5-25	
Main Point 1					
Main Point 2					
Main Point 3					
Transitions					
Explanations					___/25

SUPPORT MATERIALS	Missing 0	C 14-15.5	B 16-17.5	A 18-20	
Support Materials (3 types) **Types:** examples, statistics, testimony, analogies, metaphors, narrative, illustrations, descriptions, explanations, definitions					
Source Quality (3) **Types:** interview, book, academic journal, newspaper or magazine, website or media source					
Source Citations:					___/20

CONCLUSION	Missing 0	C 3.5	B 4	A 4.5-5	
Signals conclusion					
Restates thesis					
Reviews main points					
Memorable closer					___/5

AUDIENCE ADAPTATION	Missing 0	C 10.5-11.5	B 12-13	A 13.5-15	
Topic					
Audience Analysis					
Language					___/15

PRESENTATION AIDS	Missing 0	C 7-7.5	B 8-8.5	A 9-10	
PowerPoint					
Visual Citations					___/10

DELIVERY	Missing 0	C 10.5-11.5	B 12-13	A 13.5-15	
Extemporaneous					
Vocal Delivery *Pronunciation, Articulation, Volume, Pitch, Rhythm, Rate, Tone, Vocalized Pauses*					
Nonverbal Delivery *Apparel, Posture, Facial Expressions, Gestures, Movement*					
Eye Contact					___/15

POINT DEDUCTIONS	
Over time or under time: deduct 1 point for every 10 seconds	
Missing instructor evaluation: deduct 10 points	

Total Score: ___/100

Explanatory Speech Peer Evaluation Form

Your name:_____ Person you are evaluating:_____

INTRODUCTION	M	C	B	A
Attention getter is (C) present, (B) uses a meaningful narrative, quotation, statistic, or question that is related to the topic, and (A) involves the audience or creates information hunger				
Background and audience relevance (C) some background information about the topic is provided, (B) the significance of the topic is firmly established, and (A) topic is clearly connected to this specific audience				
Speaker credibility (C) speaker provides a reason for choosing the topic, (B) explains why they care about the topic, and (A) explains why they have compelling experience or expertise in this area				
Thesis (C) The thesis is clearly stated (B) in a clear, complete, single declarative sentence, and (A) uses carefully chosen language that sets the tone and direction for the speech				
Preview of main points (C) tells the audience what main points will be discussed, (B) uses signposts, and (A) uses concise, carefully worded phrasing				

BODY	M	C	B	A
Main Point 1 (C) is clearly stated and supports the thesis, (B) is well developed using a variety of support materials and (A) is supported by distinct, clearly worded and supported subpoints				
Main Point 2 (C) is clearly stated and supports the thesis, (B) is well developed using a variety of support materials and (A) is supported by distinct, clearly worded and supported subpoints				
Main Point 3 (C) is clearly stated and supports the thesis, (B) is well developed using a variety of support materials and (A) is supported by distinct, clearly worded and supported subpoints				
Transitions (C) speaker clearly indicates when they are moving to each new main point (B) and has an effective summary, signpost, and preview in **each** transition, and (A) include pauses, gestures, or movement to reinforce the transition				
Explanations: (C) attempts to explain complex idea to non-expert audience (B) using at least one of the strategies to help audience understand (repetition, show & tell, build on the known, humor, check understanding) and (A) at least one of the three strategies for explaining difficult concepts (elucidating, transformative, or quasi-scientific explanation)				

SUPPORT MATERIALS	M	C	B	A
Support Materials (C) uses at least **three** different types of support materials (B) that effectively support the speech and enhance understanding and (A) help to establish significance and make the speech memorable **Types:** examples, statistics, testimony, analogies, metaphors, narrative, illustrations, descriptions, explanations, definitions				
Source Quality: (C) cited **three** different types of sources (B) including an interview with an expert, and (A) all sources were high quality and had strong credibility **Types:** interview, book, academic journal, newspaper or magazine, website or media source				
Source Citations: (C) all sources had some type of oral citation and (B) each citation had the name of the person/organization/publication and date and (A) provided the credentials of the expert who provided the information when possible				

CONCLUSION	M	C	B	A
Signals conclusion: (C) transition to the conclusion is indicated (B) using a clear signpost (A) that is reinforced through vocal tone, gestures, movement, and /or a brief pause				
Restates thesis: (C) topic of speech is clearly mentioned (B) in a clear, complete declarative thesis statement (A) using carefully chosen language that reinforces the tone of the speech				
Reviews main points: (C) tells audience which main points were discussed (B) using clear signposts (A) using concise, carefully worded phrasing				
Memorable closer: (C) brings a sense of closure to the end of the speech (B) in a memorable way that has audience impact and (A) ties back to the attention getter				

How effective was the organization of this speech? Are there ways that the speaker could have more effectively communicated the organization of ideas to the audience? Why or why not?

AUDIENCE ADAPTATION	M	C	B	A
Topic (C) is appropriate for this assignment and context, (B) is clearly related to the student's major or intended career, and (A) has clear significance for the speaker and the audience				
Audience Analysis: (C) speech is appropriate for and considerate toward all members of the audience, (B) is clearly adapted for this specific audience and context, and (A) incorporates specific characteristics of the audience into the speech				
Language (C) is appropriate for the audience and occasion, (B) uses several memorable phrases, and (A) incorporates several language structures and devices				

PRESENTATION AIDS	M	C	B	A
PowerPoint (C) supports the speech, (B) utilizes images, graphs, diagrams, and other visual resources that complement the presentation rather than primarily using text that repeats the presentation, and (A) is visually appealing and utilizes blank slides when appropriate				
Visual Citations (C) some type of verbal or visual reference is made to the source of images, graphs, diagrams, etc. used on slides under the images, (B) name of source or URL appears under some of the images in the presentation, or (A) **all** images have the name of a source or URL under them				

DELIVERY	M	C	B	A
Extemporaneous: (C) reads heavily from notecards or manuscript throughout the speech, (B) occasionally reads portions of the speech from notecards, (A) student refers to notecards occasionally, but notecard use does not interfere with delivery				
Vocal Delivery: (C) speaker can be heard and understood throughout speech, and (B) vocal delivery conveys enthusiasm for the topic and keeps audience attention, and (A) vocal delivery engages audience and commands the attention of the room throughout speech *Pronunciation, Articulation, Volume, Pitch, Rhythm, Rate, Tone, Vocalized Pauses*				
Nonverbal Delivery: (C) attempts to use gestures, movement, and facial expressions a few times during the speech but may include a few distracting movements (swaying, rocking, repetitive motions, etc.) (B) speech uses gestures, movement, and facial expressions during the speech that at times complement the message, (A) speech uses intentional and effective gestures, movement, and facial expressions to enhance the speech, enhance credibility, and maintain audience attention *Apparel, Posture, Facial Expressions, Gestures, Movement*				
Eye Contact: (C) speaker looks at audience a few times during the speech, (B) makes eye contact with some audience members during significant portions of the speech, (A) makes eye contact with all members of the audience throughout the speech				

What did you learn from this speech? How will this information be useful to you in the future?

Which part of the speech did the speaker explain most clearly? Which part of the speech was most confusing? Why?

What are two things that the speaker did well and two things that could have been improved in the delivery of this speech?

Are there any other comments that you want to share with the speaker?

Explanatory Speech Peer Evaluation Form

Your name:_____ Person you are evaluating:_____

INTRODUCTION	M	C	B	A
Attention getter is (C) present, (B) uses a meaningful narrative, quotation, statistic, or question that is related to the topic, and (A) involves the audience or creates information hunger				
Background and audience relevance (C) some background information about the topic is provided, (B) the significance of the topic is firmly established, and (A) topic is clearly connected to this specific audience				
Speaker credibility (C) speaker provides a reason for choosing the topic, (B) explains why they care about the topic, and (A) explains why they have compelling experience or expertise in this area				
Thesis (C) The thesis is clearly stated (B) in a clear, complete, single declarative sentence, and (A) uses carefully chosen language that sets the tone and direction for the speech				
Preview of main points (C) tells the audience what main points will be discussed, (B) uses signposts, and (A) uses concise, carefully worded phrasing				

BODY	M	C	B	A
Main Point 1 (C) is clearly stated and supports the thesis, (B) is well developed using a variety of support materials and (A) is supported by distinct, clearly worded and supported subpoints				
Main Point 2 (C) is clearly stated and supports the thesis, (B) is well developed using a variety of support materials and (A) is supported by distinct, clearly worded and supported subpoints				
Main Point 3 (C) is clearly stated and supports the thesis, (B) is well developed using a variety of support materials and (A) is supported by distinct, clearly worded and supported subpoints				
Transitions (C) speaker clearly indicates when they are moving to each new main point (B) and has an effective summary, signpost, and preview in **each** transition, and (A) include pauses, gestures, or movement to reinforce the transition				
Explanations: (C) attempts to explain complex idea to non-expert audience (B) using at least one of the strategies to help audience understand (repetition, show & tell, build on the known, humor, check understanding) and (A) at least one of the three strategies for explaining difficult concepts (elucidating, transformative, or quasi-scientific explanation)				

SUPPORT MATERIALS	M	C	B	A
Support Materials (C) uses at least **three** different types of support materials (B) that effectively support the speech and enhance understanding and (A) help to establish significance and make the speech memorable **Types:** examples, statistics, testimony, analogies, metaphors, narrative, illustrations, descriptions, explanations, definitions				
Source Quality: (C) cited **three** different types of sources (B) including an interview with an expert, and (A) all sources were high quality and had strong credibility **Types:** interview, book, academic journal, newspaper or magazine, website or media source				
Source Citations: (C) all sources had some type of oral citation and (B) each citation had the name of the person/organization/publication and date and (A) provided the credentials of the expert who provided the information when possible				

CONCLUSION	M	C	B	A
Signals conclusion: (C) transition to the conclusion is indicated (B) using a clear signpost (A) that is reinforced through vocal tone, gestures, movement, and /or a brief pause				
Restates thesis: (C) topic of speech is clearly mentioned (B) in a clear, complete declarative thesis statement (A) using carefully chosen language that reinforces the tone of the speech				
Reviews main points: (C) tells audience which main points were discussed (B) using clear signposts (A) using concise, carefully worded phrasing				
Memorable closer: (C) brings a sense of closure to the end of the speech (B) in a memorable way that has audience impact and (A) ties back to the attention getter				

How effective was the organization of this speech? Are there ways that the speaker could have more effectively communicated the organization of ideas to the audience? Why or why not?

AUDIENCE ADAPTATION	M	C	B	A
Topic (C) is appropriate for this assignment and context, (B) is clearly related to the student's major or intended career, and (A) has clear significance for the speaker and the audience				
Audience Analysis: (C) speech is appropriate for and considerate toward all members of the audience, (B) is clearly adapted for this specific audience and context, and (A) incorporates specific characteristics of the audience into the speech				
Language (C) is appropriate for the audience and occasion, (B) uses several memorable phrases, and (A) incorporates several language structures and devices				

PRESENTATION AIDS	M	C	B	A
PowerPoint (C) supports the speech, (B) utilizes images, graphs, diagrams, and other visual resources that complement the presentation rather than primarily using text that repeats the presentation, and (A) is visually appealing and utilizes blank slides when appropriate				
Visual Citations (C) some type of verbal or visual reference is made to the source of images, graphs, diagrams, etc. used on slides under the images, (B) name of source or URL appears under some of the images in the presentation, or (A) **all** images have the name of a source or URL under them				

DELIVERY	M	C	B	A
Extemporaneous: (C) reads heavily from notecards or manuscript throughout the speech, (B) occasionally reads portions of the speech from notecards, (A) student refers to notecards occasionally, but notecard use does not interfere with delivery				
Vocal Delivery: (C) speaker can be heard and understood throughout speech, and (B) vocal delivery conveys enthusiasm for the topic and keeps audience attention, and (A) vocal delivery engages audience and commands the attention of the room throughout speech *Pronunciation, Articulation, Volume, Pitch, Rhythm, Rate, Tone, Vocalized Pauses*				
Nonverbal Delivery: (C) attempts to use gestures, movement, and facial expressions a few times during the speech but may include a few distracting movements (swaying, rocking, repetitive motions, etc.) (B) speech uses gestures, movement, and facial expressions during the speech that at times complement the message, (A) speech uses intentional and effective gestures, movement, and facial expressions to enhance the speech, enhance credibility, and maintain audience attention *Apparel, Posture, Facial Expressions, Gestures, Movement*				
Eye Contact: (C) speaker looks at audience a few times during the speech, (B) makes eye contact with some audience members during significant portions of the speech, (A) makes eye contact with all members of the audience throughout the speech				

What did you learn from this speech? How will this information be useful to you in the future?

Which part of the speech did the speaker explain most clearly? Which part of the speech was most confusing? Why?

What are two things that the speaker did well and two things that could have been improved in the delivery of this speech?

Are there any other comments that you want to share with the speaker?

Explanatory Speech Outline Grading Rubric

This assignment will be uploaded to Blackboard and graded online using the rubric shown below:

	Missing 0	C 17.5-19.5	B 20-22	A 22.5-25
Level of Detail	Outline includes only key word and phrases.	Outline is written in complete sentences, but has far too little detail for the type and length of speech	Outline is written in complete sentences and has almost everything the speaker plans to say in the speech, but is not quite as detailed as a speech of this type and length should be	Outline is written in complete sentences and has adequate detail for a speech of this type and length. Everything that the speaker plans to say in the speech is included in the preparation outline
Outline Format	The outline is not formatted using the appropriate symbols, indentions, spacing, and labels	The outline is complete and includes some outline formatting (symbols, indentions, spacing, labels), but is missing some of these components	The outline mostly uses appropriate formatting, including the correct outline symbols, indentions, spacing, and labels	The entire outline uses appropriate formatting, including the correct outline symbols, indentions, spacing, and labels
Proofreading	Final preparation outline is unreadable, illogical, made up only of key words, or not turned in	Final preparation outline is written in complete sentences and contains several significant grammar, syntax, or spelling errors	Final preparation outline is written in complete sentences and contains a few minor grammar, syntax, or spelling errors	Final preparation outline is written in complete sentences and contains no grammar, syntax, or spelling errors
Source Citations in Outline	No source citations are included in the final preparation outline	Sources are included in the outline, but are not cited the way they should be in an outline	Sources are integrated throughout the outline in the places that they will be cited orally in the speech, but are not written in the correct citation format	Sources are integrated throughout the outline in the places that they will be cited orally in the speech. Source citations in the outline are written in the correct citation format
Source Citations and Support Materials Labeled	No sources or support materials are labeled in the final outline using the *Add Comments* feature.	A few sources and support materials are labeled in the final outline using the *Add Comments* feature.	At least three sources and three support materials are labeled in the final outline using the *Add Comments* feature, but there are not three separate types of each.	At least three types of sources and three types of support materials are labeled in the final outline using the *Add Comments* feature.
APA Reference List	No references list is included.	The references list is included and is consistently formatted, but is not formatted in APA style.	The references list is included and adheres closely to APA formatting guidelines, but has some mistakes.	The references list is included and adheres to APA formatting guidelines perfectly.
PowerPoint	No PowerPoint was uploaded	PowerPoint is mostly comprised of text, is visually unappealing or hard to see, and only minimally supports the speech.	PowerPoint helps to support the speech and include some diagrams, graphs, keywords, etc., but also has a lot of unnecessary text and/or only moderately supports the speech.	PowerPoint includes images, diagrams, graphs, key words, and other elements that support the speech. PowerPoint is visually appealing and includes appropriate citations for images.

232

Explanatory Speech Self-Evaluation Form

Instructions: Download a copy of this form from Blackboard. Watch the video recording of your speech. Afterward, type your answers to the following questions. Save your work as a .doc or .pdf file and upload it on Blackboard. <u>For each question, your response should include at least a full paragraph (4-6 sentences) and the time stamp</u> of a specific portion of the speech video to which you are referring.

1. After re-watching your speech, do you think you clearly explained a complex idea so that a non-expert audience could understand it? Was this a topic that will help your audience in some way? Why or why not? How could you have done this even more effectively?

2. Which strategies to help your audience understand and strategies to explain difficult ideas did you incorporate into your speech? Were you able to effectively use these strategies to share complex ideas with your audience? Are there other strategies that might have been more effective?

3. How effective was the organization of this speech? Are there ways that you could have more effectively communicated the organization of ideas to the audience? Why or why not?

4. What are two things that you did well and two things that you could have done better in the delivery of this speech?

5. What have you learned from the process of developing and giving this speech? How can you build on this experience and improve before your next speech?

Chapter 14

Nature of Formal Presentations

In addition to interpersonal communication, you may also be called upon to give a formal presentation at some point during your life. Presentations may be part of a career, one that asks you to deliver a sales report or run an orientation program. The occasion might arise in your personal life, such as giving a wedding toast, eulogy, or even a roast of a friend or colleague. Even though each presentation is for a different audience, they all have some things in common. Public communication involves a presenter speaking to a group of people for an extended period of time without interruption. In formal public presentations, the speaker also typically stands in front of a seated audience.

The roots of instruction for public speaking date back to Ancient Greece and Rome. Aristotle identified three basic categories of speeches. The first, deliberative, involved speeches about future actions that might be taken; the second, forensic, included arguments about what had happened, much like you would find in a courtroom; and the third, epideictic, included speeches that celebrate or commemorate events or people. He also provided us with the five canons of rhetoric, or the five elements of creating and presenting a speech:

1. **Invention**: identifying the topic on which you will speak
2. **Arrangement**: determining the order in which you will address points related to the topic
3. **Style**: the words and phrases you use to make the topic interesting
4. **Delivery**: the physical and vocal dimensions of speaking
5. **Memory**: remembering the entire speech (much more important during classical days than it is today)

In this chapter, we examine the nature of public speaking using what we have learned from Aristotle through today. First we will examine the process of invention or, as we call it today, topic selection. We will then discuss how to adapt messages to audiences. Third, we will define the different types of formal presentations, and then discuss the role of the research process in speech development. Finally, we will provide suggestions and guidelines for making speeches more dialogic in nature, thus creating an environment where the audience will be more likely to listen and think about your message.

Topic Selection

When you are asked to give a formal presentation, the first and perhaps most difficult task you will need to undertake is choosing and narrowing your topic. Sometimes you will be asked to speak about something very specific, such as presenting a business report in a stakeholder meeting, but more often you will have some flexibility to choose your own topic. In these situations, you should consider several questions when evaluating potential topics for your presentation.

What is the General Purpose of My Speech?

General purpose the broad intent of what your speech should accomplish; the three types of general purposes are to inform, to persuade, and to commemorate

The **general purpose** is the broad intent of what your speech should accomplish. There are three primary types of general purposes: to inform, to persuade, and to commemorate. In an informative speech, you are trying to teach your audience something. For example, in a CPR class, the instructor is trying to teach his or her audience the steps for performing CPR effectively. In a persuasive speech, you are trying to change or reinforce your audience's attitudes, actions, or beliefs in some way. In a campaign speech, for example, a political candidate is usually trying to convince you to agree with her or his stance on several issues and persuade you to vote for her or him on Election Day. In a commemorative speech, you are usually celebrating or honoring something. A wedding toast is a classic case of a commemorative speech intended to celebrate the love and marriage of the newlywed couple.

What Topics are Appropriate for the Occasion?

If you are in a speaking situation in which you get to choose your topic, you will need to consider what types of topics are considered appropriate for the occasion. Audiences typically expect certain topics to be addressed on particular occasions. We usually expect wedding toasts to focus on the couple getting married and to perhaps include anecdotes about the couple and well-wishes for a happy marriage. We presume commencement speeches will have themes related in some way to hopes, dreams, goals, and success. We anticipate a first aid training workshop to teach us something about how to help a person during a medical emergency. In these situations, there are many potential topics you could choose that would be appropriate, but there are also many that would be inappropriate. Consider that an audience might be horrified if a speaker told a story about either the bride or groom's one-night stand with a previous romantic partner during a wedding toast, talked about genocide in a graduation address, or tried to persuade an audience to take his or her side on a political issue in the middle of what was supposed to be a CPR training session. When thinking about potential topics, take time to consider what types of topics might be appropriate or even expected for the occasion.

Is the Topic Appropriate for this Particular Audience?

Just as occasions carry expectations, so too do audiences. In some situations, a particular audience may be interested or receptive to a particular message even though others might also fit the occasion. You should consider your audience's interests, needs, and level of expertise when choosing your topic, and consider how those mesh with the occasion. An audience of kindergarteners is probably not interested in listening to a speech about retirement savings options, an audience of Kansans probably doesn't need to know how to protect their homes in case of a hurricane, and a group of emergency room doctors probably will not benefit from a speech on basic first aid, since they already have extensive expertise in dealing with medical emergencies. Instead, you should consider what topics will be of interest to, connect with, and build upon an audience's existing knowledge in some way.

Is This Topic Appropriate for Me?

After you consider your audience and the occasion, you also should make sure your topic is appropriate for you. Is this topic something you care about? Is it a subject in which you are an expert, or about which you would like to know more? Is the topic choice one that reflects the person you want to be seen as? You will spend a significant amount of time thinking about, researching, practicing, and delivering your speech, so you should make sure the topic is one you care enough about to invest what will be a lot of time and work. A topic might be appropriate for you if you are already an expert in that area, or if you are interested in and want to know more about it. Be forewarned, some of the worst speeches happen when a speaker is just not interested in what he or she is talking about.

Brainstorm
the practice of creating a list of all of the possible topics you can think of, beginning by writing down every possible idea that comes to mind, regardless of how good you think the idea is, and then afterward organizing or evaluating the ideas to help you make a decision about which to choose

Concept map
a visual representation of all of the potential areas you could cover in your speech that includes circles around topics and lines that connect related ideas; also known as a mind map

Demographics
categories of definable characteristics of groups of people, such as age, sex, race, ethnicity, religion, political affiliation, socioeconomic status, education level, and sexual orientation

Is This Topic Narrow Enough?

Once you have identified a potential topic that is appropriate for yourself, your audience, and the occasion, you will need to narrow your topic to make sure you can adequately explain your subject matter in the amount of time you have available. In a classroom presentation situation, you will probably be given a minimum and a maximum time frame. In professional contexts, the length of your presentations will vary. Sometimes you might have as little as 30 to 60 seconds to give an "elevator pitch," which is a quick synopsis of a complex issue. In these instances, your topic needs to be narrow and targeted. At other times you may have anywhere from five to 10 minutes, or perhaps even a full hour. When you have that much time, you can cover much more ground. If you are struggling to narrow your topic, you might find it helpful to **brainstorm** all of the various subtopics or components your broader, general topic contains. You could also create a **concept map** to help you identify the other potential areas you could cover and how they relate to one another.

Audience Analysis and Adaptation

Once you have selected a topic and have begun to narrow it to fit the parameters of the speaking occasion, you should find out as much as you can about your audience so you can adapt the speech to meet its specific needs. The amount of time you will have to prepare and the amount of information you will be able to learn about your audience will vary depending on the occasion. In some situations, you will be able to collect some information about your audience's background characteristics, knowledge, and attitudes toward your topic in advance, while other times you might need to look for clues about your audience and adapt accordingly during your speech. In this part of the chapter, we will address seven different ways you can analyze an audience.

Demographics

The first way in which you can analyze your audience is by gathering information about their background. **Demographics** are categories of definable characteristics of groups of people, such as age, sex, race, ethnicity, religion, political affiliation, socioeconomic status, education level, and sexual orientation. Different types of demographic information are collected by a variety of institutions for many reasons. For example, the U.S. Census Bureau collects some demographic data every 10 years to get an overall picture of who lives in the United States. Universities collect demographic data about their employees and students to help understand who is on campus, which programs might help to meet their needs, and to track performance data by specific groups. Marketers use demographic data to better target areas where potential clients might live. As a speaker, knowing something about your audience's demographic makeup might give you some general ideas about your audience's likely experiences, expectations, beliefs, values, behaviors, and habits. This information helps you determine how best to capture their interest and appeal to them.

Artifacts

In addition to demographics, taking a careful look at your audience and surroundings can also provide information about them. **Artifacts**, in terms of public speaking, are objects that indicate something about the values, beliefs, practices, history, and norms of a group of people. Most people have at least some artifacts that reflect things that are important to them in their offices and homes. These include everyday objects or pictures that serve as reminders of important life events or values, posters, or artwork, all of which tell you something about the person who typically occupies that space. Think about your own office, dorm room, or home. How much could an outsider learn about your experiences, knowledge, interests, beliefs, attitudes, and values from looking around for just a couple of minutes?

Similarly, you can learn a lot about a group you are speaking to by looking at the artifacts around them. Before a presentation to an organization, you might want to consider looking at its website for pictures, a mission statement, news articles, or anything else that might tell you about the group and the goals of the individuals in that group, and then show up a little early so you can pay attention to the objects in the workspace. If you are giving a speech in class, you might examine what your classmates wear, what they talk about, and what kinds of objects they carry with them, and then consider what those things communicate about your classmates' interests and values.

Informants

When you give speeches in class, you will typically know several people in your audience, but you might find yourself in other situations in which you are invited to speak to a group of people, most, if not all, of whom you do not know. In these situations, you might want to consider getting information about your audience from an informant. An **informant** is a contact person within the organization or group from whom you can obtain information about your audience. For instance, if you are invited to talk to a volunteer organization, you might ask the person who invited you to speak to tell you a little bit about the background, interests, knowledge, and needs of the audience. If you have a friend that belongs to the organization, you can also ask him or her to tell you a little bit about the audience and the organization.

Interviews

Contact persons are not always readily available and sometimes are not much help. In the event you do not have a contact person, you might want to consider asking the person arranging the speech to put you in touch with a few potential members of the audience so you can interview them. You can conduct interviews in person or via phone, email, or Skype to ask the individuals about their own experiences, knowledge, and interests, or ask them about the group as a whole. You can then get a general sense of the entire audience from the information you obtain from those interviews. This information can be enormously helpful in tailoring your message to the particular audience you will address.

Artifacts
in terms of public speaking, objects that indicate something about the values, beliefs, practices, history, and norms of a group of people

Informant
a contact person within the organization or group you can talk with to obtain information about the audience you will be speaking to

Likert scale questions
survey questions that provide statements and then ask respondents to circle a number that measures their level of agreement with the statement

Semantic differential scale questions
survey questions that ask participants to choose their position on a continuum between two polar opposites

Open-ended questions
questions that ask audience members for more elaborate written responses

Surveys

If you have enough time before your presentation, and have the ability to reach each audience member, you can send your audience a survey to fill out and return to you before you prepare your speech. These surveys can help you gather demographic data as well as information about people's attitudes regarding specific issues. You could ask multiple choice questions that give a limited number of possible responses, **Likert scale questions** that give statements and then ask respondents to circle a number that measures their level of agreement with it, **semantic differential scale questions** that ask participants to choose their position on a continuum between two polar opposites, or **open-ended questions** that allow audience members to give more elaborate written responses to a question.

Types of Survey Questions

Multiple Choice

Which of the following issues do you consider to be the most important in the upcoming presidential election?

    a.   Economy

    b.   Foreign Policy

    c.   Health care

    d.   Education

Likert Scale

I believe that the future of our national economy depends primarily on the quality of our public education system.

    1.   Strongly disagree

    2.   Disagree

    3.   Somewhat disagree

    4.   Neither agree nor disagree

    5.   Somewhat agree

    6.   Agree

    7.   Strongly agree

Semantic Differential

I believe the future of our national economy depends primarily on the quality of our public education system.

Not Valuable   1   2   3   4   5   6   7   Valuable

Open-Ended

What do you think the university can do to improve the quality of student experiences on this campus?

Polling the Audience

Oftentimes, you will not have the time or opportunity to conduct a survey with your audience in advance. This does not, however, mean it is impossible to ask your audience a question. Instead, you can informally poll your audience by asking a question, or even several questions, during your speech. You can ask audience members to raise their hands if they agree or disagree with a particular statement. This can be an especially effective strategy that will help you capture your audience's attention during the beginning of your speech, while also learning something about them you can then use later in your presentation. If you use this strategy, you should make sure you incorporate your audience's responses into your speech in some way.

Direct Observation

On the day of your speech, you will be able to learn a lot about your audience by simply observing them. During your speech, you will also be able to see your audience's nonverbal feedback, which will provide cues about how they are reacting to specific aspects of your message. You might see your audience become increasingly engaged, nod their heads, smile, make lots of eye contact, or provide other nonverbal feedback that indicates they are interested in your speech or agree with you. On the other hand, you could see your audience becoming distracted, looking at cell phones, frowning, shaking their head, looking away, or even falling asleep during your speech, which could indicate disinterest or disagreement.

Regardless of which methods of audience analysis are available—and there are always some strategies available for analyzing your audience—you should adapt your speech

MEDIATED MOMENTS

Speeches have always had a home in all kinds of movies because of their ability to generate emotional reactions in their audiences. The 1996 film *City Hall* contains a prime example of a speaker who overcomes a hostile audience with a eulogy of a young African American child who had recently been shot. The mayor, played by Al Pacino, uses artifacts commonly found in the city, as well as the boy's coffin, to generate identification with the audience and allow them to see him as an ally and not an enemy. He knew going into the situation that the audience was predisposed to be against him, yet he quickly observed things he could use in the church where he spoke to help him overcome their hostility. This use of direct observation and other audience analysis techniques serves to show that, even in movies, speakers need to be attuned to their audience to create a connection with their audience.

based on what you learn about your audience. If you find out that your audience does not know a lot about your topic, you might need to provide a little bit more background information. If your audience disagrees with your message, you might need to put in extra effort to acknowledge opposing viewpoints and provide even more evidence that supports your position using arguments that are likely to appeal to the values of your audience. If you know that specific audience members have experiences related to your topic and are open with others about those experiences, you might want to refer to them by name during your presentation. The more information you have about your audience both before and during your presentation, the better you can craft a message that will appeal to them.

Conducting Research

Knowing about your audience can also help you determine which information will be most effective in delivering your message. The most time consuming part of giving a speech is not the speech itself, but rather the research that goes into finding the information you need to make your point. Incorporating and citing research throughout your speech enhances your ability to connect with an audience, because it increases your credibility as a speaker and substantiates the claims you make. In this part of the chapter, we will identify five different types of sources you can look to for credible and useful information, describe four different types of information you will find there, and provide a way to evaluate the information you find.

Sources of Information

Despite the prevalence and utility of Google, there are a wide variety of resources for gathering information when developing a speech. Each of them has its own benefits and drawbacks, and not all will be useful for every speaking occasion. Knowing about these diverse sources of information gives you a variety of possibilities to consider when developing a presentation, adding to your ability to make an engaging and interesting message. Here are five different places you can potentially find useful information and evidence.

Peer-Reviewed Academic Journal Articles. Peer-reviewed articles are original research studies typically published in academic journals you can find in your university or college library. These studies are usually written by academic researchers, such as university professors, and are reviewed by other experts in the field before publication to ensure that the study used high-quality research methods and its results warrant the conclusions. Because the articles undergo a rigorous review process, they can provide some of the most reliable, up-to-date information, but will also usually be written with a high level of specific detail given that they are intended primarily for other experts and researchers.

Books. Like peer-reviewed academic journal articles, some books are extended research reports that investigate a topic in depth. Others provide histories, background information, and overviews intended to teach you about a broad subject (such as a textbook). While other books include stories about individuals who went through a particular experience or contain completely fictional accounts. Typically, nonfiction research-based books or text-books will be the most useful sources of evidence when you are preparing a speech, but you might find a good narrative or example in fiction books that will add some color to your presentation.

Magazines and Newspapers. Magazines and newspapers are intended for more general audiences than academic journals, and they rely heavily on subscribers and advertisers to maintain profits. Some are intended to share specialized information in a particular field, some deliver current events, while others are intended purely for entertainment purposes. Depending on your topic and your audience, there may very well be valuable information in these sources. For instance, human interest stories found in certain magazines and news-papers might provide some interesting examples to help explain a point within a speech.

Web and Media Sources. Websites and media sources such as television shows, radio pro-grams, documentaries, and movies can be good sources of quality information, but can also be highly unreliable. Generally, websites ending in .gov and .edu are more reliable than websites ending in .com, .org, or .net, but you will want to consider the credibility of the website providing the information in deciding whether a website should be considered an accurate source of information. For instance, www.mayoclinic.org is a highly credible source for medical information, since the information is provided by the Mayo Clinic, one of the top research hospitals in the United States, while www.nationalenquirer.com gets its information from gossip magazine reports and sensationalized news stories based on rumors about celebrities. The use of Web and media sources depends largely on how you approach your topic and the connections you seek to make between that information and your topic.

Interviews with an Expert or Peer. For many of your speeches, it will be helpful to talk directly with an expert or a peer. An expert might be a professor who does research or teaches about the subject, or someone who has professional experience related to your topic. For example, if you are giving a speech about common running injuries, you might want to consult with a kinesiology professor who researches running injuries, a medical doctor who frequently diagnoses injuries, or a physical therapist who helps athletes recover from injuries. These would all constitute experts on the topic. Peers, on the other hand, do not possess expertise but can offer opinions or even experiences related to the topic. Instead of a healthcare provider who has expertise, you might interview a friend who injured himself or herself running. Peers provide a different type of information than an expert can, but the stories shared by peers can help your audience better understand how your topic impacts others' everyday experiences.

Types of Supporting Evidence

Each of the sources we just discussed provides information that can be used to support the points you make in your presentation. Information comes in many forms, just as it comes

Numbers
raw quantitative
data

Statistics
quantitative reports
that summarize
and organize sets
of numbers to
make them easier
to understand and
visualize

Examples
instances that we
use to help define
or clarify concepts,
draw attention to
a particular feature
of an experience, or
elicit memories and
emotions in our
audience

Testimony
the words of other
people used to
support your point

from many outlets. Ideally, you should use several of the following types of supporting materials in your speech to add variety, interest, and credibility to your speech.

Numbers and Statistics. **Numbers** report raw quantitative data, whereas **statistics** summarize and organize sets of data to make them easier to understand and visualize. Statistics might include ratios, percentages, fractions, averages, standard deviations, or other calculations that make it easier to understand the overall impact of the data. Numbers and statistics can be especially valuable for showing the extent of a problem or the likelihood that your audience will be impacted by an issue. For example, you would be using a number if you were to say that, according to the Centers for Disease Control (CDC), 16,238 people are killed in homicides in the United States each year, but you would be using a statistic if you explained that means that 5.2 people out of every 100,000 will die as homicide victims each year.[1] You would be using a number if you said that according to seer.cancer.gov, 13,397,159 people are living with cancer in the U.S. right now, but you would be using a statistic if you said that 40.8 percent of all people will be diagnosed with cancer during their lifetime.[2]

Examples. Sometimes we use a story to personalize a number or statistic. These stories are **examples,** which are instances that we use to help define or clarify concepts, draw attention to a particular feature of an experience, or elicit memories and emotions in our audience. Examples can be brief or extended, and they can be real or hypothetical.

Testimony. Another qualitative form of evidence you might use in a speech are statements by other people. This is also called **testimony,** and it involves using the words of other people to support your point. There are two types of testimony: expert testimony and peer testimony. **Expert testimony** is information you obtain from someone who conducts extensive research on the topic, has significant experience with the topic, or holds a position that

DIALING DIVERSITY

In the library, books, journals, and magazines are often organized using one of several filing systems. You are likely familiar with the Dewey Decimal System, but the one used in most university libraries is the Library of Congress Classification System. A third system was also developed by Indian library scholar S.R. Ranganathan. In addition to a coding system, Ranganathan also is remembered for devising the five laws of library science:[3]

1. Books are for use, not storage.
2. Every patron should be able to find what they need.
3. Every book has someone who finds it useful.
4. Use business principles to improve reader services.
5. Libraries grow, and should be prepared to handle that growth.

lends credibility to his or her ideas on a subject. **Peer testimony** is information that comes from someone who is in the same peer group as the audience, and who is not necessarily an expert on the topic. Expert testimony would be valuable when explaining why climate change is occurring and how it will impact future weather patterns, while peer testimony would be valuable when talking about what the general student response to the new student union on campus has been. Often, but not always, testimony comes from interviews with these individuals, but there are times when you find testimony in an article you then use, despite not having done the interview yourself.

Definitions. If you are talking about a topic that might be unfamiliar to many members of your audience or are using terms that could have multiple meanings, it can be helpful to include definitions in your speech. You might choose to provide the **denotative meaning** of a word or phrase, which is the literal definition of that word or phrase you might find in a dictionary. Alternately, you might need to explain the **connotative meaning** of a word or phrase, which is the way that word or phrase is used in a particular context by a particular group of people. When using definitions, you might need to extend your definition to include the history of the word or phrase, explanations or descriptions of the thing being defined, or analogies and metaphors that help the audience understand a new concept by showing how it is similar to something that is familiar.

Evaluating Information

Once you have found a variety of sources and support materials, you will need to evaluate whether they effectively support your speech. As you evaluate your sources, you will want to make sure that they are sources your entire audience will view as credible. When evaluating the credibility of your sources, there are several criteria you should keep in mind.

How recent is the source? Typically, more recent sources will have more up-to-date, useful information. For example, an article about cancer treatments published in 1975 is not a good source of information about current cancer treatments, because a great deal of research and innovation has occurred that changed the way many cancers are treated today.

Is the source in a position to know the information? If the person or organization that provided the information to the source is an expert on the specific subject, then it is probably a reliable source. For example, Dr. Sanjay Gupta, a neurosurgeon and professor at Emory University School of Medicine who is perhaps best known for his work as a CNN medical correspondent, would be an excellent source of information for a speech about brain injuries and neurosurgery, but he would not be a very credible source of information about which home building materials should be used in an area that has frequent earthquakes.

Is the source biased? If your source will gain financially, or in some other way, from convincing you to adopt a particular perspective or to purchase a particular product, you should

Expert testimony information that you obtain from someone who has conducted extensive research on the topic, has significant experience with the topic, or holds a position that lends credibility to his or her ideas on a subject matter

Peer testimony information that comes from someone who is in the same peer group as the audience, who is not necessarily an expert on the topic

Denotative meaning the literal definition of a word or phrase that you might find in a dictionary

Connotative meaning the way a word or phrase is used in a particular context, potentially as slang or with an implied value judgment take that bias into account when determining whether to use the information. For instance, even though Kobe Bryant undoubtedly knows something about basketball shoes as a star basketball player for the Los Angeles Lakers, he is also a biased source because he gets paid by Nike to endorse their shoes and other merchandise. Instead, you would be better off trusting a podiatrist to help you identify which shoes might be best for you, since a podiatrist has expertise in identifying which shoes are most appropriate based on your physiology, but will likely not see any financial gain if you choose one brand of shoe over another. If you do use information from a potentially biased source, make sure the audience knows about that potential bias.

Is the information consistent with other sources? If you have a half-dozen sources that meet the previous criteria for being credible sources, and one of the sources contradicts the other five sources, it is probable that the five consistent sources are accurate, not the single source that contradicts them. Just as journalists are typically expected to have multiple sources corroborating a story before they publish it, you should have multiple sources that corroborate your claims before you try to convince your audience those claims are true.

Dialogic Public Speaking

Although many people imagine a dialogue as occurring between two people, dialogues can actually happen in the public sphere as well. Creating a dialogic environment when a large audience is involved can be difficult, and is not entirely under the control of the speaker. Nevertheless, there are some things you can do that encourage an audience to act with good will and openly exchange ideas with you as the speaker at the appropriate time. In this section of the chapter, we will provide a few suggestions for how to do this.

> *"I think a good many people have a similar desire to be freed from the obligation to begin, a similar desire to be on the other side of the discourse from the outset, without having to consider from the other side what might be strange, frightening, and perhaps maleficent about it."[4]*
>
> —*Michel Foucault*

Identify with Your Audience

Audiences can be put off very quickly if you as the speaker do not make an attempt to connect with them in terms of their interests, values, and concerns. Demonstrate early in the speech that you tried to understand the topic from their perspective, but do so without making broad sweeping statements about "what you know about them," or being disingenuous in your attempts to connect with them.

Respect Differences

Audiences, although large and seemingly homogenous, are not made up of identical people. Even among a particular demographic group there are differences in attitudes and values, so do not make the presumption that they all know or believe something just because they are members of a certain group. There are differences among members of an audience that you should respect and appreciate.

Keep an Open Mind

Even though you may believe you know what you want to say, the evidence may take you elsewhere. Search unbiased sources first, then look to those that might be supportive of and those that may disagree with your position. This allows you to take in evidence beyond that which only supports a specific agenda. You may actually uncover information that makes you change your mind—and that is a good thing.

Strive for Audience Understanding

The tendency may be to deluge an audience with statistics or testimony in the hopes that the sheer amount of what you provide will sway them. Instead, take the information and condense it into manageable units for an audience to digest. Help them understand things the way you do, rather than force them to be convinced by quantity.

Talk with, Not at, Your Audience

Formal presentations can seem like the speaker is speaking at an audience who simply absorbs the message, but in actuality the process is much more transactional. The audience brings their own experiences, knowledge, and biases to their interpretation of your message. An effective speech retains a conversational quality that invites follow-up comments and questions when it is done.

Summary

Formal public speaking presentations occur in a different communication context than interpersonal relationships. In this chapter, we explored some of the basic tenets and qualities of public speaking that make it different from a simple conversation. We first addressed the matter of topic selection, before examining how to analyze an audience for a formal presentation. We then looked at the process of researching information to use for speech construction, before offering some suggestions for making a speech to a large audience more dialogic.

Chapter 14 Key Ideas

- The five canons of rhetoric are invention, arrangement, style, delivery, and memory.
- When selecting a topic, you should consider the general purpose of your speech and whether the topic is appropriate for the occasion, the particular audience, and yourself

- You can analyze your audience through the use of demographics, artifacts, informants, interviews, surveys, polling the audience, and direct observation
- Five sources of information you might use to find information for your speech include: (1) peer-reviewed academic journal articles, (2) books, (3) magazines and newspapers, (4) Web and media sources, and (5) interviews with experts
- Supporting evidence can include: (1) numbers and statistics, (2) examples, (3) testimony, and (4) definitions
- When evaluating the credibility of a source, you should consider: (1) how recently the source was produced, (2) whether the source is in a position to know the information, (3) whether the source is biased, and (4) whether the source is consistent with other reliable sources of information

Chapter 14 Key Terms

General purpose	Likert Scale Questions	Testimony
Brainstorm	Semantic Differential Scale Questions	Expert testimony
Concept map	Open-ended questions	Peer testimony
Demographics	Numbers	Denotative meaning
Artifacts	Statistics	Connotative meaning
Informant	Examples	

References

1 Assault or homicide. Centers for Disease Control and Prevention. Retrieved from http://www.cdc.gov/nchs/fastats/homicide.htm

2 SEER Stat Fact Sheet: All Cancer Sites. Surveillance, Epidemiology, and End Results Program. Retrieved from http://seer.cancer.gov/statfacts/html/all.html

3 Ranganathan, S.R. *The Five Laws of Library Science.* 2nd ed. Bangalore, India: Sarada Ranganathan Endowment for Library Science.

4 Foucault, M. (2001). From the Order of Discourse. In Bizzell, P & Herzberg, B. (Eds.), *The Rhetorical Tradition* (p. 1460).

Chapter 15

Informative and Explanatory Speaking

Speeches can serve different purposes. One of the primary goals of some speeches is to deliver information to an audience. These informative speeches do not try to persuade an audience, though the audience may very well be persuaded; rather, they only try to convey information to an audience so they understand it. Such speeches might take place at job orientations, sales meetings, or, most commonly, in a classroom where a teacher tries to explain material to students.

Informative speeches are intended to teach the audience something new and have two key purposes: to **inform**, which is to make the audience aware of a phenomenon, and to **explain**, which is to deepen the audience's understanding of that phenomenon.[1] When you are simply informing an audience, you are likely to be using the linear model of communication. Recall that the linear model treats communication as a one-way process in which a speaker gives his or her audience information, and there is no response from the audience. For example, if you are reporting the morning's headline news, sharing information about the day's stock prices, or telling someone the year you were born as part of an identity security check, you are simply sharing information with someone else. Explaining, however, goes much further than informing.

Inform
make the audience aware of a phenomenon

Explain
deepen the audience's understanding of that phenomenon

Speakers that seek to explain something to an audience provide deeper details about how and why something is a certain way and take care to pay attention to whether an audience accurately understands what is presented. Audience members exhibit evidence of this understanding, or lack thereof, through nonverbal reactions and their ability to accurately answer certain questions during or after the presentation.

In this chapter, we investigate informative speeches, and in doing so, demonstrate how informing and explaining share similar qualities. We will first discuss the types of information speakers typically explain to audiences. Next, we will explore different ways to explain difficult concepts, and then provide strategies for facilitating audience understanding. We will conclude by providing several suggestions for how to maintain a dialogic atmosphere when explaining material in a formal presentation.

Types of Information We Explain

There are many different pieces of information we might seek to explain to an audience. We can categorize those pieces of information into a handful of types. Knowing what type of information you need to explain to an audience helps you choose a method for arranging your points. The topic itself will often suggest the way it should be organized for the most effective explanation, but in some cases you need to "invent" the organizational pattern. In this section of the chapter, we will explore four types of topics you might choose for your informative speech: objects, processes, events, and concepts.

Objects

A speech about an object is a speech about a tangible item. Objects might include artifacts, mementos, souvenirs, buildings, places, or even people. For example, you probably gave speeches about objects when you stood up to do "show and tell" in elementary school. You would also be giving a speech about an object if you explained how a mortar and pestle are used to grind spices, taught your audience about Henrietta Lacks and the role her cells have played in cancer research, described several important landmarks in Seattle, explicated the significance of prayer beads in many of the world's religions, or explained the differences between types of coffee beans.

Processes

A speech about a process is a speech that explains the steps needed to accomplish something, and these presentations are usually arranged chronologically. Often, a speech about a process is a "how to" speech intended to teach the audience how to accomplish something, such as a how to create a secure password, how to change a tire on a car, or how to roast a traditional Thanksgiving turkey. These speeches can also explain processes specific to a particular industry, such as how tea leaves are grown, how plastic is recycled and then used to create something new, or how a particular marketing plan will be used to launch a new product. Furthermore, speeches about processes are often used to explain how things happen in science and medicine, such as explaining how cells divide to grow new cells, describing the steps involved in a cancer treatment plan, or helping the audience understand how climate change is leading to the rising of the ocean.

Events

A speech about an event is a speech that focuses on something that happened, is happening, or might happen at some point in the future. Speeches about events are often organized chronologically in a way that allows the speaker to explain the event as it unfolded, but could also be arranged topically, especially when many things are happening simultaneously. For example, you might use a chronological pattern of organization to explain how the major events on Inauguration Day unfold when a new president enters office. If you are an event planner hosting a conference that has multiple things happening at the same time, however, you might present your plan topically, with each main point explaining a different element of the conference, such as the food, the programming, and the entertainment.

Concepts

A speech about a concept explains an abstract idea instead of a concrete object. Concept speeches might include presentations about theories, ideas, religion, economics, political

MEDIATED MOMENTS

Television has had a profound effect on the dissemination of information. Additionally, the advent of the 24-hour news channel concept in the 1980s has ballooned, and now there are numerous such channels domestically and internationally. This has been valuable in times of crisis because it allows for misinformation to be corrected whenever necessary. Take the 2014 Ebola epidemic in West Africa that expanded to include countries like the United States and Spain. The public, particularly in the U.S., had little understanding of the virus, and so numerous news channels contracted doctors and public health experts to explain the disease to the public and prevent a mass panic. One such station, the BBC, aired a 40-second report that explained how Ebola actually attacks human cells using visuals and a voice-over report. To further illustrate the impact media has on the ability to spread information, that report is now available on YouTube.[2]

ideology, or laws. Concept speeches can be especially challenging because they require the speaker to take something that is abstract and intangible and make it easy for the audience to understand by using vivid description, examples, or illustrations. A physicist might drop several objects of different weights from the top of a building at the same time to demonstrate the idea that gravity pulls all objects toward the Earth at the same speed, regardless of the weight of the object. A philosopher might try to explain how John Locke's theory of mind differs from Renee Descartes' rationalism. Similarly, a film producer might describe the plot for a film he or she plans to make.

Patterns of Organization for Informative Speeches

When trying to explain difficult and complex information to your audience members, the way you organize your main points is critical for helping them understand your topic. Before you begin to develop your outline, you should carefully consider which of the following patterns of organization will be most effective in helping communicate your message to your audience. The goal is to present information in the best way possible to foster understanding by the audience, and so choosing the best organizational pattern to accomplish that task is a must for any speaker.

Spatial

Spatial pattern of organization
used to describe an object by explaining how parts physically relate to one another in a defined space

The **spatial pattern of organization** is used to describe an object by explaining how parts physically relate to one another in a defined space. When you use spatial organization, you might describe something in order from top to bottom, bottom to top, right to left, left to right, front to back, or in some other physical order as you visually or physically move through the thing you are explaining. For example, you might use spatial organization to explain the layout of the National Mall by first talking about the Capitol Building, which is on the far eastern end of the Mall. Next, you might discuss the Smithsonian Museums, which lie west of the Capitol building. Finally, you might end by describing the monuments and memorials on the far western end of the Mall. In another instance, a docent at the Museum of Modern Art might describe Salvador Dali's *The Persistence of Memory* by describing the painting from top to bottom.

Chronological

Chronological pattern of organization
used to describe events or processes in the order that they occur in time, from earlier events to later events

The **chronological pattern of organization** is used to describe events or processes in the order they occur in time, from earlier events to later events. Chronological organization works especially well when describing historical events, such as the events that led to the Civil War, or processes that have several steps, such as how to build a car engine. Chronological speeches can also be used to describe objects. For example, you might give a speech about the Roman Coliseum by beginning with its construction, then discussing its purposes for the Roman Republic, before discussing what state it is in now.

Cause-Effect

The **cause-effect pattern of organization** is a variation of the chronological pattern of organization that discusses the causes that led to a specific event or effect. There are usually several causes that lead to each event, and each cause usually leads to several effects, and so in this kind of speech it is important not to oversimplify a cause-effect relationship by arguing that a single cause led to a single effect with no other factors involved. At the same time, your speech can easily become tangential if you focus on all of the possible causes of an event as well as all of the possible effects or outcomes. So in a cause-effect speech, you will want to choose whether to build your thesis around the causes or the effects. For example, you might decide to discuss how economic and social differences, views on state versus federal rights, and slavery were major factors that led to the U.S. Civil War, and then discuss the overall impact of that war. In that speech, you would be focusing on the specific event (the Civil War) and talking about several causes leading to it.

Problem-Solution

The **problem-solution pattern of organization** involves organizing your speech by first explaining a problem before teaching your audience about the solution to that problem. In an informative speech, the problem-solution pattern of organization might involve teaching your audience about a problem that occurred in the past and how it was solved in the past. For example, you might discuss why taking regular food into space on a space shuttle was a problem and how it was solved by developing freeze-dried food that could be rehydrated and eaten in space. Alternately, your speech might teach your audience about a common problem and teach them how to solve that problem. You might approach the problem of having nitrogen deficiency in soil and then explain how to solve the problem by adding compost, manure, nitrogen-fixing plants, coffee grounds, or chemical fertilizers to the soil. When giving an informative problem-solution speech, though, you need to be careful to make sure you are teaching your audience about the problem and possible solutions, not persuading them to adopt a particular solution.

Topical

The **topical pattern of organization** is used to divide your speech into categories or subtopics. Topical organization can be used when there are specific elements of your topic you want to discuss or when your topic does not fit any of the other patterns of organization. For example, you might use topical organization in an informative speech about different types of bikes and might choose to organize your main points by talking first about road bikes, second about mountain bikes, and finally about hybrid bikes. You might also choose to give a speech about effective teaching by talking first about how students learn, second about how to manage a classroom, and finally about how to assess whether and how much students have learned. Most syllabi and schedules in college courses are actually arranged topically, providing the content focus for each particular day.

Cause-effect pattern of organization a variation on the chronological pattern of organization used to discuss the causes that led to a specific event or effect

Problem-solution pattern of organization used to organize a speech by first explaining a problem and then teaching the audience about the solution

Topical pattern of organization used to divide your speech into categories or subtopics

Explaining Difficult Concepts

In many informative speeches, you will be explaining concepts that are difficult for your audience to understand, particularly if your audience is not comprised of experts in the subject about which you are speaking. There are many reasons that an idea might be difficult for an audience to understand, but according to Dr. Katherine Rowan,[3] there are three primary reasons it is hard for a nonexpert audience to understand a complex idea: (1) the language or concepts are difficult, (2) the structure or process is hard to envision, or (3) the idea is difficult to believe. When explaining difficult concepts in your informative speech, you should first identify why the concept is difficult to understand, and then choose the explanatory strategy that best helps audiences overcome that particular challenge. In this part of the chapter, we will discuss ways to overcome these three challenges to effective explanation.

Difficult Language

Elucidating explanation an explanation that helps an audience understand the definition term by distinguishing the essential characteristics that are always present from the associated characteristics that are only sometimes present in the objects, concepts, or processes that are examples of the term you are defining

When a concept is difficult to understand because the vocabulary is unfamiliar to your audience, you should use an **elucidating explanation.** Your goal in an elucidating explanation is to help your audience understand the definition of a term and distinguish its essential characteristics from the associated characteristics that are only sometimes present in that which you are defining. Rowan explains that elucidating explanations should include four parts: (1) a common *exemplar*, or ideal example, of the concept, (2) a *definition* that explains the essential characteristics of the concept, (3) several *examples* of the concept, along with some *nonexamples* that might commonly be mistaken as examples of the concept, and (4) opportunities for your audience to *practice* identifying examples and nonexamples of the concept.[4]

Take the case of the term "immediacy," which might be unfamiliar to some people who have not studied instructional communication or psychology. If you used an elucidating explanation to help your audience understand the concept of immediacy, you might say:

> "In *Dead Poet's Society*, Mr. Keating, who is played by Robin Williams, seems to draw his students in and connect with them by doing things like calling on them by name, moving around the classroom, using a lot of vocal variety and gestures, using humor during class, and having a relaxed posture. All of these behaviors show that Mr. Keating has a high level of immediacy. Immediacy is 'the degree of perceived physical or psychological closeness between teachers and students.' Immediacy represents a set of verbal and nonverbal communication behaviors that indicate a teacher's willingness to approach and be approached by students.[5] Some examples of teacher immediacy behaviors include making eye contact with students, having a relaxed body posture while teaching, allowing for small talk, using words like 'we' and 'us,' and using vocal variety and gestures. On the other hand, sarcastic humor, telling stories that embarrass students, and reading from PowerPoint slides are not examples of teacher immediacy."

Here you see how each of the components of an elucidating explanation are included. Not all elucidating explanations need all of these, but if you have the time, and the term is particularly hard to pin down for an audience, use as many as you can.

Difficult to Picture

Other concepts use familiar words but are difficult to understand because they are difficult to picture. Concepts or processes might be challenging to imagine because they are abstract ideas, or because the process or object is microscopic and cannot easily be seen. There are two ways that something can be difficult to picture. First, it might be difficult to get an overall impression of the thing being explained, and second, it might be difficult to see the parts, processes, and interrelations of the phenomenon.

When you explain something that is difficult to picture, you should use a **quasi-scientific explanation** to help the audience better understand the phenomenon. A quasi-scientific explanation should include two key parts: (1) a graphic feature that helps the audience get an overall big picture of the phenomenon, such as a model, simplified drawing, cartoon, or diagram; and (2) verbal organizational cues that indicate the relationships among the parts or subprocesses of the phenomenon, including transitions, summaries, previews, and statements that clearly state the relationships. Some of the best quasi-scientific explanations include titles that suggest what the overall structure is, analogies that help the audience organize the information by comparing it to something familiar, and thesis statements or topic sentences that suggest a model that shares similar characteristics with the unfamiliar phenomenon.

For example, it can be difficult to picture how herd immunity helps prevent the spread of vaccine-preventable diseases even when a few people cannot be vaccinated because they are newborns who are not yet old enough to receive the vaccine, or because they have a medical condition that weakens the immune system and would make getting vaccinated dangerous. To help explain how vaccinating a large proportion of a population protects those who cannot be vaccinated, you might explain that humans fighting off diseases like the measles are in some ways similar to a herd of cattle trying to fight off coyotes that prey on young calves. In both instances there is power in numbers. Along with this analogy, you might choose to provide a diagram that shows how easily diseases can spread through a population once a critical mass of people chooses not to be vaccinated.

Difficult to Believe

Sometimes concepts use simple language and can be imagined easily, but are difficult to believe because they are counterintuitive. In these cases, speakers should use **transformative explanations** to help the audience change their everyday ideas about how something works into an accurate understanding of the phenomenon. Transformative explanations have four parts: they (1) acknowledge people's everyday or "lay" theory about the concept, perhaps by asking the audience to describe the concept; (2) acknowledge why the audience members' understanding seems plausible on the surface; (3) explain why their impression is incorrect and show examples that

Quasi-scientific explanation an explanation that helps the audience get an overall picture of a phenomenon and see relationships among the parts

Transformative explanations explanations that help audience members transform their everyday ideas about how something works into a more scientifically accurate understanding of the phenomenon demonstrate why it is not adequate for explaining the phenomenon; and (4) explain the theory and illustrate why it is effective.

For example, when we think we see things, we are actually seeing reflected light off of the object, not the object we are looking at. This is counterintuitive because we think we are actually seeing the object that is in front of us. If you were to use a transformative explanation to help your audience understand how we see things, you might say something like this:

> "Most people think when we see something, we are actually seeing the object that is in front of us. This makes a lot of sense because, in our experience, when we see something, it is really there. However, if this were true, we would be able to see everything that was in front of us all of the time. But if you have ever tripped over something while walking through a dark room in the middle of the night, you know that sometimes things are in front of you that you cannot see when there is no light. Instead, when we think we see something, we are actually seeing the light that is reflected off of the object that is in front of us."

This statement includes all the elements of a transformative explanation and illustrates how you can explain and correct a misunderstanding someone might have in a logical and civil manner.

Strategies to Help Your Audience Understand

In addition to the tips for explaining difficult content to your audience, there are several other strategies available to you as a speaker for helping your audience understand your topic and remembering the key points of your presentations. These six methods may seem simple, but they go a long way in helping to ensure your audience understands and remembers the information you provided.

Repetition. If you only say something once, your audience is unlikely to remember it. If you expose your audience to the same idea multiple times and in multiple ways, they are much more likely to remember the information. Repetition is especially helpful for aiding your audience in understanding important complicated material within your speech. Often, audiences may not completely get what you are explaining with one example. They may require another, different example, or perhaps an analogy to help them understand the concept. Finding creative different ways to express the same idea helps the audience achieve understanding. The more you repeat something, the greater the chance the audience will pick up on it.

Rewards. Your audience will pay more attention to what you are saying if they perceive they will be rewarded for doing so. Rewards can be explicit, such as giving candy to audience members who can answer questions correctly, or implicit, such as telling the audience how they will benefit from the knowledge you are sharing. When you have a choice, though, the latter works better for using rewards, because the reward lasts much longer for the audience. Creating intrinsic rewards for listening to the speech also assists the audience in investing time paying attention to you, and as we have mentioned at other times in this book, when we invest time in something, it shows we care about it. The same applies for convincing an audience that investing time in listening to your speech will reward them in numerous ways.

Show and Tell. Although Show and Tell is a game played mainly by elementary school students, it also can play a vital role in helping adult audiences understand material. It essentially uses visual and verbal organizational cues to help your audience identify the most important concepts and understand how those concepts relate to each other.[6] Visual organization cues might include putting key words for each main point on a PowerPoint slide when you preview your main points, showing important definitions or quotations while you are talking about them, showing your audience diagrams or images that will help them visualize how concepts are related, or giving your audience a paper handout that will help them follow along during your speech. Using matrixes or other diagrams that summarize information and visually demonstrating how ideas are related can be especially helpful because the audience can more easily understand the connections between concepts.[7] Verbal organization cues include signposts, reviews, and previews that help draw the audience's attention to important concepts and help the audience understand how ideas are related. This is why the preview of main points in the introduction of your speech, transitions between main points, and the review of main points in the conclusion are so important.

> *"Developing your ability to inform and explain will assist you in many aspects of life, be those parenting, work, or recreation. Doing so will give you tools for learning complex material and sharing that material with others."*
>
> —*Katherine Rowan, George Mason University*

Build on What Your Audience Already Knows. When explaining concepts that are unfamiliar to the audience, you can help them understand by connecting the new information to something that the audience already knows.[8] For instance, you might use an analogy or metaphor to show the similarities between something familiar and something new. One of the most effective ways of both explaining a difficult concept and identifying with an audience is to connect your topic or information to something with which they are already familiar. This helps them make the association themselves in terms they understand, making it more likely the information will be remembered.

Use Humor. Incorporating humor that is related to the topic of your speech can help you capture and keep your audience's attention. You will want to be careful, however, to make sure that your humor enhances your audience members' attention to your topic rather than distracts from it. In short, humor must help them focus on the content and not you. You will also need to be careful that your humor can be easily understood by your entire audience through the use of idioms and terms you expect the audience will know. Just because a speech delivers information does not mean it needs to be boring and uninteresting.

Check for Understanding. Finally, you can help your audience learn by checking for understanding periodically. Ask your audience questions or provide examples to see whether they understand the concepts you have explained so far. If you find that your audience does not quite understand the ideas, adapt your speech by explaining the ideas in a slightly different way until your audience shows they understand the concepts. To plan for this, you should prepare a few different ways to explain the same point, even if you do not end up needing all of them.

Delivering Information Dialogically

Helping an audience understand something is inherently transactional. You can say something, but if you do not appreciate the fact that your audience may interpret it differently, then true understanding of what you conveyed may never be achieved. Just as it is transactional, the process of informing and explaining concepts to an audience, large or small in size, can be enhanced through dialogic principles. In this final section of the chapter, we will outline a few guidelines for ensuring your delivery of information to your audience proceeds in a dialogic manner, increasing the chances of understanding and retention.

Provide Multiple Examples

When trying to explain something you know to an audience that does not know it, you must be prepared to explain the idea several different ways. Sometimes the way you learned the material will not work for members of your audience, so if you notice they do not seem to grasp the material, try another way of approaching the subject. People who are effective at explaining ideas and complicated material to others come armed to the discussion with several different examples that illustrate the same concept. The more options they have, even if they do not need them all, simply increases the likelihood that the audience will understand what they are saying.

Notice Audience's Nonverbal Cues

A good speaker will be able to look at audience members and determine how well they seem to understand what is being said. There will be head nods, note-taking, consistent eye contact, and other signs of listening. Conversely, a good speaker also pays attention for an audience that seems lost by focusing on lack of eye contact, confused facial expressions, head shakes, and other signs that they may not completely understand his or her message. This type of awareness depends on your confidence with and ability to deliver the material in your presentation. If you know your material, you can pay attention to others, but if you are focused on reading prepared notes, then you will not be able to pick up on the subtle, but important, cues coming from your audience.

DIALING DIVERSITY

One of the more noteworthy events during the Iraq War was the March 23, 2003 capture and subsequent rescue of U.S. Army officer Jessica Lynch after she was abducted during the Battle of Nasiriyah. She was rescued on April 1, 2003, the first such rescue of an American POW since Vietnam, and the first ever rescue of a woman. Upon her return to the United States, she was invited to deliver her account to a committee of the U.S. House of Representatives. In this informative presentation, she clearly states her goal, effectively organizes her information, and employs transformative explanation techniques to help correct misinformation regarding her capture, rescue, and the status of the war in Iraq.[9]

Achieve Understanding, Not Agreement

One of the hardest things to remember with informative speaking is that the goal is not to change people's minds or get them to agree with you; rather, you simply want them to understand your point of view and why you hold it. You want your audience to understand content, not necessarily agree with it. When we focus on agreement, we delve into persuasion; and speaking persuasively when the situation calls for informative speaking can have disastrous effects on our credibility and success with the presentation.

Ask Clarifying Questions

Nonverbal indicators are just one way of determining accurate transmission of information to an audience. We may also ask clarifying questions designed to see if someone understands material. Good clarifying questions are specific, not general such as "Do you understand what I am saying?" Or "Are you following along?" These will almost universally elicit agreement from the audience. Instead, ask an audience member who appears lost to provide an example of her or his own or rephrase the definition you provided. Don't do this as a test, but rather as a check to see if your examples and speech are effectively explaining the subject matter.

Maintain Interest Throughout Your Speech

A fast way to destroy an opportunity for dialogue is to show a lack of interest in your audience or your topic. Instead, be energetic and enthusiastic when speaking and try to convey a feeling of enjoyment at the opportunity to teach, inform, or explain something to this audience. When you are interested, the audience will be more likely to be interested as well. Your interest should be both in the topic and in the audience. People are very capable of picking up on your interest in them, and if they perceive that you are not terribly interested in their understanding or reaction, they may stop listening to you.

Provide Clear Points and References

In clearly laying out the key elements of your speech in the introduction, at the beginning of each main topic, and in the conclusion, you help repeat important information for the audience. Additionally, you owe it to your audience to let them know where you gathered your information from. Citing your sources is ethical, honest, and creates an atmosphere where an audience is open to what you have to say, instead of one where they question your information and credentials.

Summary

One of the primary purposes of public speaking is to explain information to an audience. That information is often complicated, and without knowing the difference between types of information and how to convey it properly, informative presentations risk failure. In this chapter, we provided the different categories of information speakers explain, and explored several different ways you might organize that information when speaking to an audience. We also provided tips for delivering complicated material and maintaining a dialogic environment when trying to explain information to an audience that does not understand it.

Chapter 15 Key Ideas

- Informing involves making the audience aware of a phenomenon, whereas explaining is intended to deepen the audience's understanding of that phenomenon.
- Informative speeches can be used to explain objects, processes, events, or concepts.
- The most effective patterns of organization for information speeches include (1) spatial, (2) chronological, (3) cause-effect, (4) problem-solution, and (5) topical organization.
- Concepts might be difficult for the audience to understand because the vocabulary is difficult to understand, the concept is difficult to picture, or the idea is difficult to believe. You can use elucidating explanations, quasi-scientific explanations, or transformative explanations to help your audience understand these respective types of difficult ideas.
- To help your audience understand and remember your speech, try using repetition, offering rewards, showing and telling, building on what the audience already knows, using humor, and checking for understanding.

Chapter 15 Key Terms

Inform

Explain

Spatial Pattern of Organization

Chronological Pattern of Organization

Cause-Effect Pattern of Organization

Problem-Solution Pattern of Organization

Topical Pattern of Organization

Elucidating Explanation

Quasi-Scientific Explanation

Transformative Explanations

References

1 Rowan, K. E. (2003). Informing and explaining skills: Theory and research on informative communication. In J. O. Greene & B. Burleson (Eds.), *Handbook of communication and social interaction skills* (403-438). Mahwah, NJ: Lawrence Erlbaum Associates.

2 How does Ebola attack human cells? BBC News. Retrieved from http://www.youtube.com/watch?v=PvsKgpO9MaI

3 Rowan, K. E. (1995). A new pedagogy for explanatory public speaking: Why arrangement should not substitute for invention. *Communication Education, 44,* 236-250.

4 Ibid.

5 Richmond, V. P., Lane, D. R., & McCroskey, J. C. (2006). Teacher immediacy and the teacher-student relationship. In T. P. Mottet, V. P. Richmond, & J. C. McCroskey (Eds.), *Handbook of Instructional Communication* (167-193). Boston, MA: Pearson.

6 Titsworth, B. S., & Kiewra, K. A. (2004). Organizational lecture cues and student notetaking as facilitators of student learning. *Contemporary Educational Psychology, 29,* 447-461.

7 Kiewra, K. A. (2002). How classroom teachers can help students learn and teach them how to learn. *Theory into Practice, 41*(2), 71-80.

8 Bruner, J. (1960). *The process of education.* Cambridge, MA: Harvard University Press.

9 Lynch, J. (April 24, 2007). Opening statement before House Oversight and Government Reform Committee. Retrieved from www.americanrhetoric.com, http://www.americanrhetoric.com/speeches/jessicalynchopeningstatement.htm

Chapter 16

Organizing Your Presentation

A common misconception people have regarding public speaking is that it is a talent you are born with and not a skill you can refine and develop. The fact is you can become better at public presentations by using and practicing certain skills. One of those skills involves organizing your main points and evidence in a way that best supports your topic and that also allows the audience to follow along. The organizational dimensions of public speaking take a significant amount of time, but the payoff is huge when you deliver an organized and coherent speech. Organization begins after you have identified your topic and gathered research on it.

While repeating information is key to organizing a presentation, there is a little bit more to developing an effective speech. In this chapter, we will talk about how to move from a general purpose and topic to a clear thesis statement. We will then examine the different parts of a speech, and explain how outlining can assist you in crafting those elements. We will also provide you with tools to ensure you cite sources properly in your speech. Finally, we will provide tips for how to use proper organization of your presentation to encourage dialogue with an audience.

From Broad Topics to Specific Purposes

Before you can begin to develop your speech outline, you need to have a clear, specific goal for your presentation. It is not enough to say you are speaking about some broad topic; you must be able to lay out what your specific approach is to the topic. This is something you can only do after researching the topic and narrowing it to something that fits appropriately within the time you have to speak. In this part of the chapter, we will discuss the two steps involved in refining your topic from something broad to something specific.

The first step is developing a specific purpose statement. A **specific purpose statement** is a narrower version of the general purpose statement that identifies the topic you will address, what you will say about it, and what you hope the audience will take away from the speech. A specific purpose statement includes both your general purpose and topic, and it is written as a declarative sentence that states what your speech will do for your audience.

Here's an example of a specific purpose statement for an informative speech:

> **Specific purpose statement:** My speech will teach my audience to do CPR by showing them how to do compressions, open the victim's airway, and give rescue breaths.

Notice that the specific purpose statement above includes the general purpose of the speech (to teach, a variation of informing), the topic (CPR), and a preview of the main points (compressions, airway, and breaths).

The specific purpose statement is part of the speech development process that helps you plan your speech, but it is not something you explicitly say out loud during your speech. Instead, you will go through one final step to convert your specific purpose statement into a thesis statement. A **thesis statement** is a one-sentence summary of your speech that is written the way you will say it out loud to your audience during your speech, and it is followed by a preview of main points. For example, you would convert the specific purpose statement above into the following thesis statement and preview of main points:

> **Thesis:** Learning three steps of CPR can help you save a life.
>
> **Preview of main points:** Today, we will first learn to give compressions, then how to open the victim's airway, and finally how to give rescue breaths.

Notice that the thesis statement and preview of main points together include almost the same information as the specific purpose statement. Language about the audience is removed, however, since you are talking directly to them. The thesis and preview are written in two separate sentences, and the preview of main points includes **signposts**, or key words that signal to the audience you are moving from one part of the speech to another. Once you have established your general purpose, specific purpose, and thesis, you are ready to develop the remainder of your speech.

Specific purpose statement
a narrower version of the general purpose statement that identifies what you will talk about, what you will say about it, and what you hope the audience will take away from the speech

Thesis statement
a one-sentence summary of your speech that is written the way you will say it out loud to your audience during your speech

Signposts
key words that signal to the audience you are moving from one part of the speech to another

The Parts of a Speech

Every speech is different, but all good speeches contain the same three parts. They contain an introduction, a body, and a conclusion. These parts represent a modernization of the organizational structure of a speech. In Classical times, it was the Exordium, narration, and the peroration—quite similar but a bit more nuanced in structure than the contemporary approach. Nevertheless, the introduction, body, and conclusion of the speech also contain certain components. Although they may sound simple, they require careful crafting to be effective. In this section of the chapter, we will explore those things that compose an introduction, a body, and a conclusion.

Introductions

The first thing your audience hears from you is the introduction. If you do not have a clear and organized introduction, then you risk losing your audience immediately; on the other hand, a strong introduction can capture their attention for the remainder of the presentation. Introductions should be creative and memorable, since they create a first impression, help to determine whether the audience will give you their attention during the rest of your speech, and set the tone for your entire presentation. They also follow a pretty standard formula. There are six parts that should be included in every introduction: the attention getter, statement of relevance to the audience, evidence of speaker credibility, thesis, preview of main points, and a transition to the body of the speech.

Attention Getter. The first thing you need to accomplish in your introduction is capturing your audience's attention. You should try to engage the audience from the moment you begin to speak and make them want to listen to the rest of your speech. There are several strategies you can use to get your audience's attention, but you should carefully consider which will be the most effective for your particular audience, is most appropriate for your topic, and sets the tone you want to establish as you move forward in your speech.

The first attention-getting strategy is asking the audience a question. If done well, this strategy will engage the audience members immediately and give them an incentive to stay involved in your speech. The best attention-getting questions should solicit answers from the audience. One way to do this is to poll your audience and ask for a show of hands from those who have had a particular experience or hold a particular position on an issue that is related to your topic. If you are giving a speech advocating for adopting dogs from rescue organizations instead of from breeders and puppy mills, you might begin by asking everyone who has ever owned a pet to raise their hand. Another option is to ask a question and ask for audience answers. If you have limited time, however, you should be careful to ask questions that will have brief answers rather than questions that will lead to extended discussion. For instance, in a speech about romantic relationships, you might begin, "Psychologist John Gottman found there are four behaviors that predict if a relationship will end and called them the Four Horsemen of the Apocalypse. Can anyone guess what those four behaviors are?" Using a question as your attention getter will only be effective if it is a question that your audience can actually answer, not a rhetorical question that is not intended to be answered.

The second attention-getting strategy is sharing a surprising fact or statistic. Such data should startle your audience and make them want to know more about your topic. The information should pique the audience's curiosity, help them begin to realize how widespread a problem is, or challenge commonly held views about how things work. Be sure to cite your source for this information in your attention getter and make sure it is related to the topic on which you are speaking.

The third attention-getting strategy is beginning with a brief narrative, or anecdote. Stories help make issues come to life by connecting the issue to human experience and adding an emotional component to your speech. If you choose to use a narrative as an attention getter, you will need to be careful to keep it brief and to make sure it connects clearly to the topic of your speech.

The fourth attention-getting strategy is using a famous or inspiring quotation that relates directly to your topic. For example, if you are giving a speech about the importance of community service or a particular social issue, you might open your speech with Mahatma Gandhi's quotation, "You must be the change you wish to see in the world."[1] When you choose a quotation, you should make sure it is aligned with your topic and include a brief explanation about how the quotation relates to your topic.

The fifth attention-gaining strategy is using a joke to open your speech. Jokes can be risky, however, because they can easily be misinterpreted or distract from your speech if they are not planned carefully. If you use a joke that is appropriate for the audience and occasion, and that is directly related to the topic of your speech, the joke can be an ideal way to catch your audience's attention. But if your joke is not directly related to your topic, is offensive, or contains inappropriate language, you will quickly lose credibility and risk upsetting your audience and losing their attention before you have even reached the thesis of your speech.

Relevance to Audience. **After** you have captured your audience's attention, you will need to provide any necessary background information and clearly establish the relevance of the topic for your audience. This is the portion of your introduction where you tell your audience members why they should care about this particular topic. This can be an especially good place to use a statistic or other source to show the overall impact of the topic before relating it directly to your specific audience.

Speaker Credibility. **In** the third part of your introduction, you need to establish your credibility as a speaker. Explain why you are qualified to speak on this topic and why your audience should trust you. Do you have professional or work experience related to this topic? Perhaps you are qualified to speak about different types of car engines because you work in an auto repair shop and have rebuilt a couple of engines. Maybe you are qualified to speak about administering first aid because you spent five years working as a lifeguard and occasionally had to use your first aid training. If you do not have professional or volunteer experience related to your topic, then you could emphasize that you learned a lot about the area as part of your academic major or have done extensive research on the topic to prepare for the speech. Nursing majors have more expertise than most people about vaccines and how to treat common injuries, communication majors have expertise in maintaining interpersonal relationships, and computer science majors have expertise in cyber security. The key goal is to let the audience know why they should trust the information you provide on this subject.

Thesis. You should also clearly state your thesis. You learned about how to develop and write a thesis statement from your general purpose and specific purpose statements earlier in this chapter. Your thesis is a one-sentence summary of your speech that serves as an umbrella covering all of the topics you will cover. Now is the time to let the audience know what you intend to say, or what their takeaway should be from your presentation.

Preview of Main Points. After you state your thesis, you should end your introduction by previewing your main points. Your preview should include all of the main points you plan to cover in the order you plan to discuss them. Your preview of points is a roadmap for the rest of your speech. Your thesis statement provides the destination, while your preview tells your audience how you will get them there.

Transition to the Body. After you have completed your introduction, you need a transition statement that indicates to your audience that you are ending the introduction and beginning to move into the body of your speech. We will discuss transitions in more detail, but for now just remember that you need to have a transition in order to move from the introduction to the body.

> **Transition to the body:** The first step in CPR is giving chest compressions.

Overall, the introduction of your speech should only comprise 10 to 15 percent of your total speaking time. For a seven-minute speech, this means your introduction should accomplish all six of these tasks in less than one minute, while a twenty-minute speech allows up to three minutes to accomplish these tasks. Even though your introduction will be the first thing your audience will hear when you deliver your speech, it should be the last part of the speech you write, or at least revise, because you have to decide what the body of your speech will say before you can decide how to best introduce it.

Body of Your Presentation

The body of your presentation is where you share the bulk of the information in your speech. The body of your speech should take 75-80 percent of the total time in your speech, so this is where you will use the most support materials and give the most detail about your topic. The body of your speech will be divided into several main points, each of which

DIALING DIVERSITY

On August 22, 1964, at the Democratic National Committee in Atlantic City, New Jersey, an African American woman named Fannie Lou Hamer delivered a presentation on the significant challenges minorities faced when trying to vote in the South. Her talk was well organized and made several key points: she provided her own experiences trying to vote, which included being evicted from the plantation where she lived and worked because she refused to rescind her voter application and encountering resistance at registration drives where she was beaten and ridiculed by police simply for trying to help others exercise their right to register to vote. Without proper organization and a clear thesis, her testimony would have had little impact or relevance to those to whom she spoke.[2]

should help to support your thesis. Your main points should be separate categories of information, meaning they should not overlap and should be organized in a pattern that makes the most sense for the topic you have chosen. In most speeches, each main point should be divided into two or more subpoints that help to support that particular main point. Each subpoint should be a separate idea that does not overlap with other subpoints, and each subpoint should clearly support the main point under which it is organized rather than other main points in the speech.

Conclusions

The conclusion of your speech is your final chance to impact your audience, so it is important you make this final component of your speech memorable. The goal of your conclusion is to help your audience remember the points you have already made and leave them with a lasting impression. Your conclusion should only be approximately 10 percent of your total speaking time, and, in that brief time, you should do three things.

Signal conclusion. After you have delivered the body of your speech, you need to indicate to the audience you are ready to begin the conclusion. You want to make sure your audience is paying careful attention during the final moments of your speech, and you can use a signpost as a signal that you are beginning the conclusion, such as "In conclusion," "Finally," "To summarize," or "To wrap up."

Review thesis and main points. After you signal that you are beginning the conclusion, you should summarize your speech by restating the thesis and main points of your speech. You might also choose to recap the highlights of your speech and pull it all together for a few final thoughts, but your conclusion should not add any new information not already presented in the body of your speech.

End with a clincher. After you have summarized your speech, you should end your speech with a clincher. A clincher is the final statement of your speech. Clinchers can use the same devices as an attention getter, such as narratives, statistics, quotations, or audience questions, and they can even refer back to the attention getter you used to open your speech. Clinchers are the last thing an audience hears in a speech and should both provide them with a sense of closure and reiterate what they should take away from the speech.

> *"The effective wielder of public discourse, like the military man, belongs to social and political history because he is one of its makers."[3]*
>
> —Herbert Wichelns

Transitions

Although not a distinct section of a speech, per se, transitional statements are the glue that holds a presentation together, and thus warrant a discussion all their own. As you have probably already gathered from the discussion of the introduction, body, and conclusion, you will need to use transitions several times during your speech. A **transition** is a connecting statement that lets your audience know you are moving from one part of your speech to another, and, depending on where in the speech a transition occurs, you would use one of these three types of effective transitions:

> **Internal summary**: a statement that reviews or sums up what you just finished telling the audience.
>
> **Signpost**: a word that catches the audience's attention and indicates where you are in the speech, similar to the way a road sign helps to tell you where you are and provide direction when you are driving.
>
> **Internal preview**: a statement that previews what is coming up next and can even be an overview of the elements of the next main point.

There are three primary places where you will use transitions in your speech: between the introduction and body of the speech, in between main points, and between the body and conclusion of the speech. The transition between the introduction and body of the speech should include at least a signpost. Transitions between main points could include an internal summary of the previous point, a signpost, and/or an internal preview of the next point. The transition between the last main point and the conclusion only needs a signpost, such as "In conclusion," since you are moving directly into a summary of the entire speech.

Transition
a connecting statement that lets your audience know you are moving from one part of your speech to another

Internal summary
a statement that reviews or sums up what you just finished telling the audience

Signpost
a word that catches the audience's attention and indicates where you are in the speech

Internal preview
a statement that previews what is coming up next and can even be an overview of the elements of the next main point

Full-sentence preparation outline
an outline that includes everything you plan to say in your speech and is written somewhat like a manuscript in an outline format

Key Word Speaking Outline
the outline you will put on a notecard and use during your speech; it should include only key words to remind you of your main points and subpoints, as well as source citations, statistics, and direct quotations you want to make sure you say in a particular way

Outlining

Knowing your thesis and the general structure of a speech allows you to then move to the next step in speech preparation: outlining. Good speeches should be carefully organized and prepared before you deliver them, and one of the most important tools for organizing your speech is an outline. There are two different types of outlines you will develop as you prepare your speech: a full-sentence preparation outline and a key word speaking outline. The **full-sentence preparation outline** includes everything that you plan to say in your speech and is written somewhat like a manuscript in an outline format. You will use this outline to refine your speech in your early practice sessions when you are becoming familiar with the material. The **key word speaking outline** is the outline you use during your speech, and it should include only key words to remind you of your main points, subpoints, source citations, statistics, and direct quotations you want to make sure are said in a particular way. This outline is much shorter than the full-sentence preparation outline.

FIGURE 16.1   Outline Template

I.   Introduction
    A.   Attention Getter
    B.   Background and Audience Relevance
    C.   Speaker Credibility
    D.   Thesis
    E.   Preview of Main Points
    F.   Transition to First Main Point (Signpost and Internal Preview)
II. Body
    A.   Main Point 1
        1.   Subpoint 1
        2.   Subpoint 2
Transition (Internal Review, Signpost, Internal Preview)
    B.   Main Point 2
        1.   Subpoint 1
        2.   Subpoint 2
Transition (Internal Review, Signpost, Internal Preview)
    C.   Main Point 3
        1.   Subpoint 1
        2.   Subpoint 2
III. Conclusion
    A.   Signal Closing
    B.   Restate Thesis
    C.   Review Main Points
    D.   Clincher

References

As you can see in the template, Figure 16.1, outlines use symbols, labels, and indentations to help organize your speech. There are three principles, or rules, that will help to ensure you are developing an effective outline.

Subordination

The process of creating a hierarchy of ideas in which the most general ideas appear first followed by more specific ideas is called **subordination**. Each level of the outline has a different symbol set and amount of indention associated with it. As you can see in the example, the broadest ideas or categories of information, such as the main points, have a smaller indention and are represented by Roman numerals. The next level of information is indented half an inch to the right and is represented by a capital letter. These lines contain the subpoints of the speech.

Subordination
the principle of outlining that creates a hierarchy of ideas in which the most general ideas appear first followed by more specific ideas

Coordination

The second principle of outlining is **coordination**, which is the idea that all information on the same level has the same degree of significance. Each of your main points should be equally important, and each of your subpoints should be fairly equal in importance. This is indicated by both the level of the outline and the amount of time devoted to discussing each element. Each of your subpoints should be given approximately the same length of time, and each of your main points should take roughly the same amount of time in your speech.

Coordination
the principle of outlining that states all information on the same level has the same level of significance

MEDIATED MOMENTS

TED Talks have become one of the more prominent vehicles for public speaking in today's world. These talks ask experts and professionals in specific content areas to develop presentations for nonexpert audiences about their area of expertise and deliver them in usually less than half an hour. The talks are then recorded and placed online for the public to view. One of these talks was delivered by Facebook CEO Sheryl Sandberg on the topic "Why are there so few women leaders?" In order to cover the topic in the time she was given, Sandberg made sure to organize her information into three main points. She indicated each of those points using clear signposts. Her three points were simple: first, she advised women to sit at the table and not underestimate their ability to contribute; second, she asked all couples to make his or her partner a true partner; and third, she advised women not to leave the workforce too soon. All of these points were aimed to support her thesis that women and men have a lot of work to do to create balance in the workforce. Without proper organization, her points would neither be remembered nor effective.

Division
the principle of
outlining that states
if a main point
is divided into
subpoints, it must
be divided into two
or more subpoints

Division

The principle of **division** states that if a main point is divided into subpoints, it must be divided into two or more subpoints. If you are going to divide your subpoints into sub-subpoints, you need to divide them into at least two sub-subpoints. If you cannot divide your main point into more than one subpoint, then you are still simply stating the main point rather than explaining it further.

References

Once you have developed the overall organization for your speech, you will need to add supporting material to substantiate your claims. Most of these support materials will come from the sources you found when conducting research. You will need to cite a source each time you use information from it in order to give credit to the original source as well as to add to your own credibility. There are three points at which you will need to refer to your sources: in your speech, in your presentation aids, and in your references page or bibliography.

Citing Sources Verbally

When you deliver your speech, you should verbally attribute the sources for any information you found while conducting research. You should give the source citation before sharing the information from it to draw your audience's attention and to enhance the credibility of what you are saying. We recommend including your source citation in your full sentence preparation outline exactly the way you plan to say it in your speech, so you remember to attribute the source and become comfortable citing your sources while you are practicing. Each oral citation should include four components: the name of the publication or source, the date the source was published, the name of the person or organization who provided the information to the publication, and the credentials of that person or organization:

> Example: "According to Dr. William Rawlins, an expert in interpersonal communication and professor at Ohio University, in his 1992 book titled *Friendship Matters*, the type and functions of our friendships change over the course of our lives."

Sometimes you will not have information about all four of these components of a citation, and in those cases, you should just include as many of these elements as possible. For instance, if a newspaper article shares information but does not refer to the source of that information, you might only be able to include the name of the newspaper and date of publication. If you obtain information from an organization's website, the organization's name might be the primary credential you need:

> Example: "According to the Centers for Disease Control and Prevention website, last updated on May 23, 2014, diseases that are almost nonexistent today could return as epidemics if we stop vaccinating children."

In this citation, the website name also tells us the organization that provided the information, so there is no need to repeat those details multiple times.

Citing Sources in Presentation Aids

If you use an image, diagram, or other graphic in your PowerPoint presentation (or Prezi, Keynote, or any other slide deck program) from another source, you should cite that source on the slide on which the image appears. At minimum, you should include a link to the image on your slide in a small font that will not interfere with the overall impact of your slide. If the image is from an organization that lends credibility to the message (as opposed to an image that is functioning primarily as clip art), you might also want to include the name of the organization or person that is responsible for the image. In some cases, you might even want to consider including a reference to the source of the image in your speech, especially if you are also citing that source for other information you are sharing at the same time in your speech. Review Figure 16.2 for an example of how to integrate a citation into an image.

FIGURE 16.2   **Integrating a Citation Into an Image**

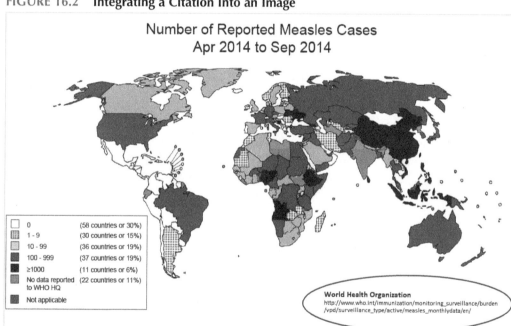

Citing Sources in Your Reference Page

The final place you need to cite your sources is on your references page or bibliography at the end of your full sentence preparation outline. Your instructor will probably require you to use APA, MLA, Chicago/Turabian, or another specific format for your references section. Citing sources in both your outline and verbally attributing them within your speech helps establish and enhance your credibility as a speaker by demonstrating that you conducted research on the topic and are not just providing an opinion. If you do not have a copy of the required style manual on your bookshelf, you can find detailed information about citing your sources at The Purdue Online Writing Lab (OWL) at https://owl.english.purdue.edu.

Using Organization to Encourage Dialogue

The goals of dialogue—encouraging people to listen and seeking to create understanding—may seem to be correlated solely with delivery, but these goals can often be achieved through the atmosphere of dialogue a speech creates. In fact, strong speech organization can go a long way toward creating a spirit of dialogue in a public setting. In this final section of the chapter, we will provide a few guidelines for organizing a speech that helps to create a dialogic environment.

Use an Interesting, Ethical Attention Getter

One common mistake made by speakers is to choose the most shocking and potentially offensive attention getter they can find to ensure the audience listens. This is not necessarily the best strategy. Instead, when creating your attention getter, try to put yourself in your audience members' places and think about what would get your interest, but not offend you, if you were them. Choosing your attention getter wisely ensures its maximum impact without risking losing the audience before you get started.

Use Personal Credibility Wisely

You may be an expert in the subject area on which you are speaking and the audience may very well not be, but this does not provide you with license to diminish their importance or abilities. Additionally, although you may know a good deal about the subject, you likely do not know everything; do not present yourself as "the authority," but rather as "an authority." If you are not an authority, but do have some knowledge, then make that clear to the audience. Be honest and modest.

Provide Credentials for All Sources

We mentioned this when speaking about references, but it bears repeating. Providing the source information to an audience is an ethical way to use information and indicates that you trust the audience members to evaluate the source veracity themselves. Giving this type of trust to an audience both enhances your credentials and also creates an environment where the audience members are invited to be active participants in the discussion of the topic.

Leave the Evaluation to the Audience

Speakers often wish to deliver content with certainty, and that is a good thing, to a point. When concluding a speech, however, particularly a persuasive speech, allow the audience to make their own decision and do not push them too hard toward a certain action or belief. Doing so can come across as suggesting to the audience "If you don't agree now then you just are not smart enough," which is the exact opposite of a dialogic and respectful environment. The discussion of the topic does not end with your speech. Instead, your speech should be treated as a contribution to a longer discursive chain that will continue well after you speak.

Acknowledge Disagreement

Disagreement exists about a great many things, and when we advise you to acknowledge disagreement, we mean for you to do so in two ways. The first is to recognize when there is contradictory research on a point you are making. You should not ignore this, but rather let the audience know there is disagreement out there and that you are siding with a particular interpretation for specific reasons. Share those reasons with the audience. Second, acknowledge that disagreements with your overall position may very well be possible. Not everyone will agree with you, and letting the audience know you are comfortable with that goes a long way toward creating a supportive and dialogic speaking environment.

Summary

One of the most important parts of speech development is determining the organization of your presentation. This chapter focused on providing the tools necessary to create an organized speech. We first discussed how to turn a topic into a specific purpose and thesis. We then explored the three primary components of every speech: the introduction, body, and conclusion. Third, we covered how to cite sources and explained why that is important for you as a speaker. Finally, we provided five clear suggestions for using organization properly to create a dialogic environment for a public presentation.

Chapter 16 Key Ideas

- When developing your speech, you should move from a broad topic to a specific purpose statement, and then to a clear thesis and preview of main points
- All speeches should include an introduction, a body, and a conclusion
- Most introductions should include six parts: (1) attention getter, (2) statement of background and audience relevance, (3) evidence of speaker credibility, (4) thesis statement, (5) preview of main points, and (6) transition to the first main point
- A conclusion should (1) signal the conclusion, (2) restate the thesis, (3) review the main points, and (4) end with a clincher
- Transitions should include an internal summary, signpost, and preview
- Outlines should follow the principles of subordination, coordination, and division
- You should cite your sources (1) out loud in your speech, (2) in your presentation aids, and (3) in the references page or bibliography of your final preparation outline

Chapter 16 Key Terms

Specific Purpose Statement	Signpost	Subordination
Thesis Statement	Internal Preview	Coordination
Signposts	Full-Sentence Preparation	Division
Transition	Outline	
Internal Summary	Key Word Speaking Outline	

References

1 Gandhi, M. Mahatma Gandhi quotes. *Brainy Quotes.* Retrieved from http://www.brainyquote.com/quotes/quotes/m/ mahatmagan109075.html

2 Fannie Lou Hamer testimony before the Credentials Committee. Retrieved from http://americanradioworks.publicradio. org/features/sayitplain/flhamer.html

3 Wichelns, H. (2010). The literary criticism of oratory. In C. R. Burghardt (Ed), *Readings in Rhetorical Criticism* (26). State College, PA: Strata Publishing.

Chapter 17

Persuasive Speaking

Most of us try to persuade others every day. In fact, all communication is capable of persuasion to some degree; what makes a speech persuasive instead of informative, however, is its purpose. **Persuasion** involves attempting to change the attitudes, actions, or beliefs of another person. When working on a group project with classmates, you might try to convince your group mates to choose a particular topic or to do a specific part of the project. At work, you might need to convince clients that your solution will best meet their needs, motivate others to complete a project, negotiate your benefits and salary, or persuade your boss that a proposal you have developed is worth investing in. At home, you might persuade someone to watch a TV series with you, eat at a specific restaurant for dinner, or choose a particular paint color for the kitchen.

At the same time, you will be faced with numerous situations when others try persuading you, whether it is a campaign ad trying to persuade you to vote for a specific candidate, a commercial trying to convince you to use a particular kind of deodorant, or an op-ed article persuading you to support a policy. This chapter investigates how to ethically persuade others while being respectful of other perspectives. Learning how to be ethically persuasive will also help you better evaluate persuasive messages from others. In this chapter, we will first differentiate between the types of persuasion. We will then provide

> **Persuasion**
> attempting to change the attitudes, actions, or beliefs of another person

organizational patterns for persuasive arguments. Third, we will explain how to use emotion and logic both effectively and ethically in a presentation, and then define numerous logical fallacies that should be avoided in a speech. Finally, we will provide guidelines for creating a dialogic atmosphere when trying to persuade an audience to do or believe something.

Types of Persuasion

Persuasive messages surround us all of the time, and they can be categorized into different kinds of persuasion that address certain questions. We encounter each of these questions, or categories, every day in our lives. Sometimes we are the ones trying to persuade others, but often we are the ones being persuaded to feel a particular way about an issue, idea, or topic. In this section of the chapter, we will examine the primary types of questions and forms of persuasive messages. The four types of persuasion are questions of fact, questions of value, questions of policy, and refutations.

Questions of Fact

Questions of fact persuasive messages that attempt to change the audience's beliefs about something

As discussed earlier in the book, people often perceive the same events in different ways. As such, determining facts about what happened can be quite difficult. Think about court cases where lawyers argue for different interpretations of what happened in a specific instance. These arguments are prime examples of persuasion regarding questions of fact. Persuasive speeches that argue **questions of fact** attempt to change the audience's beliefs about something. Persuasive messages about facts are concerned with questions regarding whether something is true or false, does or does not exist, did or did not happen, or is real and not fake. For a speech to focus on a question of fact instead of being an informative speech, it must seek to change how an audience interprets something, rather than simply teaching them or telling them about it. For example, over the last decade or so, we have often heard debates in the media about whether or not some vaccines can lead to autism, and whether or not climate change is caused by humans. Participants in these debates try to provide their interpretation of the evidence supporting their answers to these questions in a way that encourages an audience to agree with them.

Questions of Value

Questions of value persuasive messages that try to change an audience's attitudes toward a topic by convincing the audience whether or not a belief, object, or action is moral, ethical, important, or worthwhile

Facts are not the only thing people debate or see differently. People also differ in terms of what they value or how much they value something. Whenever we debate priorities with a partner or an audience, or try and advocate for the "best," we present an answer to a question of value. Persuasive speeches that argue **questions of value** try to change an audience's attitudes toward a subject by convincing the audience whether or not a belief, object, or action is moral, ethical, important, or worthwhile. Persuasive speeches about value provide arguments about whether we should place greater emphasis on something, or value it more than we already do. For example, someone might give a speech arguing that we have a moral obligation to protect our natural resources, why it is important to develop listening skills, or why human trafficking is unethical.

Questions of Policy

In the legislative wing of government, we often find examples of a third type of question: policy. These are often, but not always, focused on what to do in the present or future. Policies, however, need not be governmental in nature. We also might develop certain class-room policies, or partners may debate a family procedure for handling bonus money from their jobs. Persuasive speeches that are **questions of policy** try to change the audience's actions or convince the audience that something should or should not be done. You might persuade audience members that they personally should take some action, or that they should support an action by another organization, group, individual, or government. For example, someone might give a persuasive speech arguing that Congress should pass a law that creates a way for undocumented immigrants who arrived in the United States as children to gain citizenship. Another person might give a speech arguing that the NCAA should honor scholarships that were offered to student athletes to finish their degrees, even if students are injured and cannot continue participating in the sport.

Questions of policy persuasive messages that try to change the audience's actions or convince the audience that something should be done

Refutations

Not all persuasive efforts seek to change an audience's perspective by proposing an idea; some try to refute arguments that have already been offered by others. They are defensive and, in a way, responses to the statements of others. Persuasive speeches that are **refutations** are speeches in which a speaker defends his or her own position on an issue while respond-ing to the arguments of another person. Refutations involve persuading the audience that your position is stronger than your opponent's or that your opponent's position is flawed. In a refutation, you will need to understand and explain your opponent's argument, address each of her or his points by showing how her or his position is flawed, and propose a more

Refutations persuasive speeches in which a speaker defends his or her own position on an issue while responding to the arguments of another person

DIALING DIVERSITY

In 1851, civil rights advocate Sojourner Truth gave an address entitled "Ain't I A Woman?" Truth, who was born into slavery but eventually became a free woman and minister, used the speech—and numer-ous others—to raise issues of race and gender in the public sphere. Her one speech was not effective at changing minds, but her efforts as a whole helped raise awareness of discrimination and the com-plexities of it in American society during her time. Truth's speech, relatively short by public speaking standards, addressed a question of value, but it later led to a great many persuasive attempts address-ing the questions of policies toward women and minorities in the United States.

viable alternative solution. Refutations can involve questions of fact, value, or policy, and take a significant amount of time and research to prepare. Speeches of refutation are often given in political debates, campaign speeches, or when two professionals are proposing competing solutions to the same problem.

Organizing a Persuasive Argument

For any of the four types of persuasive speeches, you need to think carefully about how to best organize your evidence to help your audience understand the issues and your argument. Your topic and goals will help you determine which organizational pattern is most effective. In this section of the chapter, we will discuss four patterns most commonly used in persuasive speeches: problem-solution, problem-cause-solution, comparative advantages, and Monroe's Motivated Sequence.

Problem-Solution

Problem-solution pattern of organization persuasive pattern of organization in which you begin by explaining the problem and then discuss your solution

Persuasion is fairly common when more than one possible solution exists to a particular problem. In these cases, multiple voices provide arguments for different solutions to the problem, and the best organizational pattern for speeches attempting to contribute to this conversation is the **problem-solution pattern of organization.** This approach to persuasive speeches is similar to the problem-solution organizational pattern for informative speeches; you begin by explaining the problem, and then explain your solution. Persuasive speeches that use the problem-solution pattern of organization, however, are intended to convince the audience to adopt a specific solution for an unresolved problem from among several possible solutions, whereas an informative speech teaches the audience about how a past problem was solved.

When you advocate for a particular solution in a persuasive speech, you need to explain how the solution will address the problem and why it is more effective than alternative options. For example, you might explain why there is a shortage of organs available for transplants (problem), and then propose that we switch from our current process by which those who wish to donate their organs upon death must opt-in to the donor registry, to a process in which everyone is included on the donor registry by default and individuals have the option to opt-out of the registry (solution).

Problem-Cause-Solution

Problem-cause-solution pattern of organization persuasive pattern of organization in which you present the problem in the first point, the underlying causes in the second point, and the proposed solution in the final point

In some cases, problems are merely symptoms of some larger cause that needs to be addressed. The **problem-cause-solution pattern of organization** aims to address such larger causes through its organization. This pattern is similar to the problem-solution pattern of organization, except that it adds a step to explain the causes that are contributing to the problem. After presenting the problem in the first point, you explain the underlying causes in the second point, and finally propose your solution to the causes in the third point. This pattern of organization usually helps you build an even stronger argument because it allows you to show how your solution addresses the problem as well as the underlying causes that contributed to the problem in the first place. For example, if we return to the problem of having a shortage of organs available for transplant along with a growing waiting list, we might explain that one of the causes for the organ shortage is that people tend to choose default options because those require the least effort. Since the current default option is to not be a donor, most people who might be willing to donate their organs do not go out of their way to change their preferences from the default. Thus, the solution of changing the default organ donation option addresses both the problem and the cause.

Comparative Advantages

In most cases, there are a great many ways to solve a single problem, and the real issue is determining the best and most efficient solution to the problem. This often means comparing alternative solutions to identify the better one from all the options available. The **comparative advantages pattern of organization** is used to compare two or more potential solutions to a problem in an effort to argue why the solution you support is better than another solution. This pattern of organization is especially effective for refutations. In some cases, you might convince the audience that your solution is effective, while the other is ineffective, but in other cases, you might convince your audience that your solution is better than another solution that is also effective in many ways.

When you use the comparative advantages pattern of organization for a persuasive speech, each main point articulates why your position is better than the alternatives. Your first subpoint for each main point will explain how your opponent addresses that issue, and the second subpoint will explain how your solution addresses the issue more effectively. For instance, you might argue that donating money to the American Cancer Society is a more effective way to help fight cancer than donating to the Susan G. Komen Foundation by comparing how many cancers each organization is trying to cure, what proportion of donations each organization spends on research, and how many lives have been saved as a result of each organization's work.

Monroe's Motivated Sequence

The final organizational pattern for persuasive speeches is Monroe's Motivated Sequence. **Monroe's Motivated Sequence** uses five steps to persuade the audience to adopt a plan of action: attention, need, satisfaction, visualization, and action. In the first step, **attention**, the speaker captures the attention of the audience members and gets them to focus on the topic he or she plans to address. This is typically done in the attention getter at the beginning of the speech, using those same attention-getting devices discussed in Chapter 14: asking a question, sharing a surprising fact or statistic, telling a brief anecdote, using a quotation, or telling a joke.

In the second step, **need**, the speaker makes the audience aware of the problem, or need, that must be addressed. This step explains the broad significance of the problem, as well as why this problem is relevant to the speaker's particular audience. If audience members do not think they need to know what a speaker is talking about, they are less likely

Comparative advantages pattern of organization persuasive pattern of organization in which you compare two potential solutions to a problem to argue why the solution you support is better than another solution that is being proposed by someone else

Monroe's Motivated Sequence persuasive pattern of organization in which you use five steps to persuade the audience to adopt a plan of action: attention, need, satisfaction, visualization, and action to listen. The third step, **satisfaction**, presents the solution to the problem by fulfilling the need established in the prior step. The fourth step, **visualization**, uses vivid language to help the audience members see themselves adopting the solution and satisfying the need using the speaker's preferred solution. The final step, **action**, calls the audience to action by reiterating the solution and telling audience members what they specifically should do to address the problem. This pattern of organization is often used in sales presentations and commercials.

Using Emotion and Logic

Effective persuasion does not depend upon organization alone. In *Rhetoric*, Aristotle argues that there are three means of persuasion, or **artistic proofs**, that a speaker can use to persuade an audience: *ethos*, *pathos*, and *logos*.[1] Aristotle called them artistic proofs because the speaker constructs them. Any effective and ethical persuasive speech or appeal requires all three of these elements to work. In this section of the chapter, we will define and describe what *ethos*, *pathos*, and *logos* are and how they work to enhance persuasive speeches.

Ethos

Whether or not you will believe a message from a speaker depends a great deal on how you perceive the speaker's credibility. *Ethos* refers to the perceived personal character, or credibility, of the speaker. In order for a speaker to have credibility, the audience must believe the speaker has expertise and experience with the topic, is a good or moral person, and has goodwill toward the audience. As a speaker, you can enhance your *ethos* by telling your audience why you should be trusted when speaking on the topic by citing credible sources, using sound logic and arguments, and showing the relevance of your topic for your specific audience. You can also enhance your *ethos* by using good delivery, appearing confident, and dressing appropriately for the occasion. Your credibility changes throughout a presentation, and could improve or decrease depending upon how you handle the speech. As you give more and more presentations and do work on a specific topic, you will gain *ethos* through your reputation in that field.

Pathos

Credibility alone cannot carry a speech, and so Aristotle also proposed an emotional dimension to persuasive appeals. *Pathos* is the use of emotions in persuasion, specifically the generation of an emotional attachment to your position or topic. As a speaker, you have the ability to evoke emotions in your audience members that will help them be more easily persuaded. Narratives about specific people or objects are a highly effective way to get your audience to feel emotions about the topic of your speech. They work much better than a broad statistic or sweeping generalization.

For example, opening your speech about the impact of natural disasters with a story about a family that lost everything following tornados in Joplin, Missouri, might make your audience feel sympathetic or sad. A story about a young woman who was kidnapped and

Artistic proofs
Aristotle's category for credibility, emotion, and logic within a persuasive appeal; he called them artistic because the speaker creates them

Ethos
the perceived personal character or credibility of the speaker

Pathos
the use of emotions in persuasion

became a victim of human trafficking might make your audience feel anger or horror, while a story about someone who worked hard to overcome challenges to achieve something extraordinary might evoke joy or hope in your audience. An additional way to enhance this emotional connection is through showing pictures of a single representative of the larger issue (the family, not an overhead shot of Joplin). Helping your audience members connect emotionally with your topic can help you persuade them, but you must be careful to balance emotional appeals with logic so you are not manipulating your audience. Relying on *pathos* alone is a serious problem for a speech because it makes it seem as though the speaker either cannot locate evidence to support his or her claim, or is trying to trick an audience for personal gain.

Logos

In addition to credibility and emotional dimensions of a speech, logic also is of paramount importance. *Logos* is what Aristotle termed the use of logic and evidence to persuade an audience. As a speaker, a lot of your evidence will come from the information you find while doing research for your speech, such as numbers, statistics, examples, definitions, explanations, and quotations. How you use that evidence to build logical arguments, however, is even more important. As a speaker, there are two types of reasoning processes you will use to build arguments and reach conclusions in your speech: deductive and inductive reasoning.

Deductive Reasoning. **Deductive reasoning** involves using general truths to reach a certain conclusion about a specific instance. The formal structure for deductive reasoning is the **syllogism**, which sets up a series of claims that build upon each other to reach a conclusion.

There are three parts to the syllogism: (1) the **major premise**, which is a statement that is believed to be true by your entire audience, (2) the **minor premise**, which connects the statement in your major premise to the specific instance about which you are trying to make a claim, and (3) the **conclusion**, which is the logical result of both the major and minor premises and is the claim you are ultimately trying to make. Here's an example of a syllogism (Figure 17.1):

> *Logos*
> the use of logic and evidence to persuade your audience

> **Deductive reasoning**
> involves using general truths to reach a certain conclusion about a specific instance

FIGURE 17.1   **Syllogism**

Major premise: All dogs have tails.
Minor premise: Einstein is a dog.
Conclusion: Therefore, Einstein has a tail.

This example begins with a fact about a large category (all dogs) in the major premise, connects that fact to a specific instance (Einstein) in the minor premise, and then reaches a certain, logical conclusion about that specific instance.

Inductive Reasoning. **Inductive reasoning** involves using several specific instances or pieces of evidence to draw probable conclusions about general truths. There are four types of inductive reasoning.

Reasoning by cause is used when you claim that one event causes another. For example, you might notice that each time you eat peanut butter, you break out in hives, so you might conclude that eating peanut butter causes you to break out in hives.

Reasoning by example is when you use several specific instances that are related to each other to draw an overall conclusion about them. For instance, you might observe that you enjoyed watching the movie *Superman*, loved *Guardians of the Galaxy*, and liked *Thor*, so you then conclude you enjoy watching movies that are based on comic books.

Reasoning by sign occurs when you conclude that the presence of one thing indicates the presence of another. For example, when we see smoke, we usually conclude that there is a fire. When we see people walking past the window carrying umbrellas, we might conclude that it is raining outside.

Finally, **reasoning by analogy** occurs when you compare two similar cases in order to argue that what is true in one case is also true in the other, because the two cases share similar features. For example, if an anti-bullying campaign worked well in one school, you might argue that it will also be effective in another school that has similar characteristics.

When you give a persuasive speech, it is important to carefully balance your use of *ethos*, *pathos*, and *logos* so you can effectively and ethically persuade your audience. Additionally, you should take extra care to use sound reasoning. As we are about to discover, though, not all reasoning is sound.

> *"To work and live together, we must, whether we like it or not, learn to talk with each other to resolve our difficulties and decide on alternatives. At the same time, we need to be able to evaluate the persuasive activities that are directed toward us as citizens, consumers, and members of social groups. The study of persuasion is, at once, one of the oldest and most important of human intellectual activities."*
>
> —*Martha Watson, University of Nevada Las Vegas*

Logical Fallacies

Just because someone says something or presents a formal speech does not mean it is logically sound. In fact, society is rife with examples of clever arguments that make no logical sense. It is imperative that we, as speakers, avoid using such fallacious reasoning, and that, as an audience, we are able to know poor logic when we hear it. In this part of the chapter, we will identify and define 10 common **logical fallacies,** which are errors in reasoning that lead to invalid conclusions.

Ad Hominem Attack. In an ***ad hominem* attack,** a speaker tries to equate the quality of some-one's argument with the quality of his or her character. This fallacy is sometimes referred to as name-calling, and it often focuses on irrelevant elements of personal history. You would be using an *ad hominem* attack if you constructed an advertisement in a campaign that labeled the other person as uncaring because he or she does not support immigration reform.

Ad Vericundiam. The ***ad vericundiam*** fallacy is an appeal to authority. In this fallacy, a person argues that his or her positional authority, perhaps as a parent or elected official, makes the argument correct rather than relying on logical reason to make his or her case. For example, if a child asks why he needs to brush his teeth and his mom replies, "Because I'm the mom, and I said so," his mother would be relying on an *ad vericundiam* fallacy instead of using logic to explain how brushing teeth contributes to dental health. This does not mean it is a bad idea for her son to brush his teeth, but it does mean that his mother is not using sound reasoning.

Slippery Slope. A **slippery slope** fallacy argues that once a course of action is taken, a series of other unavoidable and undesirable events will necessarily take place. It assumes that there is no way to stop or turn back once we begin moving down a particular path. If we argued that banning the purchase of some automatic guns with large magazines would eventually lead to the banning of all guns, we would be using a slippery slope fallacy because one does not necessarily mean that the other will follow.

Non Sequitur. A ***non sequitur*** fallacy involves making an unjustified move from one topic to another, and is often a result of reasoning that is happening in the wrong order. This can often result from an inappropriate reasoning from sign. If you were to claim that someone had to be wealthy because of the type of car he or she drives or apartment he or she resides in you would be making a logical jump not supported by the evidence. Just because someone drives an expensive car or has a nice apartment does not necessarily mean he or she is wealthy.

Straw Man. In a **straw man fallacy** the speaker ignores the actual position of his or her opponent, misrepresents his or her position, and then attacks that made-up position instead of the actual position. Often, the speaker oversimplifies his or her opponent's position, takes his or her comments out of context, or represents an entire group's position with bad arguments from one person in that group. Imagine that David and Chris are running for political office, and David argues that we should spend more tax money on health and education. Chris responds by saying that he is surprised that David hates our country so much that he wants to leave it defenseless by cutting military spending. In this case, Chris is using a straw man fallacy.

Hasty Generalization. **Hasty Generalizations** involve using a small sample of evidence to draw unjustified conclusions about an entire group or category. This is a poor use of reasoning from example. If you were to ask two of your friends what their favorite television show is, and then use that as evidence that all college students love that particular show, you would be making a hasty generalization.

Either-Or. The **either-or** fallacy, which is sometimes called a false dilemma, happens when the speaker claims there are only two alternatives when there are really many other options available. This fallacy attempts to force audience members to make a choice between two extreme positions. For instance, we often see news coverage about abortion laws label people as pro-life (opposed to abortion in all circumstances) or pro-choice (supportive of keeping abortion legal in all circumstances) when, in reality, there are many possible positions between those two.

False Cause. Also known by its Latin name, *post hoc, ergo, propter hoc*, the **false cause** fallacy assumes that one event caused another unrelated event to occur because the events happened around the same time, even though the two events were completely unrelated. Put more succinctly, false cause fallacies use "after this, because of this" reasoning. False cause is the basis of many superstitions. For example, when deciding where to go for dinner, a couple rules out a restaurant at a nearby mall because "every time we go there it rains." This assumes that because they chose to go to that restaurant it will rain when, in fact, just because the events happened sequentially, it does not mean they were in any way connected.

Red Herring. A **red herring** fallacy happens when the speaker introduces irrelevant ideas in order to distract attention away from the real issue, but sometimes tries to make them appear related to the first issue. An example of a red herring would be, "We should increase the rigor of our classes for students. You should support this because we are in a budget crisis and do not want to be furloughed." Even though the second sentence is being used to support the first sentence, it does not address that topic. Likewise, we often see red herrings in political debates when a candidate does not want to answer a question and instead introduces a new topic that will make her or him appear more favorable. We sometimes refer to this as "dodging the question," "avoiding the issue," or "spin doctoring."

Begging the Question. **Begging the question** is the use of a circular argument in which your evidence and your conclusion are really saying the same thing, and you assume certain facts that have not yet been proven. To say, "The reason that there is such a big demand for iPhones is that everyone wants one," is an example of begging the question because the evidence used to support the conclusion is just saying the same thing in a different way. Common indicators of this fallacy include prefacing a statement with "it begs the question" and "for the sake of argument."

Engaging in Dialogic Persuasion

Persuasion can often become contentious and uncomfortable because we tend to tightly hold to our beliefs and attitudes, not allowing ourselves to be persuaded. In fact, people may

MEDIATED MOMENTS

In the 2005 film, *Thank You for Smoking*, advertising agent Nick Naylor (played by Aaron Eckart) gives several presentations before various audiences trying to convince them smoking is either not bad for them or that it should not come with a warning. In a scene where he is questioned before a committee in Congress, Naylor employs numerous logical fallacies to avoid the issue of cigarettes and confuse those who are watching. For instance, he uses the *non sequitur* when asked about warning labels on cigarettes and states that if we do that, we should also put them on jet planes and cheddar cheese, because those things are also potentially harmful. His repeated performances in the movie serve to illustrate numerous logical fallacies and how convincing they sound on the surface.

sometimes feel like being persuaded is akin to being manipulated, when that is not the case at all. Creating an environment where persuasion—true persuasion—can occur shares a number of similarities with the atmosphere needed for dialogue. In this final section of the chapter, we will provide some general guidelines for creating an open environment where persuasion can occur.

Be Open to Other Ideas

Whether you are the speaker or the listener for a persuasive message, try to put aside your personal position and allow new information to be presented. Add that new information to what you already know and see if your mind is changed. This is no small feat, and requires a mutual feeling of goodwill between you and the speaker, but it is essential for creating a comfortable environment for any speaker and audience.

Don't Prejudge Speakers or Audiences

It is one thing to gather information about a speaker and an audience; it is another to judge them and his or her message before he or she has a chance to deliver it. Believing an audience will be hostile will probably make you speak like they are, thus making them hostile. Additionally, if as an audience member you begin the presentation with the assumption you will not agree with the speaker, you likely won't.

Understand A Speaker's Perspectives

Invariably, a speaker will say something you disagree with, but that does not mean everything he or she says is contrary to your beliefs and attitudes. It is possible to disagree on specific elements of a position, but still agree with the overall argument. When you listen and when you speak, make distinctions between disagreements with the argument and with specific parts of the argument. This might allow you to begin to find common ground with the speaker.

Avoid Inciting Your Audience

On the one hand, you need to incorporate an emotional dimension to your speech to help your audience connect with it. On the other, you do not need to engender an extreme degree of a particular emotion in your audience, either. Focusing on emotion too much in a speech can increase defensiveness and aggressiveness in the audience, and that is not conducive to the exchange of ideas.

Clarify Your Credentials

When providing your experience or expertise to an audience, be clear and honest about them; do not misrepresent yourself in the hopes of appearing more credible. If you set the bar too high and then make mistakes in your address, it will damage your believability and chance to effectively persuade the audience.

Accept Disagreement

The goal of any single persuasive message cannot be to change the hearts and minds of an audience. The instances of such things happening are very difficult to find. Instead, be satisfied with an audience that simply heard and considered your ideas. Not everyone will agree with you, and if you show disdain for those that disagree, then the chances of working with those people again in the future decrease. Disagreement is good and can be the sign of a thoughtful audience. Accept that you will not win over everyone, regardless of your argument's strength.

Summary

When most people think of public speaking, they think of persuasive speaking. To many, the opportunity to change someone's mind or attitude is the most enjoyable part of speech. That said, it is also a risky endeavor and, when we persuade, we must be aware of the pitfalls and traps inherent in it. In this chapter, we explored the different types of questions persuasive arguments seek to answer. We then explored how to organize persuasive arguments and how to effectively incorporate credibility, emotion, and logic into those arguments. Finally, we discussed the 10 most common logical fallacies used by speakers today, and provided suggestions for creating a dialogic and supportive climate when trying to persuade an audience.

Chapter 17 Key Ideas

- The four types of persuasion are questions of fact, questions of value, questions of policy, and refutations.

- The most effective patterns of organization for persuasive speeches include problem-solution, problem-cause-solution, comparative advantages, and Monroe's Motivated Sequence.
- The three means of persuasion, or artistic proofs, are *ethos*, *pathos*, and *logos*.
- You might use both deductive and inductive reasoning to build arguments and reach conclusions in your speech. Deductive reasoning involves using general truths to reach certain conclusions about a specific instance through the use of a syllogism. Inductive reasoning involves using several specific instances to draw probable conclusions about general truths and can include reasoning by cause, example, sign, or analogy.
- You should avoid using logical fallacies—which lead to invalid conclusions—as support in your presentations.

Chapter 17 Key Terms

Persuasion	Artistic proofs	*Ad vericundiam*
Questions of fact	*Ethos*	Slippery slope
Questions of value	*Logos*	*Non sequitur*
Questions of policy	*Pathos*	Straw man fallacy
Refutations	Deductive reasoning	Hasty generalization
Problem-solution pattern of organization	Inductive reasoning	Either-or
	Reasoning by cause	False cause
Problem-cause-solution pattern of organization	Reasoning by example	Red herring
	Reasoning by sign	Begging the question
Comparative advantages pattern of organization	Reasoning by analogy	
	Logical fallacies	
Monroe's Motivated Sequence	*Ad Hominem* attack	

References

1 Aristotle (2001). From Rhetoric. In P. Bizzell & B. Herzberg (Eds.), *The Rhetorical Tradition* (2nd ed., 179-240). Boston, MA: Bedford/St. Martin's.

Chapter 18

Delivery

The first thing most people comment on after watching someone give a speech is the delivery, because it is the most noticeable element of a speech and can be the most memorable. Speaking in front of an audience can be intimidating. Delivery is that part of speaking that makes many people turn away opportunities to share their thoughts, beliefs, and knowledge with a larger and wider audience. It is also one of the five canons of rhetoric we noted when we began our discussion of the public speaking context two chapters ago. It has always been a point of emphasis in speech training, because sound and strong delivery can raise a presentation to new levels.

There are numerous things good delivery provides a speaker and an audience. Good delivery will help keep your audience's attention, enhance your credibility, and make your message more memorable and impactful. On the other hand, poor delivery can hurt a speech and detract from your chances of getting your message across to an audience. Poor delivery can make even the best-planned and most-researched speech easy to forget or, perhaps even worse, difficult to believe or trust. For these reasons it is important to understand the various dimensions of delivery and to practice them far in advance of delivering your presentation. You might be able to cram for a test the night before, but you cannot do the same for a presentation.

In this chapter, we turn our attention to delivery. First, we will learn about the components of delivery and the four forms of delivery. Then we will discuss a common concern for many speakers: communication apprehension or, as it is more commonly known, the fear of public speaking. We will then examine the proper ways to construct and deploy presentation aids. We will also provide strategies for practicing that will help maximize your chances of speaking success. Finally, we will discuss some ways to use delivery to create a dialogic atmosphere when giving a speech.

Components and Forms of Delivery

Delivery is a term that encompasses a great many parts. Just think about a speech you recently heard. Was the delivery simply verbal? Were there gestures and facial expressions that contributed to your interpretation of the message? Perhaps the inflection and emphasis placed on certain phrases or words made them more memorable for you? The fact of the matter is delivery involves a great many different things working together. Speeches are also delivered in different ways, resulting in different impressions of the speaker and the message. In this section of the chapter, we will discuss the components of speech delivery as well as the four ways in which people deliver formal presentations.

Vocal and Physical Delivery

Delivery can be broken into two key components: elements of speaking that deal with the voice, which we call vocalics, and elements of speaking that deal with the body, or physical delivery.

Vocal Delivery. **Vocal delivery** includes everything that affects how your voice sounds when you speak. Even though all of them are happening at once, there are several different components of vocal delivery that you should pay attention to while you are speaking.

Pronunciation is what a word should sound like when it is spoken according to regional rules and standards. If you mispronounce words in your speech, you might sound like you did not practice, and will thus lose credibility with your audience.
Articulation is the process of physically shaping the sounds that make the word. Articulation errors occur when you run words together or improperly shape vowels or consonants. While this is common in everyday, casual conversation, it can hurt your credibility in a formal speaking situation.
Volume is how loud or soft the sound of your voice is when you speak. When giving a speech, you should speak loudly enough that your audience can easily hear you.
Pitch is how high or low your voice sounds when you speak. Lower voices tend to carry through a room more easily than higher pitched voices, so if your voice has a high pitch, you might have to work even harder to increase your volume and project your voice.

Vocal delivery
everything that affects how your voice sounds when you speak

Pronunciation
what a word should sound like when it is spoken according to a rule or standard

Articulation
the process of physically shaping the sounds that make the word

Volume
how loud or soft the sound of your voice is when you speak

Pitch
how high or low your voice sounds when you speak

Rhythm is the cadence or pattern of movement in your voice. Most of us have a natural cadence, but sometimes we develop a repetitive sing-song pattern when we're nervous.

Rate is how fast or slow you speak. The typical rate of speech varies some by geographic region, but if you speak too quickly, your audience might have trouble following along. On the other hand, if you speak too slowly, you might lose your audience's interest.

Tone refers to how variable your voice is and how "warm" your voice sounds. If you vary your voice while you speak, you will more easily convey emotions and interest, but if you speak in a monotone voice, your audience will struggle to maintain interest.

Vocalized pauses are filler words that many speakers use when they feel like they should be saying something but do not have anything to say. Common vocalized pauses include "umm," "like," and "y'know." It is normal to use occasional vocalized pauses when speaking, but too many can interfere with your speech and hurt your credibility.

By now, you have probably noticed that many of the elements of vocal delivery in public speaking include the vocalics we discussed earlier in the book when we covered nonverbal communication. As you continue, you will see that the same is true for many of the elements of physical delivery.

Physical Delivery. **Physical delivery**, often called nonverbal delivery, can impact the way that your message is received as much as, or more than, anything else. Physical delivery includes all of the physical signals your body sends to your audience during your speech, and there are several elements you should consider.

Rhythm
the cadence or pattern of movement in your voice

Rate
how fast or slow you speak

Tone
how variable your voice is and how "warm" your voice sounds

Vocalized pauses
filler words that many speakers use when they feel like they should be saying something but do not have anything to say

Physical delivery
all of the physical signals your body sends to your audience during your speech, and there are several elements you should consider

DIALING DIVERSITY

Different cultures have different expectations for appropriate attire in public speaking situations. In Western countries, like the United States, proper dress for men and women includes things like a pressed suit or dress. While hats such as baseball caps are frowned upon in such scenarios, religious headscarves are expected from certain Muslim and Hindu speakers.

Women from India may wear saris when speaking, and when the Dalai Lama speaks to the UN or other audiences, he invariably wears his religious robes, not a suit. Understanding and appreciating the cultural backgrounds of speakers helps to identify appropriateness of dress for formal presentations. Although not wearing a pressed suit or dress, they still are wearing what they deem to be respectful and appropriate clothing for the speaking occasion when wearing religious or ethnic garb.

Physical appearance includes your apparel and grooming

Posture the position of your body when you are speaking

Facial expressions the way the position and movement of your facial features convey emotion and engagement

Gestures the movements of your hands and arms

Eye contact looking members of your audience in the eyes while speaking

Memorized speech a speech the speaker commits to memory and delivers without the use of any notes

Physical appearance includes your apparel and grooming and is the first element of physical delivery your audience will notice, even before you say a word. You should be dressed appropriately for the occasion, whether it is in class or at a wedding or funeral, but, generally, you should dress at least as formal, if not more formal, than your audience.

Posture is the position of your body when you are speaking and can either communicate confidence and respect, or nervousness and disinterest. When you speak, you should stand up straight, in a relaxed and natural pose. While you speak, stand on both feet; do not shift back and forth from one foot to the other or cross your feet, as this will make you look unbalanced. If there is a podium, you may rest your hands occasionally as you speak, but you should not lean on the podium.

Facial expressions convey emotion and engagement through the position of your facial features, which might include a smile, raised eyebrows, a glare, a smirk, a grimace, a frown, or many other expressions. Your facial expressions should reflect the emotional tone of the occasion and what you are saying in your speech.

Gestures are the movement of your hands and arms and should be used to add emphasis to important points and illustrate relationships between ideas. Gestures should appear to be natural, and you should work on incorporating them into your speech when you begin practicing. Excessive or repetitive gestures can be distracting, and too few gestures can make it look like you are not engaged in your speech or failed to practice. This is especially true if your gestures are limited because you are using your hands to hold your notecards where you can read it for most of your speech.

Eye contact is perhaps one of the most important elements of physical delivery. Establishing and maintaining good eye contact allows you to maintain your audience's attention, build rapport, and help your audience feel like you care about your speech and their response to your message. Instead of speaking to the wall in the back of the room, staring at one or two individuals through your entire speech, looking at the floor, or reading from your notes, try making eye contact with each of your audience members for a few seconds at a time. This allows you to treat your speech as many small conversations with individuals in your audience, instead of a presentation to a room full of people.

Forms of Delivery

Just as different speaking contexts call for different types of speeches, different contexts also call for different types of delivery. There are four primary types of delivery, and there are advantages and disadvantages that accompany each.

Memorized. In a **memorized speech**, the speaker commits the entire speech to memory and does not use any notes while delivering the speech. Memorized speeches were common in ancient Greece and Rome and are still sometimes used in public speaking competitions and during political campaigns, but are rarely used in most classroom or professional presentations today. Some of the advantages of memorized speeches are that you will be able to give your speech the same way every time, and you will be able to use eye contact and gestures to their maximum effect since you will not be holding a notecard in your hand or looking at your notes or manuscript during your speech.

However, the disadvantages of memorized speeches far outweigh the advantages for most speakers. It takes a substantial amount of time to memorize a speech, and, even if you have spent hours trying to memorize your speech, you still might forget what you intended to say. It is not uncommon for speakers who have memorized their speeches to freeze in the middle of their speech or forget a couple of words, causing them to completely lose their place or repeat a phrase over and over until they remember what was supposed to come next. Finally, it is very difficult to adapt your speech to the audience and occasion if you have finalized and memorized your speech far in advance.

Manuscript. In a **manuscript speech**, the speaker writes out his or her speech word for word in an essay format and reads the entire speech from that manuscript. It is common for political speeches, news broadcasts, and many commemorative speeches to be delivered from a manuscript. Manuscripts allow the speaker to carefully word every sentence of the speech. Manuscript speeches are difficult to adapt to the audience and context, however. It is also nearly impossible for a speaker to make eye contact with individuals in the audience or to use effective gestures when reading from a hard copy of a manuscript. Finally, unless you have a great deal of experience and training in speaking from a manuscript, your verbal delivery will probably sound unnatural and choppy.

Manuscript speech
a speech the speaker writes out word for word in an essay format and delivers by reading from the manuscript

Extemporaneous. An **extemporaneous speech** is a practiced, polished speech that makes use of a limited speaking outline. If you are giving an extemporaneous speech, you have practiced your speech often enough that you are familiar with the content of the speech and have nearly memorized the material, but you probably say the speech a little bit differently each time you deliver it. Speakers have a notecard with limited notes, such as a key word outline with source citations and statistics, but do not have their full preparation outline or a manuscript in front of them. Extemporaneous speeches allow you to use natural verbal and physical delivery, make eye contact with your audience throughout your speech, and adapt to audience feedback throughout the speech. An extemporaneous speech does, however, take time to prepare and practice.

Extemporaneous speech
a practiced, polished speech that makes use of a limited speaking outline

Impromptu. **Impromptu speeches** are presentations with little or no preparation. For example, you are giving an impromptu speech anytime you are called on to answer a question or elaborate on an idea in class. You will also be giving an impromptu presentation when you interview for a job. Politicians also often give impromptu speeches in response to questions asked during town hall meetings, and pageant contestants deliver impromptu speeches when they are asked on-stage questions. Impromptu speeches can be intimidating, since you cannot prepare and might not even know whether you will be speaking in advance.

Impromptu speech
a speech presented with little or no preparation

Communication Apprehension

Communication Apprehension
the fear or anxiety associated with real or anticipated communication with another or others

For as common as communication is in our lives and as long as we have been doing it, it does generate a great deal of anxiety for many people. **Communication Apprehension** (CA), is defined by communication scholar James McCroskey as "the fear or anxiety associated with real or anticipated communication with another or others."[1] CA can impact people in a variety of contexts, such as speaking in one-on-one interpersonal conversations or speaking in a small meeting, but many people experience this anxiety in public speaking contexts. This is not particularly surprising; most of us have less experience speaking in front of a large group than in an individual speaking context, and research tells us that we are more likely to feel anxiety when we are being evaluated, which is usually the case in a public speaking context.

Trait CA
the amount of communication you were born with and naturally have due to genetics

Everyone has some level of CA, ranging from very low anxiety to very high anxiety and, if you would like, you can evaluate your level of CA using the Personal Report of Public Speaking Anxiety.[2] There are two components that impact the level of CA that you feel. The first is **Trait CA**, which is the amount of communication anxiety you were born with and naturally have due to genetics. The second is **State CA**, which is anxiety that is related to the context in which you are communicating. While there is very little you can do to change your Trait CA levels, the good news is that you can reduce your overall CA by working to reduce your State CA.

State CA
anxiety that is related to the context in which you are communicating

Some of the symptoms of communication apprehension include sweating, feeling like you have butterflies in your stomach, slightly increased blood pressure, shortness of breath, dry mouth, flushed skin, and difficulty remembering what you planned to say. While these symptoms are hard to ignore as a speaker, in most cases, your audience probably will not even notice them.

> *"In the early years of the study of CA, a distinction was made between 'Trait CA' (TCA) and 'State CA' (SCA). TCA was seen as being a general pattern of low, medium, or high orientation of anxiety/fear across communication contexts. SCA was seen as experiencing anxiety/fear in one situation but not in others"*[3]
>
> —*J. C. McCroskey*

Strategies to Reduce Communication Apprehension

Systematic desensitization
the process by which a person is slowly introduced to something he or she fears so that each time he or she overcomes the fear the intensity is decreased

Fortunately, there are several strategies you can use to reduce your anxiety. The first strategy is to practice your presentation often. If you begin practicing your speech far in advance of your presentation and practice often, you will increase your comfort level with the material and therefore your confidence on the day you speak. The second strategy is to employ relaxation techniques. These might include breathing exercises, stretching and yoga, exercise, meditation, or any other technique that typically helps you de-stress. The third strategy is **systematic desensitization**, which is the process by which a person is slowly introduced to something he or she fears so that each time he or she overcomes the fear, the intensity of the fear is decreased. This might involve someone who is afraid of heights going up to different floors of a tall building as she or he gets comfortable with the height of the one she or he is on. The fourth strategy for reducing CA is to visualize success. Visualizing yourself being successful can help lead to the occurrence of a **self-fulfilling prophesy**, which is convincing yourself that something is going to happen before it does, thus leading to the occurrence of what you originally expected. The final strategy for reducing CA is to think about your speech as a conversation with one individual in the audience at a time, instead of as a presentation in front of an entire room full of people at once.

Self-fulfilling prophesy
convincing yourself that something is going to happen before it does, thus leading to the occurrence of what you originally expected

Using Presentation Aids

Decades ago, it was not uncommon to give speeches that relied almost entirely on their words to communicate messages, but today it is easier than ever to complement and reinforce messages through the use of presentation aids. **Presentation aids** are additional resources that engage one or more of the audience members' five senses (sight, sound, touch, taste, smell) to help them better understand the message. Depending on the topic and goal of your speech, you might choose to use one or more of the following types of presentation aids.

Presentation aids
resources that engage one or more of the five senses (sight, sound, touch, taste, smell) of the audience to help the audience better understand the message

Objects

Objects are physical items you discuss in your speech. If you bring an object to class, you bring the actual thing you are discussing into class, not a representation of it. Objects can be an excellent tool for helping your audience experience something firsthand, because an object can allow your audience to engage multiple senses at once. Using the physical object you are discussing as a presentation aid helps your audience more easily understand what you are talking about and makes it easier to visualize the processes you might be describing. In some cases, objects can also give your audience a chance to touch, taste, and smell what you are talking about; however, if you plan to use an object your audience will need to taste, touch, or smell, you should think carefully about how to best let your audience come into contact with the object, so they can experience it when you want them to during the speech. Additionally, there are some objects you should not bring when giving a speech in a class because they are banned in most university classrooms, including illegal substances, weapons, and live animals.

Objects
physical items that you are discussing in your speech

Models

Models are scaled physical representations of things. Sometimes, the object you are discussing is too small for your audience to easily see, or is too large to carry easily to where you are giving your presentation. In these cases, it can be useful to have a larger or smaller representation of the object that can be easily seen or used to demonstrate the process you are trying to show. For example, most eye doctors use a much larger model of an eye

Models
scaled physical representations of things utilized as presentation aids

to explain how the eye works and how certain conditions interfere with or damage your vision. Many architects build smaller-scale models of the projects they have designed to allow their clients to more easily visualize the building, boat, landscape, or other project.

Demonstrations

Demonstrations involve actually enacting the process you are trying to teach your audience. Demonstrations often involve using objects or models to show the audience how to do something. For example, a cyclist might bring his or her bike and cycling shoes to demonstrate how to clip into SPD pedals, and show how the use of clips increases the power that can be generated while cycling. Additionally, some demonstrations might primarily involve the use of the speaker's body. For example, an exercise instructor might demonstrate the proper form for a squat, a hip hop dancer might demonstrate several common hip hop moves by dancing for the audience, and a physical therapist might demonstrate the proper way to push off from a chair when standing by demonstrating that specific movement.

Traditional Presentation Aids

There are a variety of ways you can enhance a presentation and help an audience understand a certain concept. These can be visual, audial, or both. In this part of the chapter, we will explore some of these additions to your speech that can help an audience better understand a complicated subject.

Charts show numeric data in a series of rows and columns, as shown in Figure 18.1. Charts allow your audience to see general trends in data and are especially useful if your audience might need to be able to look up a specific value. Charts can quickly become overwhelming, however, and can be difficult to absorb quickly. If it is important to your audience to get a sense of the overall impact of the data or quickly see relationships among numbers, one of the other graphs in this section might the best choice.

FIGURE 18.1   **Example of a Chart**

Enrollment at GMU by Year[4]					
Year	2004	2006	2008	2010	2012
Full-Time Students	15,218	16,267	16,694	18,819	20,297
Part-Time Students	13,656	13,622	14,020	13,743	12,664

Line graphs use lines along two axes to show changes in values over time (Figure 18.2). Line graphs are especially useful for showing trends, losses, or growth, and are especially good for allowing the audience to compare trends for two or more groups over a particular time frame. The line graph below makes it easy to see that the number of full-time students enrolled at George Mason University increased over the last eight years, while the number of part-time students decreased during that same time frame.

Demonstrations
enacting the process you are trying to teach your audience

Charts
visual presentation aid that shows numeric data in a series of rows and columns

Line graphs
visual presentation aid that uses lines along two axes to show changes in values over time

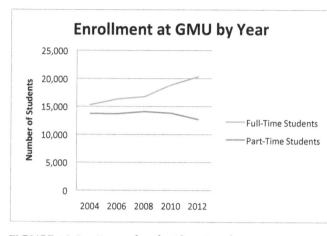

FIGURE 18.2   Example of a Line Graph

Bar graphs have two axes and either horizontal or vertical bars that show the total number of items or levels of achievement in each category. Bar graphs are especially useful for helping the audience compare the levels of several different subcategories within a larger category in order to demonstrate the relative degrees of impact of each of those subcategories. The bar graph in Figure 18.3 makes it easy to quickly identify the leading causes of death in the United States and quickly shows the audience that heart disease and cancer kill far more people each year than anything else.

Bar graphs visual presentation aids that have two axes and either horizontal or vertical bars that show the total number of items or levels of achievement in each category

FIGURE 18.3   Example of a Bar Graph[5]

Histograms are a type of frequency chart that shows the proportion of individuals that obtained a certain level of achievement along a continuum. As can be seen below, the horizontal axis shows categories based on ranges of achievement (sometimes called bins) in order from lowest to highest, such as grades on tests or number of items sold, and the vertical axis shows the frequency, or the number of individuals who obtained that level of achievement. Unlike bar charts, which represent discrete categories, histograms

Histograms a type of frequency chart that shows the proportion of individuals that obtained a certain level of achievement along a continuum do not break between the columns because the categories are continuous, as shown in Figure 18.4.

FIGURE 18.4   **Example of a Histogram**

Pie graph
a round graph that has slices that represent how large the proportion of that particular category is compared to the whole

A **pie graph** is a round graph that has slices that represent how large the proportion of that particular category is compared to the whole. Pie graphs show the proportion of individuals out of 100 percent that have a particular characteristic, and are especially useful for showing demographic data or indicating preferences among a group (Figure 18.5).

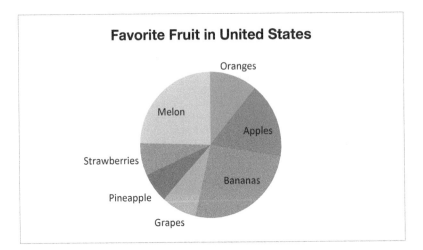

FIGURE 18.5   **Example of a Pie Graph**[6]

Scatterplot
a graph that shows the relationship between two continuous variables

A **scatterplot** is a graph that shows the relationship between two continuous variables. Scatterplots are useful for helping your audience understand the relationship, or correlation, between two variables. The scatterplot in Figure 18.6 has an upward slope and shows a positive relationship between height and weight, meaning that the taller people are, the more they tend to weigh.

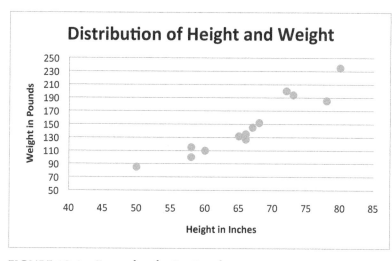

FIGURE 18.6   **Example of a Scatterplot**

Photographs can also be a valuable presentation aid for showing your audience an image of something that cannot actually be brought into the classroom. You might use a photograph to show a picture of someone or an historical event, or an object you cannot easily bring into the classroom. If you use photographs or images as presentation aids, it is most effective to show the photograph or image to your entire audience at once, perhaps by using a PowerPoint slide, a projector, or a large poster. If you try to pass a photograph or image around so that each audience member can look at it closely, it can become a distraction and will not as effectively support your speech, since each audience member will see it at a slightly different time during your speech.

Many people also like using videos within their presentations. When you need to demonstrate something that is impossible for you to exhibit on your own in the classroom, a brief video clip can be an excellent way to briefly show an idea to your audience. If you plan to use video during your speech, make sure you test the video equipment in the room before you begin your speech. You should also preset the video, so all you have to do is press play when you reach that part of your speech. Have a back-up link ready to open in case someone accidentally closes your video. You should briefly introduce the video and tell your audience what to focus on beforehand, and then debrief the video for a few moments afterward to summarize what you just showed them. Finally, you should make sure the videos you plan to use are brief and do not occupy a huge part of the body of your speech.

Another presentation aid you might use is a simple audio clip. For instance, you might want to play excerpts from two different pieces of music to demonstrate the difference between Baroque and Romantic styles. Sound can be highly valuable in helping your audience understand that topic and others like it. The guidelines for using audio in your speech are similar to those for using video in your speech: (1) keep the audio clips brief, typically under 30 seconds; (2) test and preset the equipment, so all you have to do is press play or begin to produce the sound; and (3) preview the audio to tell your audience what to listen for, and then summarize what they heard afterward.

Multimedia Technology

PowerPoint, Prezi, Keynote, or other types of slide show presentation technologies can be highly effective ways to display presentation aids for your audience. For example, you might decide to put a chart, graph, map, or photograph on a slide so your entire audience can easily see it at the same time. You might embed a video clip or audio clip into another slide so it is ready to play at the appropriate time in your speech and then easily move on to your next graph. If used poorly, however, PowerPoint and other similar technologies can distract from your speech. For instance, many speakers put too much text on their slides, choose fonts and color schemes that make the slides difficult for the audience to read, or put extraneous information on the slides that distracts the audience from the purpose of the speech. Table 18.1 shows a few guidelines for using PowerPoint and other slideshow technologies when speaking.

TABLE 18.1   PowerPoint Guidelines

Do . . .	Don't . . .
· show diagrams, charts, graphs, maps, photographs, and other visual elements that complement your message.	· fill your slides with excessive text, the outline of your speech, or entire paragraphs of writing.
· choose large (at least 28 point), serif fonts that are easy for your audience to read.	· use small, serif, or script fonts that are difficult for your audience to read.
· include blank slides in your presentation when you are not directly incorporating a slide.	· use filler slides with distracting images, animations, or anything else that takes away from your message.
· choose visually appealing color schemes and use a high level of contrast between your background and text colors.	· use colors that clash, have low contrast between the background and text, or choose colors that are commonly confused by those who are color blind.
· use animations that make images and text appear at the moment you begin to talk about them in your speech.	· use animations that introduce excessive movement, take too much time, or distract from your message.
· have a backup plan in case the technology fails, and test your presentation before you begin your speech.	· rely on extended videos or audio clips to fill time in your speech.

Practice

Practice is the final element necessary for delivering a successful speech. Public speaking is a skill that must be developed over time, and one of the best ways to become a better speaker is to do it often. In this sense, public speaking is a lot like other skills. Most basketball players shoot hundreds of baskets per week, musicians practice for several hours each day, bodybuilders do countless reps in the weight room, and most good writers spend some time writing almost every day for years. Likewise, it takes hours of practice to deliver an effective speech.

There are several ways to practice your speech. You can practice your speech by yourself in front of a mirror. This will give you a chance to become comfortable with your speech and make any needed changes while also giving you an initial opportunity to check your appearance. You can also practice your speech in front of a small group of friends or family. This is a good opportunity to get feedback from others, make additional revisions in your speech, and become more comfortable speaking in front of others. Finally, you could record a practice session of your speech and then watch it to see how you appear. This is an excellent way to identify what you are doing well and in what ways you can improve your content and delivery.

In order to make your practice sessions as effective as possible, there are several strategies you should consider.

- You should time yourself with a stopwatch every time you practice your speech. Your speech will be a little bit different every time you deliver it, and you will want to make sure the length stays within the expected time frame every time.
- Practice with your presentation aids, as you want to become as comfortable as possible using them.
- If practicing in front of friends, family, or others, give them some guidance about the type of feedback you would like to receive. You might give them some questions to consider as they listen, or even give them a grading rubric to fill out so they can help you make sure you are not missing any important elements. You could ask your audience to focus primarily on the organization of the ideas during the earliest stages of practice, on your support materials and arguments in the middle stages of practice, and on your delivery skills during your final stages of practice.

Ultimately, effective practice sessions can and should involve more than just you.

Using Delivery to Encourage Dialogue

Attitudes often come across through our body language more than even the content of what we say. A person's mannerisms influence the language and tenor of any interaction, whether they are noticed before engaging the party in a discussion or during the conversation. A person who looks grumpy or down might be approached (if at all) one way, while a person who is perceived to be happy or excited would be approached in an entirely different manner. With that in mind, good delivery can encourage a dialogic environment and invite audiences to engage you in a civil, yet critical, manner. There are some things you can do in terms of delivery that help to create a dialogic environment, and we will now provide you with a few of those methods.

Check Pronunciations before You Speak

Not only does pronouncing a word or name wrong damage your credibility, but it also can leave the audience with the impression you did not care enough to check the correct pronunciation, making them less interested in engaging with or even respecting you. As you practice, if you encounter names or words you are not entirely sure how to pronounce, check with a dictionary or even another person to learn how to properly pronounce the name or word.

Engage with Your Audience

A key element to creating dialogue is facing the audience and making eye contact with them. This helps create the perception you are talking with them, not at them, and thus makes them less likely to look away and more likely to pay attention. Standing up straight and looking people in the eye are signs of respect from a speaker, and so it is important to do so when giving a presentation. Even when using a visual aid, face the audience when explaining the aid instead of looking at the image.

Practice, Practice, and Then Practice Again

Unless you are delivering an impromptu speech where practice is impossible, you owe it to your audience to prepare your presentation well in advance. If you come across as having done this at the last minute, people will not feel you took them, or the topic, seriously and will be less likely to engage you during or after the presentation.

Choose Presentation Aids to Increase Understanding

Many speakers use presentation aids just because they look flashy or cool, but they serve no purpose in terms of helping the audience understand something complicated. Use presentation aids judiciously and with the purpose of helping the audience, not making your speech more entertaining. To that end, if you choose to use PowerPoint or Prezi, make sure the meaning is what comes across, and that the visuals are not distracting. Also, do not feel the need to have a slide or representation for everything—only those things that may require more than words to help the audience appreciate or understand.

Choose Interesting Vocal Delivery Methods

Nothing makes an audience interested in a topic and predisposed to listen to a speaker more than a presenter who is interested in the topic and who is engaging with the audience. This excitement comes across through vocal delivery that is enthusiastic, interesting, and varied. Share your interest with the audience and they will respect you for it. Often, audi-

MEDIATED MOMENTS

In the classic comedy, *Ferris Bueller's Day Off*, Matthew Broderick stars as a high school student who skips school to go on an elaborate adventure with his best friend and girlfriend. Early in the movie, there is a scene with comedian and former presidential speechwriter, Ben Stein, where one of Bueller's teachers (played by Stein) is calling attendance and interacting with his class. The performance is so monotone that as the camera scans the class it highlights students sleeping and not paying attention. Although meant to exaggerate the impact a monotone voice can have on an audience, the scene underscores the importance of varying your tone of voice when trying to engage an audience.

ences contain people who may not care about the topic initially, but through the expression of your excitement and enthusiasm you may actually reach them and ignite an interest in them for the topic. Dialogue requires presentness, and nothing makes it easier to be present with someone than interest and enthusiasm.

Summary

Delivery is often one of the most frightening elements of giving a speech, but once you understand its various components it becomes less intimidating. In this chapter, we examined the components of delivery and the four primary means by which we deliver a speech. We then explored the concept of communication apprehension, and explained how we can help manage the anxieties that accompany delivering a formal presentation. Third, we discussed various ways to use presentation aids within a speech to help an audience understand complicated material, before finally suggesting some ways to use delivery to encourage a dialogic environment.

Chapter 18 Key Ideas

- Vocal delivery includes everything that affects how your voice sounds when you give your speech, including pronunciation, articulation, volume, pitch, rhythm, rate, tone, and vocalized pauses.
- Physical delivery includes all of the physical signals that your body sends to your audience during your speech, including your physical appearance, facial expression, gestures, and eye contact.
- The four forms of delivery include memorized, manuscript, extemporaneous, and impromptu speeches.

- Communication apprehension is "the fear or anxiety associated with real or anticipated communication with another or others."
- Presentation aids can include objects, models, demonstrations, charts and graphs, photographs, video, or audio clips.

Chapter 18 Key Terms

Vocal delivery	Facial expressions	Self-fulfilling prophesy
Pronunciation	Gestures	Presentation aids
Articulation	Eye contact	Objects
Volume	Memorized speech	Models
Pitch	Manuscript speech	Demonstrations
Rhythm	Extemporaneous speech	Charts
Rate	Impromptu speech	Line graphs
Tone	Communication Apprehension	Bar graphs
Vocalized pauses	Trait CA	Histograms
Physical delivery	State CA	Pie graph
Physical appearance	Systematic sesensitization	Scatterplot
Posture		

References

1 McCroskey, J. C. (1976). Oral communication apprehension: A review of recent research. *Human Communication Research, 4,* 78-96.

2 Personal Report of Public Speaking Anxiety (PRPSA). Retrieved from www.Jamesmccroskey.com, http://www.jamescmccroskey.com/measures/prpsa.htm

3 McCroskey, J. C. (2009). Communication apprehension: What we have learned in the last four decades. *Human Communication,* 12, 157-171.

4 George Mason Enrollment Trends. George Mason University. Retrieved from http://irr.gmu.edu/10YrEnrollTrends.pdf

5 Deaths and Mortalty. Centers for Disease Control and Prevention. Retrieved from http://www.cdc.gov/nchs/fastats/deaths.htm

6 Food Availability (Per Capita) Data System. United States Department of Agriculture Economic Research Service. Retrieved from http://www.ers.usda.gov/data-products/food-availability-(per-capita)-data-system/.aspx#.VACJMvldWSo

DELIBERATIVE DIALOGUE

Overview: The purpose of this assignment is to engage in a small group discussion about a difficult topic. During the first session, your group will be given a difficult problem to explore, and during the second session, you will be asked to deliberate about several possible solutions and develop a team proposal. Finally, you will develop a group presentation in which you share your proposed solution with the entire class.

Part I: Exploration Stage (in class)

During class, your group will meet and will be given the problem that you will be working through. During this session, your group's task is to explore the issue and make sure that you understand it as completely as possible. Some of the questions that you might want to explore include the following:

- What is the problem that you are exploring?
- Why does this problem exist?
- Why are we focusing on this particular issue at this particular time?
- What are the issues that might make this a complicated situation?
- How has this problem been addressed in other places?
- What are some of the possible solutions that should be considered?
- What are the advantages and disadvantages of each option?
- What do we still need to know?

You may use your laptops to do research together during this session, and as you research, you should save and share your resources with your entire group (perhaps using Dropbox, Google docs, a group space in Blackboard, via email, or through another means). Your goal in this session is not to choose a solution; instead, your *goal is simply to understand the issue as deeply as possible* and to identify as many potential solutions as possible.

As you work through this problem together, make sure that you are practicing effective small group, leadership, and dialogic communication.

Initial Position Statement (at home, 25 points)

After class, you should take some time to think about your group discussion and consider your own perspective on the issue. Take a few notes about how your group functioned, which roles each person took on (relationship, task, and leadership roles), how dialogic communication happened (or didn't happen). Also, take a few notes about what you heard and how you felt about what you heard in your group. Save these notes for your reflection paper.

Next, take some time to review your group's research and your notes from the meeting. Conduct additional research if there is information that is still needed. Think about what you think the best solution or approach to your group's problem might be and write a position statement that articulates your position and the reasons for holding that position. Please cite **at least one source** in your position statement. Your position statement should be 1-2 paragraphs long, and you should be able to read it out loud in 1-2 minutes. Upload a copy of your position statement on Blackboard before class, practice reading it out loud a few times, and bring a hard copy with you to class.

Part II: Deliberation Stage and Group Proposal (in class, 25 points for group proposal)

Your goal today is to deliberate together as a group and develop a proposal for addressing the problem that you have been given.

First, each group member should read their position statement out loud within the group. As your group mates read, listen carefully and thoughtfully to what they have to say. Practice dialogic communication; seek to understand each person's perspective and to openly share our own. You may take notes or jot down a couple of questions in response to each position, but you should avoid distracting nonverbal feedback and should not respond verbally until after every person in your group has shared their position statement.

Next, deliberate as a group and work to develop a proposal that responds to the problem that you were given in some way. Your proposal should take all of your group members' perspectives into account and should be something that all group members are comfortable with.

Your proposal should be written as a formal letter that is addressed to someone who you believe has the ability to enact the solution that you are proposing. Make sure that you include the appropriate spacing, addresses, and punctuation required for business letters. In your letter, briefly summarize the problem, explain and provide a rationale for your solution, and describe the steps needed to implement your solution. Cite at least three sources in the text of your letter. Your group should finish writing the letter and upload it as a group assignment to Blackboard before leaving class. Only one person in your group needs to upload the letter on behalf of the entire group.

After completing and uploading your group proposal, your group will need to prepare a group presentation sharing your proposal. You might have some time at the end of class to begin this preparation, but should also plan to spend some time together outside of class preparing and practicing your presentation.

Reflection Paper and Group Assessment (at home, 50 points)

After class, you should write a 2- 2 ½ page (single spaced, 12 point Times New Roman font) paper reflecting on your group's first meeting. Each person will write their own individual reflection paper. In your paper, you should address the following questions:

1- Choose EITHER the Phase Theory of Group Development OR the Tuckman Model of Group Development. Explain how your group went through some or all of the phases/stages of this model.
2- Which group tasks did each person take on? How were these group tasks chosen, assigned, or assumed? Was your group able to effectively work together and complete all of the necessary tasks?
3- Who emerged as the leader in the group? Was the leader chosen by the group or identified in some other way? Which leadership style did they use? Provide examples that support your response.
4- Did you group engage in dialogic communication? Give specific examples of behaviors that suggest that your group was or was not engaging in dialogic communication.
5- How did you feel about the final proposal that your group presented? Did you support the proposal, and were you comfortable with what was shared? How was your perspective incorporated (or not) into the proposal? Do you believe that all group members' perspectives were considered and that all group members supported the proposal? Why or why not?
6- What grade (out of 100%) would you give each member of your group for their contributions during this project? You must give a different grade to each person in your group. Explain why you think each person earned the grade that you assigned by providing specific examples and details about how your group worked together.

Deliberative Dialogue Presentation (in class, 50 points)

Your group should prepare a persuasive group presentation in which you help your audience understand the problem that you were assigned, explain and provide a rationale for your solution, and describe the steps needed to implement your solution. Do not simply read your proposal to the class. Instead, you should prepare an outline and develop a presentation that adheres with all of the guidelines for effective public speaking that you learned earlier this semester.

- **Research:** You should verbally cite a minimum of three sources in your presentation and include at least three types of support materials.
- **Presentation aids:** You may use PowerPoint or other presentation aids.
- **Length:** 10-15 minutes for the presentation, plus 5 minutes for questions.

On your speech day, please bring a copy of the Deliberative Dialogue Presentation Instructor Evaluation Form and a final draft of your group's presentation outline.

Guidelines for Formatting a Formal Business Letter

Your street address
Your city, state, zip

Date

Name of person you are writing to
Their title
Their street address
Their city, state, zip

RE: Subject of letter

Dear Title and Name:

Start your first paragraph with a friendly opening and clear statement of the purpose of your letter. Use the following paragraphs to provide more details, argue your case, and provide examples. In your final paragraph, summarize your proposal and suggest a plan of action.

Notice that there are no indentions in this letter format. This is referred to as a formal block style letter and has become the preferred format for business letters. Formal business letters should have 1-inch margins and use 12 point Times New Roman font. If you are using letterhead, you do not need to include your own address at the top of the page. The date should spell out the name of the month and use numbers for the day and year, like this: July 3, 2015.

In the greeting or salutation, you will notice that the name is followed by a colon rather than a comma. After your final paragraph, you will want to include a formal closing (such as Sincerely,) and then leave three blank spaces (hit enter four times) before typing your name. Before you print your letter, proofread it carefully. After printing the letter, sign your name between the closing and your name.

Sincerely,

Your Signature

Your Typed Name
Your Title

Enclosures: list attachments, omit if there are none

Deliberative Dialogue Position Statement Rubric

This assignment will be uploaded to Blackboard and graded online using the rubric shown below.

	Missing 0	C 17.5-19.5	B 20-22	A 22.5-25	
Solution: (C) Statement proposes a solution to the problem that the group was assigned, and (B) the solution will directly address the problem, and (A) a clear plan for how to implement the solution is included					
Rationale: (C) Statement provides a rationale for why this solution was chosen, and (B) provides an explanation of the advantages, disadvantages, and costs of this solution, and (A) explains why this solution is likely to be more effective than other solutions considered					
Source: Position statement (C) cites a source in the text of the position statement, and (B) the source is a high quality, reliable source, and (A) an accurate APA format reference for the source is provided after the position statement.					
Proofreading: statement (C) is written in complete sentences and contains several significant grammar, syntax, or spelling errors. (B) includes 1 or 2 well-organized paragraphs and contains only a few minor grammar, syntax, or spelling errors. (A) Is free from grammar, syntax, and spelling errors. Statement also reflects careful attention to word choice and language structures.					___/25

Deliberative Dialogue Group Proposal Rubric

This assignment will be uploaded to Blackboard and graded online using the rubric shown below.

	Missing 0	C 17.5-19.5	B 20-22	A 22.5-25	
Solution: (C) Letter proposes a solution to the problem that the group was assigned, and (B) the solution will directly address the problem, and (A) letter addresses why this is a feasible solution given the constraints of the problem.					
Rationale: (C) Letter provides a rationale for why this solution was chosen, and (B) provides an explanation of the advantages, disadvantages, and costs of this solution, and (A) explains why this solution is likely to be more effective than other solutions considered					
Action Plan: (C) Letter provides steps for implementing the solution, and (B) the implementation plan is feasible and possible, and (A) the action plan comprehensively implements the proposed solution					
Sources: (C) Letter refers to at least three sources in the body of the letter, and (B) the sources are high quality, reliable sources, and (A) enough information is provided about the source that another person could find the original source with a couple of minutes of searching.					
Proofreading: (C) Letter is written in complete sentences and paragraphs, but contains several significant grammar, syntax, or spelling errors. (B) Paragraphs are well-organized and contain only a few minor grammar, syntax, or spelling errors. (A) Letter is free from grammar, syntax, and spelling errors. Letter also reflects careful attention to word choice and language structures.					
Format: (C) Proposal can be recognized as a formal business letter, though there are several formatting errors. (B) Proposal adheres closely with formal business letter format, but has one or two minor formatting errors. (A) Proposal is formatted perfectly as a formal business letter.					___/25

Deliberative Dialogue Reflection Paper & Grou[

This assignment will be uploaded to Blackboard and graded online using the r

	Missing 0	35-3!			
Phase Theory or Tuckman Model: (C) Paper identifies whether it is analyzing the group using either the Phase Theory of Group Development or the Tuckman Model of Group Development, and (B) clearly and accurately identifies the steps associated with the selected model, and (A) provides detailed evidence that shows how the group went through each step, including details about specific interactions.					
Group Tasks: (C) Identifies which group tasks were taken on by each person and provides details of how each individual carried out those tasks, and (B) identifies whether the tasks were chosen, assigned, or assumed, including details of how that process occurred, and (A) evaluates the effectiveness with which those tasks were carried out.					
Leader: (C) Identifies who was the leader in the group and explains how they were chosen for or emerged into that role, (B) explains which leadership style that individual used, and (A) provides detailed examples that support the argument for who the leader was and which leadership style was used.					
Dialogic Communication: (C) Explains whether the group used dialogic communication, and (B) identified specific behaviors or interactions that illustrated the use or exclusion of dialogic communication behaviors, and (A) uses key terminology from the textbook to identify specific dialogic behaviors or nondialogic behaviors.					
Feelings about Final Proposal: (C) Describes the degree to which the writer supported the final proposal and was comfortable with what was shared, (B) describes the degree to which other group members' perspectives were considered and were supportive of the final proposal, and (A) provides detailed explanations of interactions to support why they do or do not believe to proposal was inclusive of the entire group's perspectives.					
Group Evaluation: (C) Gives a unique grade (out of 100%) to each group member for their contributions, (B) explains why each person earned the grade assigned, and (A) provides specific examples and details about how the group worked together to support arguments about grades earned.					
Proofreading: (C) Paper is written in complete sentences and paragraphs, but contains several significant grammar, syntax, or spelling errors. (B) Paragraphs are well-organized and contain only a few minor grammar, syntax, or spelling errors. (A) Paper is free from grammar, syntax, and spelling errors. Writing also reflects careful attention to word choice and language structures.					___/50

Deliberative Dialogue Presentation Instructor Evaluation Form

Give this form to your instructor before you give your speech

Names:_____

Topic:_____ Length of Presentation Only:_____ Total Length:_____

INTRODUCTION	Missing 0	C 3.5	B 4	A 4.5-5	
Attention getter is (C) present, (B) uses a meaningful narrative, quotation, statistic, or question that is related to the topic, and (A) involves the audience or creates information hunger					
Background and audience relevance (C) some background information about the topic is provided, (B) the significance of the topic is firmly established, and (A) topic is clearly connected to this specific audience					
Speaker credibility (C) speaker provides a connection to the topic, (B) explains why they care about the topic, and (A) explains why they have compelling experience or expertise in this area					
Thesis (C) The thesis is clearly stated (B) in a clear, complete, single declarative sentence, and (A) uses carefully chosen language that sets the tone and direction for the speech					
Preview of main points (C) tells the audience what main points will be discussed, (B) uses signposts, and (A) uses concise, carefully worded phrasing					__/5

BODY	Missing 0	C 14-15.5	B 16-17.5	A 18-20	
Main Point 1: problem (C) is clearly stated and supports the thesis, (B) is well developed using a variety of support materials and (A) is supported by distinct, clearly worded and supported subpoints					
Main Point 2: solution & rationale (C) is clearly stated and supports the thesis, (B) is well developed using a variety of support materials and (A) is supported by distinct, clearly worded and supported subpoints					
Main Point 3: action plan (C) is clearly stated and supports the thesis, (B) is well developed using a variety of support materials and (A) is supported by distinct, clearly worded and supported subpoints					
Transitions (C) speaker clearly indicates when they are moving to each new main point (B) and has an effective summary, signpost, and preview in **each** transition, and (A) include pauses, gestures, or movement to reinforce the transition					
Quality of Arguments: (C) speech has some good arguments, along with a few fallacies, (B) speech uses sound reasoning and argumentation and is free of fallacies, and (A) arguments are well-supported and persuasively constructed					__/20

SUPPORT MATERIALS	Missing 0	C 3.5	B 4	A 4.5-5	
Support Materials (C) uses at least **three** different types of support materials (B) that effectively support the speech and enhance understanding and (A) help to establish significance and make the speech memorable **Types:** examples, statistics, testimony, analogies, metaphors, narrative, illustrations, descriptions, explanations, definitions					
Source Quality: (C) cited **three sources** (B) including a variety of types of sources, and (A) all sources were high quality and had strong credibility **Types:** interview, book, academic journal, newspaper or magazine, website or media source					
Source Citations: (C) all sources had some type of oral citation and (B) each citation had the name of the person/organization/publication and date and (A) provided the credentials of the expert who provided the information when possible					__/5

CONCLUSION	Missing 0	C 7-7.5	B 8-8.5	A 9-10	
Signals conclusion: (C) transition to the conclusion is indicated (B) using a clear signpost (A) that is reinforced through vocal tone, gestures, movement, and /or a brief pause					
Restates thesis: (C) topic of speech is clearly mentioned (B) in a clear, complete declarative thesis statement (A) using carefully chosen language that reinforces the tone of the speech					
Reviews main points: (C) tells audience which main points were discussed (B) using clear signposts (A) using concise, carefully worded phrasing					
Memorable closer: (C) brings a sense of closure to the end of the speech (B) in a memorable way that has audience impact and (A) ties back to the attention getter					__/10

DELIVERY (Use initials to evaluate each speaker on each criteria) and then average those delivery scores to obtain a group delivery score	Missing 0	C 7-7.5	B 8-8.5	A 9-10	
Extemporaneous: (C) read heavily from notecards or manuscript throughout the speech, (B) occasionally read portions of the speech from notecards, (A) students refer to notecards occasionally, but notecard use does not interfere with delivery					
Vocal Delivery: (C) speakers can be heard and understood throughout speech, and (B) vocal delivery conveys enthusiasm for the topic and keeps audience attention, and (A) vocal delivery engages audience and commands the attention of the room throughout speech *Pronunciation, Articulation, Volume, Pitch, Rhythm, Rate, Tone, Vocalized Pauses*					
Nonverbal Delivery: (C) attempts to use gestures, movement, and facial expressions a few times during the speech but may include a few distracting movements (swaying, rocking, repetitive motions, etc.) (B) speech uses gestures, movement, and facial expressions during the speech that at times complement the message, (A) speech uses intentional and effective gestures, movement, and facial expressions to enhance the speech, enhance credibility, and maintain audience attention *Apparel, Posture, Facial Expressions, Gestures, Movement*					
Eye Contact: (C) speakers look at audience a few times during the speech, (B) make eye contact with some audience members during significant portions of the speech, (A) make eye contact with all members of the audience throughout the speech					___/10
QUESTION AND ANSWER PERIOD					
Question and Answer Period: (C) speakers are able to answer questions from the audience, (B) are able to include additional relevant information that was not included in the presentation, and (A) show a deep understanding of the topic					
POINT DEDUCTIONS					
Over time or under time: deduct 1 point for every 10 seconds					
Missing instructor evaluation: deduct 10 points					
				Total Score:	___/50

Deliberative Dialogue Presentation Instructor Evaluation Short Form

Give this form to your instructor before you give your speech

Names:_____

Topic:_____ Length of Presentation Only:_____ Total Length:_____

INTRODUCTION	Missing 0	C 3.5	B 4	A 4.5-5	
Attention getter					
Background and audience relevance					
Speaker credibility					
Thesis					
Preview of main points					___/5
BODY	Missing 0	C 14-15.5	B 16-17.5	A 18-20	
Main Point 1: Problem					
Main Point 2: Solution & Rationale					
Main Point 3: Action Plan					
Transitions					
Quality of Arguments					___/20
SUPPORT MATERIALS	Missing 0	C 3.5	B 4	A 4.5-5	
Support Materials Types: examples, statistics, testimony, analogies, metaphors, narrative, illustrations, descriptions, explanations, definitions					
Source Quality Types: interview, book, academic journal, newspaper or magazine, website or media source					
Source Citations					___/5
CONCLUSION	Missing 0	C 7-7.5	B 8-8.5	A 9-10	
Signals conclusion					
Restates thesis					
Reviews main points					
Memorable closer					___/10
DELIVERY (Use initials to evaluate each speaker on each criteria and average those scores to obtain a group delivery score)	Missing 0	C 7-7.5	B 8-8.5	A 9-10	
Extemporaneous					
Vocal Delivery *Pronunciation, Articulation, Volume, Pitch, Rhythm, Rate, Tone, Vocalized Pauses*					
Nonverbal Delivery *Apparel, Posture, Facial Expressions, Gestures, Movement*					
Eye Contact					___/10
QUESTION AND ANSWER PERIOD					
Question and Answer Period					
POINT DEDUCTIONS					
Over time or under time: deduct 1 point for every 10 seconds					
Missing instructor evaluation: deduct 10 points					

Total Score: ___/50

318

Chapter 19

Small Group Communication

Human beings have depended upon groups to survive throughout their history, so it should come as no surprise that such associations are important today. Without successful and positive group associations people would be left to fend for themselves, and likely would never have survived as a species. Men and women worked together to hunt for food, develop farms, and even to raise families. Even today many of the communication situations we find ourselves in occur with groups of people, especially those tasks we complete for work. Today groups come in various forms with different names, like "units," "departments," or "committees."

Groups are fundamental to society, government, and business organizations as each of these depends on the successful completion of group work that benefits the entire collective. The ability of any group to be successful is predicated upon the members' communication skills. Poor communication is the death knell of any group, while successful, dialogic group members can facilitate quality work and an enjoyable experience for the entire group. In this chapter, we explore the nature and characteristics of group work. We will first spend some time defining the qualities consistent within any group before exploring two different models of group development. We will then examine the different roles or tasks performed by group members in any situation. Next, we will lay out some of the common challenges and rewards to group work before finally providing some guidance on how to employ dialogue to maximize the effectiveness, productivity, and efficiency of a group.

Defining Small Groups

The phrase "small group" can be tricky to define, as some of the contexts we have already explored in this book might seem to fit the bill for a small group. For example, a family or even a large company may seem to constitute a group. As we will see in this section, however, the various aspects that define small groups do not apply to these scenarios, thus making them unique contexts. In this section, we will discuss six characteristics that, taken together, define a small group and illustrate how a small group differs from families and public speaking engagements.

Vary in Size

Researchers who specialize in small group communication admit there is some debate over how to define the size of a small group; however, they all concede small groups consist of between three and 15 people.[1] To maximize the effectiveness of the group, the magic number appears to be somewhere between five and seven members.[2] It is important to note, though, that group size is not a necessary characteristic of all small groups, and that ultimately the number that allows interaction and role recognition between members should determine the size of the group. The larger the group, though, the more likely there will be subgroups, as is the case within academic departments where certain members of the department form committees to do specific work on behalf of the larger group. Although it may seem important, group size is actually not the most central characteristic of the definition of a small group.

Function as Systems

Much like families, small groups function as interdependent systems whereby something one member does impacts all other aspects of the group. When one group member does not complete something he or she was tasked with, it falls to another member to do so; conversely, when a member finishes a task early, he or she can then help someone else in the group finish another task. For small groups to function properly, members need to coordinate their efforts with each other so things are completed how and when they should be.

Maintain Task-Oriented Goals

Whereas families and small groups are both interdependent in nature, small groups are task oriented, whereas families are not always so. This means that small groups focus on completing a specific action or goal and then likely disband, whereas families do not dissolve or disband when something they worked together to achieve is finished. The task can be the creation of something, the completion of a project, or the resolution of some problem, but groups are always aware they have a limited lifespan that ends when their job is completed.

Governed by Their Own Norms

Every group is different, but each expects certain behaviors from group members. Some of these norms concern the ways in which group members act toward each other, while others pertain to the processes groups follow. For instance, some groups formalize votes for important decisions with the understanding that everyone will respect the outcome, and some groups expect that members will support one another in a variety of ways when a member is in need. These are just some examples of norms that might govern the members of a group. What makes small-group norms different from the norms of families and companies is that the norms of small groups contain the force of all members and are not driven by one person's authority.

Create Their Own Identities

One way groups maintain themselves is by crafting their own identity out of all the unique qualities of its members. This identity serves as a boundary for membership, as it protects the group from anyone else joining and destroying its cohesiveness. Sometimes groups create codes or languages that only members know, while other times they use uniforms or physical labels. Communication scholar Ernest Bormann referred to the times when groups coalesce around a theme or particular group experience as "fantasies" and he points out that particularly strong fantasies can "chain out" and be applied to other events.[3] **Fantasies** are creative interpretations of shared events that help define a group's identity, and fantasies become so powerful that they can be used and applied to various other experiences the

Fantasies
creative interpretations of shared events that help define a group's identity

MEDIATED MOMENTS

Small groups are often a powerful narrative vehicle for television and movies. One such example can be found in the NBC sitcom *Community*, about a group of seven community college students from a variety of different backgrounds. In each episode of the critically acclaimed show, the group works through challenges to accomplish some sort of task, whether it is related to their college coursework, the survival of their school, or even maintaining their group. The seven individuals each have unique identities, but over the course of the show's five-year run they develop a cohesive group identity that is so powerful that other people at the school— including the dean— desperately want to join.[4]

group may have to remind them of their common identity. In 1999, the Providence College baseball team was discontinued, but in its final season the team generated a great degree of cohesiveness by creating special warmup T-shirts inspired by the movie *Major League*. Whether it is through code languages, membership cards, or some type of apparel defining membership, the identity of the group is always protected. The group identity also influences the way individual members define their own identity, making group identity a powerful internal and external influence on individuals.

Preserve Member Cohesiveness

The bond that links group members is ephemeral and largely depends upon each member feeling connected to each other. The more connected they feel, the stronger the group, the weaker the connection, the poorer the work. This form of unity represents what Gerald L. Wilson calls "a special kind of interpersonal attraction."[5] Members of high functioning groups typically like each other, but they like the group with those people in it even more. The attraction becomes less about something in the person on an interpersonal level, and more about what positive qualities that person brings to the group as a whole. In some cases, it is entirely possible to not like a person on a one-on-one basis, but truly appreciate him or her as a member of a group.

Good group cohesion comes from a sense of fairness in the group, equal opportunity to participate, the sharing of similar attitudes—especially about the task the group confronts—and the actual work being done. This latter point refers to success in accomplishing tasks, and a feeling of progress throughout the experience with the group. Good groups have clear direction, specific goals understood by all members, and a plan for how each member is to act to achieve those goals. The better the group, the stronger the work, and the more successful the work, the stronger the group's sense of cohesion.

How Groups Develop

Despite their importance to organizations and society, it is almost impossible to predict how most groups will emerge. We have several useful models for understanding how groups function and develop once they form. In this section of the chapter, we will discuss two models for group development. The first, Phase Theory, focuses on four distinct stages for groups and connects well to some of the ideas we discussed in Chapter 12 regarding conflict management. The second, the Tuckman model, which is named after the scholar who devised it, argues that a group's lifespan follows five stages.

Phase Theory of Group Development

The Phase Theory of Group Development is built upon the findings of several scholars.[6] These researchers consistently found that groups naturally progress through four phases, each addressing different elements of the needs of the group at a particular time. In defining the four phases of group development, you may see some similarities to groups you have worked with in the past.

Phase #1: Orientation. As we have discussed, it is important for individuals to develop cohesion in a group for it to be effective. One step essential for forming cohesion is getting to know everyone in the group—their desires, their aims and vision for the group, and their understanding of the task before them. During this initial phase, members define themselves and perhaps how their experiences or expertise connects to the larger goal of the group. Orientation also involves group members reaching a consensus on the nature of their task because without a clear universal understanding of this, group members cannot achieve cohesion or even know what it is they are brought together to do.

Phase #2: Conflict. After group members get to know one another and identify the task before them, the group progresses to the conflict stage. This does not necessarily mean that negative feelings emerge, but rather that the group members examine the issues related to their task and debate the best way to move forward. The more robust the discussion about the different aspects of the task and how it might be solved, the better the group functions. The less debate and exchange of ideas at this point, the less likely the group will find the most efficient and effective solution. Some group members may attempt to bring those with different views together with a compromise, others may pose alternatives, and still others may inquire about the reasoning behind different positions taken by those in the group. The important thing at this point is to maintain a constructive approach to discussing different ideas and not take things personally or attack group members.

Phase #3: Emergence. After a good discussion and examination of the task and its associated issues, the group ultimately produces a decision. The emergence phase occurs as the group moves from conflict to a decision. As ideas are exchanged during this phase, group members identify the things upon which the group agrees and use those as building blocks to form a decision. When there are disagreements, the reasons for the disagreements are explored until ultimately the group has built a way forward with which everyone is comfortable. It is also important during emergence that any damage done between group members during the conflict stage is repaired, thus allowing individuals to retain the cohesion of the group and create a consensus.

Phase #4: Reinforcement. This final phase of group life serves to note the effectiveness and success of the group. The completed work is praised, thus creating a strong degree of satisfaction for members regarding the work they put into addressing the task. This phase is especially important in groups within companies because when members feel their work was done well and appreciated, it increases their future commitment to the company as a whole. Failing to praise good work makes group members feel as though their contributions were not important, and so they become less likely to participate at a high level in the future. Good groups need to have their qualities reinforced so that they live on in the future.

The Tuckman Model of Group Development

The Phase Theory of Group Development is not the only potential description of the lifespan of a group. One of the more recent alternative understandings of group development was proposed by Bruce Tuckman,[7] who argued groups move through five stages in their lifespan. The Tuckman model of group development is a bit more robust than the phase theory, and it also allows for the possibility that groups may skip stages and still be successful at accomplishing their tasks or goals.

Stage #1: Forming. The forming stage is very similar to the orientation phase in Phase Theory. This is when group members meet and engage in conversation in an effort to learn about each other. During this stage relationships form between group members as everyone explores what their potential roles and contributions could be to the larger group task. These interactions are colored by prior knowledge of other group members, and also by each individual's experiences with group work in the past. In today's mediated environment, many groups go through this stage through email or perhaps virtual meetings and conference calls, but nonetheless it is important to form the group before progressing to completing the task.

Stage #2: Storming. Once group members establish a rapport, the group turns its attention to the task at hand. During the storming stage, group members express open disagreement over what it will take to complete the task, who is best suited to what role, and what processes the group will follow to make decisions and accomplish assignments. This is very similar to the Phase Theory phase of conflict, but the Tuckman model adds more definition to the conflicts that take place, especially those that occur when group members have trouble assimilating to the group at the expense of their own identity and positions. During the storming stage, it is essential that the group members work through these difficulties.

Stage #3: Norming. The norming stage represents one of the differences between the Tuckman model and Phase Theory of group development. Rather than progressing from conflict to the emergence of a decision, the norming stage represents a move from conflict to cohesion. During this stage, disagreements have passed, the group focuses on the task, and group roles and norms for behavior take shape.[8] This new focus on the mission of the group promotes trust, honesty, and cohesion where once there was conflict and disagreement. Groups that go through norming ultimately develop stronger bonds than those that do not.

Symbolic convergence occurs when groups create a unique meaning for a term, experience, or event in the group's life that serves to further strengthen the bond between group members

Stage #4: Performing. Once conflict is resolved and people settle into their roles, they focus on completing the task assigned to the group. During the performing stage, group members expend their efforts in developing solutions, finishing tasks, and working together to complete their particular assignments. Individuals also become fully acclimatized to the group culture and procedures, a process that sometimes leads to what communication scholars call symbolic convergence. **Symbolic convergence** occurs when groups create a unique meaning for a term, experience, or event in the group's life that serves to further strengthen the bond between group members.[9] During the performing stage, group members report to each other on their progress, work through task and relationship challenges that may come up, and ultimately ensure the group accomplishes its objectives.

Stage #5: Adjourning. This last stage represents yet another signature difference between Tuckman's model and Phase Theory. Phase Theory focuses on reinforcement, which occurs while groups are still together, but it never discusses what happens when a group's task is complete. The adjourning stage of Tuckman's model does just that. This last stage accounts for when the group is finished with its task and moves to disband, which could be for a variety of reasons, including successful or unsuccessful completion of their assigned task. This stage may be met with a variety of emotions, depending upon the experience of individual members, but whether they wish to work together again in the future likely depends upon a positive experience and feeling like their work was valued.

Group Member Tasks

Communication scholars typically focus on the roles played within groups; however, these roles are merely the arbitrary labeling of responsibilities carried out by various group members during the lifespan of a group.[10] The principle behind role assignment is that if groups arrange themselves according to tasks, then the member who accomplished that task is thus assigned that particular role. The most significant issue with this approach is that members often complete multiple and overlapping tasks within a group. In this section of the chapter, we will examine some of the various tasks and responsibilities group members fill when working together, knowing that individuals can do more than one in any given group.

Recording

Groups often need a transcript of meetings and a list of decisions made at those meetings, and this recording responsibility often falls to one person. Some groups officially designate a secretary to perform this role, but it is good practice for all group members to take notes and record what transpires during group meetings because even an official secretary may miss something. The record allows the group to reflect on what they accomplished, and keep track of what still needs to be done and who needs to do it.

Commentating

An essential function of any group member is offering opinions and ideas to the larger group. This commentary can be in the form of constructive criticism or playing the devil's advocate. Additionally, comments can also include suggestions for ways to manage tasks or ideas on potential solutions to the problem the group faces. In a well-functioning group, all members feel as though they are able to offer ideas and comments to the rest of the group, and this commentary is shared with a spirit of good will.

Researching

The problems groups are brought together to overcome are complex in nature, hence the need to bring various perspectives and expertise to bear on finding a solution. The complexity of the problem requires researching what will be the best way to move forward. Each group member has a responsibility to the larger group to adequately research the problem the group takes up as well as the potential solutions offered by group members. This research can vary in nature, but is essential in identifying the best way to move forward.

Encouraging

One of the foundations of cohesiveness within groups is a feeling of support and an openness to participate in deliberations. A key way to develop this atmosphere within a group is by encouraging the participation of other group members. This can be done by seeking out thoughts from quiet members, or thanking those who do participate for sharing their ideas, even when they are not adopted by the group. Often, groups lose sight of this emotional dimension of cohesiveness and focus too much on the task at the expense of encouragement. It is a responsibility of all group members to make sure everyone feels valued and welcome in the group.

Challenging Ideas

Although seemingly the complete opposite of encouragement, challenging ideas brought forth by group members is another essential part of a high-functioning group. The challenges should not be aggressive or nasty, but they must be aimed at ensuring the group considers all potential aspects of an idea before it is adopted. If a member has questions regarding something the group discusses, she or he must feel welcome to challenge the idea and inquire about those things that give him or her pause. By challenging ideas, each group member ensures the group does not move too quickly or lose sight of some important detail that may have been missed.

Coordinating

No group can be successful without coordinating the deliberations and efforts of its members. This coordination may seem like the responsibility of one member, but it is more than that. Each member, when assigned a task, should know with whom he or she is working and, if there are other tasks being completed by other group members, how their efforts overlap. This involves constant communication between group members to update one another on progress. Without such coordination it is entirely possible the work will be done in a vacuum and will not coalesce into a clear and consistent group effort. This can lead to irresolvable conflict and problems with the group output. A group is more than just the sum of its parts.

It is also important to note that while many group roles are focused on getting work done, other group roles emphasize building and maintaining relationships within the group and making sure that all members are included. Both of these types of roles are necessary for groups to function well, and ignoring either type of role can lead to negative outcomes for the group as a whole. Groups that only emphasize the task roles and do not take time for social interaction and building interpersonal relationships within the group might find that group members do not enjoy their time working together and become less productive over time. On the other hand, groups that only emphasize relationship maintenance roles and do not balance those with task roles tend to enjoy the group interaction, but spend so much time socializing that very little work is actually accomplished.

In a high-functioning group, every group member performs each of these tasks. Compartmentalizing the tasks may seem like a good option, but that approach treats members as individuals doing tasks rather than a group working on parts of one task.

The Challenges and Rewards of Group Work

Working in groups is not always the easiest thing to do, even when you know and like those with whom you will work. There are numerous challenges to group work that, if not managed well, can derail the work of the entire team. These challenges can involve conflicting personalities, the pressures caused by deadlines, and even in some instances groups that get along too well and do not focus on the tasks at hand. There are also tremendous rewards that can be reaped from working together in a positive manner. Working and succeeding in teams allow people to feel a sense of joint accomplishment, share common experiences with others and in some cases, to develop bonds that survive beyond the life of the group. In this section of the chapter, we will explore what the challenges and rewards of successful group work are.

Challenges to Working in Groups

There are five primary challenges groups face when conducting work. Sometimes groups encounter several of these difficulties, but other times it can be only one, or even none. Nevertheless, it is essential group members enter into the project aware of these types of pitfalls so they can work to avoid them.

Groupthink. Many groups seek, or even demand, a unanimous decision where all members agree. This can be problematic in terms of process because the pressure to conform and reach such a decision may force certain people who harbor doubts to remain silent and acquiesce in the name of unanimity. Some groups where members know each other well fail to examine ideas critically and believe in the power of their collective abilities to come to the best decision. Still other groups have members who actively prohibit seeking evidence that may change the group's course. All of these situations illustrate **groupthink**, or the willful seeking of unanimity despite individuals who harbor doubts.[11]

Grouphate. Scholar Susan M. Sorenson proposed a concept called **grouphate**, which occurs when people have strong negative feelings about the prospect of working in a group.[12] Individuals who wish to avoid working in a group, but must do so nonetheless, tend to

Groupthink
the willful seeking of unanimity despite individuals who harbor doubts

Grouphate
when people have strong negative feelings about the prospect of working in a group

detract from the potential cohesion and success of the group. These individuals tend to be independent people who either do what they want regardless of the will of the group, or they withdraw almost entirely from the project and do not participate.

Nonparticipation. Sometimes groups contain members who do not do their fair share of work. They also fail to participate in group deliberations regarding the decision making process, assignment of tasks, or even the decision itself. As groups are systems, their lack of effort forces changes in other group members that include taking on additional work not completed by the nonparticipant, as well as developing negative feelings toward the group as a whole, thus damaging the cohesiveness of the group.

Domination. The opposite of the nonparticipant is the dominator, a person who seeks to control the discussion and the decision the group is tasked with making. Dominators speak over others, never seek input from group members, and often interrupt people when they speak. They have a vision of how to proceed and where they want the group to go and do not deviate from it. Often these people lack listening skills.

Irresponsibility. The final challenge to effective group work that we will discuss is the irresponsibility of some members. Suffice it to say, group work depends upon members trusting each other when they say they will be somewhere or do something. Sometimes that trust is violated by individuals who fail to hit deadlines, forget about meetings, or produce inferior work for the group. This irresponsible behavior is perhaps driven by a person feeling like she or he does not fully belong to the group, or she or he does not have an appropriate incentive for participating (e.g., students working on a group project may all receive the same grade, so there is no cost for irresponsible behavior). Of all the challenges to group work, this may be the hardest to deal with.

The Rewards of Group Work

Although there are numerous challenges to group work, there are also some rewards that make the effort of working alongside others worthwhile. In this section, we will briefly explore three of those rewards.

Efficiency. Groups often come together to accomplish complicated tasks that require expertise in several different areas. Others groups form simply because of the amount of work that needs to be accomplished. Properly using resources and individual talents can make the completion of a complex and difficult task much more efficient and effective. This allows people to know what their time commitment will be as part of the group and feel comfortable with what they are asked to do.

Opportunity to Learn from Others. When people with different experiences and expertise come together to accomplish a task, there is an opportunity to broaden your understanding of various areas of specialization. Being open to the idea that expertise in different areas can

DIALING DIVERSITY

The workforce is becoming increasingly diverse each year, and companies recognize the importance of training employees to collaborate with diverse sets of colleagues and clients. Perhaps no industry is more attuned to this need than the hospitality industry, where guests and employees come from around the globe. Since 2002, MGM Resorts International has run a program designed to prepare its employees for working with people of diverse backgrounds. To date, more than 4,000 employees have participated in the "Diversity Champions" initiative, developing skills such as respecting differ-

ences through an emphasis on inclusive teamwork and being aware of their own reactions when interacting with people of diverse backgrounds. Employees have continually cited the value of this workshop, saying things like, "this class has brought us closer to each other." The skills in the Diversity Champion program help facilitate successful work within departments and groups of MGM Resorts International.[13] It is also important to note that this initiative is not restricted to MGM Resorts International, as numerous other companies also have instituted similar programs.

add to your own knowledge of how best to accomplish something can provide you with the chance to grow in your own sphere of work.

Exposure to Diverse People. In today's global environment, groups are often composed of people in different states, regions, or even countries. One can look at this and see a challenge in that each of these people brings different cultural expectations and perspectives to the collective, but that need not be a challenge. Learning from and adapting to people with diverse backgrounds can be an enriching experience that allows you the chance to sharpen your interpersonal skills and worldview. Groups present a unique opportunity for learning about various cultures.

Group work is not easy, but it is also not something you can avoid. Whether it is during your college career or after graduation in your workplace or community, you will work with other people in a larger group. Knowing what the rewards can be from such participation and how to avoid the challenges that can accompany it will help you make the experience as beneficial as possible.

Dialogue in Groups

Dialogic communication can help establish and maintain a positive atmosphere for small group communication. It can help facilitate the exchange of ideas, the critical examination of those ideas, and the building of strong relationships between group members. Whenever groups work together, there are bound to be disagreements and tension, but dialogic communication in these environments can turn these moments of stress into productive opportunities to advance the group goal. In this final part of the chapter, we will provide you with six guidelines for employing dialogue within small groups to help make these exchanges constructive and not destructive. They are not easy to do, but the more you make an effort at building an atmosphere where dialogue is encouraged and rewarded, the stronger the cohesiveness of the group, and the more positive the experience will be.

> *"People think that communication is a 'magic bullet' for group success. I like to remind people that groups can, and often do, talk themselves into trouble. The key to group success is for groups to communicate effectively about the right things—whether it be understanding the problem, evaluating alternatives, or working through interpersonal disagreement or conflict."*
>
> —Randy Hirokawa, University of Hawaii at Hilo

Allow for Non-task Talk

Building a cohesive group necessarily involves cultivating trust and comfort between the members, and the best way to do this is to allow individuals who will be working together to get to know each other. This means that the initial meeting of the group should encourage conversation not related to the group task so people can grow to feel comfortable with one another. Non-task talk also takes place during the work of the group, and it should be taken as a sign that people are working well together. A dialogic atmosphere within the group depends upon people not feeling like they are a cog in a machine, or only able to speak about certain topics, and so allowing for, and even encouraging, non-task talk is important for developing a successful group.

Paraphrase Contributions to Ensure Understanding

As we have discussed, people do not always understand and interpret statements made by other people as they were intended. In groups, it is important to ensure that everyone is on the same page, and so when comments are made, or questions asked by others, you should paraphrase what was said to make sure you interpreted it correctly. Paraphrasing statements and repeating questions to clarify the other person's inquiries help create mutual understanding and avoid miscommunication that can derail the group's efforts.

Exercise Turn-Taking

The risk of people talking over one another increases when several people are talking about a topic. To that end, it is essential to employ the use of nonverbal regulators to organize the conversation. It is also imperative to allow people to finish their statements or questions and not interrupt them, even when you feel like you have something important to contribute. If group members are allowed to speak over or interrupt each other, then a negative climate within the group will develop and people will be less likely to contribute in the future. Respecting the person whose turn it is to speak goes a long way toward creating a successful group.

Take Good Notes

Earlier we discussed the various tasks members of the group engage in, and we advised that all members of the group should take notes during meetings. This is a very good way to ensure the group stays on task and that everyone understands what needs to be done by whom. People cannot remember every detail of what was said during a meeting, but fewer things get lost when everyone takes notes.

Be Flexible

Everyone has his or her own talents, and good groups leverage those talents to achieve their goals. Sometimes people wish to do the same task within a group, however, and so maintaining flexibility is important when determining what you will contribute to the group's work. You may wish to take on one particular item, but when someone else is perhaps better suited to do so, you must be open and flexible to doing something else that will benefit the group. A good way to avoid conflict over these issues is to have conversations early in the group's lifespan about what needs to be done and what the expertise and desires are for those in the group. This will allow for dialogue about matching people's skills and wishes with the group's work needs.

Engage in Constructive Conflict

Every group will encounter disagreements, whether they are over the processes the group will follow, the tasks assigned to individuals, or the ultimate decision at which the group arrives. For a group to be effective, it cannot avoid these conflicts. Members must feel like they can express dissent when they have a different opinion. These disputes should be engaged constructively, with other group members seeking to identify what the reasons are behind the differing opinions and working to understand the concerns of that group member. After the group understands the rationale behind the different opinions, they can work toward bridging the gap and potentially creating a consensus. Conflict in groups should be viewed as a positive occasion, when ideas can be critically examined and improved, not as an impediment to concluding the group's work.

Summary

In an increasingly global communication environment, small group communication skills are more important than ever. In this chapter, we defined small groups, illustrating how they are different from interpersonal and public speaking contexts. We examined two theories of how groups develop and explored the various tasks group members complete when working together. We then explored the various challenges and rewards of group work, before finally providing six guidelines for using dialogue to facilitate a positive and effective group experience.

Chapter 19 Key Ideas

- There are six characteristics that can be used to define small groups: (1) effective small groups range in size, (2) small groups function as systems, (3) small groups are task-oriented, (4) small groups are governed by their own rules and norms, (5) small groups create their own identities, and (6) small groups are cohesive.
- The Phase Theory of Group Development includes four phases: orientation, conflict, emergence, and reinforcement.
- The Tuckman Model of Group Development includes five stages: forming, storming, norming, performing, and adjourning.
- Group members fulfill various group tasks, and it is important for groups to balance task- and relationship-maintenance work.
- Some of the challenges associated with working in groups include groupthink, grouphate, nonparticipation, domination, and irresponsibility.
- Rewards of group work include efficiency, learning from others, and exposure to diverse styles.

Chapter 19 Key Terms

Fantasies

Symbolic convergence

Groupthink

Grouphate

References

1 Socha, T. J. (1997). Group communication across the lifespan. In L. R. Frey & J. K. Barge (Eds.), *Managing group life: Communicating in decision making groups* (3-28). Boston: Houghton Mifflin.

2 Cragan, J. F. & Wright, D. W. (1999). *Communication in small groups: Theory, process, skills* (5th Edition), Belmont, CA: Wadsworth.

3 Bormann, E.G. (1972). Fantasy and rhetorical vision: The rhetorical criticism of social reality. *Quarterly Journal of Speech* 58: 396–407. doi:10.1080/00335637209383138

4 Krasnoff/Foster, Universal Entertainment (2009). *Community* [Television series]. Los Angeles, CA: NCB.

5 Wilson, G. L. (2002). *Groups in context: Leadership and participation in small groups* (6th Edition). New York: McGraw Hill.

6 Caple, R. B. (1978). The sequential stages of group development. In *Small Group Behavior* 9 (470-476); Bell, M. A. (1982). Phases in group problem solving. In *Small Group Behavior* 13 (475-495); Bales, R. F. (1976). *Interaction process analysis*. Chicago: University of Chicago Press; Fisher, A. (1970). Decision emergence: Phases in group decision-making. *Speech Monographs*, 37, 1.

7 Tuckman, B. (1965) Developmental sequences in small groups. *Psychological Bulletin*, 63, 384-389; Tuckman, B. & Jenson, M. A. (1977). Stages of small group development revisited. *Group and Organization Studies*, 2, 419-427.

8 Wheelan, S. A. (2010). *Creating Effective Teams: A guide for members and leaders* (3rd Edition), Los Angeles, CA: Sage.

9 Bormann. E. G. (1972). Fantasy and rhetorical vision: The rhetorical criticism of social reality. *Quarterly Journal of Speech*, 58: 4, 396-407.

10 Myers, S. A. & Anderson, C. M. (2008). *The fundamentals of small group communication*. Thousand Oaks, CA: Sage.

11 Janis, I. L. (1972). *Victims of Groupthink*. Boston: Houghton-Mifflin.

12 Sorenson, S. M. (1981). *Grouphate*. Paper presented at the meeting of the International Communication Association (Minneapolis, MN).

13 Our Diversity Champion Initiative. MGM Resorts International. Retrieved from http://www.mgmresortscareers.com/diversity/diversity-champion-initiative.aspx

Chapter 20

Leadership

Groups of all sizes organize themselves in various ways, but one consistent component of any group is a leadership structure. In some cases, this takes the form of a small group representing the larger group, but in most cases there is one person who ultimately makes the decisions. Serving in leadership roles is something many employers look for in job candidates, and it is often an indicator that an employee is highly regarded by his or her colleagues or supervisors. It is important to understand, though, that the role of leader is one of service to the group. In effect, the leader works for the group; the group does not work for the leader. In this way, leadership is different from other roles in groups and organizations where individuals report to supervisors.

Simply having people report to you does not make you the leader, despite your oversight responsibility. A leader is different from a manager, supervisor, and even a boss in this way. A leader supplies vision, generates support for the task, and inspires a belief in others that she or he will take the group where they want to go. Leaders see the status quo and seek to change parts of it for the betterment of the group. Managers maintain the status quo, follow policy, conduct reviews, and do other tasks defined by the group or organization, but do not have a clearly articulated vision or mission that the members of the group understand and support. The term "manager" is a title given to someone, while leadership is a set of qualities and characteristics displayed by an individual in a group setting. In this way, managers can be leaders, but not all leaders are managers. The same can be said for bosses and supervisors because not all of them are leaders, but they are all managers.

Leaders are often chosen by groups based on their ability to effectively communicate with the group about their goals and how they will be achieved. In this chapter, we explore the communicative foundations of leadership. We will first identify the three primary ways groups identify their leaders. Second, we will explore the types of power that help groups recognize leaders, and which of those types leaders can also use to support the group. Next we will examine a host of characteristics exhibited by strong leaders before exploring six leadership communication styles. Finally, we will provide a set of suggestions and guidelines for using dialogue within groups to encourage good leadership, and, perhaps, take on those responsibilities yourself.

Leader Selection Process

Despite what many people might believe, leaders are not born, nor is the role of leader something everyone wants or should take on. In fact, there are several old adages that warn of the burden leadership may place on people like, "Heavy is the head that wears the crown." Nevertheless, groups always find leaders among their members, and they do so in a variety of different ways. Sometimes these leaders are elected, and when this happens they typically have sought the position. Other times it is less formal, and people may simply be viewed as, and thus ultimately behave as the leader of the group. In this section, we will detail three of the common ways groups identify their leaders.

The Elected Leader

Many groups large and small use a democratic method for selecting their leaders. The larger the group, the more likely this method will be employed because it helps manage the size of the gathering much better than direct discussion. There are typical patterns groups use to elect leaders. In some groups, for example, to be elected a person has to choose to run for the position of leader, whatever the title may be (e.g., president, chairperson). Additionally, the elected leaders typically serve fixed terms before having to run for the position again. The election model has a degree of appeal because it makes the leader responsible to the group, and if he or she fails to live up to the needs or expectations of the organization, then he or she can be replaced in the next election cycle. On the other side, the election model can lead to the creation of factions of supporters within a larger group by favoring certain members over others. Additionally, the best people do not always choose to run for the leadership positions, leaving the group to choose their leader from less than ideal candidates.

The Appointed Leader

In some organizations, leaders are appointed by someone or a body outside of the group. Committees and task forces, for example, often are created with a chairperson already identified by the person who convened the group. Appointed leaders usually come with some form of expertise that qualified them to lead the group, whether it is knowledge about the task or a reputation for good group communication and management. The challenge for appointed leaders, however, is that they may not be respected by the group and may have to spend a significant amount of time generating support before they can move forward with the job the group is tasked with completing.

The Emergent Leader

The third method for leadership selection is through the emergence of a leader within the group. In these situations, there might also be an appointed or elected leader, but if that person is not providing vision or direction, then someone within the group may step forward to do so. This type of leader is identified by the group, but not officially; rather, an emergent leader demonstrates qualities that everyone else in the group sees as both needed

MEDIATED MOMENTS

There are few better examples in film and television of an emergent leader than the 1957 classic film, *12 Angry Men*, starring Henry Fonda as a man who argues for reasonable doubt with his fellow jurors in what appears initially to be a sure-fire guilty verdict. Fonda's character, Juror #8, is not the foreman nor is he the smartest or strongest person in the room, but through encouraging others to examine evidence in a critical manner he eventually convinces them to let go of their own biases and think critically about the case. Fonda uses dialogic techniques such as asking questions aimed at understanding, not agreement, to overcome individuals who do not care about the case and simply want to leave, who are enacting their own personal biases on the defendant, and who do not wish to abandon their own initial verdicts. As the story unfolds, he moves from the lone holdout juror to the spokesperson and leader of those who see reasonable doubt in the case against the defendant. Such emergent leadership would not have been possible without his strong communication skills and calm demeanor.

and positive, and so they give their support to this person when she or he makes suggestions or decisions. Emergent leaders do not typically focus on the positional benefits of being a leader and do not seek to dominate or control the group, but instead provide structure, vision, and energy to a group that needs it. An emergent leader is accepted because he or she is already a part of the group and was not placed in a position of authority by an outside entity; therefore he or she is not beholden to segments of individuals within the group to keep the leadership position. These are leaders by example, and they treat their colleagues as equals—one of the reasons they emerge as leaders!

Leadership and Power

Leaders often gain their position due to a certain degree of power they either hold or are given. They also maintain their positions through the judicious exercise of that power. Leaders who abuse power will lose the respect of the group, and despite whatever title they may hold, they will lose their ability to lead the group in a certain direction. A leader's power can come from one or multiple places, and in this section of the chapter, we will explore five sources of power for leaders in a variety of different situations.[1] Keep in mind that leaders can, and often should, derive their power from several of these sources, but they need only one to be seen as the leader.

Reward Power

Reward power
power linked to the ability to either provide a good thing or take away a negative thing from someone for doing a task

The first type of power a leader might have is **reward power**, or the ability to either provide a good thing or take away a negative thing from someone for doing a task. Some managers and bosses have this type of power over employees because they control your salary and how much of a pay increase you will receive. Teachers also employ reward power through giving good grades, extra credit, or even candy to students who do their assignments or projects well. If teachers could not give candy or provide extra credit for students, and if managers lost the ability to determine raises, then they consequently would lose power over their charges. Such is the nature of reward power; it only exists so long as an individual can give something positive (e.g., award a bonus) or take something negative away from people (e.g., decrease their workload) as a result of doing something well.

Referent Power

Referent power
power derived from the charisma of a leader, and it can be seen when people follow someone they like, admire, look up to, or otherwise are attracted to

Unlike reward power, referent power does not emanate from the leaders' ability to provide a benefit to employees. **Referent power** is power derived from the charisma of a leader, and it can be seen when people follow someone they like, admire, look up to, or otherwise are attracted to. When your friend is leading a group you're in, you are likely to follow her lead because you like her, thus acquiescing to her referent power over you. Referent power, though, is tricky because as a leader you may do something that even the people who like you disagree with, and if that disagreement is strong, their attraction to you may diminish, thus reducing your referent power. Referent power is also something advertisers and politicians use when

DIALING DIVERSITY

Much to American society's benefit, people tasked with important leadership roles in companies, government, and schools are increasingly from historically marginalized groups. One such individual whose leadership style has been well respected at every stop in her career is Condoleezza Rice. Rice was born in Birmingham, Alabama in 1954 and quickly made her mark by ascending to the second highest office at Stanford University, becoming the first woman and first African American in the school's history to serve as provost. Rice left the position only to break another barrier when she was appointed by President George W. Bush as the first African American woman to serve as National Security Advisor. In President Bush's second term, he appointed her as Secretary of State, the United States' chief diplomat, and she was again the first African American woman to serve in the position. Rice's quiet leadership style gained the respect of those on both sides of the aisle as she helped navigate American foreign policy during a time of crisis and turmoil.

they seek endorsements for their products or campaigns. Ultimately, referent power works best when it is coupled with another power source. Just think about an instructor you really admired or liked. You worked hard in his or her class because of that respect, and when he or she also issued good grades, you increased your already strong effort.

Coercive Power

Leaders who have reward power also usually have its opposite: coercive power. **Coercive power** involves the ability to introduce something negative or take away something positive from group members. Coercive power often is perceived as the strongest form of power leaders can employ, but in fact using it can be very destructive to the group and diminish one's standing as leader. Coercive power needs to exist in certain situations, however. In the military and in prisons, for example, coercive power is necessary to keep order.

Legitimate Power

Some power emanates from a position, and so the person occupying that position is imbued with authority that must be followed. This type of power, otherwise called **legitimate power**, is often spelled out in a governing or organizational document that delineates exactly what authorities are associated with the position. It is important to

Coercive power power linked to the ability to introduce something negative or take away something positive from group members

Legitimate power power that emanates from a position, and so the person occupying that position is imbued with authority that must be followed remember that legitimate power is not derived from the individual or a person's style, but rather from the position he or she occupies; therefore, when the person no longer occupies that position, he or she no longer has that authority. The classic example of legitimate authority involved President Jimmy Carter, who in the middle of his failed re-election campaign in 1979-1980 was trying to negotiate the release and return of American hostages in Tehran. President Carter was able to inquire and be briefed on the progress of efforts to return these citizens until his successor, Ronald Reagan, took the oath of office. In the limo ride following the inauguration, Carter tried to ask for an update on the hostages and was told he no longer could be briefed on their status because he was no longer president. Thus, his legitimate authority expired and transferred to the new occupant of the position.

Expert Power

Expert power
power gained through specific knowledge of a topic or content area, thus providing the person with that knowledge power over those who do not have it, but who need it nonetheless

A final common source of power is expertise. **Expert power** comes from having specific knowledge of a topic or content area, thus providing the person with that knowledge power over those who do not have that knowledge. You may have heard someone being interviewed called "a leader in her field," or perhaps you have seen or heard of expert witnesses or expert testimony. In times of medical emergency, such as the 2014 Ebola outbreak, we defer to the CDC or other medical experts to tell the public what we need to do to avoid getting ill. These are examples of people using expert power. Within groups, sometimes we assign certain tasks to people who are experts, or at least more well versed than others in the area related to the task. This gives them expert power. Experts, however, do not always make the best leaders, so knowledge in an area alone does not necessarily qualify one to automatically become a leader.

Leadership Styles and Responsibilities

Just as there are different ways to become a leader and different sources of power and authority, so too are there several unique styles of leadership. In this part of the chapter, we will highlight six different conceptions of leadership identified by scholar Daniel Goleman, a leading expert on the concept of emotional intelligence.[2] Emotional intelligence can best be understood as the ability to manage ourselves and our relationships effectively.[3] There is not necessarily one best type of leadership style; instead, each leadership style works well in some situations, but not in others. Good leaders know that the situation often dictates the leadership style that works best and adjust their leadership style to best match the needs of the situation. Additionally, in this section, we will briefly explore eight responsibilities of leadership. These run the gamut from responsibilities to manage interpersonal interactions within the group to keeping everyone focused on the task at hand.

Coercive

Coercive leadership style
a top-down approach to decision making that stifles individual ingenuity and participation and neglects motivating the group

The first type of leadership style we will discuss actually has perhaps the most negative impact on a group. The **coercive leadership style** is a top-down approach to decision making that often stifles individual ingenuity and participation, as well as destroys any type of rewards system because it is not driven by motivating group members to succeed, but rather by pushing them to do what the leader wants. The coercive leadership style often manifests in those with strong drives to achieve and desires for control. With a "Do what I say" approach, the coercive leadership style can erode a group's cohesion and ability to perform.

Despite its negative qualities, Goleman believes it does have its place in certain situations. In business, he believes the coercive style can be effective in helping companies engineer turnarounds when they are underperforming, or when there is a genuine emergency where discussion and group consultation are not feasible. Nevertheless, the coercive style should be used sparingly and only when its benefits are clear.

Authoritative

On the surface this style may sound similar to coercive power because to apply coercion one needs authority, but these two styles are actually quite different. The **authoritative style** comes from a place of confidence and empathy, not control and enforcement. This style can have a very positive impact on a group if used in the right moments, specifically when a new vision or direction needs to be supplied and workers lack motivation. The authoritative leadership style helps mobilize people toward a particular vision they lacked before.

Goleman's research found that this style is by far the most effective. Authoritative leaders provide clarity of vision in an enthusiastic way that infects the rest of the group. People who work for leaders who exhibit this style know what they do matters, and feel that their colleagues respect their participation and input. Despite its overwhelming positive impact, Goleman cautions it does not work in every situation. For instance, if members of a group are more experienced, the authoritative style can come across as condescending and overbearing, defeating the benefits it might have otherwise achieved.

> **Authoritative leadership style** comes from a place of confidence and empathy, not control and enforcement

Affiliative

If the coercive leader is exacting and rigid, and the authoritative leader is inspiring, then the **affiliative leader** is flexible and encouraging. By this we mean he or she allows risk-taking, values relationship building, and builds trust with his or her group members. This style maximizes group harmony and generally creates a positive environment for the group to complete their work. Affiliative leaders are, in essence, people persons.

When groups encounter stressful situations, or have undergone major structural changes that have caused rifts and sewn distrust among the group, then the affiliative style works at its best. The risk with this style is ignoring poor performance and encouraging an atmosphere of lax work ethic, and so Goleman advises to not use this style alone, but to mix it with another leadership orientation that allows constructive criticism and clarity of expectations.

> **Affiliative leadership style** flexible and encouraging, allowing group members to take risks and work on their own to engender trust; a "people person" leadership style

Democratic

Another positive approach to leadership is the democratic style, where leaders try to build consensus and collaborate with their team or group members. To be clear, democratic does not mean everyone votes, but rather everyone has an equal share in decisions and collaborates on potential solutions. The simple truth behind this approach is that through participation, consensus can form around the best solution or way forward. The democratic approach works well when trying to generate buy-in from multiple constituencies, or when leaders want to collect input from valuable and invested employees.

This approach to leadership takes time, patience, and an open mind—it is also not always the best way to move a group forward. One of the drawbacks to this approach lies in the risk of too many meetings between parties because consensus becomes difficult to forge. It also is not as effective when group members or employees are just not knowledgeable or skilled enough to provide good feedback and input. When leaders do not know the best way forward or want a fresh perspective on their particular plan, however, the democratic style can yield substantive benefits.

Pacesetting

The fifth style of leadership Goleman identified is what he calls pacesetting. In the **pace setting leadership style**, a leader is focused on setting a high standard and modeling that standard for his or her team members. It is indicative of a desire to achieve the most in the fastest time possible, and the leader expects everyone to "keep pace" with him or her in terms of energy and dedication. It may or may not surprise you to find this type of high-octane approach to leadership results in a negative impact on the group climate because people get overwhelmed and morale drops, but like the coercive style, it does have a place in a leader's options.

The pacesetting approach, according to Goleman's research, can be most beneficial when the members of the group are already highly motivated and very competent in their

Pacesetting leadership style focused on setting a high standard and modeling that standard for his or her team members

TABLE 20.1 **The Six Leadership Styles at a Glance**[4]

	Coercive	Authoritative
The leader's modus operandi	Demands immediate compliance	Mobilizes people toward a vision
The style in a phrase	"Do what I tell you."	"Come with me."
When the style works best	In a crisis, to kick start a turnaround, or with problem employees	When changes require a new vision, or when a clear direction is needed
Overall impact on climate	Negative	Most strongly positive

tasks. In these situations, people require little direction and work to complete tasks at a good pace. Much like the affiliative style, however, Goleman cautions to use this approach sparingly and that it should never be the sole style of any leader.

Coaching

The final style Goleman identified was the **coaching style**, which is focused on helping individuals improve and grow through training and constant feedback. Not surprisingly, many in the business world surveyed by Goleman and his team did not employ this style because of the time commitment necessary to invest in each employee's development. The benefits of this approach include a positive group climate and an increased feeling of worth within individuals.

Despite the benefits, many in business are just not familiar with how to help people identify and improve upon their weaknesses. In fact, for the coaching style to work the leader needs to be competent enough in the areas in which he or she is coaching employees, and the employees need to be open to hearing constructive criticism and trying new ways to improve their weak areas. When leaders are not familiar with what they are coaching, their credibility evaporates quickly, just as it is impossible to coach the "uncoachable," or people who are not aware of and unwilling to work at their deficiencies.

Leadership Responsibilities

Leaders exhibit common responsibilities regardless of which style they employ in a given situation. These serve to illustrate the communication skills necessary for good leadership, whether it be democratic, coercive, or anything in between. In this section of the chapter,

Coaching leadership style focused on helping individuals improve and grow through training and constant feedback

Affiliative	Democratic	Pacesetting	Coaching
Creates harmony and builds emotional bonds	Forges consensus through participation	Sets high standards for performance	Develops people for the future
"People come first."	"What do you think?"	"Do as I do, now."	"Try this."
To heal rifts in a team or to motivate people during stressful circumstances	To build buy-in or consensus, or to get input from valuable employees	To get quick results from a highly motivated and competent team	To help an employee improve performance or develop long-term strengths
Positive	Positive	Negative	Positive

we will examine eight communication behaviors that serve as the foundation of leadership in many different groups and organizations.

Leaders must remain well informed. Leaders are usually given information about the task and the backgrounds of group members. They are also aware of any work being done outside of the group that may impact or be impacted by their own group's work. If leaders are not knowledgeable about the task, issues, or people with whom they work, then they seek out that information. In short, leaders know more than group members.

Leaders provide direction and structure to their group. One of the primary responsibilities of leaders is to establish the work structure for group members and assign each person his or her responsibilities. How he or she chooses to do this is a matter of style and situational demands, but leaders must make both the structure and specific assignments clear to the group to avoid confusion.

Leaders must be flexible to the demands of the situation. Despite laying out a clear structure and delivering directions to group members, the group might need to change its approach when presented with new information or factors. Leaders must be flexible to the demands of their group and adjust as needed.

Leaders must be able to manage complex situations. The larger the group or more involved the task, the more complexity for a leader to manage. Leaders need to keep track of what is expected and being accomplished by the group, as well as how that will impact other elements not within the group.

Leaders must recognize the strengths and weaknesses of group members. One of the primary characteristics of a leader is his or her ability to recognize the skills and abilities of those in his or her group. Knowing what people can do, and what they cannot, allows leaders to place their group in the best position possible to accomplish their tasks and achieve their goals. This is also something that may invite some conflict within a group when members do not appreciate or agree with a leader's assessments.

Leaders promote group cohesiveness. Not every responsibility of the leader relates to the group task; some responsibilities also concern the maintenance of a positive communication climate and strong relationships between group members. Leaders need to stay tuned in to the atmosphere of the group and determine when to engage in activities that can help people release stress or reengage with the group's mission and identity. These non-task related functions are just as important as anything else a leader must do.

Leaders manage conflict amongst group members. A fundamental responsibility of all leaders is to adjudicate and resolve conflict between group members whenever it arises. Group members look to leaders to be fair, impartial, and responsible for handling disputes in a way that all parties continue to feel comfortable working with each other. Conflict management serves both task and relational purposes for the group because when individuals are fighting, they are not working to achieve the group's goal, and they also create a negative experience for everyone else. Leaders must help resolve these situations.

Leaders consider multiple perspectives. Group members have the benefit of stating their opinions, positions, and critiques whenever they wish to. Leaders, on the other hand, take all of those statements and consider them before attempting to make a decision or weighing in with the group. Even autocratic leaders make decisions by taking input from a variety of sources and perspectives, but they are the only people with decision-making authority.

Leaders are responsible for a great many things; they are not just the decision makers. Each of the eight responsibilities we discussed necessarily involve good communication skills, because without the ability to effectively communicate with the group and outside parties, then groups deteriorate and goals are not achieved. Leadership is challenging work, and both becoming and maintaining the position as leader of a group requires the ability to skillfully interact with others.

> *"Leadership in a democracy depends upon the articulation of a shared goal or set of goals, and a shared willingness to make both sacrifices and compromises in pursuit of that goal or set of goals. Leadership, then, isn't something leaders do to others; it is something leaders do with others."*
>
> —Mary Stuckey, Georgia State University

Leadership and Dialogue

Given the numerous responsibilities, group member personalities, and pressures that come with the position, it should come as no surprise that dialogue skills are paramount in succeeding when leading a group. In this section of the chapter, we will detail seven suggestions for effectively employing dialogue in a leadership position.

Openly Talk Through Group Processes

One of the greatest pitfalls facing leaders occurs when leaders do not discuss or detail the processes that will govern group meetings, assignments, and other functions. To be an effective leader, regardless of which style you employ, it is important that members of the group understand such things as how decisions will be made, how meetings will be managed, and how other assignments are determined. Understanding does not mean simply laying out this information, but also allowing group members a chance to ask questions and provide feedback that may improve how the group functions. Open dialogue that results in a group understanding of rules and procedures will reduce the likelihood of missteps and conflict in the future.

Encourage Alternatives, Suggestions, and Questions

Simply providing an opportunity for feedback is not enough to facilitate dialogue between group members. Effective leaders find ways to encourage participation by group members either during a group meeting, or privately afterwards. It also is essential to encourage disagreement so there is a critical analysis of ideas and suggestions that hopefully results in a better decision. Leaders must take initiative in promoting participation in discussions and assignments, sometimes by directly asking individuals for specific thoughts.

Divide the Task into Manageable Units

Groups convene to confront complex issues, and any group member can feel overwhelmed by the task's complexity. To help mitigate this confusion and stress, good leaders break down the goal and task into manageable units for group members so they see the steps that need to be taken to achieve success. Leaders can turn complex tasks into simple steps, thus reducing the tension group members may feel by focusing on a large, complex task.

Continually Communicate with Group

Even when there is information you cannot share with the group, let them know that you cannot share it instead of hiding the fact you know it. Additionally, and most importantly, maintain open lines of communication throughout the life of the group. Give opportunities for feedback, share developments that may affect the group, and give status updates about any subgroups to each member. In doing these things, good leaders must also be accessible themselves, as well as responsive. It is both respectful and a good practice for leaders to respond in a reasonably quick time frame when members make inquiries. What is challenging is knowing the most effective way to communicate information. Some messages should be delivered face to face, while other information can be relegated to email or even a text message.

Don't Let Emotions Get the Better of You

Make no mistake, being a leader does not make you more or less human. You will have emotional reactions to statements and events, but these reactions must not govern your decisions or impact the way you interact with group members. It is important to stay consistently calm when interacting with others, despite any emotions you may feel inside. This is especially true of anger and frustration, but also applies to excitement and joy. Too much of an emotional display can be read the wrong way by group members and thus may create false perceptions for those who work with you in the group. Group leaders should be stable and consistent, the rock upon which the group is built, even when they might want to erupt with emotion. Remember that emotional displays can create a defensive communication climate and are therefore inconsistent with dialogic principles.

Provide an Agenda Before Group Meetings

The next guideline for leaders who wish to effectively encourage dialogue is to provide a clear agenda in advance of any group meeting. The agenda does a number of positive things for the leader and the group. First, it demonstrates that someone is tracking where the group is headed. Second, it provides direction and structure for group members and group activities. Agendas also help focus dialogue by setting out topic areas the group will engage. This can help reduce the chances of the meeting being hijacked or going off on an unrelated tangent. There are numerous ways to construct an agenda, but they all list the order of events and topics the group will cover during the meeting, what materials are needed for the meeting, and who is expected to lead discussions on what during the gathering. This focus maximizes the time spent together and helps the leader manage the group.

Take Minutes at Every Meeting

The final guideline we will suggest for leading groups is making sure someone takes clear and detailed minutes of the meeting and that this record is kept for as long as the group works together. Minutes allow for an accurate record of who attended meetings, what was covered, how topics were discussed, what decisions were made, and who is responsible for doing what. Meeting minutes can go a long way toward solving disputes between group members by allowing people a record to examine when disagreements over decisions or assignments come up. It also promotes honesty and good behavior in colleagues when they know that what they say is being recorded.

Summary

Groups do not function without a leadership structure, and the success of the leadership structure depends largely on the leader's communication skills. In this chapter, we explored the power dimension of leadership, and examined the three primary ways through which groups choose their leaders. We also described the dimensions of the six major leadership styles, emphasizing that not all are appropriate all the time. We then briefly discussed some of the responsibilities that fall to leaders and provided seven guidelines for leaders to effectively employ dialogue in groups.

Chapter 20 Key Ideas

- Leaders can be elected, appointed, or emerge.
- The five bases of power include reward power, referent power, coercive power, legitimate power, and expert power.
- The six leadership styles that were discussed are coercive, authoritative, affiliative, democratic, pacesetting, and coaching.
- Leaders have numerous responsibilities within the group.

Chapter 20 Key Terms

Reward power	Expert power	Democratic leadership style
Referent power	Coercise leadership style	Pacesetting leadership style
Coercive power	Authoritative leadership style	Coaching leadership style
Legitimate power	Affiliative leadership style	

References

1 French, J. R. P., Jr., & Raven, B. H. (1959). The bases of social power. In D. Cartwright (Ed.), *Studies in social power* (pp. 150–167). Ann Arbor, MI: Institute for Social Research.

2 Goleman, D. (2000). Leadership that gets results. *Harvard Business Review,* p. 79-90.

3 Ibid.

4 Adapted from Goleman, D. (2000). Leadership that gets results. *Harvard Business Review*. Retrieved from http://www.haygroup.com/downloads/fi/Leadership_That_Gets_Results.pdf

Chapter 21

Group Presentations

In many professions you will find yourself working in teams, and often those teams will be asked to deliver their findings or project results to an audience. When this happens it is as a part of a group, not as an individual. The type of presentation may be informative, as in a corporate board report, or it may be persuasive, such as sales teams trying to persuade a client to purchase a particular product. Regardless of the type or topic of the presentation, there are certain elements of a group presentation that differ from individual performances.

In this brief chapter we will explain the requirements and expectations of group presentations and provide some guidelines for how to handle question and answer sessions at the end of a group presentation.

Group Presentation Formats

A common mistake that novice group speakers make is not seeing the presentation as one speech. Instead, they see a group presentation as a loose connection between multiple individual performances. For instance, if there are five speakers in the group, they often make the mistake of seeing the group presentation as five distinct speeches rather than one whole performance. This error is often made early in the development of a presentation, and comes from not clearly establishing the most appropriate format for the presentation. To better equip you in making this determination early and thus avoiding the error of a loose connection between participants, we will explain the two effective formats for group presentations: the bookend approach and the panel approach.

In the **bookend approach** the first speaker is also the last speaker. Their responsibility in this role is to introduce the topic and overview which group members will explain each component and why they will do so. The "why" helps explain each individual's credibility on their topic. For example, suppose Kris, Jarrod, Liz, and Brian are giving a presentation proposing a parking shuttle system to and from campus. They are going to use the problem-cause-solution organizational pattern for the body of the presentation. Kris will introduce the topic and the qualifications of each group member and then conclude by introducing Jarrod, who will speak next. Jarrod will detail the problem, and when he is finished, he will introduce Liz, noting that she will discuss the cause of the problem. When she finishes discussing the cause, Liz will present Brian by explaining that he will provide a solution that addresses the cause of the problem. After Brian presents the solution, Kris will again address the audience by delivering a conclusion that summarizes the group's talk. There are several benefits to the bookend approach for a group presentation. The bookend approach gives a nice sense of closure by having the same person begin and end the presentation. It also gives the performance continuity by having each speaker connect their topic with the next. Additionally, the bookend approach allows for a degree of individuality in performances by giving each person a specific focus to develop on their own and then connect to the other parts developed by the group. It is important, however, that the individual aspects of each presenter do not overshadow the need to have a fluid connected overall presentation. Be sure to have clear transitions between speakers and have all speakers work together as they develop their individual components of the presentation. Keep in mind that in a group presentation every speaker is still required to provide evidence, cite sources, and use logic, just as they would in an individual speech.

The **panel approach** is another common approach for giving a group presentation, and it is structured differently from the bookend model. Panel presentations occur in both formal and informal settings and are most appropriate when audience interaction is expected or encouraged. Panel presentations are individual performances, but all cover the same topic in different ways. Each member of a panel may present his or her ideas on a single topic, or each may have a specific subset of a topic. Panel speakers may agree or disagree with one another, and sometimes even challenge other speakers on their content or positions. To handle transitions between speakers, panels need to have a person play the role of moderator.

Moderators are unique participants in a group presentation using the panel approach. First, they should be objective and should not present their own opinions, ideas, or thoughts on the topic or speaker presentations. Second, they introduce the entire panel at the start, establish the order of speakers, and transition between speakers when each individual completes his or her remarks. It is important that panelists and the moderator talk before the panel convenes so that there is no miscommunication when the performance is delivered to the actual audience. Moderators also serve the important role of handling interactions between speakers and the audience. They indicate when individuals may ask questions and let the speakers know when they reach the time for their talk to be done. Ultimately, their task is to maintain an orderly presentation and keep the interaction on topic. It should be obvious that the panel approach does not have as much structure as the bookend approach, but it has the advantage of being more interactive and covering more material than the bookend model.

Q&A Sessions

After all the information has been presented to the audience, they may be given the opportunity to offer feedback and ask questions. This practice is most common in the panel format of group presentations, but it is not unrealistic for it to happen in bookend style talks as well. This part of the presentation can be stressful for members of the group; think about it as a conversation rather than an interrogation and it will help reduce your anxiety. Here are some other tips for handling Q&A sessions.

First, you should always allow the audience member sufficient time to ask their question or offer their comment. In doing so, you should never interrupt people when they are making their point. If the person's points are not easily discerned and their statements seem unclear, ask for clarification. Whatever you do or say, remain polite. Even if an audience member becomes agitated, you should "keep your cool," as you have the obligation to the rest of the audience and to your group to do so. Just because an audience member is emotional does not mean that you have to behave in the same manner.

It is also a good idea to take notes when a person asks a question or makes a comment, especially if the comments are somewhat long. You may learn some things from the audience and might want to consider those points in a later presentation. Taking notes also signifies that you value the feedback that you get from the audience and that you paid careful attention to them when they spoke.

It is also important to be comfortable with the fact that you do not know everything and may even get stumped by a question from the audience. This is not a bad thing, as delivering a presentation is not a quiz show, and you will not be eliminated for not knowing the answer. In fact, it is far worse to lie or make up an answer than to state the honest truth. The audience does not even expect you to always know everything. There is nothing wrong with saying, "I do not know the answer to that question, but I will find out and get back with you. Make sure I have your contact information before we leave here later." Audiences usually respect this answer.

Conclusion

In this chapter we have discussed several aspects of group presentations. We went over the two different formats and discussed how to handle a question and answer session after a group presentation. Group projects and even presentations can be rewarding, and you may discover skills of which you were unaware, but they are not easy. In fact, group presentations often take a lot more work and effort than individual presentations because of the constant interaction between different people.